ANGLO-SOVIET RELATIONS, 1917-1921

Volume II

Britain and the Russian Civil War

November 1918-February 1920

PUBLISHED FOR THE CENTER OF INTERNATIONAL STUDIES

PRINCETON UNIVERSITY

A LIST OF OTHER CENTER PUBLICATIONS

APPEARS AT THE BACK OF THIS BOOK

ANGLO-SOVIET
RELATIONS, 1917-1921

Britain
and the
Russian
Civil War

NOVEMBER 1918 -
FEBRUARY 1920

BY RICHARD H. ULLMAN

★ ★

PRINCETON, NEW JERSEY
PRINCETON UNIVERSITY PRESS
1968

To

ELLIOTT PERKINS

for his friendship and his example

PREFACE

LIKE its predecessor, this second volume of what has now become a three-volume work comprises an account of how the British government dealt with the problems created by the fact that a communist administration, militantly hostile to the world of bourgeois states, had come to power in Russia during the last cataclysmic year of the World War. The first volume explored the making of British policy during that year, culminating in the beginnings of a military intervention whose implicit (if not avowed) purpose was the overthrow of the Soviet government in Moscow. The present volume commences with the Armistice which ended the war with Germany. It treats the making of British policy during the following fifteen months, the critical months of the Russian Civil War. Of all foreign governments, that of the United Kingdom was the one most heavily involved—both directly, through the use of its own military, naval, and air forces, and indirectly, through the provision of material assistance and advice—in the campaign to unseat the Bolshevik regime. By February 1920 this campaign, along with the hopes of the more realistic anti-Bolshevik Russians, had been almost entirely abandoned. Then it was the British government which led the effort to reach an accommodation between Russia and the West. That effort, made much more difficult by the Polish-Soviet War of 1920, will form the subject of the third and final volume of this study of British statecraft.

My aim in the pages that follow has been to focus quite precisely on the Russian Civil War as a problem for British policy makers, and to examine the process by which Great Britain's commitment to the anti-Bolshevik side was first enlarged and then liquidated during 1919 as the perceived costs of intervention, and still more the predictable costs of achieving any outcome that might have been labeled "success," became increasingly apparent. As in *Intervention and the War*, I have sought to place emphasis upon the making of policy within the government in London and the relationship to that process of the perceptions and actions of British public servants, military and civilian, in the field. Once again, I have not attempted systematically to describe the course of British domestic politics and the handling of other contemporaneous problems of foreign policy, or to trace in detail the development of British public opinion regarding Russia. Neither have I discussed any aspects of the Russian problem at the Paris Peace Conference other than those whose examination is necessary for an understanding of British policy. These several tasks would have vastly lengthened a long book and would only have gone over ground already very well covered by Arno J. Mayer in his remarkable work on the politics and diplomacy of 1918-19, or by John M. Thompson in his solid study of the Russian problem at the Peace Conference.[1] Grateful for their efforts, I refer readers to them. Where their concerns have seemed directly relevant to mine, I have of course encompassed them. But I have sought to run narrow and deep, rather than wide. My focus —I emphasize once again—is on the process by which the government of a Great Power extricated itself from a civil war in which it was the leading foreign participant, after it became clear that the war could not be won without the payment of a wholly unacceptable price.

❖

As I indicated in the preface to *Intervention and the War,* my original intention was to complete this study in two volumes, the second describing both the liquidation of British intervention in the Russian Civil War and the process of accommodation which culminated in the Anglo-Soviet Trade Agreement of March 1921 and London's extension of *de facto* recognition to the Soviet government. By late 1965 I had finished what I thought was a final draft. But early in 1966 the government of Prime Minister Harold Wilson announced that it was departing from the previous "fifty-year rule" restricting access to official papers and, as a preliminary measure on the way towards an eventual thirty-year closed period, would allow access to all papers through 1922. Therefore, I suspended pub-

---

[1] Arno J. Mayer, *Politics and Diplomacy of Peacemaking: Containment and Counterrevolution at Versailles, 1918-1919,* New York, 1967; John M. Thompson, *Russia, Bolshevism, and the Versailles Peace,* Princeton, 1966. For a treatment of one important segment of British political life, see Stephen R. Graubard, *British Labour and the Russian Revolution, 1917-1924,* Cambridge, Mass., 1956.

lication of the second volume and spent three summer months working at the Public Record Office in London and in private collections to which access also became possible due to the new government policy.[2]

Once I began, I realized that the new materials—particularly the Cabinet, Foreign Office, and War Office papers in the Public Record Office—would enable me to treat the making of British policy on a scale so different from that on which my earlier manuscript was written that minor revision would be impossible and that, indeed, a fundamentally different book would result. A glance at the footnotes of this volume will indicate the importance to my purposes of these new materials.[3] Along with a decision to rewrite the original manuscript drastically came a decision to divide it in two. This seemed good sense, and not only because of the bulk of the rewritten work: in fact, the events with which it dealt had never fit easily together, and I had in any case divided the earlier manuscript into two parts, one treating the end of intervention, the other the process of reaching the Anglo-Soviet accord of March 1921. Now the two parts will be separate books, each one, like *Intervention and the War*, presuming to stand alone.

❖

This book has been written in the interstices of a full-time teaching schedule at Harvard and at Princeton. Many individuals at both of these universities, and elsewhere, have assisted me in many ways. It is my pleasure to acknowledge these debts.

I am grateful to the Milton Fund of Harvard and the Center of International Studies and the University Research Fund of Princeton for enabling me to spend summers in England doing research. Mrs.

[2] The most valuable of these collections for the purposes of the present volume were the Curzon Papers and the Balfour Papers. Other collections, principally the Milner Papers, had previously been placed at my disposal without restriction. Two most important collections—those of Lloyd George and Churchill—remain unavailable for general scholarly use at the time of going to press for the present volume.

[3] In citing materials from the Public Record Office I have used the standard Record Office notation system to indicate the department of origin: Cab. (Cabinet and Cabinet Office), F.O. (Foreign Office), and W.O. (War Office). Cabinet papers, of course, include those from all departments which the Cabinet Office circulated (either at its own volition or by ministerial request) to members of the Cabinet. Because of the thoroughness with which the Cabinet Office went about the task of sifting departmental papers for wider circulation, I have not felt it necessary for the purposes of this study to use the files of additional departments, such as the Home Office and the Admiralty.

Preface

Faith Henson and Mrs. Dorothy Rieger, my secretaries at Lowell House, Harvard, and the Woodrow Wilson School of Public and International Affairs, Princeton, cheerfully did the bulk of the typing of the two successive versions of the manuscript. Robert Bunselmeyer, of Yale, came to my rescue by doing for me a piece of research which I had overlooked. Invaluable assistance with Russian translation was rendered by Alastair N. D. McAuley and my wife, Yoma Crosfield Ullman, who has also done much to see the manuscript through the press. Robert I. Rotberg and Paul M. Shupack read and criticized the earlier version of the manuscript; Ernest R. May and Arno J. Mayer brought their unrivaled knowledge of the politics and diplomacy of the First World War and its aftermath to the criticism of the present version. I am indebted to them all.

Crown-copyright material in the Public Record Office, London, is published here by permission of the Controller of Her Majesty's Stationery Office. The overworked staff of the Record Office were unfailingly helpful to me during my work there in the summer of 1966; I am most grateful to them. Material from the Curzon Papers is published here by permission of Viscount Scarsdale, who kindly allowed me to use them at Kedleston before their shipment to the India Office Library, where they are now housed. During a previous summer's visit, Mariott, Lady Ironside, allowed me to use and to quote from the unpublished diaries of her late husband, Field-Marshal Lord Ironside; to her and to Colonel R. Macleod, who did much to facilitate my access to the diaries, I am much indebted. Similarly, I wish to express my gratitude to Major Cyril J. Wilson, who allowed me to use and to quote from the unpublished diaries of his late uncle, Field-Marshal Sir Henry Wilson.

I should also like to express my indebtedness to the following:

to Mr. Mark Bonham-Carter for permission to use and to quote from the Asquith Papers in the Bodleian Library, Oxford;

to the Trustees of the British Museum for permission to use and to quote from the Balfour Papers and those of Lord Robert Cecil;

to the Library of the University of Birmingham for permission to use and to quote from the Austen Chamberlain Papers;

to Viscount Davidson of Little Gaddesden for permission to use and to quote from his own papers;

to the Warden and Fellows of New College, Oxford, for permission to use and to quote from the Milner Papers now in the Bodleian Library;

and to the Library of Yale University for permission to use and to quote from the papers of Colonel E. M. House, Frank L. Polk, and Sir William Wiseman.

Princeton, New Jersey   R.H.U.
June 1967

CONTENTS

xiii

MAPS AND ILLUSTRATIONS

CHRONOLOGY OF PRINCIPAL EVENTS

1918

30 October—Armistice between Allies and Turkey

31 October—War Office orders occupation of Baku and oil fields

6 November—Sixth All-Russian Congress of Soviets proposes peace to Allies

7 November—first anniversary of Bolshevik seizure of power

11 November—Armistice between Allies and Germany

14 November—Cabinet decides to occupy Batum-Baku railway

17 November—coup at Omsk establishes Kolchak as "Supreme Ruler of All Russia"

14 December—General Election returns Coalition with vastly increased majority

18 December—French expeditionary force lands at Odessa

24 December—Litvinov addresses peace note to President Wilson

December-January (1919)—Czechs abandon front in Siberia, saying they will not fight for Kolchak

1919

12 January—Peace Conference opens at Paris

23 January—Allies invite all Russian factions to attend peace conference on Princes Islands (Prinkipo) in Sea of Marmora

24 January—Bolsheviks call for a congress at Moscow to found new revolutionary International (the Comintern)

January-March—Britain torn by industrial unrest and riots by servicemen awaiting demobilization

4 February—Soviet government accepts Prinkipo invitation; it is rejected by the several anti-Bolshevik administrations

15-17 February—Churchill, in Paris, unsuccessfully tries to get Supreme Council agreement for massive effort of intervention

4-6 March—decision for early withdrawal of British troops from North Russia and Caucasus

8-14 March—Bullitt talks with Soviet leaders in Petrograd and Moscow, gets peace terms from them

22 March—Communist regime under Bela Kun established in Hungary

25 March—Lloyd George's "Fontainebleau Memorandum" warns that harsh terms will foster Bolshevism in Germany

6 April—French withdraw all troops from South Russia

9 April—200 M.P.'s send telegram to Lloyd George in Paris urging government to have no dealings with Soviet regime

9 April—War Office recruits two-brigade relief force for North Russia

16 April—Lloyd George assures House of Commons that government will have no dealings with Soviet regime

27 May—Council of Four sends Kolchak note assuring him of support and hinting at recognition provided he pursues liberal policies

9 June—Red Army takes Ufa, marking beginning of Kolchak retreat

June—U.S. troops leave North Russia

11 June—Cabinet approves Churchill plan providing for offensive by relief force in North Russia in order to bring about link with Kolchak

25 June—Denikin takes Kharkov

26 June—Labour Party annual conference passes strong resolution against intervention in Russia, hinting at industrial action to stop it

28 June—signing of Treaty of Versailles

3 July—Denikin, at Tsaritsyn, launches Volunteer Army on "Moscow campaign"

9 July—Reichstag ratifies Treaty of Versailles, ending state of belligerence and removing legal foundation for blockade of Russian coasts; Allies nevertheless continue blockade

7-23 July—mutinies among White forces convince Ironside that they will not be able to hold front against Red Army in North Russia; he decides upon early and complete British evacuation

29 July—Cabinet decides that North Russia evacuation will be military operation, unaccompanied by attempt at negotiations with Bolsheviks; it decides also to curtail British aid to Kolchak and to concentrate it instead on Denikin

1 August—Kolchak's retreat has taken his forces more than half distance from Urals to Omsk

12 August—Cabinet decides on "final packet" of aid for Denikin

8 September and 1 November—the two British battalions in Siberia depart

24 September—Cabinet decides upon change in policy toward Baltic

states; it can send no more aid, nor can it advise them not to make peace with Moscow

27 September and 12 October—British forces depart from Archangel and Murmansk

12 October—Yudenich begins offensive aimed at taking Petrograd

13 October—Denikin takes Orel, 250 miles from Moscow

20 October—Red Army recaptures Orel from Denikin and turns back Yudenich in outskirts of Petrograd

mid-October—British troops withdraw from Caucasus, leaving only small garrison at Batum

8 November—Lloyd George, speaking at Guildhall, implies that intervention had failed and that government would pursue new policy toward Russia

12 November—Kolchak abandons Omsk to Red Army

17 November—attempt at coup by leftist opposition to Kolchak at Vladivostok is easily put down

20 November—Cabinet decides that British warships on blockade duty in Baltic, now to be withdrawn for winter, will not return in spring

25 November—last remnants of Yudenich's North-Western Army flee to Estonia

25 November—negotiations begin in Copenhagen for Anglo-Soviet agreement on exchange of prisoners

1920

16 January—Lloyd George secures agreement of Supreme Council to permit trade with Russian cooperative organizations, now controlled by Soviet government

19 January—Supreme Council agrees on *de facto* recognition, and aid, for Caucasus states

7 February—Kolchak executed at Irkutsk

12 February—signing of Anglo-Soviet agreement on prisoner exchange

20 February—Red Army enters Archangel and Murmansk

26 March—Denikin and Volunteer Army abandon mainland, take refuge in Crimea

1 April—last U.S. troops leave Siberia; Czechs depart during summer, while Japanese remain until late 1922

ANGLO-SOVIET RELATIONS, 1917-1921

Volume II

Britain and the Russian Civil War

November 1918-February 1920

EUROPEAN RUSSIA
1919

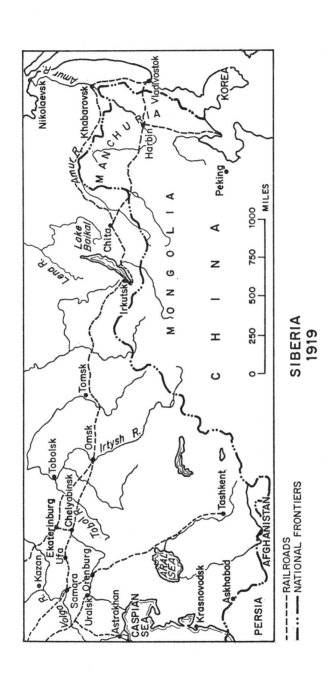

SIBERIA
1919

- - - - - RAILROADS
·—·—· NATIONAL FRONTIERS

CHAPTER I

INTERVENTION AND THE ARMISTICE: THE MILITARY CONFRONTATION

If there was ever the slightest doubt as to the intentions of the Allied Governments, there can be none now. The purpose of the Allied invasion of Russia is to crush the Socialist Republic and to re-establish the reign of capitalism and landlordism.—Soviet leaflet "To British and American Soldiers," December 1918[1]

On the evening of 7 November 1918, the first anniversary of the Bolshevik Revolution, Edmund Ironside—Major, Royal Artillery, temporary Brigadier-General and Acting Commander of a 7,500-man mixed Allied force spread in a wide arc south of the North Russian port of Archangel—made his daily entry in his diary. Ironside used his diary not only to record events but for rumination; newly arrived in Archangel, with rank and responsibilities beyond his thirty-eight years, he preferred solitude to the company of the officers he found there and often spent his evenings in lengthy, discursive writing. On this occasion it was not the anniversary of Soviet rule which he found worthy of comment: anniversaries, after all, grow in importance with the passage of years, and in November 1918 there seemed little likelihood that the Bolshevik regime, its hegemony confined to only a small portion of the former Russian Empire, would survive to celebrate the passage of a second year. Instead, he reflected on the impending end of the war in Europe—news of the negotiations then proceeding between the Allies and the Germans had reached even isolated Archangel. "If the war comes to an end," Ironside wrote, "we shall be in a curious position here." And he continued:

[1] "Kommunisticheskie listovki i vozzvania k soldatam antanty" (Communist Leaflets and Appeals to the Soldiers of the Entente), *Istoricheskii arkhiv* (Historical Archive), 1958, no. 1, pp. 29-31. It is worth noting that this particular appeal, printed in English, was headed "Why Have You Come to Ukraine?" This was an error: no English-speaking troops participated in the Ukrainian intervention (see below, pp. 46-48).

The original objectives of the expedition appear to have been to stop the Germans from taking Murmansk and Archangel, ports from which they might direct submarine action against us. We had a suspicion of the Bolshevik Government and did not trust them not to make common cause with the Germans. Now the German menace is over . . . we find ourselves opposed to the Bolsheviks only. The Czechs in Siberia have to be liberated and we have been trying to entice them westward. We are now backing a White Russian Counter-Revolution against the Bolsheviks and are actually committed to staying here in Archangel. We could not evacuate the place even if we wanted to do so, for the ice may come at any moment, being late already.[2]

Here, in a paragraph, Ironside put down the circumstances which had brought him and so many others to Russia during the last months of the Great War.[3] They had come initially to fight Germans, not Bolsheviks, as part of a desperate effort to reconstitute the Eastern Front which had collapsed when the Soviet regime, by signing the Treaty of Brest-Litovsk, had taken Russia out of the war. In this effort neither the Archangel force nor the larger Allied force up on the Arctic Ocean at Murmansk had been assigned a principal role. Their function, as Ironside wrote, was to guard the two ports to prevent the Germans from making use of them and from seizing the vast quantities of war materials which the Allies had landed during the preceding several years, but which had not been shipped inland owing to the wretched condition of the Russian transportation system.

Instead, the plans drafted in London and Paris during the spring and summer of 1918 assigned the main part in this effort to reconstitute the Eastern Front to forces moving west from the Siberian Far East. These forces, according to the plans, would be principally Japanese—the figure of half a million men even made the rounds at one point—in order to make use of Japan's vast manpower resources, the only sizable reserve not already committed to the war and one which, moreover, could not practically be used on the Western Front. The Japanese would be joined in their 6,500-mile journey across Siberia and European Russia by smaller contingents from the other Allies and also by the so-called Czechoslovak Corps,

[2] MS diary of Field-Marshal Lord Ironside, entry for 7 November 1918.
[3] Except where otherwise noted, the following introductory material is drawn from Volume I of the present work, *Intervention and the War*, Princeton, 1961, *passim*.

some 60,000 strong, formed during the period of the Provisional Government from Czechs and Slovaks, either previously resident in Russia or recently captured as prisoners of war, who wished to fight against the Dual Monarchy for an independent Czech and Slovak state. These were the Czechs mentioned by Ironside in his diary entry. In particular, all of these forces coming west from Siberia would serve as a rallying point for "loyal" Russians anxious to drive the German invader from Russian soil. Although it was realized that the Bolshevik regime in Moscow, subject as it was to German threats and pressures, could not give its open approval to such a scheme, it was nevertheless hoped that at least its tacit acquiescence might be forthcoming.

All the assumptions behind these plans were wildly unrealistic, the product of a frantic search for some means of forcing the Germans to divert troops from the Western Front as, after Brest-Litovsk, they had diverted them from the East. The Japanese had no interest in reconstituting an Eastern front (a fact they did not try to conceal from their Allies), but they were not unwilling to establish their control over the Maritime Provinces of Siberia: of the 70,000 Japanese soldiers in Siberia by the time of the Armistice, only one battalion ever ventured west of Harbin, and it got no farther than Irkutsk.

If it was absurdly wishful thinking to expect the Japanese to bear the brunt of an offensive against the Germans in European Russia, it was perhaps even more unrealistic to think that the Bolsheviks would acquiesce in what amounted to a series of foreign invasions of the territory they claimed to rule. In mid-May 1918 hostilities erupted between Soviet forces and units of the Czechoslovak Corps scattered over central Siberia. In early July, Red Army detachments heading north from Petrograd became embroiled with a small British force patrolling south from Murmansk. By the following month, when a British, French, and American force under British command landed at Archangel and Japanese and American troops began to flow into Siberia (President Wilson agreed to American participation in order to rescue the Czechoslovak Corps), it was openly acknowledged that they were going into combat against the Bolsheviks, not the Germans, who had already begun withdrawing troops from Finland and the Ukraine in order to bolster their crumbling positions in the West.

In this manner, during the final months of a four-year global war, the Allied governments committed military forces to an enterprise whose purpose and nature bore little resemblance to the underlying purpose and nature of the plans drawn up by the general staffs. Of all the assumptions upon which these plans were based, the only one even remotely valid was that "loyal" Russians would rally around the foreign invaders, and it was valid only in the sense that the various foreign forces inevitably served as protective screens behind which anti-Bolshevik forces—whose primary purpose, of course, was the defeat of Bolshevism, not the renewal of war against the Central Powers—could form. This was the "White Russian Counter-Revolution" about which Ironside wrote in his diary. Its focal points were Archangel in North Russia (the Murmansk region was too sparsely populated and too remote ever to be more than an outpost), Omsk in central Siberia, and the Don country in South Russia. In the South, however, it was not Allied intervention but German occupation which provided the screen—in this case one of confusion, rather than assistance—behind which resistance to Moscow took shape.

Readers of the first volume of this work will recall that, although the Japanese contributed the most troops and the French were the most outspoken in their professed hostility to Bolshevism, the Power which actually was most deeply involved in the whole effort of intervention was Great Britain: the French were vociferous in principle but parsimonious in practice, the United States was from the outset a reluctant participant, while the Japanese in fact threatened not the existence of the Soviet regime, but only the extent of the territory it ruled. For this British predominance there were strategic reasons. Unlike the French, who, understandably enough, viewed the war in terms of territorial gains and losses on the Western Front, the British—with their imperial and naval concerns—saw it as a global encounter. They sought to prevent German domination of the Baltic provinces of Russia and the oil fields of the Caucasus, both areas of importance for British investors. More urgently, they feared the spread of German influence and Turkish pan-Islamic agitation across the Caspian Sea down into Persia and even into Afghanistan and India, the heart of the British Empire. These motives impelled the British to take the lead in devising schemes for intervening in order to re-create an Eastern front against

Germany. Once intervention had begun, their global concerns led them to exercise the dominant foreign influence upon the various anti-Bolshevik forces, and to contribute the largest share of material assistance to them in every sector. This dominant role extended even to Siberia, where Japan's influence was limited, despite the number of Japanese troops involved, by the parochial nature of Japanese interests.

For the British government the intervention only gradually, and imperceptibly, became an effort whose purpose was to overthrow the Bolshevik regime at Moscow. No one date can be singled out as a turning point, except, perhaps, 31 August, when an armed mob in Petrograd, the former capital, invaded the British Embassy, killed the naval attaché, Captain F.N.A. Cromie, and seized all of the Embassy's records; in response, Arthur James Balfour, the Foreign Secretary, announced in London that, unless full reparation were immediately made, the British government would hold members of the Soviet government individually responsible for the outrage and would "make every effort to secure that they shall be treated as outlaws by the governments of all civilized nations and that no place of refuge shall be open to them."[4] One would use such language about no one but an enemy.

By then, however, Allied forces at Murmansk and Archangel had already begun their undeclared war against Soviet units sent to drive them out, and the first Japanese and American troops, together with a British battalion, had arrived in Siberia. Yet, before all these events occurred, it was by no means certain that enmity would necessarily develop between the Soviet regime and the Allies. Throughout the spring of 1918 Allied agents in Moscow, in particular R. H. Bruce Lockhart, who represented the British government, tried desperately to bring about cooperation, rather than hostility, between the two sides. To Lockhart and his colleagues, cooperation meant Soviet agreement to the entry into Russian territory of Allied troops in order to fight against the Germans. But to Lenin and Trotsky such cooperation held out only the prospect of certain—and much more rapid—German retaliation. Why should they take such a risk for the sake of a relationship with the Entente Powers (the *other* bourgeois coalition) which, according to Bolshevik doctrine, could be only temporary at best? At the time, Ger-

---

[4] Volume I, p. 290.

man forces were deep in the Ukraine, while the Allies—even the Japanese—were thousands of miles from the centers of Soviet power. It may be argued that the Bolshevik leaders misread the military situation, and that they in fact had more to fear from the Allies than they did from the Germans. But they were not the only ones who overestimated German power: the sudden collapse of the Second Empire took the world by surprise.

The German collapse, of course, served to underline all the inconsistencies of Allied policies in Russia. On 17 October, Ironside reported from Archangel that the battalion of French infantry under his command had been seriously disaffected by rumors of the impending armistice on the Western Front; once the armistice was actually signed, he said, he would no longer be able to rely on these troops to take part in combat operations.[5] Ironside's report was brought to the British War Cabinet the following day by General Sir Henry Wilson, the Chief of the Imperial General Staff. It raised the whole question, Wilson said, of Britain's future military policy in Russia. Balfour agreed that the question was serious; the end of the war with Germany would remove the whole justification for intervention in Russia. But he added: "If we now withdrew our forces from European and Asiatic Russia we should suffer a serious loss of prestige, and should be letting down our friends."[6]

Balfour did not elaborate upon his remarks about British "prestige." Nor did the Cabinet at this meeting on 18 October do more than call attention to the necessity of giving serious consideration to the problems of Russia. Other matters—the inter-Allied negotiations concerning the terms of the armistices with the Central Powers—were more pressing. Not until four weeks later, after the Armistice with Germany, did the War Cabinet return to a discussion of Russian problems. In the meantime, these problems, and possible British responses to them, received definition in a series of papers sent to the Cabinet by the Foreign Office and the War Office, the two departments of state which since the outbreak of revolution in Russia in 1917 had been most involved.[7]

These papers differed in tone and in approach, but through them all ran a recognition that the current situation contained two dis-

[5] Ironside's telegram of 17 October 1918 is cited in Volume I, p. 256, n. 87.

[6] War Cabinet minutes W.C. 489, 18 October 1918, noon; Cab. 23/8.

[7] For a discussion of the different approaches toward Russian problems taken by the Foreign Office and the War Office, see Volume I, pp. 82-84.

tinct threats to the security of the Western democratic powers. The first was the westward spread of Bolshevism "with [as one Foreign Office paper put it][8] its doctrine of irreconcilable class war." Germany itself might well succumb to revolution spurred on by hunger and military defeat. On the other hand, if the war were to end with German society and German industry essentially intact, the second danger might appear. Given her geographical position, Germany—and not the Western Powers—might eventually "restore Russia to order." In doing so she would earn the gratitude of all Russians thus "delivered from the nightmare of Bolshevism" and thereby regain much of the position in the East which the war had cost her. The specter of a revived, reactionary Russia in league with a revived, reactionary Germany was little more cheering to contemplate than was that of a revolutionary Germany allied with a revolutionary Russia. In either event the Allied victory would be a chimera.

In one form or another, arguments such as these appeared in all of the papers about Russia circulated to the Cabinet during October and November 1918. Yet none of them, whatever their source, went on to advocate what Lord Robert Cecil, Parliamentary Under-Secretary at the Foreign Office, called in a paper on 20 October "a crusade against Bolshevism."[9] Cecil himself stated flatly that it would be "impossible" after the end of the war in Europe to maintain any British force in Russia, "at least for fighting purposes." General Sir Henry Wilson, on behalf of the War Office, reached the same conclusion in a "Memorandum on our Present and Future Military Policy in Russia" he submitted on 13 November.[10] Wilson wrote that there were three possible courses of action open to the Allied governments. The first was to withdraw all forces and simply build up a ring of states—Wilson called it a *cordon sanitaire*—around Russia. From a military point of view, he said, this was "indefensible," for it would leave the advantage of initiative entirely to the Bolsheviks, while the surrounding states would have to maintain themselves indefinitely in a condition of readiness. Moreover, for some time these states—many of them newly created—would need the support of Allied garrisons in order to maintain such a cordon. But it would be virtually impossible to find troops for this

[8] Political Intelligence Department, Foreign Office, "The Growing Danger of Bolshevism in Russia," Cabinet paper G.T. 6106, 25 October 1918; Cab. 24/68.
[9] "Memorandum on Russian Policy," Cabinet paper G.T. 6050; Cab. 24/67.
[10] Cabinet paper G.T. 6311; Cab. 24/70.

sort of duty; most of the British Army, for instance, was serving on a duration-of-war basis and would soon have to be demobilized.

A second course, Wilson continued, would be to "grasp the nettle firmly" by taking active military measures with a view to crushing Bolshevism at the earliest date. This would also be the surest way to prevent the expansion of German influence, for it would be the Allies, and not the Germans, to whom the Russians would owe their liberation. Moreover—and here Wilson briefly touched on one of the most vexing aspects of the Russian problem—a Russia thus liberated would be able to reestablish control over the border nationalities which had declared their independence. This re-created, powerful, united Russia would be an effective barrier to Germany's eastern ambitions.[11] Nevertheless, desirable as such a solution might be, Wilson could not recommend it: the Allies did not have the military manpower available for a war of intervention in Russia at the conclusion of the long, exhausting war against Germany.

"One course only remains," Wilson wrote, "namely, to do all we can in the way of material to give our friends a fair start, and then to withdraw." The "friends" were the anti-Bolshevik forces in Siberia, in North Russia, and in the South, who had remained "loyal" to the Allied cause. Here the C.I.G.S. sounded as if he were a sportsman arranging a match: provided that Britain were to place its friends in an initial position to defend themselves from the Bolsheviks, it would be giving them a fair chance. He justified such detachment with a paragraph of muddled Darwinism which deserves quotation in full:

> Bolshevism is a cult if not a religion. It flourishes in rank soil such as exists in Russia owing to complete isolation from the outside world for several years, involving stoppage of trade and of all peaceful avocations; conditions which are abnormal, even in Russia. Like all cults, if radically unsound, as we think it is, it cannot long survive the re-establishment of normal conditions in the rest of the world. If, however, it is better than we are prepared to admit, it will gradually develop into a higher organism and we cannot permanently stifle it by military action.

Wilson went on bluntly to state the consequences of such an argu-

[11] A particularly forceful statement of the argument that Germany would aim at dismembering Russia in order to bring the weak separate units into its own orbit, and that therefore it was imperative for the Allies to strive for the restoration of a united, great Russia came from Sir George Buchanan, formerly Ambassador at Petrograd, in a memorandum to Balfour on 28 October 1918; F.O. 800/205.

ment for Britain's Russian friends: "If the Bolsheviks are the better men, we cannot indefinitely continue to protect the others."

Wilson submitted his paper on 13 November, in time for it to serve as the basis for discussion at a small meeting that same day at the Foreign Office. Besides Balfour, who was chairman, and Cecil, the Foreign Office was represented by Lord Hardinge, the Permanent Under-Secretary, and Sir George Clerk, a senior official. Wilson himself could not be present, but from the War Office came Lord Milner, the Secretary of State, Major-Generals Percy de B. Radcliffe and William Thwaites, the Directors (respectively) of Military Operations and Military Intelligence, and Lieutenant-Colonel F. H. Kisch, a General Staff officer who specialized in Russian matters. The only other participant (and the only Admiralty representative) was Admiral Sir W. Reginald Hall, the Director of Naval Intelligence. From this meeting came the first specific decisions regarding British policy in Russia for the period following the Armistice; they were formally approved by the War Cabinet itself on the following day.[12]

Wilson's paper had recommended that Britain should "liquidate" its "commitments in troops" at the earliest possible moment, aiming at the complete withdrawal of British forces from European Russia, at least, by the time the treaty of peace with Germany was signed. At the meeting, however, Wilson's goal quickly became blurred. Balfour enunciated the principle that "the British Government cannot embark on an anti-Bolshevik crusade in Russia." So vague a statement could find universal agreement, but Milner quickly qualified it with the observation that, while of course they could not "crusade against the Bolsheviks in countries where Bolshevism already prevailed," they should nevertheless do their best "to protect other countries from Bolshevik attack, particularly when invited to do so." And in Milner's eyes "other countries" included not only what Balfour had called "the border States of West Russia from the Baltic to the Black Sea," but all other regions of the former Russian Empire which now were in non-Bolshevik hands. Unlike Balfour, who implied a willingness to send British troops to help the Baltic states of Estonia, Latvia, and Lithuania defend their newly proclaimed independence, Milner was unwilling to send land forces

---

[12] The minutes of the meeting at the Foreign Office on 13 November, 3:30 p.m., were appended to those of the following day's War Cabinet—W.C. 502, 14 November 1918, noon; Cab. 23/8.

there. "On the other hand," he said, "considerations both of honour and of interest demanded that we should keep Bolshevism from the regions East of the Black Sea, i.e., the Caucasus, the Don country, and Turkestan." Here, after all, the borders of the British and Russian Empires had marched together; here, for Milner, was the focus of British "interests."

The decisions that resulted from this meeting reflected Balfour's feeling that "the people of this country would not consent to [an anti-Bolshevik] crusade," Milner's concern for the British Empire's strategic interests, and Cecil's view that "our object should be to help the Russians to stand by themselves, and we should therefore do everything possible to support and strengthen existing [anti-Bolshevik] organizations." In summary, they were the following:

To remain in occupation of Archangel and Murmansk.

To retain in Siberia the British force and military mission already there; to encourage the Canadian government to adhere to its earlier, pre-Armistice decision to send out a sizable force of its own; to endeavor to induce the Czechoslovak Corps to remain at the front in western Siberia instead of demanding repatriation; and, finally, to recognize the "Directorate" at Omsk[13] as the *de facto* government for Siberia.

To establish contact with General A. I. Denikin, who had assumed command of anti-Bolshevik forces in South Russia and the Don country, and to give him all possible assistance in military material.

To occupy with British troops the railway line running between Batum, on the Black Sea, and Baku, on the Caspian.

To supply the Baltic states with military materials, if and when their governments gave evidence that they would be able to make effective use of such support.

This set of decisions received ready endorsement at the War Cabinet's meeting the next day. There Milner once again urged the support of "friendly" forces in those regions "which most closely affected the interests of the British Empire and were most easily got at." Edwin S. Montagu, the Secretary of State at the India Office, thereupon asked if there was general agreement to the "principle, stated by Lord Milner, that where there was in existence a friendly anti-Bolshevik Government which it was to our advantage to support, we should support it, and we ought to support it, even though

[13] For the Directorate at Omsk, see Volume I, pp. 267-69.

it entailed anti-Bolshevik action." The minutes of the meeting laconically record that the Cabinet decided "that the principle stated by Lord Milner should be accepted."[14]

Here, of course, was no "principle" at all; indeed, it was precisely the absence of any overriding "principle" which had given rise to the piecemeal decisions that emerged from the session at the Foreign Office on the previous day. Most of these decisions amounted, in essence, to the maintenance in being, without any explicit changes in goals, of a number of operations originally conceived as part of the anti-German war which had just ended; the others—limited aid to the Baltic states and the occupation of the Batum-Baku railway—scarcely gave evidence of a central purpose. The very *absence* of a principle underlying these initial post-Armistice decisions on Russian policy received justification in a memorandum which Arthur Balfour had written a few days earlier.[15] He was concerned, he said, about a "very insufficient apprehension" —on the part not only of Russians or of the British public, but also of British civil and military officials dealing with Russia—of the British government's aims regarding that troubled land. It seemed to be commonly supposed that, with the defeat of the Central Powers, Great Britain would use its military expeditions already in Russia as the basis of an effort "to carry out a campaign against Bolshevism, and to secure, by foreign intervention, the restoration of decent order and stable Government." This supposition, the Foreign Secretary wrote, indicated a "complete misapprehension" of what the British government either could do or desired to do. On the contrary, he said, the nation "would certainly refuse to see its forces, after more than four years of strenuous fighting, dissipated over the huge expanse of Russia in order to carry out political reforms in a State which is no longer a belligerent Ally."

The British government, Balfour said, had constantly asserted that it had no desire to interfere in Russian domestic affairs, and that it was for the Russian people themselves to choose their own government. If, in the course of military operations "essentially directed against the Central Powers," Britain had had to act "with such Rus-

---

[14] The minutes are cited above, n. 12.

[15] Balfour's memorandum, dated 1 November 1918, is appended to War Cabinet minutes W.C. 511, 10 December, noon; Cab. 23/8. A copy is in the Milner Papers in the Bodleian Library, Oxford, box C-1. Most of it is printed (but incorrectly dated 29 November) in Winston S. Churchill, *The Aftermath*, London, 1929, p. 165.

sian political and military organizations" as were "favourable to the *Entente*," such cooperation did not imply that the British government deemed itself "to have any mission to establish or disestablish any particular political system" in Russia.

The government still adhered to these views, Balfour asserted, and its military policy in Russia was governed by them. Yet it did not follow from this argument that with the end of the War it could wholly turn its back on Russian affairs. On the contrary, the Foreign Secretary continued,

Recent events have created obligations which last beyond the occasions which gave them birth.... In the South-east corner of Russia, in Europe, in Siberia, in Transcaucasia and Transcaspia, in the territories adjacent to the White Sea and the Arctic Ocean, new anti-Bolshevik administrations have grown up under the shelter of Allied forces. We are responsible for their existence and we must endeavour to support them.

During the twelve months following the Armistice this argument —that the British government was bound by obligations of honor to assist those Russians who had remained loyal to the Allied cause— was repeatedly put forward in justification of continued British involvement in the Russian Civil War. It was not only a public justification, but one used, as we have seen Balfour, Milner, Cecil, and Henry Wilson use it, at the highest levels of government. In a governmental system in which decisions are jointly made and for which ministers are held collectively responsible, such a justification had much to recommend it. It sounded politically neutral: although British ministers might personally prefer a non-Bolshevik regime, they would not presume to make this choice for the Russian people. Instead, by furnishing assistance, they would simply make certain that the non-Bolshevik governments did not immediately fall before the attacking Red Army but would survive, presumably to allow the Russian people an alternative to Bolshevism—should they want one.

Against those, within and without the British government, who argued for an effort to destroy the Bolshevik regime, such a justification made possible the reply that the government was doing all it could, commensurate with available resources. As Balfour put it in his memorandum: "Such a policy must necessarily seem halting and imperfect to those who on the spot are resisting the invasion of militant Bolshevism, but it is all that we can accomplish or ought in existing circumstances to attempt." On the other hand, to those who argued for noninterference in Russian internal affairs, the policy outlined by Balfour could be presented as essentially that—allowing two disputants to fight out their differences, only making sure that one of them did not have the unfair advantage of seeing his opponent suddenly deprived of nourishment on which he had long fed and on which he had come to depend.

Yet if the domestic utility of such a justification was high—it could blunt criticism from both sides—its effect on the substance of British policy was surely deleterious, for it encouraged the government to behave like a spectator instead of the participant it actually was. Here was no "principle," as Montagu had supposed, but the habit, so ingrained in British politics and administration, of making a virtue of the lack of a "principle." R. H. Bruce Lockhart, who had represented the British government in Moscow during much of 1918 and who had just returned from imprisonment in Russia, urged in a memorandum written at the same time as Balfour's that the Allies should either mount a massive military expedition to overthrow Bolshevism (the policy he preferred), or else come to terms with it.[16] A middle course between these two, Lockhart wrote, would almost certainly end badly. Without large-scale assistance from foreign armies the anti-Bolshevik forces in Russia would not succeed in overthrowing the Soviet regime. By giving the anti-Bolsheviks financial aid and material support the Allies would only prolong the civil war without changing its eventual outcome. The Bolsheviks would ultimately win, and one day the Allies would need to come to terms with them. But then the task would be much more difficult: as Lockhart pointed out, they would be unlikely to distinguish between massive and middling contributions to the effort to unseat them. Therefore, he wrote, unless the Allies were willing to commit several divisions to a campaign against Moscow, they should abandon the cause of the Whites and actively seek a settlement with Bolshevism. A clear choice was necessary, and it was just such a choice that was made more difficult by the sort of rhetoric

[16] For Lockhart's memorandum of 1 November 1918, see Volume I, pp. 296-300. It was circulated to the Cabinet as paper G.T. 6662; Cab. 24/73.

about noninterference in Russian internal affairs that characterized Balfour's memorandum.

✧

Although Balfour wrote his memorandum on 1 November, it did not come before the Cabinet until 10 December. During the interval the decisions of 13 and 14 November represented the sum of the British government's *articulated* Russian policy. Underlying it was no explicit doctrine, nor any precisely defined goals. Clearly, there was a profound hostility to the Bolsheviks, who—by the lights of most Englishmen—had come to power illegally, had maintained it through the widespread use of terror, had employed it on one occasion to betray Russia's allies, and who aimed at a reconstitution of society according to the precepts of an "unnatural" political and economic philosophy. Yet hostility was no guide for action. Such was the British government's concentration on events in Germany and on urgent domestic affairs that not until December did the Cabinet get down to protracted discussions of the Russian problem and the position which the British delegation would take concerning it at the coming Peace Conference in Paris. We will examine these discussions in the following chapter. In the circumstances, the delay was understandable. But while time passed British military forces on every side of the encircled Bolsheviks became more and more deeply enmeshed in the Russian Civil War. Even had there been a clear-cut disposition in London to remove these forces from Russia —which there was not—the task of doing so became steadily more difficult.

British involvement was greatest in North Russia. Allied operations in the zone spreading south from Archangel, and in the more remote and less fiercely contested region around Murmansk, were wholly under British command. Once the White Sea approaches to Archangel froze, as they did in late November, extrication of the sizable forces there became almost impossible. Even though he had no precise knowledge of what plans were taking shape in London, General Ironside had no choice but to dig in and prepare for winter. There were two main lines of communication from Archangel into the interior—the Dvina River, leading southeast to Kotlas, and the railway line directly south to Vologda. Virtually all settlement in the region was either along the Dvina and its tributaries, or along the railway. Whether in winter or in summer, movement of military units of any size could only take place along these arteries: beyond them lay thick forests and mosquito-infested swamps through which small infantry units might with some difficulty pass, but which precluded the passage of larger forces with heavier weapons.

Accordingly, Ironside established his front-line positions some 180 miles from Archangel down the Dvina, and at a somewhat lesser distance down the railway. His mixed British-American-Canadian-French force constructed a string of large log blockhouses in which they mounted machine guns and mortars. The blockhouses were lighted and comfortably heated and were surrounded by formidable coils of barbed wire hidden from sight in the deep snow. They were defensive positions of enormous strength. Around these strongholds, throughout the dark northern winter, isolated but fierce patrol actions took place as the Bolsheviks probed for weaknesses. They never found any of significance. Later, when the rivers thawed in the spring, each side could bring up heavy artillery mounted on river gunboats. Then the blockhouses would not offer such security. But while the winter lasted, Archangel was secure.[17]

Behind this barricade, Ironside worked to repair the political damage that had been done by his predecessor, Major-General Frederick C. Poole. Poole had been in charge of the initial Allied force which had landed at Murmansk in May 1918, and he had moved his headquarters to Archangel in early August, when an Allied landing combined with an uprising by local anti-Bolshevik elements had removed the area from Moscow's control. Civilian authority was then formally established under a government headed by N. V. Chaikovsky, one of the great figures of Russian populism. The government was little more than a façade, however; Poole in fact retained all important powers himself, ruling by decree on all but the most trivial matters. E. H. Carr, then a young member of the Foreign Office specializing in Russian problems, succinctly commented at the time that Chaikovsky was "one of the few Russians for whom one can feel much sympathy politically." But Carr added: "Un-

---

[17] Field-Marshal Lord Ironside, *Archangel 1918-1919*, London, 1953, pp. 90-91. For a vivid picture of life in the blockhouses and of the winter fighting, see E. M. Halliday, *The Ignorant Armies*, New York, 1960, esp. pp. 84-85, 111.

fortunately he is old, and though well-meaning not a particularly strong character."[18] In effect, the British military command took control of the life of the city.[19]

Poole was immensely unpopular with the local population (except for a certain number of former Tsarist officers who could not stomach Chaikovsky) and with the diplomatic corps—what remained of the Allied diplomats who, during the spring and summer of 1918, had fled first from Petrograd to Moscow, then to the provincial town of Vologda, and finally to Archangel. The British "Commissioner in North Russia," F. O. Lindley—formerly Chargé d'Affaires in Petrograd—had complained bitterly to London about Poole's heavy-handedness and had insisted that real authority be vested in a popular Russian government.[20] Complaints about Poole came flooding into London, and in late September the War Office pulled Ironside from a divisional command in France and sent him to Archangel as chief of staff. At the same time it asked Poole to come home for consultations. He was never to return to Russia. Ironside was, first, Acting Commander-in-Chief, and then, on 19 November, he was promoted to temporary Major-General and given full command. Chaikovsky, who was outspoken in his criticism of Poole, later described Ironside as "a man of courage and understanding, thoroughly realising the scope and nature of his duties, as well as the character of the problems he had to handle, and [enjoying] the respect and esteem of all with whom he came into contact."[21]

The force which Ironside was given to command had been strengthened shortly after the Armistice by the addition of nearly 4,000 British troops. At last the British in the Archangel region outnumbered the Americans, with 6,300 men as opposed to 5,200. By the end of 1918 some 2,700 local Russians had been recruited, bringing Ironside's total strength (including 1,700 Frenchmen) to nearly

[18] Carr's minute, undated but written in early 1919, is in file 598/2/1/1656; F.O. 608/188. Carr was then a member of the British delegation at the Peace Conference. During 1919 much of the important work of the Foreign Office took place at Paris, and Carr probably did more to shape the discussion of Russian problems within the delegation than any other member: as the junior officer dealing with Russian affairs in Paris, he was expected to comment first on any matter, and his superiors would thus respond to his minutes and, therefore, to the terms in which he cast a problem.

[19] See Volume I, p. 237.   [20] See Volume I, p. 239.

[21] Chaikovsky's comment came during a conversation in London (he was on his way to the Peace Conference) with Curzon at the Foreign Office, reported in Curzon to Lindley (Archangel), despatch 6, 4 February 1919, file 602/1/2/2046; F.O. 608/195.

16,000.[22] The force was not as strong as its numbers, however. The Americans were poorly trained, and the British were virtually all conscripts who had been classified as physically fit for garrison duty but not for combat. Moreover they were all, especially the British, poorly led. Ironside's diary for the autumn and winter months is filled with despairing comments on the low quality of the officers he inherited from Poole. He found them unimaginative and unresourceful. Large quantities of whiskey had been sent from England, and many of them had taken to it as a means of passing the Arctic winter. Drunkenness was bad enough among staff officers at Archangel; it was worse when it appeared at the front. Ironside dealt severely with these cases, but he could not eliminate them entirely. And he moved firmly to stop another abuse—the selling of whiskey to Russians at vastly inflated prices.

He was most distressed, however, by the way in which British officers openly sympathized with the most reactionary monarchist Russian officers. Within a week of his arrival he called a meeting of all the officers in his mess and told them (he recorded in his diary) that "there was far too much open criticism" of Chaikovsky and his government, and that "there was to be no further political interference or even a suspicion of meddling in the affairs of the country." In particular, he directed, "there must be no further espousing of the Tsarist cause." After the meeting Ironside noted bitterly: "They none of them have the least idea of the serious business which is in front of us."[23]

Ironside could keep his own officers from openly supporting the restoration of Tsarism, but he could not—much as he wished to—control the Russians. At Archangel, as all over Russia, the cause of anti-Bolshevism was fatally weakened by the fact that leaders such as

[22] "North Russia," memorandum by General Sir Henry Wilson, C.I.G.S., Cabinet paper G.T. 6589, 2 January 1919; Cab. 24/72. It should be noted, however, that the *fighting* strength of the Americans remained higher than that of the British until the spring, when the former were withdrawn and additional British troops arrived, because nearly half of the British were non-combatants serving at Archangel in administrative positions.

[23] Ironside MS diary, entries for 3, 4, 7 October; 26 November; and 21 December 1918. For a report of the drunkenness of a British lieutenant-colonel commanding an important sector of the front, see Ironside (Archangel) to War Office, telegram E.917/G., 7 January 1919; W.O. 33/962, no. 874. See also Ironside, *Archangel*, pp. 87 and 90, and De W. C. Poole (U.S. Chargé d'Affaires, Archangel) to Secretary of State, telegram 786, 24 January 1919; *Papers Relating to the Foreign Relations of the United States: 1919, Russia*, Washington, 1937, p. 608 (hereafter this Department of State serial publication will be referred to simply as *Foreign Relations*).

Chaikovsky, who could command popular support, had to rely upon the old Tsarist officer corps for the military skills necessary to defeat the Red Army. Some of these officers genuinely sympathized with democratic notions, but most still yearned for the restoration of the old regime. And the peasantry, who necessarily formed the bulk of the rank-and-file forces, were scarcely enthusiastic about the prospect of fighting for the restoration of the Tsarist autocracy. Ironside found to his dismay that the population of the Northern region looked upon the civil war as not at all their affair but, instead, as a struggle between the Bolsheviks and the Allies. In these circumstances, local recruitment was extremely difficult. The Bolsheviks, for their part, could also represent the civil war as, in fact, one against foreign aggressors in league with Russian reaction. Their recruitment efforts were notably more successful than those of their enemies.[24] Ironside found the Russian officers at Archangel both lazy and effete, in marked contrast to their men, whose qualities he admired. "All these Russian officers," he wrote in his diary on one occasion, "can only think of the restitution of a Tsarist Russia just as it was in the old days." Another time he wrote: "I really begin to doubt whether we are doing right in saddling Russia once more with all the riff-raff of Tsarism. They seem to have learnt nothing and to care nothing." And a third entry stated: "They want other people to save Russia for them and then to hand it back to the useless creatures who spoilt it in the time of the Tsar."[25]

Ironside did his best to place military authority in the hands of less reactionary Russian officers. At his request, General V. V. Marushevsky, who had commanded Russian troops fighting on the Western Front in France, was sent out from Paris to take charge of all Russian troops in the Archangel region. Marushevsky was not a reactionary, but he was a stern disciplinarian. Immediately after his arrival in mid-November he organized a call-up which added several hundred conscripts to the nearly 2,000 Russians already recruited. Barely three weeks later, however, he had to quell a potentially serious mutiny by force. It was not an auspicious beginning.[26]

[24] This argument is developed in Volume I, pp. 249-50.

[25] Ironside MS diary, entries for 7, 16 and 26 November 1918.

[26] *Ibid.*, entry for 11 December 1918. Also, Ironside (Archangel) to War Office, telegram E.857/G., 12 December; W.O. 33/962, no. 751. There is a discrepancy between these versions and that in Ironside's book (*Archangel*, pp. 68-70). There

The mutiny was a clue to the real condition of things at Archangel. Although the Allied forces kept the town well under control,
the population was permeated with Bolshevik sympathizers. Bolshevik agents easily slipped through from Moscow bringing vast quantities of printed propaganda. Every day fresh Bolshevik posters
appeared on walls and billboards, and letter boxes were filled with
pamphlets and leaflets. The local town guard was totally ineffective
in dealing with this propaganda, and the few British patrols that
Ironside could spare for police duty never caught any of the Bolshevik agents.[27]

The Bolsheviks also directed propaganda at the Allied troops. In
many cases, Ironside wrote in his diary, their leaflets and broadsides
were well written and had "the most extraordinary effect upon bad
troops." The British, in turn, produced their own propaganda materials to be dropped from aircraft or fired in shells. Ironside's comment on these operations is worth noting:

There is something peculiarly un-British in pouring out counter-propa-
ganda, but we are doing something distinctly peculiar in messing about
with civil war in some one else's country. Personally, I cannot see that any
good will come of it, but then the Bolsheviks are something more than
mere revolutionaries. They are trying to make revolution in all other
countries.[28]

The effect of Bolshevik propaganda upon the troops under Ironside's command cannot be precisely assessed. But there is no doubt

---

he states that the ringleaders of the mutiny were tried by court-martial, found guilty,
and sentenced to death, but that he himself was able to commute the sentences to
terms of imprisonment. But both his diary entry and his report to the War Office
state that he signed their death warrants, and that the men were immediately
executed by a Russian firing squad and buried where they fell.

[27] Ironside, *Archangel*, p. 58. For a detailed firsthand account of Bolshevik in-
filtration behind Allied lines, see G. Mymrin, M. Pirogov, and G. Kuznetsov, *Razgrom interventov i belogvardeitsev na severe* (The Defeat of the Intervention and
the White Guards in the North), Archangel, 1940.

[28] Ironside MS diary, entry for 21 December 1918. This passage is extraordinarily
revealing of the set of attitudes with which Ironside approached his role. They were
attitudes both very British and very military. A highly professional soldier himself,
Ironside regarded his mission as one of performing a specific set of military tasks.
When he arrived at Archangel, he found that Poole's intelligence staff, headed by
Col. C.J.M. Thornhill, a thoroughly Russianized Englishman, who before the Bolshevik seizure of power had been head of British military intelligence in Russia, was
spending its time in intrigues rather than in providing the information upon which
military operations depended. "I have told Thornhill that it is much more interesting
to me to know when the frost will begin than what Trotsky is saying in Moscow,"
Ironside noted in his diary on 6 October.

that there was serious unrest. They were, after all, taking part in difficult operations under unpleasant conditions far from their homes at a time when the war for which they had been conscripted had ended. Ironside did what he could to counter this unrest. Neither Poole nor the American and French commanders under him had ever ventured out of Archangel. Ironside paid repeated visits, by pony sleigh or by aircraft, to the fighting fronts, and he insisted (with little success) that the others do the same.[29] Discontent was particularly widespread among the French and American contingents. The American chargé d'affaires at Archangel reported to Washington that both nations' troops felt that their continued presence in North Russia would serve only British interests, which they suspected of being "imperialistic."[30]

There was some—but only some—truth to these suspicions. There had long been important British financial interests in North Russia. Now, each ship that came from England with supplies for the town and for the Allied forces returned with a cargo of lumber or flax.[31] As the Power with overall command of the Northern intervention, the British felt constrained to take charge of the region's economy. Most urgent, especially given the large amounts of labor and materials which were purchased locally by the British command, was the need for a stable currency. The British therefore proposed a scheme for the introduction of a new ruble backed by the Bank of England and redeemable for gold in London. Chaikovsky's govern-

[29] Ironside, *Archangel, passim.* In his diary Ironside constantly despaired that subordinate officers of all nationalities were not taking sufficiently firm control over matters for which they were responsible. On 6 January 1919 he noted: "The fault of most of these people . . . is that they will not go out and see for themselves how things are going and what is the final result of their orders. They really are frightened to be faced with something untoward and would rather remain at home and imagine things."
This particular comment was prompted by Ironside's distress at conditions in the concentration camp on Mudyug Island, in the mouth of the Dvina, where Bolshevik prisoners were interned. The camp was run by Russians, under the command of a French officer who evidently visited it seldom, if ever. Ironside raged at reports of scurvy and of maltreatment of prisoners. "We cannot have a scandalous camp. I am responsible that the Russians treat their people well . . . ," he noted in his diary. But he was evidently unsuccessful in radically changing the camp's wretched conditions, which have since justifiably figured large in Soviet accounts of the North Russian intervention (cf. *Istoriya grazhdanskoi voini v SSSR* [History of the Civil War in the U.S.S.R.], vol. III, Moscow, 1957, pp. 200-201).

[30] Poole (Archangel) to Secretary of State, telegram 572, 13 November 1918; *Foreign Relations, 1918, Russia*, Washington, 1932, vol. II, p. 567.

[31] See Isaak I. Mints, *Angliiskaya interventsiya i severnaia kontrrevoliutsiya* (English Intervention and Northern Counter-Revolution), Moscow, 1931, pp. 136-40.

ment rejected the original British proposal that this currency be issued directly by British representatives on the ground that it allowed for no Russian participation. It was then agreed that the issue of currency should be in the hands of a special State Commission of Emission composed of four Russian members and a chairman appointed jointly by the British government and the Provisional Government of the Northern Region. The British were to buy currency for their needs, crediting the Commission's account in London with sterling at the fixed rate of 40 new rubles to the pound. The Commission could thereupon issue to the Provisional Government a sum equal to one-third of the rubles purchased. This amounted to a British loan; the total to be thus loaned was limited to 200 million rubles, and the loan was to be guaranteed by the timber resources of North Russia.[32]

As soon as it was introduced—in late December 1918—the new currency caused confusion and resentment. The peasants and working classes could not understand why one "ruble" should be worth more than another, and, when the British consulate started exchanging the new for the old at the rate of 40 to 48, it found few buyers among the mass of the population despite the fact that the pound sterling was actually selling in the streets of Archangel for 70 old rubles. But the bankers and merchants were fully aware that they could profit by such a disparity, and they proceeded to do so at the expense of their more ignorant countrymen. The new scheme thus incurred the wrath of the poorer people, who accused the British of trying to devalue their old currency, and at the same time swelled the wealth of the rich.[33]

[32] The currency scheme was proposed on 5 September in a British memorandum to the American government; *Foreign Relations, 1918, Russia*, vol. III, Washington, 1932, p. 66. Its actual workings are well summarized in Leonid I. Strakhovsky, *Intervention at Archangel: The Story of Allied Intervention and Russian Counter-Revolution in North Russia 1918-1920*, Princeton, 1944, pp. 127-30. The first head of the Commission of Emission was E. M. Harvey of the British Treasury.

The initial consignment of notes, printed in England, arrived in mid-November. Unfortunately, they bore the crown and double eagle of Imperial Russia and the declaration that they were legal tender "throughout the Empire." Chaikovsky was naturally indignant, and British officials at Archangel had to go through the whole lot of millions of rubles—many in notes of small denomination—and mark out each of these objectionable features with a stamping machine, a process requiring weeks. (Ironside MS diary, 23 December 1918; Poole [Archangel] to Secretary of State, telegram 586, 18 November 1918, *Foreign Relations, 1918, Russia*, vol. III, p. 89.)

[33] The prevailing rate of exchange in London during the fall of 1918 was about 48 rubles to the pound (the pre-war rate was 10 to the pound), but this bore little

The new currency also aroused the resentment of Britain's allies. The Americans were suspicious of the scheme from the very beginning, and, although they did not try to prevent it from being carried out, they regarded it as simply a device for making North Russia a British financial protectorate. Joseph Noulens, the French Ambassador, represented the scheme in his memoirs as a means through which Britain could exploit the timber resources of the North. Moreover, he alleged, because it promised a steady depreciation of the old currency, it gravely prejudiced the interests of many Frenchmen who owned important sums of old rubles. These objections aside, it is undeniable that the so-called British rubles did achieve their purpose of providing North Russia with a stable currency. But the fact that the enterprise was so poorly understood made the British no more popular and supplied the Bolsheviks with yet another theme for propaganda.[34]

Lindley, the British Commissioner, was considerably disturbed by the British failure to win the sympathy of the Archangel population, and he felt that his own efforts at creating good will were handicapped by the lack of any definite policy on the part of his own government regarding the widespread fear that, now that the Armistice had come, Allied troops would soon withdraw from North Russia and leave the region to the mercy of the Bolsheviks. These fears, Lindley said, made friendly Russians hesitate to cooperate with the Allies. He therefore asked London for some "clear declaration of policy" which he could use to calm the inhabitants, and for some public explanation of why Allied troops were in North Russia. In

---

relation to Russian realities. The Bolsheviks had retained the Kerensky ruble (the Tsarist ruble had been nearly driven out of circulation) and had resorted to the printing presses to meet their expenditures. As a result the old ruble had dropped sharply in value, and a pound could have bought around 70 of them in Archangel by the end of the year. The American chargé d'affaires commented that the British could have prevented all of the confusion had they not called their new monetary unit a ruble, but a fortieth of a pound, or a six-pence, which it actually was. (Poole [Archangel] to Secretary of State, telegram 704, 30 December 1918; *Foreign Relations, 1918, Russia*, vol. III, pp. 98-100. See also Mints, *Angliiskaya interventsiya*, p. 134.)

[34] See the protracted Anglo-American correspondence on this subject, dating from September 1918 through the end of the year, in *Foreign Relations, 1918, Russia*, vol. III, pp. 66-100. The views of the Americans at Archangel are most clearly expressed in an unsigned "Memorandum re New British Plan of Ruble Issue," 30 November 1918, in the records of the Archangel consulate (U.S. National Archives, Washington, Russian Embassy 800 file). For Noulens' views, see his *Mon ambassade en Russie soviétique, 1917-1919*, Paris, 1933, vol. II, p. 205.

reply, Lindley was told that he could announce that, although the Allied occupation was not likely to terminate in the near future, it was not intended to endure indefinitely. But it was undesirable that he should enter into any explanation of Allied policy.[35]

Here was little comfort for Lindley. Nor did he find any in Balfour's memorandum to the Cabinet stating that the basis of the British government's policy in Russia was the necessity to discharge its obligations to the "new anti-Bolshevik administrations" which had "grown up under the shelter of Allied forces." For Lindley, the crucial question was the nature of these anti-Bolshevik administrations. A summary of Balfour's memorandum reached him in Archangel at about the same time he received news of the formation in Siberia of a military dictatorship under Admiral Aleksandr V. Kolchak. This conjunction prompted him to write a private and confidential letter to the Foreign Secretary. He could imagine no more unfortunate occurrence. "I do not believe that any dictator, relying for support on the officers and upper classes only, has any chance of success," Lindley wrote. "He will only serve to alienate the mass of the population from the cause of order and throw the waverers into the arms of the Bolsheviks." It was not enough for the British government to wish to support its "friends." Instead, he wrote,

We have to choose between supporting the old officers and upper classes, who, thoroughly discredited under the old régime, have learned nothing and dream of a return to the old order, and supporting people who are unpractical and difficult to work with but who have a real following in the country and wish to see a new order arise out of the present chaos.[36]

Lindley's own suggestion was that the Allies should use as their rallying cry the Constituent Assembly, which had been dissolved by the Bolsheviks when it met in Petrograd in January 1918—and which was scarcely more popular with the supporters of the old Tsarist autocracy than it was with the Bolsheviks. The Powers should state, Lindley said, that their only object in Russia was that the Assembly should be allowed to meet freely and to decide on the future of the whole country. Only an announcement of this

[35] A summary of Lindley's telegram and the government's reply were sent as a memorandum to the State Department on 20 November 1918; *Foreign Relations, 1918, Russia*, vol. II, pp. 569-70.

[36] Lindley (Archangel) to Balfour, 6 December 1918; F.O. 800/205.

kind would sufficiently reassure the population of the North about the purposes for which Allied troops were in their midst.[37]

Lindley put forward this proposal in a telegram of 20 December. He was, of course, allowed to make no such announcement. By this time the British government had focused its attention on preparations for the forthcoming Peace Conference at Paris. From that forum, and not from individual governments, would come all statements regarding Allied policy in Russia.

Long before this time, Lindley's colleague, Ironside, had reached conclusions of his own regarding the Allied efforts in North Russia. As he stated them in his diary:

> I am not in the least frightened, but I cannot see that we are likely to do much good here. We can keep the fort perhaps during the winter, but if the White Russians in other parts do not manage to do something, we cannot create a new Russia from this place. Russia is so enormous that it gives one a feeling of smothering.[38]

The decisive sectors for Ironside—and for the War Office as well[39]—were Siberia and the South.

❖

In Siberia, Allied intervention took a form sharply different from that which it took in the North. The actual number of Allied troops in the field in Siberia was much larger. Besides the 60,000 Czechs and the 70,000 Japanese, there were, in the months following the Armistice in Europe, nearly 9,000 Americans, more than 4,000 Canadians, some 2,000 British, and smaller contingents from France, Italy, and Poland. Yet, with the exception of the Czechs, none of these foreign forces ever engaged in anything more than brief skirmishes with the Bolsheviks—and most of them not even that. By the end of 1918, moreover, nearly all the Czechs had withdrawn from the front, embittered and disillusioned.[40] Thus, whereas in North Russia the Allies took charge of combat operations (and of many aspects of civil administration as well), with local Russian

---

[37] Lindley (Archangel) to Balfour, telegram 536, 20 December 1918, Milner mss, box C-1. For the dissolution of the Constituent Assembly, see Volume I, pp. 68-69.

[38] Ironside ms diary, entry for 31 October 1918.

[39] "Allies now recognize that Murmansk and Archangel are of secondary importance owing to climate conditions and above all failure of Russians in North Russia to rise to our call. . . ." War Office to Colonel Blair (Vladivostok), telegram 70888, 15 November 1918; W.O. 33/962, no. 593.

[40] See Volume I, p. 266, and below, pp. 35-36.

forces serving only to augment their efforts, in Siberia their role was almost entirely restricted to training and supplying White Russian troops, and to guarding some of the towns and lines of communication behind the zone of operations.

At the time of the Armistice, the fighting front between the Bolsheviks and their enemies lay between the Volga and the Urals. The only Allied detachments to get this far west—some 6,000 miles from Vladivostok, where the great bulk of the Allied forces was concentrated—were British, and they did so with little effect. Shortly after the Armistice, Lieutenant-Colonel John Ward, a trade-union leader and Labour member of Parliament in command of the 25th Middlesex battalion, journeyed with 100 of his infantrymen and a brass band from their encampment at Omsk, the political center of anti-Bolshevik Siberia, to Ekaterinburg for the presentation of colors to the Czechs in appreciation of their services to the Allied cause. After an elaborate ceremony, Ward and his men entrained for the front at Kungur, some 120 miles to the west. When they arrived, the smartly equipped British soldiers clambered off their train and stood around in little groups while their band played the National Anthem, "Tipperary," and the "Colonel Bogey March." The Bolsheviks retaliated by laying down a fierce artillery barrage. Thereupon Ward decided that the weather was too cold for his men, and they marched back to their train and departed without firing a shot. The tired and ragged Czechs, who were left to face the Bolshevik barrage, were furious.[41]

A more serious effort was made by the Royal Marine crews of eight naval guns which were taken from British warships in Vladivostok, mounted on railway carriages, and shipped across Siberia. Two of these guns arrived at Ufa on 12 November. Their crews were the first (and, with the exception of Ward's musical tour, the only) fighting men from any of the Allies to reach European Russia from Siberia—which had, after all, been the whole purpose of the Siberian intervention as it was planned in London and Paris during the spring of 1918. The date should be noted, however: it was the day after the Armistice, and the enemy, of course, were Bolsheviks, not Germans. On 19 December these two guns reached Tisichma, 6,105 miles from Vladivostok. For the next five days, in

[41] Colonel John Ward, *With the "Die-Hards" in Siberia*, London, 1920, p. 119; Gustav Bečvar, *The Lost Legion: A Czechoslovakian Epic*, London, 1939, pp. 186-87.

temperature forty degrees below zero, they supported an attack by White troops. But the attack was too poorly organized to take advantage of the British shelling, and the guns had to retire. Of the other six guns, one saw brief action in December, and five more the following May and June.[42] Such was direct Allied participation in the Siberian civil war.

This was hardly an impressive record. Such limited Allied participation had come about, however, because of the American government's refusal to allow its forces to engage in combat now that the war in Europe was over and now that the Czechs no longer needed to be rescued, and also because of the unwillingness of the Japanese to move west of Eastern Siberia and the Maritime Provinces, where Japan's interests were concentrated. The restricted British role was scarcely in accord with the wishes of Major-General Alfred W. F. Knox, the senior British military officer in Siberia, formerly the military attaché at the embassy in Petrograd, who wished for nothing so much as a crusade against Bolshevism, an attitude epitomized in a telegram he sent to London on 4 November, stating: "Civilisation demands that we should intervene to prevent the horrors now committed every day in Russia."[43]

Acting on his own authority, Knox had allowed Ward and his small detachment to go to the front, but the War Office then stepped in to make clear to him that, unless specific orders came to the contrary, no other British troops were to go west of the Urals, and that the government's policy was "opposed to definite offensive action against the Bolsheviks."[44] As Henry Wilson told the Cabinet in a memorandum dated 30 November, even operations of a defensive nature west of the Urals would "increase our commitments in Siberia and would necessarily involve demands for personnel, which, in view of the uninstructed state of public opinion as to Russia and the approaching demobilization of the bulk of our forces may meet with much opposition in this country."[45]

In any case, it had never been intended that British troops in Si-

---

[42] General Sir Herbert Edward Blumberg, *Britain's Sea Soldiers: A Record of the Royal Marines during the War, 1914-1919*, Devonport, n.d. (circa 1927), pp. 94-102.

[43] Knox (Omsk) to War Office, telegram 30, 4 November 1918 (relayed as Vladivostok telegram 173, 7 November); W.O. 33/962, no. 544. For the Japanese unwillingness to move west, see Volume I, pp. 251, 263-64, 275-76.

[44] Noted in "The Military Situation in Siberia," memorandum by General Sir Henry Wilson, 30 November 1918, Appendix A to Cabinet paper G.T. 6460; Cab. 24/71.

[45] *Idem.*

beria should take part in major combat operations. The plans drawn up during the spring and summer of 1918 had left that role to the Japanese and the Americans. Instead, the chief British contribution to the Siberian intervention was to be the training and supplying of Russian forces. This was the function of the large British military mission under the command of General Knox. Colonel Ward's 25th Middlesex battalion was simply a garrison detachment, composed (like most of the British detachments in North Russia) of "C" class soldiers, declared physically unfit for strenuous combat, that had been rushed to Vladivostok from Hong Kong in August to help keep order.[46] Until the Armistice it was the only large British unit in Siberia. On 27 November, however, a battalion of the Hampshire Regiment arrived in Vladivostok from India. A crack formation of experienced soldiers, it was sent specially at Knox's request to act as an example to the Russian troops he was training; Ward's men, Knox felt, were not of sufficiently high caliber to maintain British prestige.[47]

The Hampshires were attached to a 4,000-man Canadian Expeditionary Force which Ottawa had begun to mobilize in mid-August in response to unrelenting British pressure since June. When the Canadians reached Siberia, however, the war in Europe was over, and the Canadian government had serious doubts whether the newly arrived force should not immediately be withdrawn. Further British pressure, applied by the War Office to the Canadian General Staff and also to Sir Robert Borden, Canada's Prime Minister, who was then in London, led to a decision that the troops should remain in Siberia at least temporarily. The expedition became increasingly unpopular in Canada, however, and on 23 December the Cabinet in Ottawa decided that the troops should be withdrawn in the spring, and that in the meantime they must not engage in combat operations or even leave their base at Vladivostok without express Cabinet consent. During the winter months before their evacuation, the Canadian troops grew restive. According to Ward they were inclined to insubordination, and their discontent also affected the battalion of British Hampshires that had been combined with them into one brigade.[48]

[46] See Volume I, p. 262.

[47] War Office to Commander-in-Chief, India, telegram 66597, 18 September 1918; Milner MSS, Box D-3.

[48] The circumstances surrounding the Canadian expedition are treated in Gaddis

Much the most important aspect of the British effort in Siberia was the work of Knox's mission in training troops and distributing military supplies. By the end of November 1918 London had sent to Siberia 200 field guns and complete sets of equipment for 100,000 men; on 6 December arrangements were made for the dispatch of equipment for yet another 100,000 men.[49] On an island in the bay off Vladivostok, Knox established a training school for Russian commissioned and noncommissioned officers. The school's commander was a thoroughgoing monarchist reactionary, General Konstantin B. Sakharov. The training staff, although largely Russian, included a number of British instructors and a platoon from the Hampshire battalion used to demonstrate British methods. All of the school's equipment was British, and the cadets wore British uniforms. On 15 February 1919 the first "class" of 500 officers and an equal number of NCO's was graduated. According to Churchill, they were of "indifferent quality."[50]

Although Knox first received orders to begin training Russians at the end of August 1918, when he was still in Tokyo waiting to go to Siberia,[51] the establishment of the school was delayed because of a disagreement with the French, who insisted that they, and not the British, should be in charge of training the new Russian army. The French maintained that this duty was theirs by right of the fact that France was Russia's oldest ally. Behind this attitude, which Knox termed a "weak and dishonest . . . piece of pleading,"[52] there lay the transparent motive that, if France trained what was destined

Smith, "Canada and the Siberian Intervention, 1918-1919," *American Historical Review*, vol. LXIV, no. 4 (July 1959), 866-77. To the materials there cited, from the Public Archives of Canada, should be added others in the Milner MSS, boxes E-2 and J-2, and in W.O. 33/962 at the Public Records Office, London. See also Ward, *With the "Die-Hards,"* p. 162.

[49] War Office to Chief of Canadian General Staff (Ottawa), telegram 71361, 22 November 1918; W.O. 33/962, no. 637. Entry for 6 December 1918 in "Diary of Events in Russia and Siberia, December, 1917, to December, 1918," appended to the paper by the General Staff, War Office, "Short History of Events in Russia from November 1917-February 1918" [hereafter cited as "Diary, Short History of Events"], Cabinet paper P. 111; Cab. 29/2.

[50] *The Times*, 28 February 1919. Sakharov's memoir of this period, *Belaya Sibir* (*Vnutrennyaya voina 1918-1920 gg.*) [White Siberia (Internal War, 1918-1920)], Munich, 1925, contains almost nothing of interest concerning the school and its operations. See Churchill, *Aftermath*, p. 164.

[51] War Office to Knox (Tokyo), telegram 65390, 31 August 1918; W.O. 33/962, no. 188.

[52] Knox (Vladivostok) to Director of Military Intelligence, telegram 74, 22 September 1918; W.O. 33/962, no. 328.

to be the future Russian army, French influence would be ascendant in the Russian state that would be organized after the Bolsheviks were defeated. The French case was considerably weakened, as Knox pointed out, by the fact that he and his mission were already on the scene in Siberia, whereas General Maurice Janin, the French officer who had commanded Czech forces fighting in France and who was coming out to Siberia to take command of Czech troops there as well as to head the French military mission, would not arrive until the middle of November; "in Russia's interests," Knox telegraphed to London on 22 September, "we have a right to ask when the Frenchmen propose to commence work."[53]

The British government at least partially gave way to the French on this question, however, by suggesting that Knox should go ahead and train a maximum of 3,000 Russian officers and men on the condition that his doing so would not provide a precedent affecting future arrangements among the Allies regarding control of the Russian army. The French government agreed to this proposal but insisted that any Russians trained by Knox should be drafted into new formations as soon as Janin arrived. On these conditions, the War Office told Knox to begin his work.[54]

By the time Janin arrived, Knox's training program was well under way. Moreover, the political situation in Siberia had radically altered. During the spring and summer of 1918 there had existed a number of independent and competing anti-Bolshevik "governments" in Siberia. In early November the most important of these came together in the so-called All-Russian Provisional Government, an uneasy combination of moderates and Socialist-Revolutionaries, with its seat at Omsk. On the night of 17-18 November, however, a group of officers staged a *coup d'état* placing all power in the hands of Admiral Aleksandr V. Kolchak, the Provisional Government's Minister of War, who took for himself the title of Supreme Ruler of All Russia and Chief Commander of All Russian Forces of the Land and the Sea. The coup met with the warm approval of the British military authorities in Siberia. There are some indications that British officers at Omsk actively

---

[53] *Idem.*

[54] See: British Embassy (Washington) memorandum to State Department, 23 September 1918, *Foreign Relations, 1918, Russia*, vol. II, p. 386; Lord Derby (Paris) to Balfour, telegram 1145, 24 September, Milner MSS, box D-3; War Office to Knox (Vladivostok), telegram 67317, 27 September; W.O. 33/962, no. 352.

connived at it, and there is no doubt that Ward's 25th Middlesex battalion covered the streets of Omsk with machine guns during the hours immediately following the coup, thus effectively discouraging possible interference by any other armed force, such as Czech units garrisoned nearby.[55]

Knox had met Kolchak the previous August and had been much impressed by him. He had warmly approved of the Admiral's acceptance of the portfolio of Minister of War in the Provisional Government at Omsk. Although in early November he had warned Kolchak that it "would at present be fatal" for him to give in to the urgings of rightist officers around him and seize supreme power,[56] Knox was not displeased when the coup actually took place. "This bloodless revolution was necessary because the Socialist-Revolutionaries were intriguing to undermine discipline in the army," he commented three days following the coup in a memorandum to the general commanding Canadian forces in Siberia. And he added:

From the allied point of view it is a matter of indifference of what complexion the Government may be so long as it is strong and just and willing and able to defend the new Russian army from internationalist and other harmful propaganda. Kolchak is honest, patriotic and capable. He is the best man for the post in Siberia.[57]

Knox's influence with Kolchak was so great—greater than that of

[55] For a detailed discussion of the various allegations that have been made about British involvement in the coup which brought Kolchak to power, see Volume I, pp. 279-83. See also Peter Fleming, *The Fate of Admiral Kolchak*, London, 1963, pp. 112-17.

On 1 December 1918, General Sir Henry Wilson, C.I.G.S., ordered Knox to inform Colonel John F. Neilson, his representative at Kolchak's headquarters, that the Foreign Office regarded his "recent activity in political matters" as "highly indiscreet" and "tending to compromise" the British government. While the War Office appreciated Neilson's "energy and zeal," he was to be "cautioned against any further activity of this nature." (Wilson to Knox [Vladivostok], telegram 71873 C.I.G.S.; W.O. 33/962, no. 684.)

Wilson's telegram did not specify the nature of Neilson's "activity," but in March, troubled by allegations of British complicity in the November coup at Omsk, the War Office asked Knox to report in detail on Neilson's actions. Knox replied immediately that he did not consider that either Neilson or his junior colleague, Captain Leo Steveni, had committed any "folly." (War Office to Knox [Vladivostok], telegram 75875, 5 March 1919, and Knox to War Office, telegram 1480, 9 March; W.O. 33/966, nos. 1260 and 1291.)

[56] Knox (Omsk) to War Office, 7 November 1918 (relayed as Vladivostok telegram 208, 13 November); W.O. 33/962, no. 573.

[57] Knox (Vladivostok) to Brigadier-General J. H. Elmsley, "Notes on the Military Situation in Siberia," 21 November 1918; Public Archives of Canada, Canadian Expeditionary Force, Siberia, Records, folder 17:2.

any other foreigner—that once General Janin had arrived it quickly became clear that, no matter what might be agreed between London and Paris, the French could not take the place of the British in training the new Russian army. After protracted negotiations in London, Paris, Vladivostok, and Omsk, it was agreed that Knox would continue to be in charge of the training of Russian troops and would direct the distribution of all military material from abroad, while Janin would assume the office of Commander-in-Chief of all Allied forces operating west of Lake Baikal. For his part, Kolchak agreed to work closely with Janin in order to assure unity of direction, and to keep both Janin and Knox informed of all his plans. These arrangements were agreed to after an exhausting final three days of negotiations in Omsk on 12-14 January 1919 and were published by Kolchak as an army order on the 21st.[58]

The agreement was in fact a total victory for Knox. Janin had the title of Commander-in-Chief, but Knox retained the critical power and influence. For Janin's command was almost nonexistent. It had originally been the intention of both the French and British governments that Janin should command Russian as well as Allied troops west of Lake Baikal, but Kolchak refused to allow it.[59] So Janin was left only the Czechs, who, in any case, were the troops he had originally come to Siberia to command. There were no other Allied fighting forces of any significance in western Siberia.

By the time Janin took command, the Czechs had almost ceased to be a factor in the Siberian military situation. The Czech National Council, meeting at Ekaterinburg on 21 November, issued a declaration stating that the *coup d'état* which had brought Kolchak to power was an act contrary to the principles for which they were fighting and against all their ideas of good government, and that, "as representatives of the army that is bearing the brunt of the struggle with the Bolsheviks," they would tender neither assistance nor

[58] See the following telegrams exchanged between Knox and the War Office during the period 18 November 1918-14 January 1919 in W.O. 33/962: nos. 630, 687, 707, 729, 740, 769, 799, 908, 921, and 933. Janin's version is in his *Ma mission en Sibérie, 1918-1920*, Paris, 1933, pp. 59-66. See also "Foreign Office Memorandum on Siberia," December 1919, in E. L. Woodward and Rohan Butler, eds., *Documents on British Foreign Policy 1919-1939*, First Series, vol. III, London, 1949, no. 613, p. 717. [Hereafter volumes of this official serial publication will be referred to simply as *British Documents*. All references will be to the First Series, and therefore the series will not be specified.]

[59] Janin, *Ma mission*, p. 19; Ward, *With the "Die-Hards,"* pp. 140-43.

sympathy to the new regime at Omsk.[60] Rudolf Gajda, the Czech general who had been commanding the Corps, told the British consul at Ekaterinburg that the combination of the coup at Omsk and the failure of the Allies to send any troops to share the fighting had made it impossible any longer to hold Czech troops at the front. Already there had been cases of soldiers refusing to obey orders.[61]

In succeeding weeks these cases multiplied. There were even cases of Czech troops forming soldiers' councils within their detachments. Gajda himself resigned in disgust and joined Kolchak when the Czech National Council would not let him punish agitators within the Corps. Soldiers began leaving the front. In early January 1919, when they were ordered up to the front again, whole units refused to move rather than fight for Kolchak. By the end of the month, it was apparent that, while some Czech officers might still wish to fight, their men had effectively taken matters into their own hands. Accordingly, it was arranged that all the Czechs should be withdrawn from the front and stationed as guards along the railway from Ekaterinburg and Chelyabinsk to Irkutsk.[62]

Thus, Janin's front-line command was liquidated from the moment he assumed it. So was any influence he might have had on the course of the civil war in Siberia, for the French contribution to the Siberian intervention was slight. Janin's military mission was the only French detachment in Siberia. There were no fighting units of any kind. And the French government sent Kolchak relatively few supplies. Thus it was scarcely in any position to stand in the way of British policy.

With Japan, of course, the case was altogether different. Japan's interests in Siberia were greater than Britain's. Moreover, Anglo-Japanese relations in Siberia were vastly complicated by the fact that the United States government was concerned to limit Japanese

[60] T. H. Preston (British Consul at Ekaterinburg) to Sir Charles Eliot (British High Commissioner, Vladivostok), telegram 20, 22 November 1918; Canadian Expeditionary Force, Siberia, Records, folder 17:2.

[61] Preston (Ekaterinburg) to Eliot (Vladivostok), telegram 21, 23 November 1918; Canadian Expeditionary Force, Siberia, Records, folder 17:2.

[62] See: E. L. Harris (U.S. Consul-General, Irkutsk) to Acting Secretary of State, telegrams 52 and 58, 25 and 27 January 1919; *Foreign Relations, 1919, Russia,* pp. 274-76; Ward, *With the "Die-Hards,"* pp. 146-49; Bečvar, *Lost Legion,* pp. 200-204; David Footman, *Civil War in Russia,* London, 1961, p. 118; George Stewart, *The White Armies of Russia: A Chronicle of Counter-Revolution and Allied Intervention,* New York, 1933, pp. 245-46.

action anywhere on the Asian mainland.[63] The Japanese-American antagonism placed the British government in a dilemma from which it never entirely escaped: Japan, after all, was formally Britain's ally, while the United States was not. Painfully, the British government tried to steer a course between them. During the early autumn of 1918, when the Americans and the Japanese could not agree on how the Trans-Siberian and Chinese Eastern railways should be controlled, London informed both Washington and Tokyo that it was concerned only to see efficient administration of the railways. Since the Japanese and American governments were the "primarily interested" parties, Britain would gladly accept any arrangement upon which they could agree.[64] And in mid-November, when the American government expressed concern over the great number of Japanese troops in northern Manchuria and eastern Siberia and asked Great Britain to join in a protest at Tokyo,[65] the British reply, on 9 December, stated:

His Majesty's Government have always been anxious for the active participation of American and Japanese troops in Siberia and they see no reason therefore for criticizing, from their own point of view, the mere presence of considerable bodies of Japanese troops in Russian territory. They are, however, quite unable to understand for what purpose these troops have been concentrated in such large quantities in Eastern Siberia, or to what use it is proposed to put them. So far they seem to have made no serious effort either to help the Czechs or to protect in a friendly manner the inhabitants against military aggression by the Bolsheviks, the object in which His Majesty's Government is chiefly interested.[66]

[63] For a careful analysis of this policy, see A. Whitney Griswold, *The Far Eastern Policy of the United States*, New York, 1938 (reissued, New Haven, 1962), pp. 223ff.

[64] C. A. de R. Barclay (British Chargé d'Affaires, Washington) to Secretary of State, 3 October 1918; *Foreign Relations, 1918, Russia*, vol. III, p. 272.

The details of the Japanese-American dispute over the control of the railways need not concern us here. Although the actual terms of argument concerned procedures, and not substantive matters, the real issue at stake was whether or not Japan would be given control over the Chinese Eastern Railway and thus achieve a great part of her eventual object of extending Japanese suzerainty over Manchuria. The Japanese-American agreement of 10 February 1919 was a great success for American policy; control of all of the railway system was to be in the hands of inter-Allied boards, and the task of guarding the Chinese Eastern Railway fell entirely to China. See section III (iii), "The Inter-Allied Railway Agreement," of the "Foreign Office Memorandum on Siberia," cited above, n. 58, and Betty Miller Unterberger, *America's Siberian Expedition, 1918-1920: A Study of National Policy*, Durham, N.C., 1956, pp. 107-17.

[65] Secretary of State to Page (London), telegram 2856, 16 November 1918; *Foreign Relations, 1918, Russia*, vol. II, p. 433.

[66] The British note, telegraphed to Washington by the U.S. Chargé d'Affaires in

In other words, the British government shared Washington's concern over the concentrations of Japanese troops, but it was not prepared to protest about them in Tokyo. This equivocation dismayed the Americans.[67]

Even in matters more directly affecting its own interests in Siberia, the British government proceeded with extreme caution in approaching Tokyo. Such a matter was the continued Japanese diplomatic and financial support of the Cossack Ataman Gregorii M. Semenov and other lesser but equally notorious brigand leaders who tried to carve out individual spheres of power in eastern Siberia. The object of British policy in Siberia, on the other hand, was to establish a single authority at Omsk which might unify the whole vast country and eventually grow powerful enough to drive Bolshevism from European Russia as well. Semenov was not only disruptive but savagely brutal. Readers of the first volume of this work will recall General Knox's intense anger at the assistance which Japan had given the bandit leader.[68] Knox's anger continued throughout the autumn and winter months. A paper he wrote on 21 November clearly stated his view:

> The Japanese do all in their power to weaken Russia by subsidising every freebooter in the Far East and so enabling them to defy the central government which the other allies wish to strengthen. They irritate the local population beyond endurance and among the allies they have made nothing but enemies. Their opposition to the American railway scheme has indefinitely postponed the provision of economic assistance and so immeasurably increased the difficulties of the much tried Russian Government; Russia and the Allied cause would benefit if every Japanese were withdrawn and 10,000 Americans only were left to garrison along the railroad from Vladivostok to Baikal.[69]

On 3 December Knox urged bluntly that London should present

London on 9 December 1918 and repeated by the State Department to the U.S. Ambassador in Japan, Roland S. Morris, on the 12th, is to be found in Morris' Papers in the Library of Congress, Washington, container 4. Excerpts are printed in *Foreign Relations, 1918, Russia*, vol. II, p. 433, but the last two sentences here quoted are omitted, thus altering the entire sense of the note.

[67] Thus, Frank L. Polk, the Acting Secretary of State, recorded in his diary on 7 January 1919 that he had that day received Barclay, the British Chargé d'Affaires, and "told him rather bluntly that if his Government had shown more patriotism and had not been neutral Japan would have come to terms long ago." (Frank L. Polk Papers, Library of Yale University.)

[68] See Volume I, pp. 272-76.

[69] From Knox's "Notes on the Military Situation in Siberia," cited above, n. 57.

the Japanese with a flat ultimatum to cease their financial support of Semenov.[70]

The British government's methods were not so drastic, however. As early as 11 November, Sir William Conyngham Greene, the British Ambassador in Tokyo, had sent the Japanese foreign minister a memorandum asking that support of Semenov be stopped. Greene received no reply, so he raised the matter in a conversation with the vice-minister for foreign affairs on 30 November. The latter admitted that Japan was subsidizing Semenov and the leaders of other irregular forces in Siberia, but he maintained that this was a "matter of history" and that, if Japan should cease these subsidies, it would appear to the world that she had been coerced into doing so by Britain and France. Greene replied that the British government was convinced that Japanese support of the various irregular bands was detrimental to the organization of a Russian national army. But instead of pressing the British demands, Greene merely suggested that the Japanese "at any rate make a beginning" and drop "one or two" of the subsidies, else he might have to make further representations.[71]

These efforts were to no avail. In a memorandum to Greene on 6 January 1919, the Japanese foreign minister stated that, *as soon* as a stable and united government was established in Siberia, Japan would use her influence with Semenov to arrange for his forces to be placed under its control. But since no such government yet existed, the Japanese were

confident that their assistance to him may well be continued without in any way hampering the object of establishing an acceptable Government in Siberia. To withdraw peremptorily all support to him at the present moment would . . . not only be premature and unwise under existing conditions in Siberia, but would also involve to a certain extent a question of honour for the Japanese authorities.

And lest the British should argue that Kolchak's regime at Omsk was just such a government, the memorandum concluded:

The Japanese Government trust that, in view of the foregoing explanation, it will not be urged upon them to sever at once their relations with

[70] Knox (Vladivostok) to War Office, telegram 312, 3 December 1918; W.O. 33/962, no. 698.
[71] Greene (Tokyo) to Balfour, telegram 1189, 30 November 1918; Milner MSS, box E-2.

Ataman Semenov and to leave him helpless and in disgrace, by mere considerations of expediency due to the proclamation of Admiral Koltchak as Dictator, or to the contemplated formation of a new army in the service of a Russian political group which has not yet been recognised by any Power.[72]

To this declaration the British once again returned a soft reply. In a memorandum to the Japanese ambassador on 14 January, the Foreign Office stated that Semenov's depredations had reached a point where there was a clear risk of disaster unless he was checked at once. Therefore, it continued, "His Majesty's Government feel that the Japanese Government will realise the vital issues involved and that they can be relied upon to take such further measures as they alone are in a position to do to bring further pressure on General Semenov."[73]

This was scarcely the ultimatum Knox requested. Japanese support of Semenov continued virtually unabated, as did Semenov's banditry. And although the Japanese soon withdrew 31,000 of the troops they had initially sent to Siberia and Manchuria (maintaining so large a force in the field was not cheap), nearly 40,000 still remained. They were to provide no assistance to Kolchak.

Meanwhile, during the last days of 1918, a curious episode occurred in the relations between the British government and Admiral Kolchak. On 29 November, Colonel John F. Neilson, Knox's chief representative at Omsk when he himself was at Vladivostok and the British officer perhaps most deeply involved in the events which brought Kolchak to power, telegraphed to Knox:

> Do they realize at home that Admiral Kolchak can only be kept in power by the strongest support of the English and French? Is it impossible to recognize him in some way? Cannot some more visible outward sign of our inward approval be given?[74]

Knox relayed Neilson's appeal to London, and on 6 December

---

[72] The text of the Japanese memorandum of 6 January 1919 was sent to Balfour by Greene (Tokyo) as despatch 13, 10 January, file 598/2/1/3220; F.O. 608/188. Greene also telegraphed a summary in telegram 8, 7 January, file 591/1/3/114; F.O. 608/178.

[73] Curzon (Acting Foreign Secretary) to Greene (Tokyo), telegram 28 (repeated as no. 35 to High Commission, Vladivostok), 14 January 1919; Canadian Expeditionary Force, Siberia, Records, folder 17:2.

[74] Neilson (Omsk) to Knox (Vladivostok), unnumbered telegram, 29 November 1918, relayed to War Office as Knox's telegram 302, 1 December; W.O. 33/962, no. 683. For Neilson's activities, see above, n. 55.

it was sent to the Foreign Office by General Thwaites, the Director of Military Intelligence, along with a note strongly urging on behalf of the War Office that the government publicly express its support of Kolchak's regime. Such support, Thwaites said, would strengthen Kolchak's hand against his enemies; any further drastic change of government in Siberia "would seriously prejudice the military situation in that region."[75]

At the Foreign Office, Sir George Clerk produced a draft note to Kolchak, stating that, now that he had "assumed control of the Government at Omsk," the British government wished to assure him that it was "watching with sympathetic interest" the endeavors of himself and his associates to "establish a Russian administration on a solid basis." While it was "for the Russians alone" to decide upon their form of government, Clerk's draft continued, the British government nevertheless hoped "to see an end put to the disunion and disorder which have prejudiced the welfare and happiness of Russia," and therefore Kolchak would assure himself of London's good will by striving "to secure a Russian Government based on democratic principles and to bring about the union of all parties who have the future prosperity of Russia at heart."[76]

This was scarcely a ringing endorsement. Lord Hardinge, the Permanent Under-Secretary, accurately characterized it as "somewhat lukewarm." But Hardinge's minute went on to say that he did not think that more could be said at present.[77] Balfour disagreed, however. In his own hand the Foreign Secretary wrote out what he called a "different draft." Absent were any references to "democratic principles" or to a "union of all parties." The message stated:

> On the occasion of the assumption by Your Excellency of administrative control at Omsk, His Majesty's Government desire to express their warm sympathy with every effort to establish a free Russian Government on the solid basis of public confidence. Nothing short of this can restore Russia to her proper position among the nations of the world, or enable her to take her full share in the work of civilisation and progress.[78]

On 23 December Balfour telegraphed his own version to Sir Charles Eliot, the British High Commissioner in Siberia, with in-

[75] Thwaites's memorandum, 6 December 1918, is in file 201170/6/38; F.O. 371/3365.

[76] Clerk's undated draft (a revision of an earlier draft by a junior official) is in *idem.*

[77] *Idem.* [78] *Idem.*

structions for Eliot to present it to Kolchak "if and when" he considered it desirable.[79] Almost immediately, however, the Foreign Secretary had second thoughts. On the mimeographed file copy of the telegram he pencilled: "I think this tel. should be held up or cancelled," and he put a check mark through the word "cancelled." Accordingly, on 24 December a "very urgent" telegram went out to Eliot stating simply: "Please suspend action in regard to message for the present."[80]

Balfour's message would have been the British government's first formal gesture of support for Kolchak since the Admiral's assumption of power on 18 November. The files make clear that the decision not to present it was Balfour's own, but they contain no clue to why he suddenly changed his mind.[81] There are no indications that anyone, within the Foreign Office or elsewhere in the government, expressed an objection to the message, and the message itself was hardly less cautious than Clerk's original draft. Presumably the Foreign Secretary felt that British (or, indeed, Allied) Russian policy was still so vague and unformed that even as hesitant a commitment as this would have been premature.

In any case, such caution accorded with Sir Charles Eliot's own preferences. On 29 December he telegraphed to Balfour a long report on the political situation in Siberia. Kolchak's government, he said, had met with the general acceptance of the military, official, and propertied classes, but not with that of the population as a whole. The military officers upon whom Kolchak depended to remain in power were reactionaries as a class, and to a great extent monarchists. This meant that in the eyes of the population the regime had become identified with principles much less liberal than those which it professed to uphold. On the other hand, any demonstration of actual liberal tendencies, or curbs on the shocking degree of license enjoyed by some of the officers, might cost Kolchak his military support.[82] Eliot concluded:

[79] Balfour to Eliot (Omsk), telegram 230 through High Commission, Vladivostok, 23 December 1918; *idem*. [For Eliot's appointment, see Volume I, pp. 269-70.]

[80] Balfour to Eliot (Omsk), telegram 233 through High Commission, Vladivostok, 24 December 1918; *idem*.

[81] Neither does the weekly "Eastern Report," no. C, 26 December 1918, which simply summarizes the two telegrams without any explanation; Cab. 24/145. The "Eastern Report" was a summary circulated weekly to the Cabinet during the War and the period immediately following.

[82] Eliot referred specifically to an incident in which a group of officers murdered some Socialist-Revolutionary political prisoners who had voluntarily returned to

It will be seen that the Kolchak Government is likely to have difficulty in satisfying at the same time the moderate liberal and the military elements; that it has difficulties with the Czechs and some Cossacks and that it cannot trust its own army to keep order. It must also count on a period of hostility of Japan. I cannot consider it as a strong government or recommend that we should back it unreservedly unless it can improve its position by its own efforts. But I see no danger in giving military and other support to its operations against the Bolsheviks.

General Knox's views were more simple. He stated them in a telegram to the War Office on 10 January:

I confess that all my sympathy is with Kolchak, who has more grit, pluck and honest patriotism than any Russian in Siberia, and whose difficult task is being made almost impossible by the selfishness of the Japanese, the vanity of the French, and the indifference of the other Allies. You have to take what you can get in Russia, and if you find an honest man with the courage of a lion he should be supported, although he may not appear to have the wisdom of the serpent.[83]

By January 1919, however, the question of the precise degree of endorsement to be given to Kolchak's regime was not a matter for the British government alone to decide. The Peace Conference in Paris was about to begin. Russian policy was now a matter for joint, rather than unilateral decision. Thus, on the same day on which Knox telegraphed his appeal for support of Kolchak, the War Cabinet in London deferred decision on Henry Wilson's contention that the two British battalions at Omsk constituted a force too weak to influence the Siberian situation effectively, and that, therefore, they should either be strongly reinforced or withdrawn from Siberia altogether in order to remove them from jeopardy; Wilson's own preference, on the ground that public opinion made it difficult to send additional troops to Russia now that the war was over, was for withdrawal. The Cabinet, however, refused to give Wilson the guidance he sought. Such a question would have to await a decision in Paris as to the general policies the Allies would follow.[84]

---

prison after being freed in an abortive rising: Eliot (Omsk) to High Commission (Vladivostok) for relay to Foreign Office, telegram 23, 29 December 1918; Canadian Expeditionary Force, Siberia, Records, folder 17:2. For the incident of the murder of the S-R's, see Fleming, *Kolchak*, pp. 121-22.

[83] Knox (Omsk) to War Office, 10 January 1919, relayed as telegram 662 from Vladivostok, 12 January; W.O. 33/962, no. 899.

[84] War Cabinet minutes W.C. 515, 10 January 1919, 11:30 a.m.; Cab. 23/9. At this meeting Bonar Law presided: Lloyd George and Balfour had already left for

Of all the regions of Russia where Allied intervention took place, the end of the World War made the most difference to the South. With the opening of the Straits—required by the very first article of the Armistice with Turkey—this hitherto unapproachable area became at one stroke the easiest channel to the heart of European Russia. Under the Armistice with Germany the German troops which occupied the Black Sea coast, the Crimea, and much of the Ukraine were required to withdraw, but not immediately. Instead, Marshal Foch, the chief Allied negotiator, agreed with the German delegation's contention that "the immediate evacuation of former Russian territory now occupied by German troops would leave the inhabitants there defenseless against the horrors of Bolshevism." Therefore, the Armistice provided for German withdrawal "as soon as the Allies shall think the moment suitable, having regard to the internal situation of these territories." This was scarcely an enforceable provision. The collapse of the Kaiser's government brought on the disintegration of authority within the occupying German armies: the rank and file were concerned only to return to their homeland as rapidly as possible. This was long before the Allies could replace them. With the departure of the only forces capable of maintaining order, the entire region of the Ukraine and the Crimea became the scene of a bitter struggle for power among the Bolsheviks, their White Russian opponents, and the Ukrainian nationalist movements. As one historian of these events has remarked, "The year 1919 in the Ukraine was a period of complete anarchy."[85]

Into this turmoil, in late 1918 and early 1919, came the Allies. As we have seen, one result of the British government's discussions of 13 and 14 November 1918 was a decision to furnish assistance to the anti-Bolshevik forces in South Russia and the Don country

---

Paris. Wilson presented his views at the meeting and in a memorandum, "Military Situation in Siberia," Cabinet paper G.T. 6598, 4 January; Cab. 24/72.

[85] Richard Pipes, *The Formation of the Soviet Union: Communism and Nationalism 1917-1923*, 2nd edn., Cambridge, Mass., 1964, p. 137. For a brilliantly drawn picture of the civil war in the Ukraine, and also of the German role, see Arthur E. Adams, *Bolsheviks in the Ukraine: The Second Campaign, 1918-1919*, New Haven, 1963, *passim*. For the Armistice agreements as they affected Russia, see John M. Thompson, *Russia, Bolshevism, and the Versailles Peace*, Princeton, 1966, pp. 28-32. For the relevant clauses of the armistices with Turkey and Germany, see Harry R. Rudin, *Armistice 1918*, New Haven, 1944, pp. 410 and 431.

led by General A. I. Denikin. A War Office memorandum submitted on the 13th urged "the great importance of insisting from
the outset on the recognition of the supremacy of British interests
in any undertaking in the North or South Caucasus and the Don
country," arguing that not only the military, political, and economic
importance of these regions for the whole British position in the
East, but also the fact that British troops, virtually unaided, had
defeated the Turks who had occupied these lands during the War,
entitled Great Britain to the predominant position.[86] Accordingly,
at the meetings on 13 and 14 November it was also decided to re-
affirm the British government's adherence to the Anglo-French convention of 23 December 1917, a wartime agreement which assigned
to France responsibility for the direction of activities "against the
enemy" in the territories west of the Don River—the Ukraine, the
Crimea, and Bessarabia—while the British were to take charge of
operations "against the Turks" in the "Cossack territories,"
Transcaucasia, and Central Asia. The meaning of the term "Cossack
territories" was not made clear. In the original agreement, the
French were given temporary responsibility for aid to the anti-
Bolshevik Russian forces of General M. V. Alekseyev, then located
at Novocherkassk, on the Don. But these forces, the nucleus of what
came to be called the Volunteer Army, had been driven eastward
into the Kuban country on the northeast shore of the Black Sea,
where Alekseyev had died, his place being taken by Denikin. In
reaffirming its adherence to the Anglo-French convention the British
War Cabinet asked that the British sphere include the territory between the Don and the Volga. This was perhaps unnecessary; being east of the Don, this territory already lay within the
British sphere. But in making such a stipulation, the British government implicitly took upon itself responsibility for assistance to
the Volunteer Army. This was a most important step, for it determined the whole pattern of Allied intervention in the South.[87]

[86] The memorandum, by Major-General P. de B. Radcliffe, Director of Military
Operations, was Cabinet paper G.T. 6274; Cab. 24/69.
[87] For the Anglo-French convention, see Volume I, pp. 53-56. Its text (in French)
is in *British Documents*, vol. III, pp. 369-70.
  It should be emphasized that in the eyes of the British government, at least, the
convention of 23 December 1917 was strictly an agreement governing the conduct
of military operations and did not accord Britain or France any political rights over
the territories it delimited. This point was strongly put by both Lord Curzon and
Lord Robert Cecil at meetings of the War Cabinet's Eastern Committee on 5 and 9
December 1918, in opposition to suggestions that the British might trade some of
the "rights" they acquired over Transcaucasia under the convention for some of

The region between the Don and the Volga, north of the Caucasus mountains, had never been occupied by the Central Powers. In it, by the end of the War, Denikin had established a considerable degree of authority. To the west, on the Don itself, were the Cossacks under General P. N. Krasnov, who had briefly come to terms with the Germans in order to preserve the autonomy of the Don country.[88] The common Bolshevik enemy brought Denikin and Krasnov into an uneasy partnership. To the south of their forces, beyond the mountains, lay the states of the Caucasus. Georgia, Armenia, and Azerbaijan had all declared their independence during the spring of 1918; all, in turn, had then come under at least partial occupation by German or Turkish troops. Now, with the end of the War, they could again assert their independence—repugnant as the notion might be to Great Russians like Denikin. Finally, across the Caspian Sea, north of Persia, in the vast desert territory of Transcaspia, a Menshevik and Socialist-Revolutionary group calling itself the "Ashkhabad Committee," supported by a small British-Indian force, had established itself as a "government" of sorts.[89] This, then, was the portion of southern Russia (the Anglo-French convention of 23 December 1917 applied only to "la Russie méridional") for which the British government had made itself responsible.

The zone allotted to the French presented a sharp contrast. The territory west of the Don had been entirely under German and Austrian occupation. In it there remained no established sources of authority like the forces of Denikin or Krasnov. When the Germans left, Soviet forces began to come into the Ukraine from the north. In this situation, the only way the French could keep their sphere from being overrun by the Bolsheviks was by sending in their own troops. This, then, was the difference between the problems facing the British and the French in South Russia in the months following the Armistice: the French had to commit their own forces, while the British had only to send material assistance. It was a development

France's claims to the Arab Countries under the Sykes-Picot Agreement of 1916. (Minutes, Eastern Committee, 41st and 42nd meetings, 5 and 9 December 1919; Cab. 27/24.)

[88] Stewart, *White Armies*, pp. 63-68.

[89] British intervention in Transcaspia, and relations with the "Ashkhabad Committee," will not be discussed in this volume at all; for thorough treatment, see Volume I, pp. 315-28, and C. H. Ellis, *The Transcaspian Episode 1918-1919*, London, 1963, *passim*.

which surely had not been foreseen by the signers of the Anglo-French convention nearly a year before.

The French occupation of South Russia began when some 1,800 infantrymen went ashore at Odessa on 18 December 1918, less than a week after the Germans had left the city. These French troops were soon joined by two Greek divisions and a brigade of Polish volunteers and later by more French detachments, including large numbers of Senegalese and Algerian troops, some 60-65,000 men in all. Their occupation covered the whole Black Sea coast from the Rumanian border through Odessa and Nikolaev to Kherson, and extended inland at some points nearly 50 miles.[90]

Yet they stayed only five months. The French occupation was ill-fated from the outset; expecting to find themselves simply doing garrison duty while local forces mounted a campaign against the Bolsheviks, the French immediately became involved in a confusing tangle in which Ukrainian nationalist forces, loosely under the direction of the so-called Directory headed by Simon V. Petlyura, were fighting detachments from Denikin's Volunteer Army, and both forces were fighting the Bolsheviks. In addition, there were the partisan bands led by the Cossack adventurer, Ataman Grigorev—at this time an ally, later an enemy, of the Bolsheviks. Finally, there was the Anarchist leader Nestor Makhno, whose smaller but equally fierce forces fought first on one side, then on another. The French and their Greek allies soon had to face savage attacks. On 10 March 1919 they were driven from Kherson by Grigorev, leaving at least 400 dead behind. Two days later Grigorev seized Nikolaev, which had been garrisoned chiefly by a much larger German force that had been marooned there (due to Grigorev's having earlier broken the rail lines between Nikolaev and the west) and ordered by the French to defend the town. Instead of obeying these orders, the Germans surrendered to Grigorev. With his forces vastly strengthened by huge quantities of weapons taken from the Germans, the Ataman could now turn his attentions to Odessa.

[90] The following paragraphs on French intervention in South Russia are based upon: Adams, *Bolsheviks in the Ukraine*, pp. 95-212; John S. Reshetar, Jr., *The Ukrainian Revolution, 1917-1920: A Study in Nationalism*, Princeton, 1952, pp. 239-49; Jean Xydias, *L'intervention française en Russie, 1918-1919: souvenirs d'un témoin*, Paris, 1927, *passim*; General A. I. Denikin, *Ocherki russkoi smuty* (Sketches of the Russian Turmoil), vol. IV, Berlin, 1925, pp. 31-71. For Makhno, see the chapter devoted to him in Footman, *Civil War in Russia*, pp. 245-302.

The French, Greek, Rumanian, and White Russian defenders of Odessa vastly outnumbered their attackers, but the morale of the French was broken. They had failed to win the support of the town's population, and now they found themselves unable to furnish the food and fuel necessary for a siege. For months, from his head-quarters at Constantinople, General Louis Franchet d'Esperey, the commander of French forces in the Near East, had advised against the South Russian intervention. Until the fall of Kherson he had been overridden; now Paris took his advice. At the beginning of April he received orders to proceed with immediate evacuation. By the 6th the French and all forces under their command had fled, leaving Odessa to Grigorev and his partisans. On their heels came the Red Army, and the apparatus of Soviet control. Less than a fort-night later, the French Black Sea flotilla was torn by a major mutiny.

Because of the division of reponsibilies under the Anglo-French convention, British troops took no part in these ill-fated land opera-tions, but the French fleet was powerfully reinforced by vessels of the Royal Navy. In the Crimea, however, 500 British marines (as the nearest available Allied force) landed at Sevastopol on 1 De-cember to supervise the evacuation of German forces and to make sure that the remaining vessels of the Russian Black Sea fleet did not fall to the partisan detachments which were menacing the city. The marines remained only twenty-five days; in late December they were relieved by a much larger French force. There, too, the French remained only until April.[91]

Except for this single episode, British intervention in South Russia during the months following the Armistice was limited to giving material assistance to Denikin. British and French military missions reached Denikin's headquarters at Ekaterinodar (now Krasnodar) on 26 November 1918. At the head of the British mission was Gen-eral Poole (the qualities which had wounded the sensibilities of Chaikovsky and his civilian colleagues at Archangel would be less abrasive in a purely military context, such as Denikin's). Poole's assignment was to report upon every aspect of the Volunteer Army, so that the War Office could determine the sort of supplies it would send out.[92]

Poole was quickly impressed by Denikin, and on 15 December

[91] Admiral Sir A. Calthorpe (High Commissioner, Constantinople) to Balfour, despatch 37/1038, 9 January 1919, file 602/1/4/1623; F.O. 608/196. See Blumberg, *Britain's Sea Soldiers*, pp. 481-82, and Adams, *Bolsheviks in the Ukraine*, p. 211.
[92] Poole's instructions were put before the Cabinet as Appendix A to General

he reported that large-scale assistance to the Volunteer Army was the only way in which the Allies could put a stop to the Bolshevik terror which was "depopulating large tracts" and "destroying civilisation." He recommended not only material support, in the form of large quantities of arms and ammunition, including tanks and aircraft, but also the dispatch to Denikin's headquarters of a British infantry brigade and an artillery brigade. These forces would give Denikin the sure knowledge that his rear was secure and thus enable him to use his own troops in more extended and daring operations against the Bolsheviks.[93] In his final report, written in January 1919 after he had left Ekaterinodar, Poole repeated these recommendations and also advised that a somewhat smaller British force should be sent to the Don for the same reasons. These forces, Poole said, should be used not only to garrison headquarters areas, but also to occupy many strategic points behind the combat zones.[94]

During his stay in South Russia, Poole was instrumental in persuading Krasnov, the Ataman of the Don Cossacks, to agree to place his forces under Denikin's command.[95] This was a considerable political achievement, for the goal of the Cossacks was an autonomous government of their own, while Denikin was completely committed to the restoration of a Great Russia that would include all of the territories of the former Russian Empire. Poole could get the Cossacks to ally temporarily with Denikin because the military situation in the South was so grave. Even including the Cossacks, according to Poole's report, Denikin could bring to bear against the Bolsheviks a fighting strength of only 51,400 men. He had to employ some 30,000 additional troops to keep order in base areas, and to protect his lines of communications from the depredations of irregular bands such as those of Makhno. Against him were ranged Bolshevik forces with a fighting strength of 75-80,000.[96]

Radcliffe's memorandum of 13 November 1918 cited above, n. 86. They were slightly modified by Cabinet paper G.T. 6274 A of the following day; Cab. 24/69. Poole was cautioned not to make any definite promises of support to Denikin.

[93] Poole (Ekaterinodar) to War Office, despatch K 11, 15 December 1918, sent by G.H.Q., Constantinople, as telegram I 4103, 21 December; Milner MSS, box H-7.

[94] General Staff, War Office, "Report of a Visit to the Headquarters of the Volunteer Army in South Russia by Major-General F. C. Poole, C.B., C.M.G., D.S.O.," January 1919, Cabinet paper P. 112; Cab. 29/2 (hereafter cited as "Poole Report"). For Denikin's version of Poole's visit, see his *Ocherki russkoi smuty*, vol. IV, pp. 36-37.

[95] *Ibid.*, pp. 71-73.

[96] Poole Report. Denikin's own estimate of his fighting strength was only 32-34,000, but he did not include the Don Cossacks in this figure (*Ocherki russkoi smuty*, vol. IV, p. 81).

Poole brought together Denikin and Krasnov, but he did not even attempt to bridge the gap, as wide as the Caucasus mountains, which existed between Denikin and the three independent states of Transcaucasia. As Poole indicated in his report, the interests of the Great Russians, such as Denikin, and those of the Caucasian separatists were diametrically opposed. The Volunteer Army could expect no help from Transcaucasia; by the same token, the governments of the three republics felt the White Russians to be a more immediate menace to their independence than the Bolsheviks, who were further removed. The British government, Poole wrote, would somehow have to formulate a policy that would satisfy both Denikin and the Transcaucasian states.[97] But he did not say what such a policy might be.

As we shall see, the British government met only one of Poole's principal recommendations: it supplied Denikin with vast quantities of all sorts of materials. But it did not commit to South Russia the infantry and artillery brigades for which Poole asked. British forces in large numbers did come to the Caucasus, however. On 31 October, the day following the Armistice with Turkey, the War Office instructed the British command in Mesopotamia (Iraq) to occupy the Azerbaijani capital of Baku and its surrounding oil fields. Thus on 17 November, scarcely two months after an earlier British force led by Major-General L. C. Dunsterville had abandoned Baku to the Turks and retreated by sea to Persia, another force of 1,200 British and 800 Indian troops under Major-General W. M. Thomson retraced Dunsterville's steps and landed at Baku on the heels of the departing Turks.[98] Meanwhile, as we have seen, the War Cabinet decided on 13 and 14 November to proceed with the occupation of the railway between Baku on the Caspian and Batum on the Black Sea in order to assure the safety of this important line of communication and to enforce the terms of the Armistice with Turkey. For this task the War Office earmarked an entire British division from Salonika.

These were the largest commitments of British troops anywhere across the vast domains of the former Russian Empire. Yet they

---

[97] Poole Report.
[98] *History of the Great War Based on Official Documents, The Campaign in Mesopotamia 1914-1918* (Brig.-General F. J. Moberly, compiler), vol. IV, London, 1927, pp. 329-30. See also Firuz Kazemzadeh, *The Struggle for Transcaucasia (1917-1921)*, New York, 1951, pp. 163-67. For Dunsterville's mission, see Volume I, pp. 305-10.

were made almost as if by reflex as part of the closing moments of the World War, after only the most cursory discussion about why British forces should be going to the Caucasus, or what policy objectives they should pursue there. Not until after they had begun to arrive did the highest policy-making bodies in London find time to consider questions of this sort. Throughout December 1918 the War Cabinet's Eastern Committee was seized with them. Its deliberations offer an important insight into the way in which, during the autumn of 1918, with the abrupt end of the War, the goals and nature of British intervention in the tangled affairs of Russia were transformed. We will follow these deliberations—and see something of their relation to the actual operations which brought Transcaucasia under military occupation—in the next chapter.

❖

Before we turn to these discussions, and to preparations in London for the coming Peace Conference, we must note the course of events in yet another region of the former Russian Empire where British power became engaged during the months following the Armistice: the Baltic. There, as in South Russia, the pattern of involvement was completely altered by the capitulation of the Central Powers. Until the Armistice the Baltic Sea was as closed to Allied shipping as the Black Sea had been. German control of the sea, and of much of its coasts, had been absolute. Indeed, German occupation had saved the three provinces on the southern shore from being taken over by the Bolsheviks. Lithuania and southern Latvia had been occupied by German troops since 1915; Estonia and the rest of Latvia were absorbed only during the renewed German advance in late February 1918 that had shattered Trotsky's illusion, at Brest-Litovsk, that there could be a condition of "no war-no peace."

With the defeat of Germany, each of the three provinces reasserted its claims for recognition as an independent state. Their weak position, however, strikingly contrasted with that of their northern neighbor, Finland. Indeed, by the autumn of 1918, Finland's position as an independent state was virtually secure. Neither Germany nor Soviet Russia—the two powers which menaced the other three Baltic provinces—had designs on Finnish territory. Both had recognized Finnish independence early in 1918. Moreover, when local Bolsheviks within Finland attempted to seize power later in the year, they were decisively defeated by White Finnish forces. Although the Whites had sought assistance from Germany, the German troops which thereupon came to southern Finland withdrew long before the Armistice of 11 November.[99] Thus, at the end of the War, Finland's independence was threatened only by the fact that Admiral Kolchak and other anti-Bolshevik leaders in Russia maintained that such a question would have to await a decision by a future constituent assembly.

Given Finland's secure position, however, there was never any real doubt that, despite the views of the Russian Whites, its independence would receive international recognition. Unlike the three Baltic provinces, it had enjoyed semi-autonomous status even under the Tsarist regime, and the Finnish declaration of independence on 6 December 1917 was greeted warmly abroad. Paris, indeed, rashly accorded the new state *de jure* recognition on 4 January 1918. This move—a marked exception to later French reluctance to agree to any measures which would make formal the division of the former Russian Empire—was taken precipitously in order to counteract German influence in Finland. It failed to do so. London acted more slowly, however, and British recognition was then put off for the remainder of the War when the Finnish government called in German assistance against its Red opponents. After the Armistice the approach of the Peace Conference, with its presumption of joint Allied action, delayed British recognition still further, but that it would eventually be accorded was never in dispute.[100]

Finland had been under the rule of the Tsars since 1809; Estonia, Latvia, and Lithuania for a century longer. Like Finland, they too had a long history of movements for independence. But of the three, Estonia alone, as the only one completely unoccupied at the time, was able to profit from the opportunity of the March Revolution. In April 1917, Prince Lvov promulgated a decree giving Estonia local autonomy. Elections were duly held for a national council from which a provincial government was chosen. Roughly one-third

[99] See Juhani Paasivirta, *The Victors in World War I and Finland: Finland's Relations with the British, French and United States Governments in 1918-1919*, Helsinki, 1965, pp. 10-27.
[100] Britain accorded *de facto* recognition to the Finnish government on 6 May 1919; the United States and Japan did so on 9 and 13 May. See *ibid.*, pp. 78-109, and Malbone W. Graham, *The Diplomatic Recognition of the Border States*, Part I: *Finland*, Berkeley, California, 1939, *passim*. Concerning British recognition, see the extensive correspondence in file 598/1/3; F.O. 608/187.

of the votes cast in these elections went to the Bolsheviks, however, and after the November Revolution the new provincial government easily succumbed to a Bolshevik rising. Yet Bolshevism lasted only until the German invasion. On 24 February 1918, after the Bolsheviks had fled Reval (Tallinn) and just before German forces occupied the capital, the Estonians once more proclaimed the independence of their country. Despite the German occupation, Estonians in exile in the West continued to assert Estonia's independence. By virtue of the progress already made by the Estonian independence movement, its representatives in the Allied capitals were given more sympathetic hearings than were those of either Latvia or Lithuania.[101]

The British government, receptive in general to the idea of the independence of the Baltic provinces, reacted warmly to these Estonian developments. On 3 May, Balfour wrote to an Estonian delegation visiting London that the government greeted "with sympathy" the aspirations of the Estonian people and would give provisional recognition to the Estonian National Committee "as a *de facto* independent body" until the Peace Conference should take place, and that at the conference the British government would do its utmost to secure the application to Estonia of the principle of self-determination.[102] On 10 September, Sir Ronald Graham of the Foreign Office sent the Estonian representative in London a note formally assuring him that the British government "would be entirely opposed to any attempt to impose on Estonia, either during or after the war, a Government which would not be in accordance with the desires of her population, or which would limit her claim to self-determination."[103] Balfour sent similar assurances to the Latvian National Council on 11 November, the day of the Armistice.[104] The case of Lithuania, however, was complicated by Polish claims. Here London adopted a prudent silence.

The basis of British policy in the Baltic region was set down in a memorandum given to the State Department in Washington on 2

[101] Stanley W. Page, *The Formation of the Baltic States*, Cambridge, Mass., 1959, pp. 69-82; M. W. Graham, *The Diplomatic Recognition of the Border States*, Part II: *Estonia*, Berkeley, 1939, pp. 239-46.

[102] Balfour's note is printed in *Foreign Relations, 1918, Russia*, vol. II, p. 829.

[103] Graham, *Diplomatic Recognition: Estonia*, p. 252.

[104] M. W. Graham, *The Diplomatic Recognition of the Border States*, Part III: *Latvia*, Berkeley, 1941, p. 406.

November 1918.[105] It was apparent, the memorandum stated, that Russia's recovery and return to "normal political conditions" would take a long time. Therefore, it was difficult to insist that "these smaller nationalities" should become "units in a federation of Russian states" instead of achieving independence themselves. The paper made clear that the British government felt that independence for the Baltic provinces was desirable, but it also pointed to the political risks that would be involved. Chief among these was the prospect that,

in proportion as we encourage the independence of Finland and the Baltic states, whether they remain apart or grow into a larger Baltic league, we probably at the same time encourage the drawing together again of certain elements in Great Russia and Germany, particularly if the former country becomes strong again and once more develops an aggressive centralising tendency.

The memorandum went on, accepting the risk and proposing steps for meeting it:

To combat the latter eventuality there appear to be only two lines of counter-move, either the break-up or thorough democratisation of Germany, or the full encouragement and support of these Baltic states and Lithuania, in particular, as a buffer.

Here was an assertion that would be repeatedly made at the Peace Conference—that a German-Russian combination, if it were brought about, would gravely menace the postwar world. (It was assumed —and it continued to be assumed for some time—that the Russia in question would be a "restored," non-Bolshevik Russia.) The strength of the British commitment to the idea of independence for the Baltic states is seen in the fact that the memorandum did not even mention a third "counter-move": that the Allies should rebuff demands for recognition from the border states and hold the Tsarist patrimony intact in order to ensure that the restored Great Russia of the future would be sympathetic to themselves, and an effective bulwark against Germany. This, of course, was what the French wanted to bring about, and it explains why they were always much more reluctant than the British to recognize the independence of the border nationalities (except Poland), and why they simultaneously pursued the

[105] The memorandum is printed in *Foreign Relations, 1918, Russia*, vol. II, pp. 841-42.

first of the two "counter-moves" cited in the British memorandum—
the break-up of the German Reich. Finally, it should be noted that
the memorandum left unstated perhaps the most important motivation underlying British policy: that British investment in, and trade
with, the Baltic maritime provinces (as with Scandinavia) had long
been great, and that, once they were politically independent of the
Russian hinterland, and therefore even more outward looking, it
would surely be greater. The Baltic would, ideally, become a British
lake.

But all this was in the future. In the late autumn of 1918 it
seemed more than likely that the fate of the Baltic provinces would
be settled by the Red Army as it followed on the heels of the withdrawing German troops. To oppose a Bolshevik invasion the British
government could only offer military material—if and when the
Baltic states had governments which could receive and make use of
such material[106]—and the guns of the Royal Navy. The dispatch of
ground troops was out of the question. Even the use of naval power
offered certain severe problems, however. As Balfour told the Imperial War Cabinet on 20 November, he had been pressing the Admiralty for some time for "a show of force in the Baltic" in order to
"strengthen the populations of that part of the world against
Bolshevism." The Admiralty had objected, principally on technical
grounds—the Baltic was filled with uncharted minefields and with
many mines which had broken loose from their moorings, creating
circumstances of great potential danger.[107]

The Imperial War Cabinet decided that the risks were worth taking. Accordingly, on the following day the Admiralty ordered
Rear-Admiral Edwyn Alexander-Sinclair, commanding a fleet consisting of five light cruisers, nine destroyers, and seven mine-
sweepers, to proceed to the Baltic; his primary aim, according to
his orders, was "to show the British flag and support British policy
as circumstances dictate."[108] These orders were scarcely sufficient,
however, and a week later Rear-Admiral Sydney R. Fremantle, the
Deputy Chief of Naval Staff, returned to the Imperial War Cabinet

[106] This had been decided at the meetings of 13 and 14 November; see above, p. 14.
[107] Minutes, Imperial War Cabinet, 37th meeting, 20 November 1918, noon; Cab.
23/44. Also Geoffrey Bennett, *Cowan's War: The Story of British Naval Operations
in the Baltic, 1918-1920*, London, 1964, pp. 32-33. For the distinction between the
War Cabinet and the Imperial War Cabinet, see below p. 65.
[108] Bennett, *Cowan's War*, p. 34. Bennett's account is based upon original materials.

to try to discover precisely what sorts of action Balfour had in mind.[109] Fremantle later summarized the Admiralty's dilemma as follows:

It was extremely difficult to get the Foreign Office to understand that, to frame orders for a naval force, the officer in command must be told whether he is at war or not. It may be possible under some circumstances to tell a land force: "We do not want war if we can help it, and therefore you must let the other man fire first before you fire on him." But with a naval force you cannot do that. The first time the other man fires it may be a torpedo, and then you may not have very much more to say, if the torpedo hits. So you must be told whether when you see a suspect you are entitled to open fire on him at once.[110]

Fremantle achieved his objective. Orders went out to Sinclair stating: "A Bolshevik man-of-war operating off the coast of the Baltic provinces must be assumed to be doing so with hostile intent and should be treated accordingly."[111]

Sinclair took the bulk of his small fleet to Reval, where he was met with a request from Konstantin Paets, the head of the Estonian government, for the establishment over his country of a British protectorate, including the stationing of a British battalion to garrison the capital and a British military mission to train the Estonian army. Sinclair replied, of course, that such an arrangement was out of the question. But naval support was not. British bombardment forced the Red Army to retire from positions menacing Reval, and British command of the sea enabled small Estonian raiding parties to land behind Bolshevik lines to harass them in their retreat. Moreover, Sinclair's ships helped ferry across the Gulf of Finland two regiments of Finnish volunteers who played an important part in the Estonian counter-offensive. The naval squadron also supplied the Estonians with large quantities of arms and foodstuffs. Thus assisted, Estonia managed to preserve its territorial integrity throughout the winter and spring of 1919.[112]

Latvia was not so fortunate. When the British squadron arrived in

[109] Minutes, Imperial War Cabinet, 39th meeting, 28 November 1918, 11:45 a.m.; Cab. 23/44. Also Bennett, *Cowan's War*, p. 34.

[110] From a lecture by Fremantle to the Royal United Services Institutions, 15 February 1934; quoted in *ibid.*, p. 34.

[111] *Ibid.*, p. 34.

[112] *Ibid.*, pp. 37-38; Page, *Baltic States*, p. 128; Carl Gustav Emil Mannerheim, *The Memoirs of Marshal Mannerheim*, London, 1953, pp. 206-8.

the Baltic, Riga, the Latvian capital, was still under German occupation. Sinclair sent a senior officer, together with a cruiser and two destroyers, to request that the Germans in Latvia remain temporarily—as they were obliged to do under the terms of the Armistice—in order to prevent the formation of a power vacuum into which the Bolsheviks could step. However, August Winnig, the German Commissioner for the Baltic provinces, refused, asserting that there was no fighting spirit left in his troops, and that Berlin would not send him any replacements. By the end of December 1918 the Germans had entirely evacuated the Baltic provinces. In so doing they removed all supplies of arms, food, and railway rolling stock, another violation of the Armistice and one which left the Baltic states even more at the mercy of the Bolsheviks.[113]

The British naval force at Riga did what it could to stop the Red Army's advance. It issued machine guns to Latvian troops and instructed them in their use. Late in December, when two Latvian regiments mutinied, British ships shelled their barracks until they surrendered—much against the Admiralty's orders to Sinclair, which stated that he should not interfere in internal affairs. And when all of the small Latvian army was sent to the front on 29 December in a last desperate effort to stop the Bolsheviks, patrols from the British ships went ashore to maintain order in Riga. These efforts proved futile, however: the Red Army was not halted.[114]

When news of these events reached London, Admiral Fremantle once again went before the Imperial War Cabinet to obtain a statement of government policy. The Admiralty's view, he said, was either that Sinclair's force should be withdrawn or else the government should be prepared to face the prospect of intervention in the Baltic on a much larger scale. If the latter were decided upon, there would be need for a land expedition of considerable strength—not only in order to fight the Red Army but, in Latvia at least, to suppress local Bolshevism, which had many adherents. Existing policies, Fremantle said, were half measures, exposing to considerable

---

[113] See the report by Captain H. H. Smyth, commanding H.M.S. *Princess Margaret*, to Admiral Sinclair, no. SOM. 126/1814, 6 January 1919, file 591/1/5/608, F.O. 608/178, and V.H.C. Bosanquet (Consul at Riga) to Balfour, despatch 5405, 5 January, file 591/1/5/1228, *ibid*. Winnig's own version is in his *Am Ausgang der deutschen Ostpolitik: Persönliche Erlebnisse und Erinnerungen*, Berlin, 1921, pp. 75-76.

[114] For these events, and the Admiralty's orders, see Bennett, *Cowan's War*, pp. 49-50. See also Page, *Baltic States*, pp. 122-23.

risks a naval force that was itself too small to have a decisive effect on the outcome of the war between Soviet Russia and the seceding Baltic states. If the decision were for withdrawal, he warned, it would have to come quickly. Riga—and Reval as well—would be ice-bound before the middle of January. Yet he also felt obliged to add that, once the British had left Riga, the local Bolsheviks would in all probability massacre their political opponents. Given Fremantle's arguments, and the fact that a commitment of British ground forces in the Baltic states was out of the question, the Imperial War Cabinet had no alternative but to order the withdrawal of Sinclair's squadron. Yet the Admiralty got little long-term satisfaction from this decision; it was subsequently decided that another, even smaller force—two light cruisers and five destroyers—would be sent out to relieve Sinclair and to prepare for the prospect of an even more active role once the ice broke up in the spring.[115]

Sinclair withdrew his ships from Riga at dawn on 3 January, taking with him a number of refugees, including most of the Latvian government. Within days nearly all of Latvia (except for Libau in the south) and much of Lithuania was under Soviet control.[116]

On 13 January, in a memorandum to the Imperial War Cabinet, the Admiralty drew what it considered to be the lessons of these Baltic events:

It is abundantly clear that the only means of securing the integrity of these provinces is by the landing of a considerable military force, and the placing of the provinces under a British or Allied protectorate.

The use of naval force alone serves only to raise false hopes of more thorough assistance and is injurious to our prestige as laying us open to deserting the provinces in their hour of need.[117]

These were lessons which, it need scarcely be said, did not apply to the Baltic alone. The problem of relating force levels to policy objectives was one which would plague the British government throughout the dismal history of its intervention in the Russian Civil War.

[115] Minutes, Imperial War Cabinet, 48th meeting, 31 December 1918, 11 a.m.; Cab. 23/44. Also Bennett, *Cowan's War*, pp. 51-53.

[116] *Ibid.*, pp. 50-51.

[117] "Naval Position in Russia," by Admiral Sir R. E. Wemyss, First Sea Lord, 13 January 1919, Cabinet paper P. 95; Cab. 29/2.

CHAPTER II

INTERVENTION AND THE ARMISTICE:
DISCUSSIONS IN LONDON

Have we a Russian policy? We are killing Russians after we have
ceased to kill Germans, and our Ministers are ransacking the diction-
ary for abusive terms to apply to the Bolsheviks. All this expresses
a strong dislike, but it does not constitute a policy. Yet we can hardly
enter the Peace Conference without a policy, for a good third of the
problems of peace are Russian problems.

—Manchester Guardian, *23 November 1918*

THE Armistice which ended the World War also ended the decisive
influence exerted by the General Staff over the British government's
Russian policies. This influence stemmed from the General Staff's
claim—irrefutable in the circumstances—to expert knowledge of the
military requirements for victory over Germany, the policy goal to
which all others were subordinated. The primacy of this goal meant
that, during the year between the Bolshevik seizure of power and
the Armistice, Allied intervention in Russia was justified by reference to strategic "necessities" of the war with Germany, such as
the need to reestablish an Eastern front after Lenin had removed
Russia from the war, or the need to keep Russia's resources out of
the hands of the Central Powers. This did not mean that there were
not those within the British government, and particularly within its
military establishment, who were anxious to destroy the Bolshevik
regime. Rather, it meant that, consciously or unconsciously, they
rarely chose to argue the case for intervention in such political terms,
against which there could be equally authoritative political counter-
arguments questioning the wisdom of interfering in a foreign revolution. After 11 November 1918, however, the wartime rationale for
intervention was no longer valid. The whole British government,
and not merely the military establishment, had to confront the political question: why were British troops remaining in Russia?

We have already seen one answer to this question—Balfour's statement, in his memorandum to the Cabinet, that Allied forces had to remain because they were morally obligated to assist those Russians who had stayed "loyal" to the Allied cause and who were now fighting for their lives against the Bolsheviks.[1] This was, of course, a confidential paper, circulated only within the government. But precisely the same argument lay at the heart of the most important public statement on Russia made by a member of the government during the autumn and winter of 1918-19. The statement took the unusual form of an open letter released to the press on 18 December by Lord Milner, the Secretary of State at the War Office.[2] Replying to an unnamed correspondent[3] who had asked why British troops continued to fight in Russia after the end of hostilities in Europe, Milner wrote that intervention had originally taken place to rescue the Czech Corps in Siberia and "to prevent those vast portions of Russia which were struggling to escape the tyranny of the Bolshevists from being overrun by them and so thrown open as a source of supply to the enemy." And he continued:

In the course of this Allied intervention thousands of Russians have taken up arms and fought on the side of the Allies. How can we, simply because our own immediate purposes have been served, come away and leave them to the tender mercies of their and our enemies, before they have had time to arm, train, and organise so as to be strong enough to defend themselves? It would be an abominable betrayal, contrary to every British instinct of honour and humanity.

Milner assured his correspondent (and the public) that the troops would not remain in Russia a day longer than necessary to "discharge the moral obligations" Britain had incurred. But if the Allies "were all to scramble out of Russia at once," the "barbarism" which then reigned in only part of the country would spread to the rest, and the resulting disaster would put a much greater strain on the resources of the British Empire.

Milner released his letter to the press, as he subsequently explained to his colleagues, because he was constantly receiving letters showing "complete ignorance" of the nature of British intervention in Russia,

[1] See above, pp. 15-16.

[2] Milner's letter was published in most daily newspapers on 19 December 1918; cf. *The Times.*

[3] The letter to which Milner's published statement purported to reply is not to be found in his papers in the Bodleian Library.

and he was convinced "that misconceptions as to the origin and objects of the Siberian and Murmansk-Archangel expeditions were being allowed to grow up on all hands without contradiction and were calculated to do much harm."[4] So far as Milner himself was concerned, the arguments he put forward in his open letter were the real ones. A week before its publication he had complained in the War Cabinet that "our own people at home thought that the British troops were being used for the suppression of Bolshevism, which was not actually the case, as they were there simply to protect those people who had been friendly to us during the war."[5] Yet Milner's letter raised many more questions than it answered. They were put most succinctly by the *Daily Telegraph* on the same day it printed his letter:

The country is entitled to more information than that. It ought to be told what prospect there is of these protégés of the Alliance "arming, training, and organizing so as to be strong enough to defend themselves." We ought to hear something reliable about the mutual differences of the various anti-Bolshevik elements with whom the Allies are co-operating, and whether there is any ground for the allegation that their intervention is turning to the advantage mainly of the partisans of the regime which the revolution overthrew. We have at present a war on our hands in Russia such as would have filled the newspapers at any normal time; and the nation is entitled to know how the war is going, and what end to it is contemplated by the Government.[6]

Normal times, in the *Telegraph*'s sense of the term, were still several months away. There had not been anything resembling a full Parliamentary debate on Russia during the whole of the period

[4] Cabinet paper G.T. 6590, 1 January 1919; Cab. 24/72.

[5] War Cabinet minutes W.C. 511, 10 December 1918, noon; Cab. 23/8.

[6] *Daily Telegraph*, 19 December 1919. Here the conservative *Telegraph* found itself in the unaccustomed company of the radical *Manchester Guardian* and *Daily News*, while its usual allies, *The Times*, the *Daily Mail*, and the *Morning Post*, approved Milner's statement uncritically. It is worth noting that Milner himself rather agreed with the *Telegraph*'s comments. In a private letter on 22 December to Konstantin Nabokov, Chargé d'Affaires of the Russian Embassy in London, who had written to thank him for his statement, Milner noted: "Personally, I should like to see a more vigorous Allied intervention. . . . As things stand, I feel that we are all fumbling. We try to help, here and there, anybody who seems to be trying, with the slightest chance of success, to stem the Bolshevist tide. But that is a purely provisional opportunist policy. It is better than nothing but it is not nearly enough." The difficulty, Milner continued, was that the Allies did not know whom to support. The anti-Bolshevik cause among the Russians had not achieved anything like cohesion. "If there was only one Russian authority, representing the real Russia, with whom the Allies could make an alliance, the problem would be immensely simplified." (Milner MSS, private letters, vol. VII.)

since the Bolshevik seizure of power, nor would there be until the spring of 1919. Except for Milner's letter, the government was almost completely closemouthed about its Russian policy. On 18 November, when asked in the House of Commons to state the objects of British military operations in Russia, Ian MacPherson, the Under-Secretary of State at the War Office, replied that it was not in the national interest that any such information should be given.[7] Members on both sides regarded this answer as so unsatisfactory that Lord Robert Cecil, MacPherson's counterpart at the Foreign Office, was forced to concede that the government was "certainly not disposed to en-tangle this country at the close of a great war in serious military operations." Beyond that statement, he said, he could not go. But he added his opinion that the Bolsheviks had "committed offences against this country which, if they had been committed by any civilised Government, would have more than justified this country in seeking redress by arms." Yet Cecil could only cite a single example of these "offences": the killing of Captain Cromie in Petrograd.[8]

During the winter and spring of 1918-19 the Labour Party, and some of the more radical Liberals, began to speak out with increas-ing vigor against British intervention in Russia. While the war continued, the issue of Russia had emphasized the division between Labour's pro-war and anti-war factions and thus had been an em-barrassment to the party. The great body of trade-unionists, who were almost uniformly pro-war, had remained silent on Russia. Although few of them fully approved of intervention as it took shape during 1918, most were reluctant to speak out against it while it was being represented as so much a part of the war effort against Germany.[9]

But just as the end of the war had forced the government to find new grounds on which to justify its policies, so it also freed the hand of the Labour Party and allowed it to unite in criticism of those policies. Labour's changed attitude was typified by a *New Statesman* editorial which declared: "We feel that the time has come to break the self-imposed silence which we have observed with respect to

---

[7] 110 *H.C. Deb.*, col. 3197 (all references here to Parliamentary debates are to volumes in the Fifth Series; this notation will henceforth be omitted).

[8] *Ibid.*, col. 3263.

[9] See Graubard, *British Labour and the Russian Revolution*, p. 63.

the British Government's attitude towards Russia."[10] Although most of the Labour Party—especially the trade-unionists—fully appreciated the vast gulf that separated the British socialist parliamentarian from the Russian Marxist revolutionary, they were quick to demand that foreign forces should be recalled from Russia and the Russian people allowed to work out their own political future.[11] There is no better example of this point of view than the statement made in the House of Commons on 31 March 1919 by J. R. Clynes, an official of the National Union of General and Municipal Workers and the government's Food Controller during 1918:

Bolshevism is an ideal. It is mistaken. It would be ruinous. It is tyrannical in its effects and in its application. But it is an ideal, and if it is thought that working men in this country can be compulsorily recruited for the purpose of interfering with the internal affairs of the Russian people . . . there will be even stronger and more vehement protests in working-class quarters than has [already] been shown with regard to the Government policy on this Russian question.[12]

By March 1919—after riots by soldiers over the slow pace of demobilization[13]—views like Clynes's were undoubtedly widespread, but the autumn of 1918 was a poor time for effective protests of any kind. The criticism of a few were drowned by the wave of elation that engulfed the vast majority of the British people on their release from four years of war. In an atmosphere of overblown patriotism and a popular desire to punish Germany for the war, the Prime Minister, David Lloyd George, dissolved the eight-year-old Parliament and went to the country to seek an endorsement that would strengthen the British government's position at the coming Peace Conference—and solidify his own position as the dominant figure in British political life. Out of 541 candidates who received the "coupon" signed by Lloyd George and Andrew Bonar Law, the leaders of the Coalition, no less than 478 were returned. To their ranks were added some 48 Conservatives who had not received the coupon, but who could scarcely sit with the Opposition. The official

---

[10] *New Statesman*, 21 December 1918, p. 232.

[11] This is one of the principal theses of Graubard's book.

[12] 114 *H.C. Deb.*, cols. 953-54. See also the remarks by Joseph King and Arthur Ponsonby on 18 November 1918; 110 *H.C. Deb.*, cols. 3197, 3263, 3294.

[13] See T. H. Wintringham, *Mutiny*, London, 1936, pp. 313-27. For a discussion of the unrest in Britain during the winter following the Armistice, see Arno J. Mayer, *Peacemaking*, pp. 604-23.

Opposition party, for the first time, was Labour with only 59 seats —so great was the Coalition's triumph.[14]

In the turbulent election campaign which ended with polling day on 14 December, the government virtually committed itself to a policy of hanging the Kaiser and making Germany pay the full cost of the war, although Lloyd George, who was more moderate in his personal statements, doubted the feasibility of either proposal. The bogey of Bolshevism, too, played its part in the election. Both Lloyd George and his colleagues repeatedly asserted that a vote for the Coalition would help keep Bolshevism out of Britain, and the Prime Minister did not hesitate to tar the Labour Party with the Bolshevik brush.[15] Yet about Russia, as distinguished from "Bolshevism," very little seems to have been said during the election campaign. Although the Labour Party's election manifesto, issued on 27 November, contained the statement, "Labour demands the immediate withdrawal of the Allied forces from Russia," the government did not rise to the challenge: Russia was perhaps the one major issue on which the Coalition made no promises. In none of Lloyd George's major addresses, nor in the Coalition's election manifesto (issued on 5 December), was Russia even mentioned.[16] On the issue of a Russian policy, at least, the British government entered the Peace Conference with no prior commitments.

✧

While the election campaign was in progress, and during the month which lay between polling day and the commencement of the Peace Conference in January, the British government undertook its first systematic efforts to determine a postwar policy regarding Russia. These efforts took place in two forums, the Imperial War Cabinet and the Eastern Committee of the War Cabinet, and not in

---

[14] See Trevor Wilson, "The Coupon and the British General Election of 1918," *Journal of Modern History*, vol. XXXVI, no. 1 (March 1964), pp. 28-42. For the campaign itself, see Charles Loch Mowat, *Britain Between the Wars*, London, 1955, pp. 2-9, and R. B. McCallum, *Public Opinion and the Last Peace*, Oxford, 1944, pp. 30-42.

[15] In his final speech, to an election-eve mass meeting at Camberwell, Lloyd George said: "The Labour Party is being run by the extreme pacifist, Bolshevist group. . . . It was they who pulled Labour out of the Government at the moment when we need the help of Labour to reconstruct in this country. . . . Why? What they believed in was Bolshevism." (*The Times*, 14 December 1918.)

[16] Lloyd George's principal addresses in the campaign are printed in *The Times*, 9, 10, 12, and 14 December 1918. The Labour and Coalition manifestoes are in the issues of 28 November and 6 December.

the War Cabinet itself. Although the membership of all three of these bodies to a considerable extent overlapped, each performed a different function.

The parent body, of course, was the War Cabinet. Founded at the end of 1916, just after Lloyd George became Prime Minister, it was his device for making certain that supreme control of the British war effort remained firmly in his own hands. With the exception of Bonar Law, who was Chancellor of the Exchequer and Leader of the House of Commons, its members had no departmental responsibilities. In its small size—it varied from five to seven members—and in its overseeing role, it differed sharply from the conventional British peacetime Cabinet.[17] Lloyd George retained it as a formal model until the autumn of 1919. After the Armistice, however, its meetings were less frequent, and the practice, begun during the War, of inviting departmental ministers and service officers to attend those meetings relevant to their responsibilities grew so prevalent that the distinction between it and a conventional cabinet became blurred.

The Imperial War Cabinet was the name given to those meetings of the War Cabinet attended by representatives—generally the prime ministers—of the governments of the Dominions and of India. This was Lloyd George's way of imposing common policies on the Empire's vast war effort. The Imperial Cabinet met during March and April 1917, and June and July 1918. Then, on 20 November 1918, it reassembled for a series of meetings which continued until it adjourned for the Peace Conference, where it became the British Empire Delegation. When it was sitting, the Imperial War Cabinet dealt with virtually all important questions of foreign policy; the members of the British War Cabinet would remain after its meetings, or sometimes meet on other occasions, to handle British domestic matters. Thus the question of preparations for the Peace Conference, and of the future direction of intervention in Russia—which, after all, involved large numbers of Dominion and Indian troops—fell to the Imperial Cabinet.[18]

Just as the War Cabinet gave rise to its Imperial alter ego, so it also

---

[17] See Cmd. 9005 (1918), *The War Cabinet: Report for the Year 1917*, London, 1918, pp. 1-3, for the official explanation, and (among many accounts) A.J.P. Taylor, *English History, 1914-1945*, Oxford, 1965, pp. 74-76, for the unofficial.

[18] Cmd. 9005, pp. 5-9. Cmd. 325 (1919), *The War Cabinet: Report for the Year 1918*, London, 1919, pp. 7-11. W. K. Hancock, *Smuts: The Sanguine Years, 1870-1919*, Cambridge, 1962, pp. 427-29, 489ff.

bred the network of specialist committees of which the Eastern Committee was an important example. During the first year of the War Cabinet's existence, particular problems of all sorts would be referred to individual members, or to *ad hoc* committees chaired by individual members, for investigation, recommendation, and sometimes decision. During 1918 this practice was extended through the establishment of standing committees. With only, one exception, all of these committees dealt with essentially domestic matters, undoubtedly because the War Cabinet felt that foreign policy problems were so inextricably bound up with the most central problems of the conduct of war that their devolution to a committee was usually impracticable.[19]

The exception was the Eastern Committee, established in March 1918 to take over the work of two *ad hoc* committees, one dealing with Persia, the other with the Middle East. The chairman of the new standing committee was Lord Curzon, himself once Viceroy of India, whose passions were engaged by the East, and by his conception of Britain's mission in the East, as they were by no other subject. Its other members were General Jan C. Smuts of South Africa, like Curzon a full member of the War Cabinet; Balfour, the Foreign Secretary, who often sat with the War Cabinet but who, because of his demanding daily responsibilities, was not a member; Cecil, his deputy; Edwin Montagu, the Secretary of State for India; and General Sir Henry Wilson, the Chief of the Imperial General Staff. They were often joined by others who had a particular interest in the problem at hand at any given moment, such as Lord Hardinge, the Permanent Under-Secretary at the Foreign Office, or Major-General William Thwaites, the Director of Military Intelligence.

The province of the Eastern Committee was all "the multifarious problems that arose between the Eastern shores of the Mediterranean and the frontiers of India."[20] This vast area included the Caucasus. During November and December 1918, as we have seen, British and Indian troops replaced the Germans and Turks who until then had occupied these borderlands of Russia. Far from least among the "multifarious problems" faced by the Eastern Committee was the question of why British forces had come to the Caucasus, and what future British policy regarding those lands would be. On 2 December Curzon initiated a series of discussions of the Caucasus in

[19] Cmd. 325, pp. 1-6.   [20] *Ibid.*, p. 3.

order to determine a policy for presentation to the coming Peace Conference. We shall examine these discussions in great detail: they were enormously revealing of the attitudes and assumptions with which British statesmen and military officers approached the radically altered circumstances of the postwar world.[21]

The War, Curzon told his colleagues on 2 December, had demonstrated that it was essential to the interests of the British Empire, and of India in particular, that Britain should exercise some measure of political control over Transcaucasia.[22] The presence there of military forces hostile to the British Empire would turn Britain's flank in Asia as it so nearly had been turned during the summer of 1918. Furthermore, disorder in the Caucasus would make the region an Asian Balkans. "Any sort of anarchy, disorder, or Bolshevism there," Curzon said, would "inevitably react" upon the whole British position from Persia eastward.

Curzon then briefly reviewed the position of each of the separate nations of the Caucasus. Georgia, he thought, was the most progressive, highly developed, and cultured, and therefore the most entitled to independence; hence Britain should encourage Georgian independence by every means possible. As for that part of Armenia formerly in the Russian Empire, he thought it would be made part of the larger Armenian state which the Allies would create out of Turkish Armenia. The one "really embarrassing factor" in a general policy of support for the independence of the Transcaucasian nations, Curzon said, was Azerbaijan, because it was "violently pro-Turk, anti-Armenian, anti-Persian"—everything the British govern-

[21] Minutes of all meetings of the Eastern Committee from its inception in March 1918 until its termination as a Cabinet committee in January 1919 (it then became a Foreign Office committee) are in Cab. 27/24; there is also a set in the Milner MSS. For all meetings in which British policy in the Caucasus was under discussion, the highly unusual practice was followed of making a shorthand record, and a verbatim transcript of each discussion was printed as an annex to the usual brief third-person minutes of the session. These verbatim transcripts are a uniquely valuable source for the historian: they offer not only the usual record of decisions taken, but insight into the argument and methods of thought employed by each participant. For this reason the discussions are followed at length here.

[22] Eastern Committee 40th meeting, 2 December 1918 (no time stated), minutes and verbatim annex; Cab. 27/24. All of the committee's meetings took place in Lord Curzon's rooms in the Privy Council Office (Curzon was Lord Privy Seal). In its discussions (and in this account) the terms "Transcaucasia" and "the Caucasus" were used interchangeably to mean roughly the same territory—except that the latter may at times imply the inclusion of Daghestan, on the northern side of the Caucasus mountain range, while "Transcaucasia" invariably refers only to those lands south of the mountains.

ment did not want it to be. Finally, there remained the "wild little Moslem state" of Daghestan which lay on the northern side of the mountains and was therefore not properly a part of Transcaucasia. Its importance, Curzon said, stemmed from the fact that its territory included the Caspian ports of Petrovsk (now Makhachkala) and Derbent, and the oil wells around Groznyi. Every factor drew Daghestan toward Russia but one—national sentiment, which drew it southward. Curzon then put forward his notion of a general British policy regarding the "rising republics" of the Caucasus. They were, he said, "furiously anti-Russian and furiously anti-Bolshevik, and we ought to do nothing whatever to lead them to suppose that we are ignoring their claims to independence in favour of a possible revival of Russia in the future."

Yet apart from questions of diplomatic action, such as recognition, Curzon said, Britain's interests made necessary certain additional measures in the Caucasus. Batum must once again be made a free port, as it had been under the Treaty of Berlin of 1878 until Russia had "shamelessly" annexed it. The new free port of Batum would become the principal commercial port for Persia and the main outlet for the oil of Baku—two matters in which Great Britain was vitally interested. In addition, in order to assure the safety of both these streams of trade, Britain must control the railway from Batum to Baku. Finally, Baku and its surrounding oil fields should be "internationalised" and placed under some form of government "more secure" than any around them. "The idea that the Tatars [the Azerbaijanis], the Armenians, or the Bolsheviks, or any other party could permanently hold Baku and control the vast resources there," Curzon asserted, "is one that cannot be entertained for a moment."

These were Curzon's initial arguments. There was a pause during which General Thwaites, the Director of Military Intelligence, informed the committee that one British division had already reached Batum and another was awaiting shipping, and Sir Louis Mallet of the Foreign Office added that the British consul at Baku had reported that 60,000 troops would be needed to occupy the vital portions of all three Transcaucasian states. Then the attack on Curzon's position began when Montagu, the Secretary of State for India, sharply asked: "What is the point of it all? Why do we want to take any responsibility?" Lord Robert Cecil agreed; his view was that Britain should simply hold Baku because of the immense value of the oil deposits. Curzon replied that Baku could not be made secure unless "some Power with prestige" were in the Caucasus to keep order and thus prevent conflict among the various states. By guarding the railway—Transcaucasia's spinal cord—British troops were keeping order there at that very moment.

Cecil demurred. British troops were stationed along the railway in order to keep open the lines of communication with India. They had nothing to do with the "general political atmosphere" of the Caucasus. So far as he was concerned, the French could come in to keep order. At this point General Smuts entered the discussion. Such talk of France worried him. France was a great military power; someday, he thought, France might be the British Empire's "great problem." He then went on to propose a system of mandates operating through the League of Nations.[23] One of the Powers would take charge of the Caucasus and be responsible to the League. Smuts suggested the United States: the Americans had no selfish objects regarding the region.

Cecil again objected. The Americans were perhaps less selfish than the French, he said, but they would never take permanent responsibility for the Caucasus, and, whenever Russia recovered, she would try to reclaim her former place in the region. The Russians would be much more formidable to Britain than the French, who would be so far from their home base that they could never seriously threaten Britain from the Caucasus. Here Cecil was taking a line that would be characteristic of British policy at the coming Peace Conference and afterward: Russia was to be feared not so much because she was Bolshevik as because she was a Great Power whose interests placed her astride the lifelines of the British Empire. The theme, for British foreign policy, was scarcely new.

Curzon was much disturbed by Cecil's suggestion that France should be responsible for the Caucasus. Under the Sykes-Picot Agreement of 16 May 1916, France was already scheduled to receive control over Syria, the Lebanon, and the Turkish province of Cilicia.[24]

[23] At this time, plans for a League of Nations were fairly far advanced, and Smuts assumed that a League would come into being. Only a fortnight later he put forth a general scheme for a League system of mandates under the title, "The League of Nations: a Practical Suggestion." See Alfred Zimmern, *The League of Nations and the Rule of Law, 1918-1935*, London, 1936, ch. VIII, "The Smuts Plan," pp. 209-14, and Hancock, *Smuts*, pp. 501-3.

[24] The Sykes-Picot Agreement was negotiated at a critical moment in the war in order to reassure France that the Arab revolt, which Britain had sponsored, would

She would also probably be given a mandate over Turkish Armenia, which had been promised to the Russians in September 1916 in exchange for their approval of the Sykes-Picot Agreement. If the Caucasus, also, were in French hands, French power would extend from the Mediterranean to the Caspian, making Britain's position extremely vulnerable. He had spent much of his public life dealing with the political ambitions of France. Their national character was different—they had a certain way with Eastern peoples—and their political interests conflicted with Britain's in many cases. "Trouble in Persia means trouble in Afghanistan," Curzon said, "and then you are brought right up to the borders of India." Rather than place France in authority over one of the main approaches to India, he "would sooner the States fought it out among themselves, and that Russia ultimately come back."

Curzon's remarks brought from General Thwaites the brief comment: "We ought to be sitting there ourselves, and nobody else." Yet Curzon himself seems to have been taken aback by the bluntness of this notion. As if in disagreement, he mused:

> We are getting so much already. We are going to get the [German] colonies in Africa; we are going to get, under some disguise or other, the whole of Mesopotamia—that seems absolutely certain. If anybody looks after Persia it must be ourselves; and really, to go into the Caucasus, quite apart from whether it would be possible or not—

Curzon broke off in mid-sentence, and the discussions themselves were broken off a few moments later. They were resumed in a week's time, on 9 December. During the intervening period the General Staff prepared a memorandum putting forward its position in a stronger, more connected form than General Thwaites had been able to do in the give and take of discussion. Primarily, the paper was a response to the suggestion, made by Cecil and others in the Foreign Office,[25] that France might be given responsibility for the Caucasus.

---

not give rise to an independent Arab state that would deprive France of Syria and Cilicia, previously promised her. For Britain, Sir Mark Sykes secured Mesopotamia (Iraq). The Arab territories south of the British and French territories were to be divided into zones of British and French influence. Finally, Russia was to receive Turkish Armenia. It was this latter territory, abutting as it did on the territory assigned to France, which caused Curzon so much anxiety in these Eastern Committee meetings.

[25] The principal statement of this position (to which the General Staff paper was a direct reply) was "Memorandum on a Possible Territorial Policy in the Caucasus

Although it was several pages long, its argument was summarized in one paragraph, which stated:

> From the military point of view it would be most undesirable for the approaches to India from South Russia, the Black Sea and Turkey in Asia, which converge at Baku, to be placed at the disposal of *an ambitious military Power, which, although friendly to us at the moment, is our historical world rival.* In fact, it does not appear to the General Staff that any other Power except herself can be permitted by Great Britain to function in this manner.[26]

The dangers presented by a France astride Britain's imperial lifelines, the memorandum continued, would be made still greater by "a potential alliance between a reconstructed Russia and France." The French had already asserted that their alliance with Tsarist Russia had given them the right to take charge of the new Russian army that was being raised in Siberia. "Can it be said that the imagination of the French Eastern School fails to visualize such a situation in the future?"

At the Eastern Committee's meeting on 9 December[27] the issue was squarely put by Major-General Sir George M. W. Macdonogh, the Adjutant General, who asked: "What is the value of Caucasia to us? Do we or do we not want it? Is it an important link of the communications with India, or is it not?" He was answered by Balfour. The Foreign Secretary had not been able to attend the committee's meeting on the 2nd, but now he emerged as Curzon's leading antagonist, stating:

> I am against a mandatory Power, and against Great Britain taking it, although we may be driven to it. It would be a most serious thing. I am much alarmed at our having sent a division there. It may be necessary, but I was never consulted about it. I was rather shocked when I heard it, and am still. I think you are going to find it a great military burden. I cannot get a platoon for places much nearer home because there are no troops to give, and then I find that troops are being sent to the furthest parts of the world. Putting that out of account, I believe the very suggestion that

---

Regions," 7 November 1918, by Sir Eyre A. Crowe, who at the time was an assistant under-secretary at the Foreign Office (Cabinet paper P. 31; Cab. 29/1).

[26] General Staff, War Office, "Future Settlement of Trans-Caucasia. (The military aspect of the case.)," 5 December 1918, Eastern Committee paper E.C. 2632; Cab. 27/38 (emphasis added).

[27] Eastern Committee 42nd meeting, 9 December 1918, 3 p.m., minutes and verbatim annex; Cab. 27/24.

Great Britain is for an indefinite time . . . intending to occupy militarily the road to the oilfields of Baku . . . is damning and settles the question.

Cecil made the same sort of moralistic argument. "If we are to take the whole of the Caucasus areas," he said, "that would be a profound imperialistic policy, and is quite out of the question now." Yet Cecil's moralism went only so far; as we have seen, he was perfectly willing to take charge of the Baku oil fields, if not the rest of Transcaucasia.[28] Curzon replied to Balfour and Cecil with some moralism of his own: if the British government did not take responsibility for the Caucasus, he asked, how could it prevent "these little peoples" from being crushed by the Russians? Balfour answered: "If Russia is in a position to crush them, why not? We should not go there to protect them from the Russians. It would be folly, from a purely military point of view, for us to try and keep a military force there." Curzon's reply begged the issue: "I do not want to protect them against anybody; I want to give them a chance of standing on their own feet."

Balfour did not pause to point out the inconsistencies in Curzon's argument. Instead, he turned to the relationship between the Caucasus and the defense of India. Here he chose to challenge the soldiers (and also Curzon) on their central contention—that Batum was one of the main approaches to India. The following sections of the discussion speak for themselves:

MR. BALFOUR: . . . when we come to the point of the defence of India, I hope the General Staff will be a little more careful about the demands they make upon us about India. Every time I come to a discussion—at intervals of, say, five years—I find there is a new sphere which we have got to guard, which is supposed to protect the gateways of India. Those gateways are getting further and further from India, and I do not know how far west they are going to be brought by the General Staff. Remember, before the war there was a really great military Power in occupation of these places, not a military Power, separated as the French would be, by the whole vulnerable length of the Mediterranean. . . . It was a great military Power which we could not hit, which we of all people were helpless against. They had it and we did not tremble. . . . Trans-Caucasia . . . is far safer now, from the Indian point of view, than it ever was, because it is either going to be occupied by the French, whom I think we can manage, or by these little nations themselves. It is not going to be occupied by Russia, which was the military Power you had to fear. I would not commit

[28] But see below, n. 38.

this country to military action under necessities which have not yet arisen, and which I most earnestly trust never will arise.

LORD CURZON: . . . I do not think anything can alter the fact that somebody must be there; and if so I do not see why we should wring our hands, our interests being so closely involved, and propose anybody but ourselves. Are we so unsuspicious that we are prepared to let the French, the most imperialistic people in the world—?

MR. BALFOUR: . . . Of course the Caucasus would be much better governed under our aegis than it would be under French aegis. But why should it not be misgoverned?

LORD CURZON: That is the other alternative—let them cut each other's throats.

MR. BALFOUR: I am in favour of that.

Montagu then intervened to ask just what dangers there were in a French occupation of the Caucasus that should cause Britain to occupy the region herself. The discussion continued:

LORD CURZON: You ask why should England do this? Why should Great Britain push herself out in these directions? Of course, the answer is obvious—India. I put it to you, why should the Caucasus be given to France? France has no interest, except a sentimental or a chauvinistic one, in those parts of the world. She is going, as the result of a campaign to which she only contributed 1,000 black men—"niggers," as the Prime Minister called them—to get the greater part of the coast of Syria and the Lebanon. She must be given Armenia, because nobody else wants to have anything to do with that singularly unattractive people! . . . Having given her that, you say we must be disinterested, everybody suspects us, and therefore you propose to clap on to the French this area in which she is not interested, and to which she has no claim, and which she may use to our disadvantage. She certainly would in the event of hostilities, and in respect of oil she would be sure to reap considerable profit in the interim. I think that perhaps we are not drawing enough attention to the importance of the oil and the pipeline.

. . . If you have a friendly France there is no danger, but if you have, as one day you may, a hostile France, why add to her power of offence?

LORD ROBERT CECIL: If we occupy this region we should occupy Trans-Caspia, I suppose?

LORD CURZON: I hope not. We are talking only of staying in the Caucasus to set the people on their legs there.

LORD ROBERT CECIL: You ought not to be taken in by that phrase. We get there so often, and we always remain.

Sir Henry Wilson then suggested, facetiously, that the whole problem would solve itself if only Cecil could establish the League of Nations he had long advocated.

LORD ROBERT CECIL: Then we need not trouble about it.
MR. BALFOUR: That is my view. Why worry about it?

. . . .

GENERAL WILSON: We want to know what we are to do. This is the telegram to which I have to send a reply: "It would be the greatest assistance if I could be informed of the general lines which the policy to be adopted in the Caucasus will follow, in view of the early departure of troops to occupy Batoum and the extension of my command to Baku and Krasnovodsk...."[29]
MR. BALFOUR: This unhealthy curiosity on the part of our pro-consuls in distant parts of the world is embarrassing.
LORD ROBERT CECIL: What that means is this. The unhappy man there very naturally wants to know what kind of things he is to say to the local tribes: are we going to be here permanently, or are we going to leave it as soon as we can?
MR. BALFOUR: I should put it all upon the [Peace] Conference.
LORD CURZON: I thought we were preparing the case for the Conference. That is the object of these meetings. . . . I am trying to help you at the Peace Conference, Mr. Balfour, for you will be our chief representative there.
MR. BALFOUR: I do not think it is our business to have a policy with regard to these places.
LORD CURZON: We shall get on very badly if we do not. I think we must have an idea of what we are working for.

. . . .

GENERAL SMUTS: I should not like to go to the Conference undecided, because the result might be in the end that the French may be all over this area. . . .
GENERAL WILSON: Cannot we bribe France in some other way?
LORD ROBERT CECIL: How?
GENERAL WILSON: I do not know; that is not my part of the business.
LORD ROBERT CECIL: How can we if you do not like this arrangement?
GENERAL WILSON: That is a Foreign Office affair.
LORD ROBERT CECIL: Then I answer we cannot. I know that if Mr. Balfour or myself makes any proposition with regard to Africa, we shall

[29] This was telegram G.C. 660, Lieutenant-General Sir George F. Milne (Salonika) to War Office, 3 December 1918; W.O. 33/965, no. 2836.

be told that there is an aeroplane station, or a submarine base, or that it is the oldest colony, or it will bitterly offend some New Zealand politician if we do it, or something of that kind. It is always the same.

GENERAL WILSON: Quite.

GENERAL SMUTS: Should we not put Italy in the place of Russia, as we are bound to some extent to support her against France? Evidently those two are spoiling for a fight, and why should we not put Italy somewhere?

GENERAL MACDONOGH: She would be better than France.

Smut's proposal was not discussed further, but, as the events of the following summer would show, it was not forgotten.[30] These remarks ended the Eastern Committee's session of 9 December. Curzon announced to his colleagues that he would take the stenographic record home with him, read through it, and try to formulate some general conclusions to put to the committee at its next meeting a week later.

Before then, however, two more figures entered the debate: Lloyd George and Milner. The question of the Caucasus came before the Imperial War Cabinet on 12 December in the form of a paper submitted by Henry Wilson on the military commitments which the British Empire would have to bear after the signing of the peace treaties with the Central Powers.[31] The only forces which Wilson envisioned serving anywhere on the territory of the former Russian Empire were two divisions—some 40-50,000 men—along the Batum-Baku railway. The War Office's justification of this commitment, made by Milner, was wholly in terms of imperial defense. Holding the Batum-Baku railway would provide the "greatest possible economy of force"; it would "screen great tracts of territory," thus making it possible to station fewer troops in Persia and perhaps none at all in Turkestan, and it would remove any anxieties the Allies might have about Armenia.

Lloyd George was not convinced. Once troops were committed to operations in the Caucasus, he said, he could see no possibility of their being able to withdraw for some time, and he did not know where the British Empire could find two divisions that could be tied down for so long. Moreover, he disagreed with Milner's estimate of the benefits of such a commitment. He did not think that a Bolshevik

[30] See below, pp. 227-29.
[31] Cabinet paper G.T. 6434; Cab. 24/71.

Russia "was by any means such a danger as the old Russian Empire was, with all its aggressive officials and millions of troops." The present situation was not nearly so difficult as that of previous years. Thus Lloyd George came down firmly on Balfour's side. At the Prime Minister's urging, Wilson's paper was approved *except* for its provisions regarding the Caucasus; these (so the meeting's conclusions read) would be considered at some future date by a "full Imperial War Cabinet, at which time Lord Curzon would be asked to explain the situation."[32]

Whether or not Curzon's own thinking was influenced by arguments such as those of Lloyd George and Balfour, he was politically sensitive enough to appear at the next meeting of the Eastern Committee, on 16 December, with a draft containing thirteen propositions whose tone, at least, was much more moderate than his statements at the committee's previous session had been.[33] He read them to his colleagues, assuming that they approved each proposition unless they voiced objection. The first seven were as follows:

1) We desire to see strong independent States—offshoots of the former Russian Empire—in the Caucasus.

2) Of these States Georgia is the most advanced and has the strongest claims to early recognition.

3) Recognition of the remaining States . . . must depend on the march of events and their successful assertion of an autonomous existence.

4) Whether Russian Armenia shall have a separate existence (as distinct from Turkish Armenia) will be determined in the main by the attitude of the people themselves.

5) Whether the independent States of the Caucasus combine hereafter in a Federation or prefer to remain separate is a matter for their own determination.

6) Similarly their relations to the present or future Government or Governments of Russia is a matter that in the main concerns themselves.

7) If it is decided at the Peace Conference, either as a result of a request from the States, or at the instance of the League of Nations (should such be set up) that the services of a Great Power are required for a period to protect international interests in the areas concerned, the selection of America would be preferable to that of France, but is not in itself desir-

[32] Minutes, Imperial War Cabinet, 12 December 1918; Cab. 23/42.
[33] Eastern Committee 43rd meeting, 16 December 1918, 5 p.m., minutes and verbatim annex; Cab. 27/24. The text of the resolutions here given is as finally approved by the committee. However, the approved version was virtually identical with Curzon's draft, the committee having made only very minor changes in form.

able. The selection of France would on broad grounds of policy and strategy be undesirable. Only in the last resort, and reluctantly if pressed to do so, might Great Britain provisionally accept the task.

At this point Cecil raised the first objection. If Curzon did not want either the United States or France in the Caucasus, and if he were now genuinely reluctant to commit British forces there, did his seventh proposition not mean that the British government would willingly see the Transcaucasian states return to Russia? He himself thought that any other possibility would be preferable, for a powerful Russia would be the greatest menace of all to the British Empire. Cecil was answered not by Curzon but by General Macdonogh. The Caucasus, he said, offered an avenue to India for Western Powers but not for the Russians, who could move much more easily down the railroad which ran from Samara through Orenburg (now Chkalov) to Tashkent. In Macdonogh's opinion it was dangerous for the Caucasus to be in the hands of a *Western* Power.

Now it was Montagu's turn. Once again, the Secretary of State for India—the realm whose defense was the object of the discussions —declared himself opposed to any British involvement in the Caucasus at all. Britain had not the slightest concern there, he said, and added: "Why should we go there, even reluctantly?" Curzon answered:

We are there entirely against our will and because we have been forced to go. . . . Whatever resolution is arrived at at this table or at the Conference, we cannot take those troops away immediately any more than we can take them away from the other places in which we are involved. It is Murmansk one day, Siberia another. You cannot take them away and have everybody cutting everybody else's throat.

Montagu disagreed:

Why not? With very great respect I suggest that it is possible to take them away. That is my view. It may be wrong-headed and obstinate, but that is what I think.

Balfour, of course, supported Montagu. To attempt to keep order throughout the Caucasus would require an immense military commitment, he said, and he continued:

I feel much disposed to say with Mr. Montagu . . . if they want to cut their own throats why do we not let them do it . . . as I understand we do let the tribes of the North West Frontier, outside our own [Indian] frontier, cut each other's throats in moderation. We make expeditions ... of a punitive character when they attack us, but when they merely attack each other we leave them alone. We do not try to introduce good order there. ... I should say we are not going to spend all our money and men in civilising a few people who do not want to be civilised. *We will protect Batum, Baku, the railway between them, and the pipe-line.*[34]

With Balfour's statement even Curzon could agree. Certainly, he said, he had no idea of British troops "wandering up into the mountains and civilising the tribes or anything of that sort." Like Balfour, he attached great importance "to holding Batum at one end, Tiflis at the centre, and most of all holding Baku at the eastern end." And he added: "As our troops are already on the spot in occupation of all these places, it seems to me inevitable that they should stay there for a time." With that comment, Curzon moved on to the next resolution. Yet it was apparent that, although the committee had let his seventh proposition pass without amendment, the text did not mean what Curzon had implied. It stated that Britain would "only in the last resort, and reluctantly if pressed to do so" take up a mandate for the Caucasus. But, as Curzon plainly told his colleagues, British troops were already on the scene (although pressed by no one), and it was "inevitable" that they should stay for a time, guarding the vital line of communication and making sure that Britain would continue, as before the War, to have a large share of Baku's oil.

Curzon then read two more propositions:

8) In any case we have no intention of annexing any of these territories, or converting them into a British Protectorate, or of accepting any commitments which will involve the permanent maintenance of large British forces in the Caucasus.

9) It is important for the time being to maintain British naval control of the Caspian.

Here again, the strongest objection came from the Secretary of State for India, who could see no necessity for Britain to keep control of the Caspian. It might be necessary to retain it for a brief period until General Malleson's small force in Transcaspia was safely withdrawn (its withdrawal had already been decided upon),[35] but the Government of India had sent telegrams saying that further control

[34] Emphasis added. [35] See Volume I, p. 327.

of the Caspian was unnecessary so far as India's interests were concerned. Curzon replied that continued naval control was necessary to keep influences "in the main Bolshevik, but at any rate hostile" from crossing the sea to Persia. With this every member of the committee but Montagu agreed. Even to Balfour and Cecil, control of the Caspian seemed necessary (as Macdonogh phrased it) "to keep the Bolsheviks and Bolshevism from getting hold of Persia."

Finally, Curzon read out the last four of his propositions. They were unchallenged:

10) The ultimate settlement should provide, if possible, for the declaration as free ports of Batum, Poti, Trebizond, and Baku, and for free transit on the railway from Batum to Baku.

11) Special steps may require to be taken for the safeguarding of international interests in the city and oil fields of Baku.

12) In the reconstitution of Georgia, it will be desirable to include within its boundaries the Moslem Georgians of Batum and Lazistan.

13) If an independent Armenian State be constituted . . . and if a Great Power be called upon . . . to act as protector . . . [we] should support the case either of America or France, preferably, in the interests of a revision of the Sykes-Picot Agreement of 1916, of France.

With the endorsement of these thirteen resolutions, the Eastern Committee concluded its discussions of British policy for the Caucasus. Curzon, the chairman, thus had his way—at least to the extent that the resolutions were so imprecisely phrased that Balfour and Cecil did not press their dissenting views. Only Montagu chose to take such a step. On the following day he addressed a sharply worded memorandum to the Cabinet.[36] The wartime circumstances which had led Great Britain to intervene in the Caucasus and in Transcaspia were entirely temporary, he said. During the War even a small German-Turkish force on Afghanistan's borders might have rendered the position of the Amir impossible and have thrown Afghanistan and the northwest frontier tribes against India. In those special circumstances it was essential to do what was possible to assist such anti-German and anti-Turkish forces as could be found in the Caucasus. Now, however, the whole situation was altered. "So far as the defence of India is concerned," Montagu wrote, "it does not seem to me necessary for us to give a thought to the Caucasus. I feel that this region is entirely outside the range of our interests."

[36] Cabinet paper G.T. 6529, 17 December 1918; Cab. 24/72.

Even the "temporary" commitment endorsed in Curzon's seventh resolution, Montagu insisted, was "unwarranted on either political or strategic grounds." And he continued:

I feel confident that public opinion in this country will view with grave suspicion any new military commitments when the war has ceased, and I do not think we should take the role of preserving law and order in all countries where without our intervention law and order may be jeopardized. When a *de facto* Government or group of Governments have emerged from the present chaos [in the Caucasus], it will be time enough to consider what our relationship to each should be, though in view of our very nebulous interest in those regions, it is difficult to see that any such arrangements will be called for, provided that the integrity of Persia is respected.

In conclusion, Montagu turned to the question of oil, which seemed to have quieted the objections of Balfour and Cecil to Curzon's proposals. He had not forgotten the "allegation" that the Baku oil fields were of "international interest." If that were really the case, then their protection should be in the hands of an "international force." Britain's own interests in their security did not warrant her taking on such a task by herself.

Montagu brought these same arguments—and his contention that, since India had no interests in the Caucasus, it should not be required to bear any of the costs, in men or money, of occupying the region—to the Imperial War Cabinet a week later when that body, in "full" session, heard Curzon offer the explanation of British policy which had been asked of him on 12 December.[37] The discussion which followed went over much of the same ground already covered in the Eastern Committee, albeit more briefly. But the most important question—precisely how much responsibility a "reluctant" British government would take for the Caucasus if pressed by the Peace Conference or the League of Nations—was still unanswered. A solution of sorts was proposed by Milner. It was unnecessary to come to an immediate decision, he said. One division landing at Batum was scarcely a sizable force for controlling a region as large as the Caucasus. Nor was there any intention that British forces remain permanently. But they should stay, to enforce the withdrawal of Turkish and German troops and to forestall the outbreak

[37] Imperial War Cabinet 45th meeting, 23 December 1918, 3 p.m., minutes; Cab. 23/42.

of chaos, at least until the Peace Conference had settled the future status of the Transcaucasian states. The "spread of chaos," Milner said, was the greatest danger threatening the Peace Conference—should "large tracts of the world be in blaze," the Conference would be powerless and its decrees worthless. He would rather that British troops not occupy Germany at all than that they should abandon the countries in which they secured order.

In effect, the Imperial War Cabinet agreed to disagree. The minutes of this meeting stated:

> Although no definite conclusions were agreed to, the general trend of the above discussion was that the British forces should not be withdrawn from the Caucasus until after the Turkish and German forces had been withdrawn; that a second British division should not be sent to the Caucasus without Cabinet authority; and that British forces should not be maintained there longer than could be avoided.

In other words, the troops would stay; but the question of their future disposition still remained to be faced.

All these discussions of the Caucasus, particularly those in the Eastern Committee, were remarkable illustrations of the attitudes which prevailed at the end of the War within the British government regarding an important aspect of the problem of Russia. For all of the participants except Edwin Montagu, the absence of Russian authority in the Caucasus presented unique opportunities for the British Empire. For everyone (again, with the exception of Montagu) there suddenly existed a chance for Britain to gain control of the enormous petroleum wealth of Baku. For Balfour, this was about as far as it went. The Great War had marked the end of the era of unabashed imperialism. Balfour could say, undoubtedly with considerable feeling, that "the very suggestion" that British troops would occupy the road to the oil fields of Baku was "damning" and that such a consideration, so far as he was concerned, settled the issue. But he could also advocate British "protection" of "Batum, Baku, and the railway between them, and the pipeline," while letting the rest of the Caucasus go its own way; whether he was aware of his lack of consistency is unclear.

Lord Robert Cecil shared Balfour's interest in the oil and his dislike for new British military expeditions and the obligations they

entailed, but he also saw in the existing situation a chance to eliminate Russia from the Caucasus forever. More than any of his colleagues, Cecil seems to have feared the rebirth of Russia as a Great
Power; thus he was willing to put France in the Caucasus in Russia's
place.[38]

For all that he dominated the discussions, and for all that his views
were incorporated into the Eastern Committee's proposals, Curzon's
ideas seem to have been even less consistent and less clearly
thought-out than those of his colleagues. Britain should only reluctantly take a mandate for the Caucasus—yet British troops should
continue to control the lines of communication to the exclusion of
all others, especially the French. The various states of the Caucasus
were to be supported in their claims for independence—Britain was
to "give them a chance of standing on their own feet"—yet Britain
was evidently not to protect them against Russia. In Curzon's mind,
Russia seems to have almost ceased to exist after the Bolshevik
seizure of power. The old Russian Empire had dissolved in chaos
so great that it would be years, perhaps generations, before "Russia"
would again pose as serious a threat to the interests of the British
Empire as, for example, France did. Within only a year's time, when
Curzon himself became Foreign Secretary, he would discover the
inadequacy of these assumptions.

In December 1918, however, it soon became clear that Curzon had
not foreseen even the immediate implications of his prescriptions for
the Caucasus. As we have seen, British troops—a mixed 2,000-man
Anglo-Indian force from Mesopotamia and a division from Salonika
—were landed at Baku and Batum, respectively, as a result of decisions taken by the War Office before the Eastern Committee had
even begun its deliberations concerning future Eastern policy.[39]
Scarcely had they arrived when their commanders began to appeal
for reinforcements. Thus, on 6 December, the commander of the
Baku force, Major-General W. M. Thomson, proposed a plan for
future operations which would have entailed not only British oc-

[38] Although, as we have seen, Cecil had argued in the Eastern Committee that
Britain should maintain a force at Baku to protect the oil deposits, he later changed
his mind. On 9 March 1919 he wrote to Lloyd George urging the withdrawal of
British forces from all of Transcaucasia. He did not know what proportion of the
oil fields were British-owned, he wrote, but in any case he did not think that the
fields were in great danger, and he added: "nor is there any serious reason to think
that if they were wiped out tomorrow it would matter very much to the British
Empire." (Cecil MSS, British Museum.)

[39] See above, p. 50.

cupation of all the important towns and communications centers of Transcaucasia, including Daghestan, but also the assumption of administrative responsibility for all administrative services, such as finances, postal and transport facilities, police forces, and the like. Later in the month, when the Georgian government announced that it was quite capable of running its own affairs, and that British troops would be allowed into the country only with its permission, Thomson recommended that its wishes should, in effect, be disregarded.[40]

Thomson's attitude deeply disturbed Curzon, and he brought the matter to the Eastern Committee on 30 December. It had never been his intention, he said, that British troops should occupy Georgia. All he had wanted to do was protect the pipeline and the railway; Thomson's proposed operations were contrary to the British government's policy. Accordingly, the committee decided that the War Office should instruct the commanders of the Baku and Batum forces that it was no part of the government's policy to embark on operations at any distance from the railway, and that their mission was simply to maintain communications between the Black and Caspian Seas.[41]

Such distinctions, easily drawn in London, seemed less obvious in the field. Once on the scene, as so often occurs when military forces are committed in distant lands among alien peoples, their involvement created demands which shaped the course of future policy just as surely as resolutions by committees in London. It was scarcely possible to occupy the two ports and the railway and pipeline between them and yet leave the rest of Transcaucasia alone. Thomson and Major-General G. T. Forestier-Walker, who commanded the division which landed at Batum, had to act to secure the safety of their own troops as well as guard the railway, and their notions of the measures necessary to safeguard their forces made it inevitable that their actions should have many of the attributes of an occupation. Because the withdrawal of the Turks from Azerbaijan had left the country in a condition of near-chaos, Thomson proclaimed

---

[40] Thomson's proposal of 6 December 1918 was summarized by Curzon in a paper, "The Caucasus," 2 February 1919; copy in the Curzon Papers at Kedleston. Thomson's recommendation for the movement of troops into Georgia was reported by General Milne (now at Constantinople) in a telegram of 26 December 1918, text appended to the minutes of the Eastern Committee's 48th meeting, 30 December, noon; Cab. 27/24.

[41] Eastern Committee 48th meeting; minutes cited above, n. 40.

martial law. He himself became military governor of Baku, and public order was maintained by British military police. This was not sufficient: in the words of a Foreign Office report, "it was necessary for the British to re-establish an administration in almost every department of the country's life."[42] They took over both the Russian and the Azerbaijan State Banks and amalgamated them, supervising a note issue. They established a system of food rationing akin to the card system then employed in England. They set up a "Labour Control Office" to investigate and settle labor disputes, particularly in the oil fields and on the railways—a procedure which involved the arrest and deportation of "Bolshevik agitators."[43] And they returned to private ownership the oil and shipping industries which had been nationalized by the combination of Mensheviks, Socialist-Revolutionaries, and Dashnaks (members of the Armenian party) which had ruled Baku before the Turks succeeded in capturing the town in September.[44]

Much less drastic measures were judged necessary in Georgia. The country had been little touched by the German occupation, and its administration in Tiflis, the capital, remained in the hands of experienced Georgians, many of whom had held high positions under the old Russian regime. Batum, however, was a special problem. Unlike the rest of the country, it had been given to Turkey under the Treaty of Brest-Litovsk. Moreover, the town and its surrounding province were claimed by Armenia and General Denikin (on the part of Russia), as well as by Georgia. Both because of the disorder left by the Turkish occupation and because of these conflicting claims, the town and province were placed under British military government, although of a less thoroughgoing sort than that at Baku. British influence—of a rather heavy-handed sort—extended throughout Georgia; thus, on one occasion, Forestier-Walker threatened to close down a Menshevik newspaper in Tiflis for printing articles which he found insulting to the Allied Powers. And the British, of course, exercised firm control over the railroad and the

---

[42] "Outline of Events in Transcaucasia from the Beginning of the Russian Revolution in the Summer of 1917 to April 1921," by W. J. Childs and A.E.R. McDonnell (the latter had been Consul at Baku), 31 May 1922, file E 8378/8378/58; F.O. 371/6280. This was a 34-page printed memorandum.

[43] G.H.Q. (Baghdad) to War Office, telegram X 4707, 22 December 1918; W.O. 33/962, no. 808. (At this time the British force at Baku was under Baghdad, rather than Constantinople.)

[44] This summary of British actions at Baku is from the Foreign Office memorandum cited above, n. 42.

pipeline. The German occupation of Georgia had been mild; the British were compared unfavorably to them.[45]

The remaining new state south of the Caucasus mountains—Armenia—saw no British occupation at all. Its condition seemed so desperate, and its future so uncertain, that the British confined themselves to relief efforts. Moreover, Armenia did not lie astride the railway or the pipeline between the two seas; here was another justification for a more distant treatment than that accorded to Georgia or Azerbaijan. Perhaps the most important service the British command rendered the Armenians was to protect them from their more powerful neighbors; indeed, the British presence was the principal stabilizing influence preventing open conflict among the separate Transcaucasian states. In late December 1918, for example, when war broke out between Georgia and Armenia over disputed territory, the British command immediately stepped in to arrange for a cease-fire and for the retirement of the opposing armies to the positions they had previously occupied.[46]

At the same time, the British government was taking first steps toward recognizing the governments of the Caucasus states. As the Eastern Committee directed, the Georgians received the most favored treatment. On 31 December, Georgian representatives in London received a letter signed by Sir Louis Mallet of the Foreign Office, stating that the British government viewed with sympathy the Georgian government's proclamation of independence, and that it would support the recognition of Georgia at the coming Peace Conference.[47] And in Baku, after the election of a parliament and the formation of a broadly based coalition government, General Thomson announced on 28 December that he would accord the government full support as the only legal power within the limits of Azerbaijan.[48] For Armenia, however, despite many declarations by members of the British government in favor of an independent Armenian state, nothing was done. Much of the territory that was

---

[45] *Ibid.* See also Kazemzadeh, *Struggle for Transcaucasia*, pp. 171-72.

[46] Batum telegram G. 6, 25 December 1918, to War Office in telegram E. 757 from G.H.Q., Constantinople; and Milne (Constantinople) to Director of Military Intelligence, telegram I. 4227, 31 December 1918: W.O. 33/965, nos. 3033 and 3050. Also Kazemzadeh, *Struggle for Transcaucasia*, pp. 180-82.

[47] Zourab Avalishvili, *The Independence of Georgia in International Politics, 1918-1921*, London, n.d. (circa 1941), p. 146. Avalishvili (Avalov) was a member of the Georgian mission in London.

[48] Kazemzadeh, *Struggle for Transcaucasia*, pp. 166-67.

inhabited by Armenians was still under Turkish sovereignty; the problem of Armenia, therefore, was not to be dealt with until the Allied statesmen came to grips with the problems of Turkey in the summer of 1920.

✧

The Eastern Committee dealt with future British policy regarding the borderlands of Russia, with little attention to what type of regime might be in power in the center. Whether the Bolsheviks or their enemies sat in Moscow, it was still desirable that there should be a tier of independent buffer states between the territory they ruled and the lifelines of the British Empire. This largely unstated assumption underlay virtually all of the policy proposals made within the Eastern Committee.

The problem of the borderlands, however, was only one aspect of the larger Russian problem which during December 1918 became one of the chief concerns of the Imperial War Cabinet and the British government. Early in the month the premiers and foreign ministers of France and Italy came to London to coordinate Allied planning for the approaching Peace Conference. On the agenda was an urgent question which cut right across the whole Russian problem—the manner in which Russia was to be represented at the Conference.[49] Since no Americans were present, no final decisions were taken, but regarding Russia, at least, some issues were clearly drawn. Georges Clemenceau, speaking for France, urged that, since Russia had betrayed the Allied cause by making a separate peace with Germany, it should have no representation at the Peace Conference. Presumably he would have felt differently had a White government succeeded in coming to power in Moscow, but he cast his argument in general terms. Nor did he argue for the representation of the border states; France, after all, was committed to the ideal of a Great Russia as a counterweight to Germany.

Within the British government Clemenceau found support from both Balfour and Curzon in his refusal to admit the Bolshevik regime as the spokesman for Russia at Paris, but each argued in favor of the representation of the various border states. Against all of them,

---

[49] The inter-Allied meetings took place on 1-3 December 1918. Russian policy was discussed principally at two sessions on the 3rd: 11:15 a.m. (Minutes I.C. 100) and 5:30 p.m. (Minutes I.C. 102); Cab. 28/5. Excerpts are printed in David Lloyd George, *The Truth About the Peace Treaties*, London, 1938, vol. I, pp. 320-22.

however, stood Lloyd George. It was here that the Prime Minister first put forward a view which he was to hold, with several notable lapses, throughout the following year. The Allies could not proceed as if there were no Russia, he said. The affairs of nearly 200 million people could not be settled without hearing them. Whatever one might say about the Bolsheviks, they "appeared to have a hold over the majority of the population," a fact which could not be neglected merely because it was unpalatable. It was impossible to say, for example, that the Finns or the Letts or the Azerbaijanis might send representatives to the Peace Conference and then not give a hearing to the Bolsheviks. Lloyd George's own thinking on the Russian problem was not sufficiently crystallized so that he could suggest precisely how the Bolsheviks might be heard. Instead, he simply urged that for the moment no "fixed attitude" be adopted toward "Central Russia." For the moment, none was.

Meanwhile, throughout the period between the end of the War and the beginning of the Peace Conference, a series of peace proposals came from the Soviet government in Moscow. Some even hinted at the prospect of economic concessions if the Allies would agree to negotiate.[50] To reinforce these proposals, Maxim Litvinov,

---

[50] The first Soviet offer, made to the British government through the Swedish Embassy in Petrograd on 3 November 1918, proposed a general armistice between Russian and British forces and the beginning of peace discussions. (Ministry of Foreign Affairs of the U.S.S.R., *Dokumenty vneshnei politiki SSSR* [Documents on the Foreign Policy of the U.S.S.R.], vol. I, Moscow, 1957, p. 549.) On 6 November, the Sixth All-Russian Congress of Soviets, meeting on the eve of the first anniversary of the Bolshevik seizure of power, proposed that negotiations be opened with all countries "who are waging war against Russia"; this offer was made by wireless on the 8th (*ibid.*, p. 556; translation in Jane Degras, ed., *Soviet Documents on Foreign Policy*, vol. I, *1917-1924*, London, 1951, p. 123).

On 2 December, Georgi Chicherin, Soviet Commissar for Foreign Affairs, broadcast a wireless message protesting against intervention to all the Allied governments; in it he again offered to make peace (*Dokumenty vneshnei politiki*, vol. I, pp. 593-95; translation in C. K. Cumming and W. W. Pettit, eds., *Russian-American Relations March, 1917-March, 1920: Documents and Papers*, New York, 1920, pp. 268-70).

Meanwhile, Maxim Litvinov had come to Stockholm as Plenipotentiary of the Soviet government. On 24 December he delivered to the British, French, Italian, and American ministers there a letter stating that he had been authorized to enter into preliminary negotiations (*Dokumenty vneshnei politiki*, vol. I, pp. 626-27; translation in *Foreign Relations, 1919, Russia*, p. 1). And on the same day, he handed the American minister a long letter to President Wilson, again protesting against the intervention and stating that the Soviet government "are prepared to go to any length of concessions, as far as the real interests of their country are concerned, if they can secure thereby conditions enabling them to work out peacefully their social schemes." (*Dokumenty vneshnei politiki*, vol. I, pp. 628-30; translation in Degras, *Soviet Documents*, pp. 133-35.)

earlier the Soviet representative in Great Britain, now the Deputy Commissar for Foreign Affairs, journeyed to Stockholm at the end of November. Technically, he came as a commercial attaché in the Soviet mission (the Scandinavian neutrals had not yet broken off relations with the Bolshevik government, although they shortly would do so); in fact he was empowered to enter into political negotiations.[51] An "informant" (probably Litvinov's close friend, the British journalist Arthur Ransome, who was then in Stockholm) told R. H. Clive, the Chargé d'Affaires at the British Legation, that Litvinov hoped to secure the end of intervention and some sort of recognition of the Soviet regime. In return, Clive reported to London, Litvinov "was understood to say Bolshevik Government was prepared to meet wishes of His Majesty's Government in any way possible e.g. by rescinding decree whereby foreign loans were repudiated, releasing detained British subjects and giving compensation for murder of Captain Cromie."[52] Three days later, on 7 December, Clive reported that Litvinov (again through an intermediary) had asked to be put in communication with some member of the British Legation. Acting on his own authority, Clive declined, on the grounds that the Swedish government now forbade the Soviet mission from engaging in "political activities," confining it instead to matters concerning trade, relief, and prisoner exchanges.[53]

Within the British government, Litvinov's request initiated a debate—over whether or not to deal directly with the Soviet regime—that was to continue in varying forms for over a year. Aside from the Cabinet itself, this question most immediately concerned the Foreign Office. For nearly all of the period, until the Bolsheviks emerged clearly as the victors in the Russian Civil War, the dominant view among the higher officials of the Foreign Office was that there should be no direct dealings with the Soviet government. As one official commented, if Moscow was in fact willing to offer the terms which Clive enumerated in his first telegram about Litvinov, the Bolsheviks were evidently "losing ground," making it even less necessary to negotiate with them. And he added: "Of course no compromise with Bolshevism is possible." Although Sir George Clerk, a

---

[51] So Litvinov told Arthur Ransome, who reported it in the London *Daily News*, 30 November 1918.

[52] Clive (Stockholm) to Balfour, telegram 3600, 4 December 1918, file 200686/169701/38; F.O. 371/3345.

[53] Clive (Stockholm) to Balfour, telegram 3632, 7 December 1918, file 202541/169701/38; F.O. 371/3345.

senior official, responded, "I fear that we may find a compromise with Bolshevism is not only possible, but necessary," his view was by no means typical, and he did not elaborate upon it. Lord Hardinge, the Permanent Under-Secretary, reflected the mood of the Office when he closed comment on this file with the assertion that "It [a compromise] can only be at the price of our withdrawal from Siberia and Archangel and that would seem to be too heavy a price to pay."[54]

The sort of argument which prevailed in the Foreign Office was perhaps best exemplified in a long minute by Sir Ronald Graham, an assistant under-secretary, commenting on yet another telegram from Clive in Stockholm, this time stating that Ransome had informed him that Litvinov had drawn up some definite proposals and wished to present them to the British government.[55] Graham wrote:

I would earnestly represent that we should not commit ourselves even to opening "pourparlers" with the Bolsheviks if we can possibly avoid it. Admitting that we are unwilling and unable to take more active measures against them and that our intervention, such as it is, must inevitably end next summer, there are, before that season, some difficult months for the Bolsheviks to pass through. Their Government, beset by internal dangers and struggles and surrounded by enemies, might well crumble to ruin in the near future. Any recognition we give, even to the extent of considering Litvinoff's proposals, will be exploited by the Bolsheviks to the full; both internally and externally, it will increase their moral strength, discourage our friends and influence the attitude of neutral neighbours.[56]

Graham's argument—in essence an appeal to do nothing—was made irrelevant on the day he wrote it, 23 December. For on that day the Imperial War Cabinet decided that Litvinov's proposals should be examined. Whether or not to do so, of course, depended on what the British government's Russian policy would be, and Lord Milner's remark at the outset of the meeting, that Litvinov "had for some days been trying to offer us terms," precipitated a long and wide-ranging discussion.[57] Its tone was set by Winston Churchill.

[54] These minutes, by Walford H. M. Selby (6 December 1918), Sir George R. Clerk (6 December), and Lord Hardinge (undated), are all in the file cited in n. 52.
[55] Clive (Stockholm) to Balfour, telegram 3731, 20 December 1918, file 210041/169701/38; F.O. 371/3346.
[56] Graham's minute, dated 23 December 1918, is in *idem*.
[57] Imperial War Cabinet minutes, 23 December 1918, cited above, n. 37.

The Cabinet must reach a definite decision, he said. For him the alternatives were whether the Bolsheviks would be left alone, "to stew in their own juice," or whether the British government would attempt "to break up" their power.

The meeting marked Churchill's first foray into Russian matters. At the time, he was still Minister of Munitions, a post he had held since mid-1917, but Lloyd George had recently appointed him as Milner's successor at the War Office. During the preceding year he had been entirely absorbed with the problems of munitions production. Moreover, he was not a member of the War Cabinet. These circumstances had prevented him from being anything more than an interested bystander of the beginnings of British intervention in Russia. At the War Office, however, he was to find himself head of the department of state which, during 1919, was the one perhaps most concerned with Russia, for during that year the intervention made Russia largely a military problem. In December 1918, Churchill was already immersing himself in the affairs of the office he would assume on the 14th of January. Like Milner, his predecessor, he felt that the effort of intervention should be pressed with vastly increased vigor, and he brought his own vigor—the vigor of a younger and much fresher man—to his advocacy. At one stroke Churchill became second in importance only to Lloyd George in the determination of Britain's Russian policy. His appointment to the War Office at the end of 1918 seemed to mark his complete emergence, at last, from the cloud which Gallipoli had cast over his reputation. Russia, however—and Churchill's identification in the mind of the public with the ill-fated efforts at intervention—was to draw the cloud back down upon him.

In the Imperial War Cabinet on 23 December, Churchill expressed his conviction that intervention "by small contingents"—such as was then taking place—could have no satisfactory results. Instead, he said, either the Russians must be allowed "to murder each other without let or hindrance," or else, in the name of order, the Allies must interfere and do so "thoroughly, with large forces, abundantly supplied with mechanical appliances." The latter was Churchill's clear preference. His statement drew immediate opposition from William M. Hughes, the abrasive Labour Prime Minister of Australia. "Great principles" were involved in the decisions on a Russian policy, Hughes insisted. Would the "new world" be one in which each nation would be allowed to lead its own life, or were the victors to prescribe the way in which the others should live? In his opinion the Allies should immediately withdraw from Russia and allow the Russians to adopt whatever sort of government they wished; "the Allied professions of fighting for justice and liberty would be entirely stultified by a continuance of intervention in Russia."

Hughes's statement aroused Balfour, who regarded it as criticism of his department. The attitude of the Foreign Office was continually misrepresented, he said. He had repeatedly maintained—in speeches, telegrams, and despatches—that Russia must choose its own regime. If Russia chose to be Bolshevik, the British government would not gainsay it. Intervention had begun purely as a wartime measure whose sole object was to reconstruct the Eastern Front against Germany. Since the Armistice, however, the Allies had found themselves "the protectors of small democratic governments, threatened by the Bolsheviks." Thus there was a moral obligation. Moreover, the Russian winter had come, and many of the intervening troops could not be withdrawn before June 1919. In any case, the British government was acting in its own defense, to prevent the spread of Bolshevism, which was a deliberately aggressive doctrine. It was one thing to let the Russians stew in their own juice, Balfour said, but quite another to submit to being stewed in it with them.

Balfour did not confront Churchill's wish for intervention on a greatly increased scale. Lloyd George did, however. Churchill had argued that, if such a decision were made, then Great Britain would have to be "stirred up," and a large volunteer army raised. In the context of the times, with troops rioting for demobilization, this was a farfetched proposition, and the Prime Minister sharply attacked it. Barely 5,000 volunteers could be found, Lloyd George asserted. He agreed with Balfour and Hughes that the British government should not try to dictate the form of government the Russian people should have. But some of his colleagues, he said, wanted to intervene in Russia precisely because of their distaste for Bolshevism. Intervention in such spirit would "certainly cause trouble at home." He had been told that all over the country people were asking why the government was interfering in Russia's internal affairs. This was not the only reason he was opposed to the sort of policies Churchill suggested, he said, but it was "a strong one."

Another reason, the Prime Minister continued, was that the Allies so far had failed to enlist the sympathy of the Russians. General Poole, at Archangel, had originally expected to gather an army of 1,000,000 men. Later he had reduced his estimate to 100,000. But thus far Ironside had recruited only 3,000 Russians—half-hearted ones at that. It was argued, Lloyd George said, that "these people" should be protected against Bolshevism. Yet Lockhart, who had represented Britain in Moscow, had reported on his return in November that the workers were loyal to the Bolsheviks, and that the peasants, although objecting to Bolshevik requisitions of food, could not be counted upon to act against them.[58] Therefore he must ask: did the British government have any right to protect a minority against a majority because it happened to have political relations with the former? He recalled to his colleagues that, at the time of the French Revolution, Britain had intervened in favor of minorities in the Vendée and in the south of France. He could find little reason to follow that example.

Finally, Lloyd George said, it was alleged that the Bolsheviks were making war by propaganda on Great Britain. Yet as there were four or five British forces on Russian territory which in the course of their operations "not infrequently shot Bolsheviks," he thought that the British government scarcely had grounds for complaint. Already, he said, there were 14,000 British troops in North Russia, 4,000 (including the Canadians) in Siberia, and one and possibly two divisions in the Caucasus. If the fighting was to continue in the spring, larger forces would be necessary. Just where, he asked, could these troops be found? The Bolsheviks had indicated that they were disposed to come to terms; surely their terms should be examined.

These were the Prime Minister's arguments. They dominated the discussions. From all the Dominion premiers, and from Edwin Montagu within his own government, he found agreement. From the other members of the Imperial War Cabinet—and this was a large meeting—he got mostly silence. Churchill said nothing, after his opening remarks, important enough to be recorded in the minutes. Curzon spoke only to point out that there were different reasons, unrelated to the question of opposition to Bolshevism, for

[58] Lockhart's report is cited above, ch. I, n. 16.

stationing British troops in the Caucasus.[59] Then Bonar Law, who nearly always agreed with Lloyd George—and on whose agreement the Coalition largely depended—brought the discussion back to its starting point by suggesting that Clive, at Stockholm, be instructed to ask Litvinov to put his proposals in writing. Balfour, who had read the Foreign Office files dealing with the Litvinov mission but who had avoided taking a position on them (he merely initialled them to indicate he had seen them), urged only that any dealings with Litvinov be managed "unofficially," with sufficient discretion so as not to alarm the Allies—which meant, essentially, the French. Milner, as well, gave his support. Bolshevism was the greatest danger faced by the civilized world, he said. He did not wish to attack it, for attacks created sympathizers abroad. But he did wish to confine the fire to the area it had already ravaged. Therefore, to keep the Bolsheviks within their "own boundaries"—to keep Bolshevism from Siberia, the Don country, and Turkestan, not to mention the border states—he would be willing to come to terms with the Soviet leaders. The meeting agreed that Clive should be authorized to obtain Litvinov's proposals "for an understanding with the British Government," and that these proposals, when obtained, should be examined by the Imperial War Cabinet. This was a policy decision of fundamental importance: thenceforward the notion of direct negotiations with the Bolsheviks, although not always dominant, was never absent from British consideration.

The Cabinet never had an opportunity to examine Litvinov's terms, however. Balfour was so sensitive to the opinions of the Allies that he telegraphed the British representatives in Paris, Washington, and Rome informing them that he proposed to instruct Clive to see Litvinov and asking them to find out how the governments to which they were accredited would react to such a move. For some unaccountable reason these telegrams were not sent until the evening of 30 December, a full week following the Imperial War Cabinet's decision that Litvinov should be approached.[60] Neither the records of the Foreign Office nor of the Cabinet, nor Balfour's own papers, contain any clues about the reasons for this delay. Perhaps Balfour

---

[59] Later in the afternoon the Imperial War Cabinet had a separate discussion entirely devoted to the Caucasus; see above, p. 80.

[60] Balfour's three identical telegrams, all sent 30 December 1918, 7 p.m., are in file 211538/169701/38; F.O. 371/3346.

himself was sufficiently ambivalent about the wisdom of entering
into talks with Litvinov that he felt no urgency. In any case, the
Foreign Secretary was never one to proceed with haste or with undue intensity of effort, and the season, after all, was that of the Christmas holidays.

Neither the American nor the Italian governments had formally
replied (although President Wilson, passing through London, had
told Lloyd George that he was in favor of sounding out Litvinov)[61]
when, on 4 January 1919, the French Minister of Foreign Affairs,
Stéphan Pichon, informed Lord Derby, the British Ambassador, that
his government was flatly opposed to dealings with Litvinov; it could
not "lend itself" to a Soviet scheme whose "obvious object" was
to strengthen the authority of the Bolshevik regime by making it
appear that the Allies were disposed to treat with it. Moreover,
under the guise of diplomacy the Bolsheviks would introduce into
the Allied countries "agents for a criminal propaganda." The whole
idea was "inopportune and dangerous," Pichon said; he hoped that
London would instruct Clive to have nothing to do with Litvinov.[62]

This French opposition was sufficient to keep the British from
pursuing further the possibility of conducting negotiations through
Litvinov. In any case, by this time Litvinov's own usefulness had
been significantly reduced by the decision of the Swedish government, early in December, to deprive him of the right of cipher communications.[63] With all his messages to Moscow going *en clair,* real
negotiation was impossible. Whether or not Litvinov and Clive even
met in Stockholm is not clear from the existing records. The only
Soviet proposal which Clive received came through the mail—a
note from Litvinov on 24 December formally notifying the British
Legation (and the other Allied missions in Stockholm) of his presence, and offering "preliminary Peace Negotiations."[64] Litvinov
himself did not expect much to come from his efforts. A few days
later he released the text of his note to the Swedish newspaper
Politiken and told an interviewer: "There is no good having too

[61] Lloyd George and Balfour had an informal talk with President Wilson on 26
December; Lloyd George reported on it to the Imperial War Cabinet on the 30th
(minutes cited below, n. 67).

[62] Derby (Paris) to Balfour, telegram 15, 4 January 1919, file 2404/91/38; F.O.
371/3954.

[63] Noted in Buckler (Copenhagen) to Lansing (Paris), telegram 116, 18 January 1919; *Foreign Relations, 1919, Russia,* pp. 15-17.

[64] Litvinov's note is cited above, n. 50. Clive telegraphed it to London in his
telegram 3759, 24 December 1918, file 211538/169701/38; F.O. 371/3346.

great hopes about this, but now that we have displayed to the world our willingness for peace, responsibility for continued war and bloodshed rests on [the] Entente."[65]

Meanwhile, in the absence of any proposals from Litvinov, the discussions of Russia in the Imperial War Cabinet on 30 and 31 December—the last meetings before the beginning of the Peace Conference at Paris—inevitably retraced old ground. One new suggestion was put forward: on the 30th Sir Robert Borden of Canada stated that, in his view, the only alternative to continued intervention, to which he was strongly opposed, was to induce the warring parties in Russia, and also the governments of the border states, to send representatives to Paris for a conference with the Allies; the latter could then apply pressure "to restrain and control aggression, and bring about conditions of stable government under the power and influence of the League of Nations." A similar proposal had in fact been made a month earlier in a memorandum to the Cabinet by H.A.L. Fisher, the President of the Board of Education,[66] but the Cabinet session of 30 December was the first on which such a notion—the basis of what came to be called the "Prinkipo policy"—was discussed. After Borden spoke, Lord Robert Cecil elaborated upon his suggestion, proposing that, as a condition of their coming to Paris, all the participants in the Russian Civil War should cease firing and hold their present territorial positions until a settlement was achieved. Milner, who was dubious, observed that, if the Bolsheviks would accept such conditions and cease "their aggression on their neighbours," they would in fact have "begun to cease to be Bolsheviks," and Lloyd George replied that Denikin and Kolchak would also have to cease their "aggression" (it is striking how frequently the minutes of the meeting employed the term)—and that measures would have to be devised to prevent the Bolsheviks from using the Peace Conference as a propaganda forum.[67]

Borden's suggestion received no further formal discussion. As we shall see, however, Lloyd George was quick to act upon it. The fol-

[65] Reported by Clive (Stockholm) to Balfour, telegram 3780, 29 December 1918, file 213558/169701/38; F.O. 371/3346.

Later, in mid-January, Litvinov did have extensive talks with an "unofficial" American representative, W. H. Buckler, but by then the question of whether or not to have dealings with the Bolshevik regime was a central concern of the inter-Allied councils at the Peace Conference. See below, p. 107.

[66] Cabinet paper G.T. 6443, "Future Military Policy in Russia," 5 December 1918; Cab. 24/71.

[67] Minutes, Imperial War Cabinet, 47th meeting, 30 December 1918, 3:30 p.m.;

lowing day's meeting of the Imperial War Cabinet saw, instead, a development and a crystallization of the arguments presented on the 23rd. Chiefly, it was marked by a confrontation between the Prime Minister and Winston Churchill. Because these two emerged as the chief proponents of opposing positions regarding Russian policy, not only within the British government but within the ranks of the Powers gathered in Paris as well, their debate is worth summarizing in some detail.[68]

Churchill argued strongly for collective intervention to remove the Soviet regime by large contingents from all five of the principal Powers or, if the United States refused (as seemed likely from Lloyd George's report of a conversation he had had with President Wilson), by the other four—the British Empire, France, Italy, and Japan. Of course, he said, he would prefer a negotiated settlement that would avoid fighting. But he considered that there was no chance of securing such a settlement unless it were known that the Allies were willing to use the force necessary to achieve it. The Russians of all factions should be told that, if they were willing to hold free elections to choose their form of government, then the Allies would help them, and that, if they refused, the Allies "would use force to restore the situation and set up a democratic Government." Churchill was confident that Bolshevism "represented a mere fraction of the population, and would be exposed and swept away by a General Election held under Allied auspices." He warned his colleagues that the matter was urgent; if the Russian problem was not tackled directly, they would "come away from the Peace Conference rejoicing in a victory which was no victory, and a peace which was no peace," and in no more than a few months they would find themselves "compelled to gather our armies again, and summon the Conference anew in order to deal with the situation." This was a grand scheme. Yet Churchill failed to state where the means to execute it might be found.

Lloyd George agreed with Churchill that the Allies should come to a decision on their Russian policy before taking up any other matter; with their small forces scattered over Russia, even a few weeks of drift might lead to disaster. He had found himself leaning

Cab. 23/42. Excerpts in Lloyd George, *Truth About the Peace Treaties*, vol. I, pp. 198-200.

[68] Minutes, Imperial War Cabinet, 48th meeting, 31 December 1918, 11 a.m.; Cab. 23/42. Excerpts in Lloyd George, *Truth About the Peace Treaties*, vol. I, pp. 325-30.

first in one direction, then in another, "owing to the absolute contradiction between information supplied from Russia by men of equally good authority." Some of the most crucial facts—here Lloyd George evidently had in mind the degree of popular support that the Bolsheviks enjoyed—had never been ascertained and were, by their nature, probably unascertainable.

Yet there were other facts only too well known. The Germans and the Austrians, with a million men at their disposal, had been stuck in the Russian "morass," unable to advance to Petrograd despite the disintegration of the Tsar's army. As for the Allied forces of intervention, they were then only on the fringes of Russia with less than 100,000 troops. The Red Army now numbered 300,000; by March it might reach 1,000,000, and its organization had greatly improved. Where were the Allies to find the troops necessary to march into the heart of Russia and occupy the country? What troops would Canada, Australia, or South Africa furnish for "conquering and keeping down Russia"? No British troops could be found without conscription, and, if Parliament were to agree to conscription for that purpose, Lloyd George said, he doubted whether the troops themselves would go. The "citizen army" would "go anywhere for liberty, but they could not be convinced that the suppression of Bolshevism was a war for liberty."

Therefore, Lloyd George said, he was "definitely opposed to military intervention in any shape." Again he raised the example of the French Revolution. There had been "horrors as bad as, or worse than, any of the Bolsheviks, perpetrated by a small fraction." But the very fact of British intervention had enabled Danton "to rally French patriotism and make the terror a military instrument." France had thus become organized "as a great military machine imbued with a passionate hatred" of Great Britain. To the Prime Minister the parallels were clear: the one sure way to perpetuate the power of Bolshevism in Russia was to attempt to suppress it with foreign troops. The best policy would be to let Bolshevism fail of itself, as it would if it did not represent Russian sentiment. He hoped his colleagues would support him in refusing to countenance any further military intervention, and in inviting representatives of all sections of Russian opinion to appear before the Peace Conference, as Borden had suggested, "with a view to composing their differences."

Once again, as on the 23rd, the minutes of this meeting do not record any significant opposition to Lloyd George's arguments, except for that of Churchill. Lord Robert Cecil, however, emphasized the moral obligation of continuing to support the various White factions already receiving Allied assistance and warned that the Allies might be called upon to prevent a Soviet invasion of the countries on Russia's western frontier, such as Poland and Rumania. The official summary of the conclusions of the meeting reflected these concerns, as well as those of Lloyd George. They stated:

> It was generally agreed that, in cases where there was an external aggression by the Bolsheviks against an existing Government with which we had been co-operating, we should be entitled to support that Government in any manner which did not involve military intervention, and that our general policy should be that, as Sir J. Cook [finance minister and deputy head of the New Zealand coalition government] expressed it, of "walling off a fire in a mine."

> Subject to the above considerations, the Imperial War Cabinet endorsed the general policy with regard to Russia outlined by Mr. Lloyd George.

❖

Here, purportedly, was a statement of policy. In fact, it was more a glossing over of a lack of policy. Even apart from the fact that the labelling of Bolshevik attacks against White forces as "external aggression" involved quite a stretching of the conventional meaning of that term, the sort of support which British troops were giving the White "existing Governments" amounted to just the "military intervention" which the statement precluded. Given the stated policy, the only possible course of action should have been to withdraw the intervening forces, while still, perhaps, furnishing material assistance to the Whites, and to wait for the blaze to die down. But as General Sir Henry Wilson, the C.I.G.S., made clear in an entry in his diary that night, British troops were to stay in North Russia, Siberia, and the Caucasus "until some Allied policy for the whole of Russia had been settled on in Paris." The official summary of the meeting could not hide the fact that, as Wilson wrote, there was still "no policy in our Russian theatre, which at this time of the day after all our discussions for months and months is an absolute disgrace."[69]

[69] MS diary of Field-Marshal Sir Henry Wilson, entry for 31 December 1918 (also in Major-General Sir C. E. Callwell, *Field-Marshal Sir Henry Wilson, Bart., G.C.B., D.S.O., His Life and Diaries*, London, 1927, vol. II, pp. 158-59).

CHAPTER III

THE PEACE CONFERENCE: PRINKIPO AND AFTER

The best fate that we should desire for Bolshevism is that it should commit suicide. If it meets the other representatives of Russia, and they succeed in devising means for ascertaining the will of the Russian people, then the suicide of Bolshevism is assured.

—The Times, *23 January 1919*

ALTHOUGH the Imperial War Cabinet had reached no real agreement on Russian policy in the course of its meetings during November and December 1918, Lloyd George nevertheless resolved to proceed himself to attempt to bring about an end to the war that was raging within the confines of the former Russian Empire, even if the act of doing so also implied coming to some sort of terms with the Bolshevik regime. Accordingly, on the second day of the New Year, the Foreign Office instructed its representatives in the capitals of the principal Powers: "Please suggest to Government to which you are accredited the propriety of transmitting following message to Soviet Government at Moscow, to General Kolchak at Omsk, to General Denikin at Ekaterinburg, to M. Tschaikowsky at Archangel and to Governments of ex-Russian states."[1]

The message which followed was the basis of what came to be called the "Prinkipo policy." One of the first tasks of the Powers gathering at Paris, it stated, would be to end the fighting in Russia, to reconcile the conflicting claims of the various groups contending on Russian territory, and to bring succor to the suffering peoples of those vast lands. It continued:

Pending decisions that will be taken in this sense great friendly Powers call upon all the Governments, parties and peoples in the States and terri-

[1] Telegram to Paris, Rome, Washington, and Tokyo embassies, 2 January 1919, file 1347/91/38; F.O. 371/3954. The resulting memorandum to the State Department, 3 January, is in *Foreign Relations, 1919, Russia*, pp. 2-3.

tories in question to abstain from further aggressions, hostilities and reprisals and require them to keep the peace both at home and with their neighbours.

If the aforesaid Governments and parties will immediately suspend hostilities on all fronts for the duration of the peace negotiations, and if they or any of them should desire to send representatives to Paris to discuss with the Great Powers conditions of a permanent settlement, the Great Powers would be prepared to enter on such a discussion with them.

The instructions accompanying this draft message told British representatives in the four capitals that the government felt that some such move was urgently needed in order to preserve the states bordering on Russia, in particular the Baltic states, from a Soviet invasion. But the call for a meeting of all parties to the Russian conflict was only a suggestion, put forward privately for discussion, and not an established, publicly acknowledged policy position. The circumstances surrounding the French government's reaction to it, however, transformed it from the former to the latter and embittered discussion of the Russian problem at Paris from the outset of the Peace Conference. Pichon, the Minister of Foreign Affairs, rejected the idea of a Russian conference which would include the Bolsheviks—he had no objection to a conference of anti-Bolsheviks —as vigorously as he had previously rejected the British suggestion for negotiations with Litvinov at Stockholm. In an *aide mémoire* on 8 January to Lord Derby, the British Ambassador, Pichon equated the proposal with recognition of the Bolshevik regime—an act which "would give the lie to those principles of Right and Justice" for which the Allies stood and would only strengthen the "truculent World Bolshevik propaganda" of which the Allies themselves might be the first victims. Therefore, much as the French government appreciated the "generous spirit of universal reconciliation" which had inspired the British proposal, it nevertheless refused "to make any pact with this criminal régime."[2]

Pichon's note had been private, but on 11 January a similar, although not identical, document appeared in *l'Humanité*, then the organ of the Socialist Party, and the London *Daily Mail*—undoubtedly the only joint venture in which these two newspapers ever participated. Historians ever since have assumed that Pichon himself released it to the press in order to discredit publicly the British policy

[2] Derby (Paris) to Balfour, telegram 43, 8 January 1919, file 5060/91/38; F.O. 371/3954.

which he so strongly opposed.[3] A long entry in Lord Derby's diary, however, indicates that this may well not have been the case, that the publication might have been the result of a leak within the ranks of the officials of the Quai d'Orsay, and that Pichon and Clemenceau were both angry and embarrassed about it.[4]

Regardless of the circumstances of its publication, Pichon's reply was an accurate expression of his government's policy, and the French brought these views with them into the council chambers even before the formal opening of the Peace Conference, when the body which came to be called the Council of Ten—the heads of government and the foreign ministers of the United Kingdom, France, Italy, the United States, and Japan, usually accompanied by expert advisers—met for the first time on 12 January.[5] Pichon

---

[3] See, e.g., Thompson, *Versailles Peace*, pp. 95-96.

[4] Derby carried on an extensive private correspondence with Balfour and later, when he took over the Foreign Office, with Curzon. With his letters he frequently sent carbon copies of extracts from his diary; these extracts provided a detailed account of rumors and intrigues at the highest levels of French politics. In his diary entry for 11 January 1919 (Balfour MSS), Derby wrote that the French government's *Bureau de la Presse* had telephoned Pichon at 1 a.m. to say that both *l'Humanité* and the *Daily Mail* had obtained a version of his *aide mémoire* and planned to publish it that day. Pichon then informed Clemenceau, and together they sent messages threatening *l'Humanité* with suppression if the note appeared, and urging the *Daily Mail* not to publish it. The latter complied to the extent of removing the item from its Paris edition, but claimed that its London edition had already gone to press. *L'Humanité* then went ahead in disregard of the threat—which, of course, was never fulfilled. The published version bore the date 5 December 1918—an attempt, Derby noted, to make it seem as if Clemenceau had been aware of the British proposal previous to making a tough anti-Bolshevik speech on 30 December. A further bizarre touch is Clemenceau's explanation, to a friend of Derby, that since both Balfour and Lord Robert Cecil had been away from the Foreign Office on 2 January, when the original British message was sent, the sender must have been a subordinate with Bolshevik sympathies; this same subordinate, Clemenceau hypothesized, angered by Pichon's response, had turned it over to the *Daily Mail* and *l'Humanité*! (A translation of *l'Humanité*'s version, incorrectly dated 5 January, is in Cumming and Pettit, eds., *Russian-American Relations*, pp. 280-81).

[5] Minutes, Supreme War Council, Paris, 12 January 1919, 4 p.m.; *Foreign Relations, The Paris Peace Conference, 1919*, vol. III, Washington, 1943, pp. 490-91.

During those meetings when the Allied military advisers were present, the Council of Ten sat as the Supreme War Council—a continuation of the form used during the War. Regardless of nomenclature, the meetings of the Ten (plus advisers, military or civilian) soon proved unsatisfactory. In gatherings so large, secrecy proved virtually impossible. As the weeks went by, frank discussions of the most important subjects were increasingly transferred to the intimate setting of informal gatherings of the heads of governments, and from mid-March until the signature of the Treaty of Versailles the British, French, American, and Italian heads of government made most of the Conference's important decisions in the so-called Council of Four. (Since Japan was represented at the conference only by two ambassadors, the Council was four rather than five.) For a detailed study of the methods and procedures of the Peace Conference, see F. S. Marston, *The Peace Conference of 1919*, London, 1944, *passim*.

immediately contended that there was no need to summon delegates to Paris. Already there, he said, were representatives of all the anti-Bolshevik Russian groupings, organized in the so-called Russian Political Conference,[6] and representatives of the governments of all of the border nationalities which had now declared their independence. Here was "every shade of opinion."

Every shade, countered Lloyd George, except the opinion prevalent in Russia. The Allies must take a realistic view, he said. Formerly they had recognized the Tsar's government, although they had known it to be rotten, because it was the *de facto* government of Russia. Now they were dealing with governments at Omsk, at Archangel, and in the South, although "none of them were good," and yet they were refusing to deal with the Bolsheviks, who were the *de facto* rulers of the country. Thus they were not allowing a great people to pick its own representatives, an attitude that was contrary to everything for which the Allies had fought. Again the Prime Minister referred to the experience of the French Revolution: the British government had then said that the *émigrés* represented France, a mistake which had led to a quarter-century of war.

The result of this conflict of views was a compromise. The Bolsheviks would not be invited to Paris. But Lloyd George insisted that, if they were not, neither could the various anti-Bolshevik factions be given an official hearing, lest the impression should arise that the Powers considered that the Whites represented Russia. Their views would be obtained instead in writing or through private conversations. Thus there would be no formal Russian representation at the Peace Conference.

We get a better idea of Lloyd George's views regarding the popular basis of Bolshevism from his remarks at a meeting of the members of the British Empire Delegation on the following day.[7] In the relatively informal meetings of the Delegation, it should be noted, the Prime Minister found little opposition to his Russian policies. The representatives of the Dominions—in particular Sir Robert Borden and William M. Hughes, the prime ministers of Canada and Australia—were consistently critical of all British involvement in Russia, and, like Lloyd George, they felt that the Bolsheviks had firmer

[6] The origins and composition of the Russian Political Conference are discussed at length in Thompson, *Versailles Peace*, pp. 66-78.
[7] British Empire Delegation, Paris, 1st minutes, 13 January 1919, 11 a.m.; Cab. 29/28/1.

popular support than did their enemies. Moreover, the British members of the Delegation—usually Balfour, Cecil, Montagu, George Barnes (Minister of Labour and member of the Labour Party, who resigned midway through the Conference), and Lord Reading (the British Ambassador in Washington)—were those members of the government who generally agreed with Lloyd George on Russian matters; his severest critics, Curzon and Churchill, were for the most part tied to departmental responsibilities in London.

At the Delegation's meeting on 13 January, in response to Hughes's contention that only external aggression by the Bolsheviks, and not their conduct within Russia, should be of concern to Britain, and to Balfour's rejoinder that the Bolsheviks had invaded areas to which they had abandoned all claims, such as Finland and Estonia, Lloyd George replied that "possibly what we took for invasion in Poland, Finland, &c., was really a spontaneous Bolshevik movement on the part of the local population." For example, he said, London had sent arms "to fortify the population of Riga against these alleged invaders." However, "it had been found that we could not trust the population of Riga with arms for the simple reason that many of them were themselves Bolsheviks." Undoubtedly, Lloyd George said, the British government must take the same view of a Bolshevik invasion of a neighboring country as it had taken of the German invasion of Belgium, but in each case the facts must first be ascertained.

The Prime Minister then proceeded to draw definite policy implications from his observations. In the coming sessions of the Conference, he said, the British Empire Delegation should advocate: 1) noninterference in the internal affairs of "the Bolshevik area"; 2) assistance to states which had declared their independence of the former Russian Empire when they were invaded from without, but noninterference when it appeared instead that the "invasion" was in fact warfare "between two political parties within such countries"; 3) as for those sections of Russia not under Bolshevik control, but which had not declared their independence, the Allies should give "any assistance, financial or material, that might be possible, excluding troops."

He would accompany these measures, Lloyd George said, with the peacemaking efforts which the British government had proposed during the first days of January. Even if the Peace Conference would not officially receive the Bolsheviks and their opponents, he still favored informally summoning them all to Paris. He pursued this objective when the Supreme Council again considered the Russian problem, on 16 January.[8] The French, he said, had misunderstood his earlier proposals. The British government had never suggested that the Bolsheviks should be recognized to the extent of offering them a seat at the Peace Conference. Rather, the Allies would ask all Russian elements to come to Paris and then help them settle their differences. The only alternatives, he said, were either to destroy Bolshevism or to isolate it. He could not imagine anyone seriously advocating the first. The task would require a million Allied troops, and he doubted whether in Britain or anywhere else a thousand could be raised. Isolation—the *cordon sanitaire*—would mean continuing the existing blockade of Bolshevik Russia; yet that would mean starving, not the Bolsheviks, who could requisition the food they themselves needed, but the ordinary Russian people, who were innocent of their leaders' excesses.[9] Moreover, Lloyd George said, even if the Bolsheviks were isolated, who could overthrow them? Denikin controlled only "a little backyard near the Black Sea," and Kolchak appeared to be headed toward a revival of the old, hated regime, which would never win popular support. Finally, Lloyd George belittled French fears that Bolshevik representatives would bring the revolution with them if they came to Paris; the surest way to make Britain Bolshevik, he said, would not be to bring Bolshevik emissaries to London, but to attempt to conscript British workers to fight in Russia.

In making these proposals Lloyd George found support from Pres-

[8] Minutes, Council of Ten, Paris, 16 January 1919, 10:30 a.m.; *Foreign Relations, Paris Peace Conference,* vol. III, pp. 582-84. Unless otherwise noted, all Peace Conference minutes here cited are the official British minutes which were later handed to the other participating delegations. For a few meetings, however, the Americans took their own minutes. There are often significant differences between the two sets. See, e.g., the American minutes of the above meeting, *ibid.,* pp. 589-93.

[9] During the War, in April 1916, the Tsarist government had formally placed the control of all shipping on the northern coast of Russia in the hands of the British Admiralty. After the Bolshevik Revolution, the British continued to maintain this control, contending that it had never been revoked by a Russian government recognized in London (see the British memorandum of 31 July 1918 in *Foreign Relations, 1918, Russia,* vol. III, p. 137). By the summer of 1918, in any case, most of the coast of North Russia was in Allied hands.

The Baltic was a different story. There the Allies imposed a blockade on Russia after the Armistice as part of their blockade of Germany. Under international law, they had a right to blockade Germany until the ratification of peace should take place. For a detailed discussion of the blockade, see below, ch. VII.

ident Wilson. American reports, too, Wilson said, showed that there was considerable support for Bolshevism within Russia. Intervention was serving only to strengthen the hands of the Soviet leaders.

At this point—noon on Thursday, 16 January—the Council adjourned discussion of the Russian question until the following Monday morning, when the French brought in Joseph Noulens, just back from Archangel, to give a wildly inaccurate recitation of the horrors of Bolshevism.[10] The official records are silent regarding what occurred during the intervening weekend, but much can be learned from a long entry in the diary of Sir William Wiseman, who was in Paris as British liaison officer with the American delegation.[11]

On Sunday, 19 January, Wiseman dined at Lloyd George's flat in the Rue Nitot. Besides Wiseman and Bonar Law, there were present only the Prime Minister's family and his secretaries. In these familiar surroundings Lloyd George gave vent to his feelings about the Russian problem, which obviously had been weighing heavily upon him. Clemenceau, he said, was adamantly opposed to allowing Bolshevik representatives to come to Paris for fear that they would spread Bolshevism in France. He had even threatened to resign if Lloyd George and President Wilson pressed him on the point.

Despairing of Lloyd George, Clemenceau put his case to Lord Derby, who was not only Ambassador in Paris, but also a figure of some importance in the Conservative Party. Derby was sympathetic, but he felt that the matter was too important for him to handle, and he advised Clemenceau to see Balfour. The French Premier did so, and Balfour wrote to Lloyd George suggesting that no Bolshevik representative be received, but that, instead, a food commission be sent to Moscow, nominally to deal with the Soviet government on the question of relief but also to sound out the Bolshevik leaders on political questions.

Lloyd George did not favor this proposal, and he was furious with Clemenceau for seeing Balfour. At dinner he heatedly accused the French Premier of trying to split the British delegation; if Clemenceau persisted, he would return to London, leaving Balfour in Paris without any real authority and making it necessary to refer everything to the Cabinet. At this point, Bonar Law commented

[10] Minutes, Council of Ten, 20 January 1919, 10:30 a.m.; *Foreign Relations, Paris Peace Conference*, vol. III, pp. 623-28 (British minutes) and 629-33 (American).
[11] Diary entry for 19 January 1919; Wiseman MSS, Yale University Library.

that such a step would only appear as implied criticism of Balfour for seeing Clemenceau. Lloyd George agreed that Balfour's feelings must not be hurt but said that, nevertheless, he would speak to Clemenceau on the subject. Bonar Law then declared that the Conservative Party felt strongly on the subject of Bolshevism; if the Prime Minister pressed his policy to the point of making an issue of it with Clemenceau, it would break the Coalition government. Lloyd George flared up at once: "If that is the case the government had better be broken." Clemenceau's intransigence over the Russian problem, he said, like so many other difficulties which had arisen, stemmed from the fact that the Peace Conference was meeting in Paris. Angrily, he continued:

I never wanted to hold the Conference in his bloody capital. Both House and I thought it would be better to hold it in a neutral place, but the old man wept and protested so much that we gave way, and this is what we get for our concession.

"The old man," Lloyd George concluded, "must be taken by the scruff of the neck."

In this mood, the Prime Minister went before the assembled British Empire Delegation the following evening, 20 January, and got unanimous consent to his proposals.[12] He asked each Dominion prime minister in turn whether his country would furnish troops for continued intervention. Each replied with a firm refusal. Here there was no dispute, but over the question of sending material aid to anti-Bolshevik forces there was some slight disagreement. Balfour raised the question of Britain's "obligation" to those Russians who had remained loyal during the War. "We had sustained them, and rightly at the time, to keep Germany occupied in the East," he said. "If we withdrew we should not be deceiving them, but it was a difficult policy to make attractive." Lloyd George, supported by Smuts and Montagu, denied that any "obligation" existed. He continued, arguing on economic grounds alone:

We had gone there to fight the Germans, not the Bolshevists. If we were going to continue we must do it to the extent of many millions. Ten millions would mean 3*d*. on the Income Tax, and would not go far. It might easily come to 1*s*.

[12] British Empire Delegation, Paris, 2nd minutes, 20 January 1919, 4 p.m.; Cab. 29/28/1.

In order to bring about the conference he sought, Lloyd George suggested that, unless some effort were made to bring together the warring parties within Russia, the British government should immediately withdraw its own troops and cease subsidizing others. This policy was formally adopted by the Delegation. No longer did the Prime Minister insist on Paris as the site of a Russian conference, however; the Delegation's resolution named Salonika or Lemnos as possible alternatives. Finally, the meeting agreed that the British Empire would cooperate with the other Allies in protecting from Bolshevik invasion any independent states that might be established on territory formerly Russian.

When the Council of Ten met the following morning, President Wilson placed before his colleagues a report of a series of conversations which had taken place in Stockholm between Maxim Litvinov and a State Department official, W. H. Buckler. The conversations had been unofficial, for the purpose of information only, and were not to be made public. Peace, the Soviet Plenipotentiary assured Buckler, could easily be achieved if the Allies wished it. The Soviet government was prepared to compromise on all points, including protection of existing foreign enterprises, the granting of new concessions in Russia, and the settlement of the foreign debt. Further, Litvinov promised that the Soviet government would grant an amnesty to those Russians who had been hostile to it; if they chose, they would be permitted to leave the country. And, finally, Bolshevik propaganda in foreign countries would cease immediately upon the conclusion of peace. Moscow realized that conditions in many Western countries were not suitable for a revolution on the Russian model, Litvinov said, and that no amount of propaganda could achieve such a result.[13]

President Wilson had passed on Buckler's report only at the end of the morning's session, so there was no discussion of it. But it fortified Lloyd George for his efforts of the afternoon. When the Council reassembled, the Prime Minister used the same tactics he had employed with the British Empire Delegation. As he had done with the Dominion premiers, Lloyd George turned to Clemenceau,

[13] Buckler's original report, dated 18 January 1919 and telegraphed from Copenhagen, is printed in *Foreign Relations, 1919, Russia*, pp. 15-17. The paraphrase which President Wilson gave his Allied colleagues is printed as an appendix to Minutes, Council of Ten, 21 January, 10:30 a.m.; *Foreign Relations, Paris Peace Conference*, vol. III, pp. 643-46.

Orlando, and President Wilson and asked each how many troops his country could provide for an Allied army to crush Bolshevism. Each answered "none." He then asked which of the others would contribute to the great cost of maintaining the anti-Bolshevik Russian armies in the field. He received no reply.

At this session both Lloyd George and President Wilson put forward the idea of a meeting at Salonika or Lemnos as an alternative to inviting the various Russian factions to Paris. Lloyd George cited Buckler's report as evidence that the Bolsheviks were ready to come to terms. Orlando agreed that an effort should be made and consoled himself by pointing out that, at any rate, only the other Russians, and not the Allies, would enter into actual negotiations with the Bolsheviks. Even Clemenceau gave his consent, although reluctantly. Litvinov's offer of peace, he thought, was very clever: now if the Allies accepted, the Bolsheviks could cite their acceptance as proof that they were after only the economic concessions that Litvinov held out. Moscow had, after all, offered to make peace on previous occasions. Had he been acting alone, Clemenceau said, he would have adopted a rigid policy of a *cordon sanitaire* for Russia. But he felt that he had to make some concessions to his Allied colleagues so that the outside world—especially the Germans—would not think they were divided. The proposals of Lloyd George and the President at least had the redeeming feature that Bolshevik representatives would not be coming to Paris. Accordingly, the Council instructed Wilson to draft a proclamation of invitation to all Russian factions.[14]

The President brought a draft proposal to the Council on the following afternoon, 22 January. The minutes of the session print only the text as it was finally adopted after being "carefully considered, amended in one or two particulars, and accepted by all."[15] The sole purpose of the Allies with regard to Russia, it stated, was to help the Russian people and not to interfere in their affairs or exploit them in any way. Disingenuously, with demonstrable lack of truth, it continued: "They recognise the revolution without reserva-

[14] Council of Ten, 21 January 1919, 3 p.m.; *ibid.*, pp. 647-53 (British minutes) and pp. 663-68 (American).
[15] The phrase is that used in the American minutes (Council of Ten, 22 January 1919, 3 p.m.; *ibid.*, p. 686); the British minutes (p. 676) are even more vague. The text of the proposal is on pp. 676-77.

tion, and will in no way, and in no circumstances, aid or give countenance to any attempt at a counter-revolution."

Moreover, the statement said, it was not the purpose or wish of the Allies to favor or assist any one of the Russian factions against any of the others. Their aim was to bring about peace, to restore order, and to enable the Russian people to relieve their own distress. To that end,

they invite every organised group that is now exercising or attempting to exercise political authority or military authority anywhere in Siberia, or within the boundaries of European Russia as they stood before the war just concluded (except in Finland) to send representatives . . . to the Princes Islands, Sea of Marmora, where they will be met by representatives of the Associated Powers, provided in the meantime there is a truce of arms amongst the parties invited, and that all armed forces . . . shall be meanwhile withdrawn, and aggressive military action cease.

The proposal was singularly vague about what would take place once the Russian representatives assembled on Prinkipo[16] (the local name for the Princes Islands), saying only:

These representatives are invited to confer with the representatives of the Associated Powers in the freest and frankest way, with a view to ascertaining the wishes of all sections of the Russian people, and bringing about, if possible, some understanding and agreement by which Russia may work out her own purposes and happy co-operative relations be established between her people and the other peoples of the world.

The proposal stated that the Allies would provide transportation across the Black Sea for the Russian representatives, who were expected to be at Prinkipo on 15 February. Accordingly, a prompt reply was requested.

On the following day, the invitation was broadcast to Russia by short-wave radio.[17] The Powers then appointed commissioners to

[16] Prinkipo is a group of islands only a few miles from Constantinople. Formerly a place of banishment, it was by 1919 a summer resort. It was chosen by the Council over Salonika or Lemnos, undoubtedly, because of the availability of plenty of vacant hotel space and its nearness to Russia. (See unnumbered telegram from Admiral Calthorpe, the British High Commissioner, Constantinople, to Balfour [Paris], 26 January 1919, file 591/1/6/820; F.O. 608/179.) It may also be that the Greek government objected to the use of the former places; the Allies could disregard any objections from the defeated Turks.

[17] In *Dokumenty vneshnei politiki*, vol. II, there are printed the texts of two broadcasts, both on 23 January 1919. The first (p. 45), from Caernarvon, Wales, is a summary of the Allied proposal. The second (pp. 45-46), from Lyons, is an exact Russian translation.

represent them at the conference[18] and settled back to await the response from Russia.

✧

Published on 23 January, the Prinkipo proposal came as a bombshell to the publics of the Allied countries. Not surprisingly, the right-wing press universally condemned it as tantamount to the recognition of Bolshevism and as a potentially mortal blow to the cause for which the Entente had fought the War. In France, where the conservative press had close ties with the Russian Political Conference, these attacks were particularly vehement and protracted, although scarcely more offensively phrased than those of the *Morning Post* in England. Radical and Socialist organs—in all the Allied countries—generally approved of the proposal, but they spoke to a smaller audience. The one universal reaction in the West was surprise: it had not been expected that the Allies would treat with the Bolsheviks.[19]

To the Soviet government, however, the news was not entirely unexpected. Litvinov, in Stockholm, had read *l'Humanité*'s report of the indignant French reaction to the original British proposal early in January and had telegraphed a summary of it to Chicherin.[20] The Commissar for Foreign Affairs immediately replied that the British plan to open peace discussions seemed highly suspicious. He reminded Litvinov that, just before the landing of Allied forces at Archangel, a British economic mission had come to Moscow to talk of trade agreements and commercial concessions.[21]

Chicherin's suspicions were not allayed by his receipt of the Su-

---

[18] At dinner on the evening of 22 January, Lloyd George offered the post of British Commissioner to Lord Hardinge, the Permanent Under-Secretary at the Foreign Office. Hardinge declined without hesitation and recommended Lord Robert Cecil, who, Hardinge said, was favorable to the plan. But Cecil also refused. Finally, at a meeting of the British Empire Delegation on 23 January, Lloyd George offered the post to Sir Robert Borden, the Prime Minister of Canada, who had been an enthusiastic proponent of the scheme from its inception. Borden accepted. (See *The Old Diplomacy: The Reminiscences of Lord Hardinge of Penshurst*, London, 1947, p. 235, and *Robert Laird Borden: His Memoirs*, New York, 1938, vol. II, p. 904.)

[19] For an excellent survey of reactions to the Prinkipo proposal, see Mayer, *Peacemaking*, pp. 432-49. See also George Bernard Noble, *Policies and Opinions at Paris, 1919*, New York, 1935, pp. 277-79.

[20] Litvinov (Stockholm) to Chicherin, 14 January 1919; *Dokumenty vneshnei politiki*, vol. II, pp. 28-29.

[21] Chicherin to Vorovsky (for Litvinov, Stockholm), 14 January 1919; *ibid.*, p. 29. For this British economic mission, see Volume I, pp. 232-34.

preme Council's radio message containing the invitation to Prinkipo. Again he telegraphed to Stockholm, the one Bolshevik outpost in the Western world,[22] to ask the Soviet representative, V. V. Vorovsky (Litvinov had returned to Russia), for his opinion about the real meaning of the "strange and improbable" proposal.[23] If the Allies really did desire the pacification of Russia, Chicherin said, there was only one way to achieve it: to cease their intervention in the Russian internal struggle. That was exactly what the Soviet government wanted.

Turning to the Allied proposals themselves, Chicherin commented that he did not see how a conference on the lines suggested could bring peace to Russia. The discussions would be held in secret on an isolated island—the worst possible place so far as the Soviet government was concerned (and, of course, precisely the reason a place like Prinkipo was chosen). Only if full publicity were assured, Chicherin said, would there be any way of guaranteeing fair treatment to the Bolsheviks. And he pointed out that the Allied proposal for the end of hostilities had come only after the tide of war had turned in favor of the Soviet regime; the "forces of reaction" were growing weaker and weaker. Lenin's response was similar, but more blunt. "I am afraid that [Wilson] wants to establish his claim to Siberia and part of the South, having otherwise scarcely a hope of retaining anything," he telegraphed to Trotsky on 24 January.[24]

Chicherin's suspicion caused him, on 28 January, to send a radio message to President Wilson stating that thus far Moscow had only heard of the forthcoming Prinkipo conference from radio broadcasts, and that the Soviet government would not reply until an invitation had been extended to it.[25] On the previous day, however,

---

[22] Stockholm soon ceased to be the Soviet western outpost. The Allies put increasing pressure upon the Scandinavian neutrals to sever all connections with the Soviet government, thus tightening the blockade (see U.S. Chargé d'Affaires [Copenhagen] to Acting Secretary of State, telegram 131, January 1919, *Foreign Relations, 1919, Russia*, pp. 33-34). During January 1919 the Scandinavian countries withdrew their legations from Russia, and the Swedish government expelled first Litvinov, then Vorovsky, from Stockholm (Louis Fischer, *The Soviets in World Affairs: A History of the Relations Between the Soviet Union and the Rest of the World, 1917-1929*, vol. I, p. 248).

[23] Chicherin to Vorovsky (Stockholm), 24 January 1919; *Dokumenty vneshnei politiki*, vol. II, pp. 42-45.

[24] Lenin to Trotsky (Kozlov), telegram 27, 24 January 1919; printed in Jan M. Meijer, ed., *The Trotsky Papers, 1917-1922*, vol. I (1917-19), The Hague, 1964, no. 145.

[25] Radiogram, Chicherin to Wilson (Paris), 28 January 1919; *Dokumenty vneshnei politiki*, vol. II, p. 52.

Zinoviev, the chairman of the Petrograd Soviet, had told that body that the Bolsheviks would indeed send representatives to Prinkipo, but only with the object of forcing the Allies and the Whites to remove their masks. The Soviet delegates, he said, would know how to evaluate the Allies' promises, just as the Bolshevik plenipotentiaries had taken the measure of the Germans at Brest-Litovsk. They would not, however, discontinue for one minute the formation of the Red Army nor its advance, "which is proving victorious on every front." The Soviet government, Zinoviev stated, would not lay down its arms.[26]

The Allies made no reply to Chicherin's request for a document of invitation. To send an "official invitation," President Wilson said on 1 February, "would be tantamount to a recognition of the Bolshevik Government." Moreover, as Lloyd George pointed out, there were no official invitations; all "recipients" were notified by the same means, press and radio.[27] Invitations or none, Chicherin nevertheless replied on 4 February to the original Allied wireless message.[28] Despite the improved military situation, he said, the Soviet government was so anxious to secure an end to hostilities that it was "even willing to make weighty concessions" to purchase peace. Elaborating on the statement which Litvinov had made to Buckler in Stockholm, Chicherin said that his government would not refuse to recognize its financial obligations to nationals of the Allied Powers.[29] It would pay interest on the loans with raw materials. And "in view of the great interest which foreign capital has always displayed in the exploitation in its own interests of the natural wealth of Russia," the Soviet regime would grant mining, timber, and other concessions to Allied nationals. Not even territorial annexation of parts of Russia by the Allied Powers would be excluded from the negotiations, said Chicherin. But, in a sort of veiled threat, he added

[26] Zinoviev's speech of 27 January 1919 was considered so important that the Political Intelligence Department of the Foreign Office circulated a full translation of it: Cabinet paper G.T. 6935, 21 February; Cab. 24/76.

[27] Minutes, Council of Ten, 1 February 1919, 3 p.m.; *Foreign Relations, Paris Peace Conference*, vol. III, pp. 835-36.

[28] The text of the Soviet reply of 4 February, issued by radio, is printed in *Dokumenty vneshnei politiki*, vol. II, pp. 57-60. Most of it is translated in Degras, *Soviet Documents*, vol. I, pp. 137-39. A complete but slightly less accurate translation is in *Foreign Relations, 1919, Russia*, pp. 39-42.

[29] This, it should be noticed, was an offer to pay debts to *individual* creditors, not the debt on the inter-governmental loans, which comprised much the larger part of the Russian foreign debt.

that the extent to which Moscow would be prepared to make any of these concessions would depend upon the military position of the Red Army in relation to the Allied forces, which, from the Soviet point of view, was improving every day. Finally, while declaring the readiness of the Soviet government to undertake not to interfere in the internal affairs of the Allied Powers, Chicherin pointed out that it could not "limit the freedom of the revolutionary press." Under these conditions, he concluded, the Bolsheviks would enter into negotiations at Prinkipo or anywhere else with all or any of the Allied governments, or with "any Russian political groups" as the Allies might wish.[30]

Of the other Russian groups to which the Allied proposal applied, only the governments of the three Baltic states and the Soviet Ukrainian government accepted. The Georgian government refused, not because of any aversion to negotiations with the Bolsheviks, but because the Georgians looked upon themselves as so much separated from Russia that they could not even sit at a Russian political conference.[31]

All the anti-Bolshevik elements which looked forward to the restoration of a unified Great Russia indignantly refused the Prinkipo invitation. At this time, it should be noted, they were coming together into one "movement" under the generally conceded leadership of Kolchak, who controlled much larger territories and

[30] The acceptance of the Prinkipo invitation represented one strand of Soviet foreign policy, the willingness—as at Brest-Litovsk—to deal realistically with a given set of circumstances, and to operate at least temporarily as a member of the world of states. Another strand was represented by the appeal, sent from Moscow on 24 January 1919, less than a fortnight before the Prinkipo acceptance, summoning the workers of the world to set up a new revolutionary International and urging the world's proletariat to use mass action, "right up to open armed conflict with the political power of capital," as its basic weapon. (See Jane Degras, ed., *The Communist International, 1919-1943: Documents*, vol. I, London, 1956, pp. 1-5.) The first congress of the Comintern met in Moscow in early March.

The Comintern appeal apparently went unnoticed by the statesmen at Paris (it is not mentioned in any of the Conference records), although the American chargé d'affaires at Archangel specifically drew the attention of the State Department to its near coincidence with Chicherin's acceptance of the Prinkipo invitation. (Poole [Archangel] to Acting Secretary of State, telegram 849, 11 February 1919; *Foreign Relations, 1919, Russia*, pp. 51-52.)

[31] The acceptance of the Soviet Ukrainian government, 6 February 1919, is in *Dokumenty vneshnei politiki*, vol. II, pp. 61-64. Those of the Latvian and Estonian governments, 10 and 12 February, are in *Foreign Relations, 1919, Russia*, pp. 49-50, 52-53. The Lithuanians made no formal reply, but an American memorandum of 22 February (*ibid.*, pp. 72-73) indicates that they would have accepted had the conference actually taken place. The Georgian reply, 8 February, is in *ibid.*, pp. 47-49.

populations than did Denikin or the Archangel government. In mid-January the British government had recognized Kolchak's primacy by allowing Sir Charles Eliot to deliver the message expressing "warm sympathy" with the Supreme Ruler's endeavors which had been put forward and then, unaccountably, withdrawn the previous month.[32] On 26 January, Eliot and his French colleague, Regnault, visited Kolchak and—acting in the absence of instructions from their governments—expressed their purely personal opinions that the Prinkipo invitation "should not be refused because it gave an opportunity to all the anti-Bolshevik governments in Russia to meet and unite." They also suggested that, since Kolchak's military situation was "distinctly bad," he might profitably use a period of armistice to prepare a new offensive.[33]

Kolchak, however, was scarcely receptive to such an idea. His response was to issue an army order stating that traitors were spreading rumors that an armistice was contemplated; no such armistice with Bolshevism was possible, he declared. Later he told Eliot that the Prinkipo idea had undermined his authority and endangered his government. Eliot was sympathetic. To London he telegraphed that the Allies must realize that Kolchak had hitherto been told that the Allies supported the anti-Bolshevik movement; now the Whites were invited to meet the Bolsheviks amicably and to "settle their squabbles as if in the eyes of the Peace Conference all Russian factions were much the same."[34] Stronger reactions came from other British representatives. From Archangel, F. O. Lindley wrote bitterly that the Prinkipo proposal contained "not a word of condemnation for the Bolsheviks." Instead, "all Russian parties are lumped together on the same footing: those who have remained loyal to their obligations to the Allies through all this terrible time, and those who have heaped abuse on them, tried to raise insurrections against them, tortured and robbed their subjects."[35] And General Knox telegraphed to the War Office from Omsk: "suddenly the whole of Russia is

[32] Curzon to Alston (Vladivostok) for Eliot (Omsk), telegram 39, 15 January 1919; file 598/2/1/913, F.O. 608/188. For the previous withdrawal of the same message, see above, p. 42.

[33] Eliot (Omsk) to Curzon, telegram 90 through Vladivostok, 26 January 1919, file 598/2/1/1384; F.O. 608/188.

[34] Eliot (Omsk) to Curzon, telegrams 90, 95, 107, and 127 through Vladivostok, 26, 27, and 29 January and 3 February 1919, file 598/2/1/—; F.O. 608/188. The quotation is from telegram 90.

[35] Lindley (Archangel) to Curzon, despatch 18, 1 February 1919, file 591/1/6/3728; F.O. 608/179.

informed by wireless that her Allies regard the brave men who are here fighting for part of civilization as on a par with the blood-stained, Jew-led Bolsheviks."[36]

In Paris, the coordinating Russian Political Conference, acting in the name of the "united governments of Siberia, Archangel and Southern Russia," formally refused the invitation in a note from the Russian Embassy on 12 February, but it had been apparent since the end of January that they would not accept.[37] The White governments were vastly reinforced in their refusal by the French government, which quietly informed the Russian Political Conference that it put no faith in the Prinkipo proposal and would continue its support of the anti-Bolshevik cause regardless, and by Winston Churchill, who assured Konstantin Nabokov in London that, unless he were given categorical instructions to desist, he would make sure that the War Office continued to provide the Whites with all necessary supplies.[38] The French attitude, in particular, effectively killed the whole Prinkipo scheme: while Philip Kerr, Lloyd George's private secretary, could tell members of the American delegation in Paris on 30 January that the British were prepared to meet Soviet representatives at Prinkipo or anywhere else, whether or not representatives of the other Russian factions were present,[39] they could scarcely have met the Bolsheviks in the absence of the other Allies.

[36] Knox (Omsk) to War Office, 29 January 1919, through Vladivostok as telegram 918; W.O. 33/966, no. 1055.

[37] The note, in *Foreign Relations, 1919, Russia*, pp. 53-54, was signed by the improbable combination of Sazanov and Chaikovsky. The former had been the Tsar's Foreign Minister; in Paris he occupied the same post for Denikin (1918) and for Kolchak (1919). Chaikovsky, who had been in exile in Tsarist times, had dropped his duties as President of the Archangel government to come to Paris to plead the White cause. For a detailed account of the White reactions to the Prinkipo proposal, see Thompson, *Versailles Peace*, pp. 119-26.

[38] This was revealed in telegrams from Maklakov, the Russian Ambassador in Paris and head of the Political Conference, to Omsk and Archangel, which later fell into the hands of the Bolsheviks. See the article "Vneshnaya politika kontrrevoliutsionnykh 'pravitelstv' v nachale 1919 g." (The Foreign Policy of the Counter-Revolutionary "Governments" at the Beginning of 1919), *Krasnyi Arkhiv* (Red Archives), Moscow, vol. 37, 1929 (no. 6), pp. 71-75. See also I. Subbotovsky, *Soyuzniki, russkie reaktsionery i interventsiya; kratkii obzor (Iskliuchitelno po offitsialnym arkhivnym dokumentam Kolchakovskogo pravitelstva)* (The Allies, Russian Reactionaries and Intervention: A Brief Outline [Exclusively from the Official Archive Documents of the Kolchak Government]), Leningrad, 1926, p. 230, and Strakhovsky, *Intervention at Archangel*, p. 144. See also Thompson, *Versailles Peace*, pp. 122-23.

[39] See W. H. Buckler's memorandum, 31 January 1919, of his conversations with Kerr; *Foreign Relations, 1919, Russia*, p. 38.

The Prinkipo policy was clearly a failure. It could not have been anything else, for the White governments could never have agreed to negotiate with the Bolsheviks. Kolchak, Denikin, and General E.L.K. Miller, who had become the head of the Archangel government (Chaikovsky having gone to Paris), all claimed collectively to be protecting the patrimony of a Great Russia (whether it was the patrimony of the Tsars or of the March Revolution was never entirely clear). For them to have sat down at a conference table with the Bolsheviks would necessarily have meant a denial of their collective claim to sole authority: once you sit down to work out a *compromise* with someone, you cannot very well take all and leave him nothing.

Even given their precarious military positions at the time, the White governments would have had nothing to gain and everything to lose by coming to Prinkipo. On the other hand, those elements which were trying to alter the old Great Russian *status quo* —and they included the Bolsheviks as well as the governments, such as those of the Baltic states, which had declared national independence on what was formerly the soil of the Russian Empire— had everything to gain. The very presence of the Bolsheviks at Prinkipo would have implied Allied recognition of their hegemony over the territory they controlled. And the Baltic states, whose independence would have been denied by the Whites, welcomed a chance to negotiate a settlement with both the Bolsheviks and the Whites. It was only natural for them to accept.

Moreover, the Prinkipo proposal itself contained a very serious weakness: although it required the cessation of hostilities in Russia, it made no provisions for enforcing the cease-fire. To have had any effect at all, given the prevailing bloody civil war, it would have had to carry its demands one step further and include a threat that the Allies would forcibly punish violators of the cease-fire. This quite obviously would have been impossible under the existing circumstances, but then so was the whole Prinkipo idea: put forward as a scheme for mediation, it was in fact a form of veiled dictation by the Great Powers, and dictation without sufficient means to enforce the will of the dictators cannot help but be ineffective. Especially was this true when one of the dictators—the French government—had no liking for the scheme at all and made clear from the outset that it would have no objection to seeing it fail. Here, in the lack of Allied unity, was the greatest flaw of all.

✧

In London, Lloyd George and Curzon, the Acting Foreign Secretary, found themselves defending the Prinkipo policy long after it had become evident that the called-for meeting of Russian factions would never take place. The Prime Minister had briefly returned to England to deal with industrial unrest (principally a threatened miners' strike) and trouble in Ireland. He was, therefore, present at the first sessions of the new Parliament. On 12 February, during the debate on the Address from the Throne, he heard Sir Samuel Hoare, a respected Conservative, say of Britain's Russian policy:

The fault of our policy with Russia has been that we have never made up our minds as to which side to back. . . . We have gone on the principle of backing one horse one day and another horse another day. We have sent people to deal with the Bolshevists and other people to deal with the anti-Bolshevists. . . . The Prinkipo proposal is the embodiment of this policy of uncertainty and hesitation.[40]

Replying to Hoare, Lloyd George made no attempt to give a full explanation of the government's policy. The only course it could follow, he said, was to try to make peace in Russia. Continued intervention after five years of war would be ruinously expensive, and the *cordon sanitaire*, the only other policy possible apart from making peace or active intervention, was both inhumane and ineffective. The Prime Minister emphasized the government's view that calling the Bolsheviks to Prinkipo was not tantamount to recognizing them.[41] This was a point which Curzon had made in more picturesque language the previous day in the House of Lords. The Acting Foreign Secretary had said:

Suppose a powerful brigand captures an innocent victim, carries him off into captivity, and demands a large ransom for him; you do not, because you enter into negotiations with him, because you consent to meet him, even because you consent to pay the price, recognise him as an honourable or as a respectable man—and it is exactly the same in the case of the Bolsheviks.[42]

[40] 112 *H.C. Deb.*, cols. 187-88.
[41] *Ibid.*, cols. 193-95. [42] 33 *H.L. Deb.*, col. 40.

But Curzon did not say that the price involved at Prinkipo would have been implicit recognition of Soviet *de facto* rule and, with the end of Allied support, the probable sacrifice of the White forces. Speaking after Curzon, the Marquis of Salisbury expressed his regret that the government had evidently decided absolutely to exclude intervention as an alternative policy. "If he succeeds at Prinkipo," Salisbury said, rather inaccurately identifying Curzon with the policy of the Prime Minister, "well and good; but if he does not, he and his colleagues will have to reconsider the situation."[43]

Within the government it was fully realized that Prinkipo had failed, and just such a reconsideration took place, immediately after Lloyd George's return to London, at War Cabinet meetings on 12 and 13 February, followed by a long discussion between Churchill, Henry Wilson, Bonar Law, and the Prime Minister on the evening of the 13th. Wilson remarked in his diary that these sessions were all marked by "great arguments"; the reader of the official minutes is struck, instead, by a sense of aimlessness and inconclusiveness, rather than one of sharp controversy.[44]

In the Cabinet on the 12th, Churchill argued strongly for a definite decision to make war against the Bolsheviks, using much larger Allied forces than were at that time in Russia. The Bolsheviks were growing stronger every day, he said, while the Whites had been greatly discouraged by Prinkipo; the Allies, they thought, had deserted them. But the records seem to show that Churchill was quickly talked out of this position by Lloyd George's reassertion (once again!) of his argument that there simply were no Allied troops available for such an effort. By the next day Churchill was agreeing that the only way to combat Bolshevism was by means

---

[43] *Ibid.*, vol. 47.

[44] Wilson MS diary, entries for 12 and 13 February 1919. The three sets of minutes are: 1) War Cabinet minutes W.C. 531, 12 February, 11:30 a.m.; Cab. 23/9. 2) War Cabinet minutes W.C. 532 A, 13 February, noon; Cab. 23/15. This is an example of the so-called "A" minutes, which were considered more highly secret than ordinary minutes: the latter were printed and fairly widely distributed, while "A" minutes were typewritten, and either carbons or mimeographs were given quite restricted distribution, usually only to senior ministers and to the departments most directly involved. It is worth noting that General Poole, home from his mission to Denikin's headquarters, attended this meeting! He said little and attended no others. 3) "Notes of a Conversation held in Mr. Bonar Law's Room, House of Commons, on Thursday, February 13, 1919, at 6-30 p.m." This was not considered a Cabinet meeting, and there seems to be no copy of these minutes in the Public Record Office. The only copy I have found is in the possession of Viscount Davidson, then Mr. J.C.C. Davidson, Bonar Law's private secretary, whose papers include many of Bonar Law's.

of Russian armies, buttressed by Allied matériel and by Allied volunteers, and also by the strengthening of the states on Russia's borders. The Secretary of State for War was far from optimistic. The situation, he said, offered a "choice between a forlorn hope . . . and a certain disaster if no such steps were taken."

Churchill made no explicit proposals. Instead, he expounded a nightmare vision he had depicted before in the Cabinet: a combination of Russia with Germany and Japan. "The Russian situation must be judged as part of the great quarrel with Germany," he said in the Cabinet on the 13th, "and unless we are able to go to the support of the Russians there was a possibility of a great combination from Yokohama to Cologne in hostility to France, Britain, and America." Once before, when he had taken this line, he had argued that the Germans themselves should be encouraged to organize an Eastern front against the Bolsheviks.[45] In the course of the next two years he would make such a suggestion on several occasions, but now he urged instead that the Allies should strive for a friendly Russia and a strong Poland, each as a bulwark against a revived Germany. For Churchill, a "friendly" Russia was by definition a noncommunist Russia.

During all of these discussions—as always when Russia was the subject—the principal arguments opposing Churchill's came from Lloyd George. It was not at all clear, the Prime Minister contended, that the Russian people did not want "something like Bolshevism." How otherwise could one explain the lack of success of the Whites? According to figures presented by Henry Wilson, they were at that moment superior to the Bolsheviks both in manpower and in material resources;[46] therefore, "if the Russian population had been behind them they would certainly have made headway." The policy prescription that Lloyd George drew from this argument was that the Allies, in discharge of their moral obligation to the Russians who

---

[45] This occurred in the last War Cabinet meeting before the opening of the Peace Conference (minutes W.C. 515, 10 January 1919, 11:30 a.m.; Cab. 23/9). Churchill briefly stated the thought in passing and got no reaction to it.

[46] During the evening meeting on 13 February, Wilson estimated that the Allied and Russian forces numbered, in all, 525,000, and the Soviet forces some 300,000. On the other hand, in the Supreme Council, on the afternoon of 15 February, General Alby of the French Army estimated that the figures were 440,000 for the Bolsheviks and 410,000 for their enemies (see below, n. 51). These estimates, and others, were all based on very imperfect intelligence and quite arbitrary definitions regarding inclusion; they therefore mean little.

had remained "loyal," should make sure that, if they failed, it would not be for lack of material. On the other hand, he said, "if the country did not want to be saved, we could not save it." Neither did Lloyd George feel that the Bolsheviks threatened neighboring states with invasion. "Armies moved towards food supplies," he explained—a hypothesis which said little for his knowledge of history or his comprehension of the nature of the Bolshevik movement. Since Central and Eastern Europe were critically short of food, he said, the Soviet armies would aim instead at conquering the grain-surplus areas of the Don country, the Ukraine, and Siberia. There was no doubt that the Bolsheviks would use propaganda to try to spread their doctrines to the border states, but they would not use force.

The Prime Minister could suggest no alternative to Prinkipo, however. As he told Bonar Law, Churchill, and Henry Wilson in their talk on the evening of 13 February, he could think of nothing which might be effective at the present moment. Therefore, he would leave a decision to the Peace Conference. Since President Wilson was about to return temporarily to the United States, it was necessary that the question be discussed and decided immediately: no decision could be taken in the President's absence, and it would be "unfair" to the Russians to postpone deciding on future Allied policy until his return. These circumstances gave rise to one of Lloyd George's more serious tactical blunders at the Conference. He had not yet dealt with the urgent domestic problems which had brought him back to England, and he could not get to Paris himself before the President's departure. Therefore, he asked Churchill to "go to Paris immediately and try to obtain a decision." So far as the British negotiating position was concerned, he would leave it up to the general sense of the British delegates in Paris. But, as his remarks on the evening of the 13th make clear, the Prime Minister seemed to expect that something like a renewal of the Prinkipo proposal—perhaps even a meeting between the Allies and the Bolsheviks alone—would emerge from Churchill's efforts. He should have known better. Churchill was a singularly inappropriate choice for such a mission: for all of his other abilities, the Secretary of State for the War Office and the Royal Air Force was ill-suited for service as a messenger.[47]

---

[47] Lloyd George is very unfair to Churchill in saying (*Truth about the Peace Treaties*, vol. I, p. 368) that he "adroitly seized the opportunity presented by the absence of President Wilson and myself to go over to Paris and urge his plans with

With Henry Wilson, Churchill crossed the Channel on the 14th and faced the Supreme Council—specially convened by Balfour—in the early evening.[48] The British government wished to know, Churchill said, if the Prinkipo policy was to be pursued further; if not, what policies would be substituted for it? The meeting had been called on account of President Wilson's imminent departure. It was he, therefore, who responded. His personal opinion, he said, was that Allied troops were doing no good whatsoever in Russia, and that they should all be withdrawn. He also proposed that, if the Prinkipo conference could not be held, an informal fact-finding commission should be sent to Moscow to gain a firsthand impression of Russian conditions. He sought, he said, not necessarily a *rapprochement*, but clear information.

Churchill demurred. The withdrawal of Allied troops would mean the destruction of all anti-Bolshevik armies in Russia. He agreed with the President that no conscript troops could be sent to Russia, but he proposed that the Allies should send "volunteers, technical experts, arms, munitions, tanks, aeroplanes." Would the Council agree to support such a policy should Prinkipo prove definitely a failure, he asked? The President, who was anxious to leave, remarked only that the others knew where he stood on such a proposal. Nevertheless, he said, he would abide by any decision they might reach.

This statement—scarcely credible in the light of what we know of Wilson's attitude—ended the session. That evening Churchill, Henry Wilson, and Philip Kerr dined together; according to Wilson's diary, they agreed to draw up two resolutions for presentation to the Allies on the following day, one a renewal of the Prinkipo proposal (but, as we shall see, a renewal on terms scarcely favorable to the Bolsheviks), the other a plan for the establishment of an Allied military council to examine what might be accomplished by making war against the Bolsheviks using available Allied resources of men and materials.[49] The next morning these three, together with Generals Percy de B. Radcliffe and William Thwaites, the Directors of Military Operations and Military Intelligence, met to draft the

---

regard to Russia" upon the Allied delegations. Churchill, after all, was sent by the Prime Minister himself.

[48] Minutes, Supreme War Council, 14 February 1919, 6:30 p.m.; *Foreign Relations, Paris Peace Conference*, vol. III, pp. 1042-43.

[49] Wilson MS diary, entry for 14 February 1919.

resolutions. Churchill and Wilson then expounded their ideas to Balfour over lunch. Wilson noted in his diary that the Foreign Secretary seemed "generally favourable" to them.[50] The C.I.G.S. may have been indulging in wishful thinking, however: Balfour was scarcely enthusiastic when Churchill presented his scheme to the Council that afternoon.

Churchill's exposition was preceded by a long statement by General Alby, Chief of Staff of the French Army, regarding the military situation in Russia. In detail, he summarized conditions on each front. The picture he sketched was bleak. On all fronts except the Estonian, the Bolshevik forces were advancing. Even so, his conclusions were encouraging. The Red Army, he said, suffered from "irremediable sources of weakness," such as leadership of a very uneven quality, inadequate communications, insufficient equipment, and the lack of any motivation making men obey orders other than fear and the hope for loot. Its successes, Alby asserted, were due "to the fact that, up to the present, it has never encountered adversaries superior to it as regards either numbers, supplies, or moral[e]." Therefore he offered hope for the future: regular Allied troops, "being better officered and equipped, even though numerically inferior," would "easily" defeat the Red Army. Moreover, he added, "such a success could be won at very slight cost, provided that powerful means (such as armoured cars and bombing aeroplanes) were employed, which equipment the Bolsheviki entirely lack and the action of which their unequal moral[e] would make it impossible for them to withstand."[51]

Here was advice which perfectly fit Churchill's prescription, made the previous day, for "volunteers, technical experts, arms, munitions, tanks, aeroplanes." Churchill followed Alby's presentation with a long exposition of his own.[52] If the Prinkipo idea were not going to come to anything, he said, the sooner it was disposed of the better, for in the meantime the uncertainty would paralyze all military action. His own view was that Prinkipo had been a mistake from its inception, but that, if the proposal were simply dropped, the Western publics would think that it had been insincerely put for-

---

[50] *Ibid.*, entry for 15 February 1919.

[51] Alby's memorandum, read aloud to the Council, is incorporated into the minutes of the session (15 February 1919, 3 p.m.), *Foreign Relations, Paris Peace Conference*, vol. IV, Washington, 1943, pp. 10-13.

[52] *Ibid.*, pp. 13-16.

ward from the outset. Therefore, he proposed that a wireless message be sent to Moscow denying that the Allies had any interest in the various concessions that Chicherin had offered and reprimanding the Bolsheviks for "verbally accepting" the Prinkipo invitation while at the same time stepping up the pace of their attacks against their enemies on all fronts. The message would go on to state that the Allies would consider the Prinkipo proposal to have lapsed unless within ten days Soviet forces had everywhere ceased to attack and had withdrawn at least five miles behind their present front lines. If the Bolsheviks had begun so to withdraw within five days, then the Allies would make a similar request to the Whites. Only after an end to hostilities could the Prinkipo discussions take place.[53]

These were stringent conditions. The Bolsheviks had, after all, agreed to come to Prinkipo, and their acceptance had implied that they would cease firing when their opponents did. They could hardly be blamed for continuing their offensive before the Whites were even asked to take a similar step. The Bolsheviks would never have agreed to such a proposal, and Churchill put it forward with precisely the intention of forcing them to reject it, thus clearing away the debris of Prinkipo.

Then the second stage of his plan would come into operation. As Churchill's draft proposal put it:

> In anticipation of the Soviet Government refusing to accept the allied terms and continuing hostilities, it is suggested that suitable machinery should be set up forthwith to consider the possibilities of joint military action by the Associated Powers acting in conjunction with the independent border States and pro-Ally Governments in Russia.[54]

He went on to elaborate a scheme for an Allied council for Russia with political, economic, and military sections responsible to the Supreme Allied Council but endowed with considerable executive freedom. Such a council would obviously have been little more than a general staff for the coordination of all efforts against the Bolsheviks.[55] In urging his plan upon the Supreme Council, Churchill once

---

[53] The draft telegram is printed in *ibid.*, pp. 13-14, and also in Churchill, *Aftermath*, pp. 172-73.

[54] *Ibid.*, pp. 173-74.

[55] Churchill's proposal was strikingly similar to one advanced by the British Military Section at the Peace Conference in a memorandum dated 11 February 1919 (W.O. 95/4958), which argued:

". . . the General Staff would advocate the setting up of an Allied Council for

again evoked the image of a resurgent Germany, with a population able to produce almost three times as many annual conscripts as that of France, in league with a powerful Bolshevik Russia. His plan, he said, would ensure that such a "terrible situation" would never come about: Russia would become a "living partner in the League of Nations and a friend of the Allied Powers." Otherwise, "there would be neither peace nor victory."

In the discussion which followed, all of the principals—Balfour, House, Clemenceau, and Sonnino—declared themselves in varying degrees opposed to the Prinkipo idea. Clemenceau and Sonnino showed some interest in Churchill's plan for an Allied council for Russia. House and Balfour, however, remained silent on this crucial point. Instead of supporting his colleague, the Foreign Secretary moved to head him off by urging that the whole question—both the telegram to Moscow and the council for Russia—be deferred over the weekend until the afternoon of Monday, 17 February.

The events which followed were exceedingly complicated and are only partially clear from the available material. It seems that Churchill sent Lloyd George a report on his proposed course of action in two separate telegrams, giving his suggested message to Moscow in the first and stating his plan for an Allied council on Russia in the second. Lloyd George was spending the weekend in the country. On Sunday morning, when he received Churchill's first telegram, he drafted a message to Philip Kerr, who had remained in Paris, telling Kerr to inform Churchill that the Prime Minister liked the proposed ultimatum to Moscow (although *why* he should have liked it is unclear) but instructing him also to warn Churchill "not to commit us to any costly operations which would involve any large contribution either of men or money." A limited contribution of a few expert volunteers for technical assignments, together with any equipment British forces might be able to spare, would be permissible. Lloyd George explained his rationale for such a limitation:

Russian affairs with political, economic and military sections. This Council should have executive power within the limits of the policy defined for it by the Allied Governments.

"If the war has taught us anything, it is that unity of effort is necessary for success, that unity of effort can only be achieved by unity of control.

"The comparative lack of success which has hitherto attended Allied political and military intervention in Russia is directly attributable to the failure to apply this principle."

The main idea ought to be to enable Russia to save herself if she desires to do so; and if she does not take advantage of opportunity, then it means either that she does not wish to be saved from Bolshevism or that she is past saving. There is only one justification for interfering in Russia—that Russia wants it. If she does, then Koltchak, Krasnov [General P. N. Krasnov, Ataman of the Don Cossacks] and Denikin ought to be able to raise much larger force than Bolsheviks....

If, on the other hand, Russia is not behind Krasnov and his coadjutors, it is an outrage on every British principle of freedom that we should use foreign armies to force upon Russia a Government which is repugnant to its people.[56]

Before the Prime Minister had actually sent this message to Kerr, he received Churchill's second telegram, and also one from Kerr reporting (according to Lloyd George's memoirs) "alarming news as to the progress made under Mr. Churchill's powerful impulse towards organising an armed anti-Bolshevik intervention in Russia."[57] Lloyd George was considerably alarmed. At dinner that Sunday evening he told his confidant, Sir George Riddell: "Winston is in Paris. He wants to conduct a war against the Bolsheviks. That *would* cause a revolution! Our people would not permit it."[58] That evening, Lloyd George drafted a message to Churchill, and, when he sent it, he sent a copy, along with his original message, to Kerr— with instructions that Kerr should show both telegrams to Colonel House. The wire to Churchill was phrased in the strongest possible language:

Am very alarmed at your second telegram about planning war against the Bolsheviks. The Cabinet have never authorised such a proposal. They have never contemplated anything beyond supplying Armies in anti-Bolshevik areas.... [A] military enquiry as to the best means of giving material assistance to these Russian armies is all to the good but do not forget that it is an essential part of the enquiry to ascertain the cost and I

[56] Sent as Foreign Office telegram 177 (Curzon to Balfour), 16 February 1919, 11 p.m. (received Paris 1:05 a.m., 17 February), file 591/1/1/2297; F.O. 608/177. Churchill published its text (but not that of Lloyd George's subsequent telegram to him) in his *Aftermath*, pp. 174-75.

[57] *Truth about the Peace Treaties*, vol. I, pp. 370-71.

[58] Lord Riddell, *Lord Riddell's Intimate Diary of the Peace Conference and After, 1918-1923*, London, 1933, entry for 16 February 1919, p. 21. The owner of *The News of the World*, Riddell was in charge of relations between the British government and the press at the Peace Conference. He functioned, not as the government's press officer, but as the appointed representative of the London and Provincial newspaper association. He performed in this capacity throughout the period covered by the present volume.

also want you to bear in mind that the War Office reported to the Cabinet that according to their information intervention was driving the anti-Bolshevik parties in Russia into the ranks of the Bolshevists. I had already drafted a reply to be sent to Philip Kerr about your first telegram[;] I am sending that reply along with this. I adhere to it in its entirety[. I]f Russia is really anti-Bolshevik then a supply of equipment would enable it to redeem itself. If Russia is pro-Bolshevik not merely is it none of our business to interfere with its internal affairs[,] it would be positively mischievous[. I]t would strengthen and consolidate Bolshevik opinion[.] I beg you not to commit this country to what would be a purely mad enterprise out of hatred of Bolshevik principles. An expensive war of aggression against Russia is a way to strengthen Bolshevism in Russia and create it at home. We cannot afford the burden. Chamberlain tells me we can hardly make both ends meet on a peace basis even at the present rate of taxation and if we are committed to a war against a continent like Russia it is the direct road to bankruptcy and Bolshevism in these islands.

The French are not safe guides in this matter. Their opinion is largely biased by the enormous amount of small investors who put their money into Russian loans and who now see no prospect of ever recovering it.

I urge you therefore not to pay too much heed to their incitement. There is nothing they would like better than to see us pull their chestnuts out of the fire.

I also want you to bear in mind the very grave labour position in this country. Were it known that you had gone over to Paris to prepare a plan of war against the Bolsheviks it would do more to incite organised labour than anything I can think of; and what is worse it would throw into the arms of the extremists a very large number of thinking people who now abhor their methods.

Please show these telegrams to the Foreign Secretary.[59]

Such a message could not help but put Churchill on the defensive. He was especially angry at the fact that Lloyd George had asked Kerr to show the two telegrams to Colonel House; as Churchill told both Kerr and Sir Henry Wilson, they indicated that the Prime Minister did not fully trust him, and they revealed to outsiders divisions within the British government.[60] Churchill took his defense of his policies to a meeting of the British Empire Delegation at noon on Monday, 17 February. His eloquence won at least partial endorse-

[59] Sent as Curzon to Balfour, telegram 178, 16 February 1919, file 591/1/1/2316; F.O. 608/177. Printed in Lloyd George, *Truth about the Peace Treaties*, vol. I, pp. 371-72.
[60] Kerr to Lloyd George, memorandum, 17 February 1919; printed in *ibid.*, pp. 372-74. Also Wilson MS diary, entry for 17 February 1919.

ment for his proposals: it was agreed that at the afternoon's Council session the British delegation would press for the institution of a military commission for Russia. But the tone of the discussions makes clear that the assembled Cabinet members and Dominion ministers were firmly opposed to any large-scale Allied intervention in Russia. Far from being a "general staff" for a war against Bolshevism, the military commission would merely investigate ways in which limited Allied resources could most efficiently be allocated to aid the White armies.[61]

Churchill went from the British Empire Delegation to the full Allied Council. The ensuing discussion of Russia was so acrimonious that the delegates decided that, rather than run the risk of a leak exposing their divisions to the world, the minutes for that portion of the meeting would be deleted.[62] Churchill's proposals were supported by Clemenceau, but they were adamantly opposed by House, who categorically stated that neither American men nor materials would be allowed to go to Russia.[63] House was supported by Balfour; in the British Empire Delegation the Foreign Secretary had taken a position squarely astride the fence dividing intervention from nonintervention, but now, to Churchill's chagrin, he came down firmly on the side of nonintervention, as Lloyd George would surely have wished him to do.[64] The opposition of both House and

[61] British Empire Delegation, Paris, 8th minutes, 17 February 1919, noon; Cab. 29/28/1.

[62] Thompson, *Versailles Peace*, p. 143. See minutes, Supreme War Council, Paris, 17 February 1919, 3 p.m.; *Foreign Relations, Paris Peace Conference*, vol. IV, p. 28.

[63] House faithfully reflected the views of President Wilson, who clearly had not meant what he said when, before his departure on 15 February, he told the Council he would go along with whatever it decided. From the middle of the Atlantic, Wilson sent House an anxious radio message when he learned of the turn the Russian discussions were taking: "Greatly surprised by Churchill's Russian suggestion. I distinctly understood Lloyd George to say that there could be no thought of military action and what I said at the hurried meeting Friday afternoon was meant only to convey the idea that I would not take any hasty separate action myself. . . . It would be fatal to be led further into the Russian chaos." (Wilson to American Commission [Paris], radiogram W-6, 19 February 1919; *Foreign Relations, 1919, Russia*, pp. 71-72.)

[64] Balfour's position in these proceedings was, to say the least, ambivalent. On 15 February, in order to "compress in as narrow compass as possible, the truths as I see them, which the Allies must keep in mind in coming to a decision," he drafted a "Memorandum on the Russian Situation," stating that there was no possibility of reinforcing the Allied troops in Russia, and predicting that, unless the Bolshevik regime were to collapse due to internal circumstances, its armies "will be in a position when summer arrives to make a formidable, perhaps an overwhelming attack on any Front they may select." And he asserted: "The assurances which at one time we were constantly receiving, to the effect that it was only necessary to

Balfour meant that Churchill's plan was dead. The meeting decided simply that each Power would ask for a report on possible measures from its own military representative at Versailles, no joint report being allowed. "I think this is the greatest depth of impotence I have ever seen the Frocks fall to," Henry Wilson wrote in his diary that night, and he added: "I advised Winston to go home as he was doing no good here and would get tarred, so he went to-night."[65]

❖

Churchill's project was dead, but so also was the Prinkipo idea. More than a month had passed, and the Peace Conference had made absolutely no progress toward solving the problem of Russia. Writing to Philip Kerr on 19 February, Lloyd George outlined a Russian policy that had scarcely changed since the Armistice three months before: the Allies would send no more troops to assist the White forces unless volunteers chose to go of their own accord, but they could continue to send material assistance on the assumption that "if these territories are sincerely opposed to Bolshevism then with Allied aid they can maintain their position." On the other hand, if they were "indifferent or very divided," the Powers should not either impose on them a government they did not want or save them from a government to which they were not particularly opposed. "Our principle ought to be 'Russia must save herself.'" However, Lloyd George was prepared to take more drastic measures to defend the states which were "to be carved out of Russia" and placed under the protection of the League of Nations. Here he referred specifically to

---

provide a disciplined foreign nucleous [*sic*] in any part of Russia for all the patriotic and orderly elements to crystallise around it in overwhelming numbers have in no single case proved accurate."

A copy of this memorandum is in the Balfour MSS; I have found it nowhere else, however, and there is no evidence that it ever was circulated. Despite the views it contained, Balfour wrote a note on the following day to Churchill, asking him to take the lead in the Russian discussions in the Supreme Council on the 17th, and promising his support. Balfour wrote: "[The Prime Minister] has sent you over here because, having been present at the Cabinet Meetings where the subject was discussed at length, you are not merely acquainted with the paper arguments on either side but you are bathed in the atmosphere which prevails in Downing Street and have received directions directly from there. I will, of course, give you all the assistance in my power, but I think in the circumstances detailed above, you have no choice but to take the lead" (Balfour MSS). Yet, in the meeting, Balfour repudiated Churchill.

[65] Wilson MS diary, entry for 17 February 1919 (Callwell, *Wilson*, vol. II, p. 170). Wilson described this meeting in detail. For other reports, see Thompson, *Versailles Peace*, pp. 143-45.

Poland and Finland (as yet, he said, the Allies had reached no definite conclusions regarding the three Baltic states, and he did not even mention Transcaucasia), and he asserted:

there I think we are bound not merely to give moral but material, and, if necessary, full military support to protect these newly established states against any Bolshevik invasion from Soviet Russia. But I see no evidence at the present moment that the Soviet Government have any intention or desire to invade these territories.[66]

Absent from Lloyd George's exposition was any reference to negotiation with the Bolsheviks. In general, the policies he sketched out were the same collection of half measures which Lockhart, on his return from Soviet captivity the previous autumn, had warned would inevitably end in disaster. Churchill could justifiably complain, as he did in a memorandum to the Prime Minister on 27 February, that the efforts which Britain was making in Russia constituted a serious drain on the nation's resources and yet were insufficient to produce any positive result. He continued:

There is no "will to win" behind any of these ventures. At every point we fall short of what is necessary to obtain real success. The lack of any "will to win" communicates itself to our troops and affects their morale: it communicates itself to our Russian allies and retards their organization, and to our enemies and encourages their efforts.[67]

Yet Churchill's own defense of the government's Russian policy, made in the House of Commons on 3 March, smacked less of the "will to win" of which he spoke than simply of the will to hold on until some positive lead should come from the Conference in Paris. Speaking in the debate on the Army estimates, he admitted that the original reason for which British troops had been sent to Russia— the war against Germany—no longer applied. Churchill said nothing about a more vigorous intervention, but neither did he say when the troops might be brought home. They had acquired certain obligations to the local populations and "to the League of Nations or to the League of Allied Nations," and they would come home, he implied, whenever these obligations had been fulfilled. It was an undistinguished recitation.[68]

[66] Letter, Lloyd George to Kerr (Paris), 19 February 1919; text in Lloyd George, *Truth about the Peace Treaties*, vol. I, pp. 375-77.
[67] Churchill, *Aftermath*, pp. 176-77.
[68] 113 *H.C. Deb.*, cols. 80-82.

Churchill was followed by Sir Donald MacLean, the Parliamentary leader of the few remaining Asquith Liberals, who stated: "there is nothing which is causing graver unrest and anxiety than the commitments of this country with regard to Russia."[69] When MacLean went on to intimate that Great Britain was carrying far too great a part of the burden of intervention in Russia, Churchill answered: "The share is not unequal. I could not say it is exactly equal, but it is not unequal. All are in it to a certain extent, and all are in it with extreme reluctance."[70]

Three days later, in the course of the same debate, William Adamson, the leader of the Parliamentary Labour Party, the official Opposition, accused the government of wishing to retain conscription in peacetime not only, as Churchill had claimed, in order to supply occupation troops for the Rhine Army and garrison forces for the Middle East until sufficient new regulars could be recruited, but also to fight in Russia. Churchill hotly denied the allegation:

There is not the slightest truth in anyone saying that we want this Bill for Conscription, for keeping 900,000 men with the Colours because of Russia, or because we contemplate sending a large mass of conscript troops to Russia. If there were not a single British soldier in Russia, or if it was possible by a gesture to withdraw every British soldier in Russia, or if there were no such place as Russia, I would be standing here this afternoon, introducing this bill in the House of Commons. And if it was decided, on the other hand, to intervene in Russia, it is not with conscript troops that anyone would be so foolish to act. I cannot conceive of anything that would be more unwise or imprudent than to use men taken by compulsion who were not volunteers for intervention in a matter of this kind.[71]

Churchill's categorical assurances that no conscripts would be sent to Russia undoubtedly owed much to the replies he had received to a "questionnaire" which the War Office had sent in mid-February to the commanding officers of all military installations in the United Kingdom. The "secret and urgent" order instructed them to report "without fail" each week on the political sentiments of their troops; the information was required, it said, "with a view to the establishment of an efficient intelligence service whereby the Army Council can keep its finger on the pulse of the troops." Spe-

[69] *Ibid.*, col. 89.　　　　　　　[70] *Ibid.*, col. 182.
[71] *Ibid.*, col. 703 (6 March 1919).

cifically, post commanders were asked to report whether there was "any growth of trade unionism" among their men; whether "any agitation from internal or external sources" was affecting them; whether any "soldiers' councils" had been formed; whether troops would "respond to orders for assistance to preserve the public peace"; whether they would "assist in strike breaking"; and whether they would "parade for draft to overseas, especially to Russia."[72]

To the Army's intense embarrassment, this questionnaire fell into the hands of the *Daily Herald* in mid-May, and it aroused a storm of protest from the Labour movement within and without Parliament.[73] Churchill justified it by reminding the House that the early months of the year had been marked by riots, by mutinies in the Army, and by great industrial unrest in which a mine strike and a sympathetic walkout by the miners' allies in the Triple Industrial Alliance —the railway workers and the transport workers—had been only narrowly averted. In these circumstances, Churchill said, "it was the duty of the military authorities to know exactly what their troops would do, and also to know what their troops would not do."[74]

One thing that the troops—mostly conscripts, inducted during the War and now awaiting demobilization—would not readily do was serve in Russia. Churchill read from a summary which he said the War Office had prepared shortly after the first replies had come in:

[72] The "questionnaire" was printed in the *Daily Herald* on both 13 and 14 May 1919. It was also read into the Parliamentary record by William Adamson, the leader of the Parliamentary Labour Party, on 29 May (116 *H.C. Deb.*, cols. 1469-70). See also Mayer, *Peacemaking*, pp. 617-19.

[73] See *Daily Herald*, 14 May 1919, and the long debate in the House of Commons on 29 May (116 *H.C. Deb.*, cols. 1470-1570). On 21 May, in his fortnightly "Report on Revolutionary Organisations in the United Kingdom," no. 4, Sir Basil Thomson (for Thomson's role, see below, p. 132) wrote regarding the "questionnaire": "The damage done by this publication can scarcely be exaggerated, and there is still much misunderstanding of its meaning both among the troops and workingmen." (Cabinet paper G.T. 7305; Cab. 24/80.)

[74] 116 *H.C. Deb.*, col. 1510. Although Churchill took full responsibility for the "questionnaire," he implied that it had originated with military men within the War Office, without his being aware of it. This seems true. Indeed, the notoriety of the document seems to have far exceeded its importance within the government. It was never discussed in the Cabinet to an extent worth noting in Cabinet minutes, and the single reference to it in all of the Cabinet's memoranda is quoted above, n. 73. I have been able to find no reference to it in the files of the War Office, the Foreign Office, and the Home Office, or in any of the many private collections I have used.

For an account of the working class unrest within Great Britain during early 1919 to which Churchill referred, see Mayer, *Peacemaking*, pp. 604-23.

"Troops will parade for drafts overseas with the exception of Russia." About which doubt exists. The chief reasons why service in Russia appears to be unpopular are:

(1) Suggestions in the Press of unpleasant climatic conditions.
(2) Ignorance of policy to be adopted about that country.
(3) Taking part in active warfare against an enemy who is, to them, undefined.
(4) They do not know what the campaign in Russia is all about, or even if it is a campaign.
(5) Men fear delay in their demobilisation.[75]

The government did not need the War Office's questionnaire to inform it of the extent of popular opposition to the use of conscript troops in Russia. Sir Basil Thomson, the Director of Intelligence at the Home Office (i.e., the head of the "Special Branch," the government's principal intelligence and counter-intelligence service), wrote for the Cabinet a fortnightly "Report on Revolutionary Organisations in the United Kingdom," based on information from his agents throughout the British Isles, which continually emphasized this theme. In his reports Thomson distinguished between opposition to the use of conscript troops and opposition, in general, to intervention in Russia. As he stated in late January, "Though the outcry against intervention is loud, the motive is apparently not sympathy with the Bolshevik regime, but the fear of individual soldiers and sailors of being sent abroad again."[76] And in late April he wrote:

Every section of the workers appears to be against Conscription and Intervention in Russia. Even mild Trades Unionists are said to be strongly moved over these two matters because they think it is the "thin edge of the wedge" towards making compulsory Military Service a permanent institution. They have no sympathy for the Russian Bolsheviks, and their objection to intervention is that they do not see any necessity for it. They say that Russia has never been any good to us as an Ally, and should be left to settle her own affairs. No British lives should be lost for her sake. On the other hand, it is not at all likely that anything drastic will be done to stop conscription and intervention, for drastic action means the loss of wages for themselves. If their Executives choose to call a strike they will

[75] 116 *H.C. Deb.*, col. 1515.
[76] "Fortnightly Report on Revolutionary Organisations in the United Kingdom and Morale Abroad," no. 31, 28 January 1919, Cabinet paper G.T. 6713; Cab. 24/74. (N.B.: from late April the "Morale Abroad" aspect of these reports was treated in a separate series, hence the difference in titles and numbering.)

come out, but their feeling is not strong enough to force the hand of their Executives.[77]

Thomson had a view of the "solid British workman" that was impressionistic, romantic, and probably accurate. At the highest reaches of the government—where ordinarily sober men like Sir Auckland Geddes, Minister of National Service and Reconstruction, could argue for the imposition of drastic penalties against sedition and revolutionary propaganda, including even the use of the death sentence against aliens guilty of these offenses[78]—Thomson's was a voice for moderation. "All the revolutionary talk on platforms about the iniquity of the newspapers in reporting Bolshevik excesses, and the wickedness of the Government in intervening against the only Socialist State in Europe, seems to have fallen on deaf ears," he wrote on 28 January. Even the "leading extremists" recognized that "they could not hope to bring out the workmen on strike for the sake of Russia." Thomson then turned to the alleged threat of "revolution" in Great Britain. There was, he said, "a considerable body of revolutionary feeling," but it was "home grown" and opposed to the use of violent methods. If revolution came to England, it would more likely come by means of the ballot box than by violence, and in any case it would not be accompanied by a "terror of the Russian type." Although the most extreme speakers, like John McLean of Clydeside, or Sylvia Pankhurst, the suffragette and leader of the Workers' Socialist Federation, undoubtedly did "great harm," Thomson wrote, "on the whole it seems better to allow the whole subject of revolution to be thoroughly ventilated than to attempt to suppress it."[79]

Not unnaturally, the Labour movement greeted with suspicion Churchill's assurance in early March that no conscript troops would be sent to Russia.[80] At the time, of course, the War Office's question-

---

[77] "Report on Revolutionary Organisations in the United Kingdom," no. 1, 30 April 1919, Cabinet paper G.T. 7195; Cab. 24/78.
[78] War Cabinet minutes W.C. 529, 7 February 1919, noon; Cab. 23/9. Geddes received little support for this suggestion. The Home Secretary, Edward Shortt, pointed out that "so many who were aliens by parentage and upbringing had been born on British soil and were British subjects" and thus would not fall within reach of the suggested sanctions! Shortt ensured that Geddes' proposal was quietly shelved.
[79] "The Progress of Bolshevism in Europe," Cabinet paper G.T. 6857, 28 January 1919; Cab. 24/75.
[80] On 26 March the Opposition again tried to tie the government's hand regarding Russia and moved an amendment to the Naval, Military, and Air Service Bill which

naire had not yet been made public. Nor did Labour know that Sir Henry Wilson, as the government's chief military advisor, had long since dismissed the possibility of sending out conscripts,[81] and that (as we have seen) Lloyd George had repeatedly told his Allied colleagues in Paris that the use of additional conscripts in Russia would be out of the question. And finally, for reasons of military secrecy, Labour could not be told that on 4 March, two days before Churchill gave the House his assurances, the Cabinet had reached a most important decision based upon the premise that large numbers of additional troops for operations in Russia would not be forthcoming. After a statement by Lloyd George—with which no one disagreed—that it was the "general intention" of the government to withdraw its forces from every part of Russia as soon as possible, and then to supply the "friendly" Russian commanders with everything they might need except troops and money, the Cabinet resolved to press the Allies to agree to the early evacuation of British forces from North Russia.[82]

The decision was due in considerable measure to the insistence of Henry Wilson. The Supreme Council's acrimonious session on 17 February had convinced him that the Allies could not jointly arrive at a satisfactory policy for coming to terms with the problem of Russia. During the following week he addressed to the Cabinet a paper whose basic assumption was that "the primary responsibility of the Allies is to ensure the protection of the following States whose integrity has been guaranteed, namely: Finland, Esthonia, Latvia, Lithuania, Poland and Rumania." Although Wilson went on to recommend that the British government continue to supply materials of war to Kolchak and Denikin, gone was any reference to

---

provided that the liability to service under the Bill's sub-section on Conscription "does not include service in any part of the territory formerly included in the Russian Empire, except as regards men who are so serving at the date of the passage of this act." The proposed amendment was, of course, roundly defeated, the government vigorously objecting to it. After a long debate, Churchill closed for the government with the following declaration: "If the House wished to prevent operations taking place in Russia they could do so at any time by bringing pressure to bear on the Government . . . but no one ever created an Army and placed legislative and statutory restriction on the use of particular soldiers in that Army, and, as I said . . . we do not contemplate using these forces either in the Russian or in the industrial sphere." (114 *H.C. Deb.*, col. 484.)

[81] Wilson remarked on the impossibility of sending conscripts to Russia in nearly all of his papers on Russia that have been cited thus far in this account. See also his MS diary entry, 26 December 1918.

[82] War Cabinet minutes W.C. 541 A, 4 March 1919, noon; Cab. 23/15.

the "obligations" of the Allies to "loyal" Russian elements. Regarding North Russia, Wilson was firm. The Allied forces at both Archangel and Murmansk should be withdrawn as soon as the weather permitted, probably commencing in June, and therefore Generals Ironside and Maynard would soon have to have definite orders. The withdrawing troops would have to take with them those members of the local Russian population who would be subject to Bolshevik reprisals if they were left. If necessary, Wilson wrote, reinforcements should be sent out to cover the operations of withdrawal.[83]

By endorsing Wilson's proposals regarding North Russia, the Cabinet took a first step toward liquidating British intervention in the Russian Civil War. Between the reaching of this decision and its implementation, however, stood Winston Churchill, who was authorized to make any arrangements he felt necessary to bring about the safe evacuation of British troops, including the despatch of additional troops to fight a rearguard action while the evacuation was in progress. Obviously these troops could not be conscripts. But they could be volunteers. As we shall see, the Secretary of State for War was to use this free hand to raise a volunteer force that would initiate yet one more Russian military adventure.

---

[83] "Note for the Cabinet on Future Military Operations in Russia," Cabinet paper G.T. 6885, 24 February 1919; Cab. 24/75.

CHAPTER IV

THE PEACE CONFERENCE: THE BULLITT MISSION AND THE PROBLEM OF KOLCHAK

No real peace can be established in Europe or the world until peace is made with the revolution.

> —*from William C. Bullitt's report to President Wilson, Paris, 25 March 1919*

. . . no real peace with [Lenin] can be hoped for. Any peace he & the Bolshevik leaders make with us will be only like Brest-Litovsk to gain breathing time. Otherwise it is war to the knife underground if not above it.

> —*Minute by E. H. Carr, Paris, 11 April 1919*[1]

THE Prinkipo proposal, on one hand, and Churchill's scheme for a massive, coordinated effort against the Bolsheviks, on the other, represented the two poles of Allied policy toward Russia. At no point was either notion entirely absent from the minds of the statesmen at Paris, but among themselves they could reach no agreement. The failure of the Powers ever to unite wholeheartedly on any one approach—even on the effective implementation of the *cordon sanitaire,* the lowest common denominator among the various approaches—ensured that whatever efforts they might make would be futile. From this futility, of course, only the Bolsheviks profited. Both the Prinkipo proposal and the offer to make peace which William C. Bullitt was to bring back from Moscow in late March would have allowed the Bolshevik regime to continue in existence, but with its territory severely circumscribed. The Allies failed to strike such a bargain. Their failure to do so at a time of drastic Soviet weakness, combined with their failure ever to make effective their

---

[1] In file 609/1/2/6499 (a report of an interview between Lenin and two Norwegian journalists); F.O. 608/203.

efforts at military intervention, ensured that Soviet power, when finally consolidated, would run from Kamchatka to the Pripyat Marshes, and from the Arctic Ocean to the Turkish frontier.

Of the interventionist schemes which came before the Supreme Council, Churchill's—calling for the use of Allied forces as well as those from the states on Russia's borders—was the most extreme. But he had only one opportunity to plead for its adoption, the trip to Paris whose consequences we have seen. The other principal advocate of armed intervention was Marshal Foch. His position as chief military adviser to the Council, and his continued presence at its deliberations, enabled him to be more persistent. Yet his persistence accomplished nothing. On three separate occasions he presented his plan, and each time, owing to British and American objections, the Council rejected it.

Foch's plan depended on his contention that, in order to defeat the Bolsheviks over Russia's vast spaces, the critical factor was the *number* of troops the Allies could raise, not their quality or degree of organization. Therefore, the Western Allies need not employ any of their own forces (thus Foch countered the argument that no Western forces were available). As he told the Council on 25 February:

The necessary conditions would be fulfilled by the employment of such armies as might be raised locally in the countries of Eastern Europe. For instance, the Polish troops would be quite able to face the Russians, provided the former were strengthened by the supply of modern appliances and engines of war. But great numbers were required, which could be obtained by mobilising the Finns, Poles, Czechs, Roumanians and Greeks, as well as the Russian pro-Ally elements still available.

These young troops, in themselves not well organized (though better organised than the Bolsheviks), would, if placed under a unique command, yield a total force sufficient to subdue the Bolshevik forces and to occupy their territory.

"If this were done," Foch assured his listeners, "1919 would see the end of Bolshevism, just as 1918 had seen the end of Prussianism."[2]

Foch's anti-Bolshevik crusade would depend on East European manpower, but on West European and American matériel. Therefore, just as the Allies had established a logistical base on the West-

[2] Minutes, Council of Ten, Paris, 25 February 1919, 3 p.m.; *Foreign Relations, Paris Peace Conference*, vol. IV, p. 122.

ern Front to defeat the Germans, so they would have to erect the same sort of supply network in the East in order to defeat the Bolsheviks. This necessity raised a second aspect of his plan: the Allies would immediately and summarily impose a settlement on the Germans. As Foch put it, "to enable the Allies to transfer their resources from the Western base to the Eastern base, an end would have to be put to all further discussions on the West by imposing on Germany the Preliminaries of Peace, which she would be bound at the present moment to accept."[3]

On the first occasion on which Foch presented his proposal, 25 February, he did so in the context of a discussion of how the Polish forces which had fought in France on the Western Front might be shipped back to their homeland. President Wilson was in America. Lloyd George was still in London. Balfour was present—and incredulous. On the "narrow foundation" of "a small and modest suggestion involving no particular question of principle at all," he said, Foch had set out to erect a gigantic structure "stretching from the Rhine to Vladivostok." The Council could not possibly cope with such a scheme in the absence of two of its principal members, the Foreign Secretary insisted.[4]

In the future Foch's presentations were more modest. But the sudden manner with which he proposed his scheme to the Council on this first occasion vastly aroused the suspicions of the British and the Americans, and on 17 and 27 March, when the Marshal tried to gain approval for seemingly less ambitious projects, he met with vehement objections from both Lloyd George and President Wilson. On 17 March, Foch urged that the Allies equip Polish and Rumanian forces in order immediately to oppose the threatened seizure of the town of Lemberg[5] by the forces of the (anti-Bolshevik!) Ukrainian Directory but, more importantly, in order ultimately to form part of an anti-Bolshevik bulwark.[6]

After Foch had spoken, Sir Henry Wilson led Lloyd George out of the room and told him that Foch intended to raise "the whole Border States question."[7] The Prime Minister thereupon returned

---

[3] *Ibid.*, p. 123.
[4] *Ibid.*, pp. 123-24.
[5] Such was its Austrian name; the Poles called it Lwow, while the Russians, in whose territory it now lies, call it Lvov.
[6] Minutes, Supreme War Council, Paris, 17 March 1919, 3 p.m., *ibid.*, pp. 379-80.
[7] Wilson MS diary, entry for 17 March 1919 (Callwell, *Wilson*, vol. II, p. 174).

and delivered himself of a tirade. Foch's proposal would mean "the perpetration of a great mischief." At bottom it "merely meant the setting up of a great army for the invasion of Russia." The Rumanians had nothing to do with Lemberg, he said, yet, "under the guise of relieving Lemberg, Russia would be invaded." He was, he continued, "entirely opposed to any such operations which could only be carried out at the expense of the Allies." And he added: "Even supposing the policy was correct, who was going to pay?"[8] Such was Lloyd George's commitment to principle. "Foch very angry," Henry Wilson wrote in his diary that night.[9]

On the occasion of Foch's third presentation of his plan, 27 March, principle was raised more directly; Lloyd George sat for much of the time in silence while President Wilson did most of the talking. The meeting of the Council (this time of the Four, as opposed to the Ten, with military advisers in attendance) came five days after the establishment of Bela Kun's communist regime in Hungary. Once again Foch appealed for the "organization of a barrier against Bolshevism." He advocated, he said, "not an offensive action, but a barrier, behind which we can proceed to clean up the region." (Precisely what "cleaning up" meant in the context of a merely "defensive" action Foch did not say.) At the center of the barrier, as in previous versions of Foch's plan, would be Poland and Rumania. Now, however, he insisted that the Allies should also occupy Vienna, in order to ensure the safety of their lines of communication.[10]

After his exposition, Foch and the other Allied generals left the room. President Wilson was the first to speak. The Council found itself on familiar ground, he said. Once again it had to decide "whether we can organize armed resistance to Bolshevism, that is to say: have we not only the necessary troops, but the necessary materials, and also the support of public opinion?" In his view, "to attempt to arrest a revolutionary movement by means of deployed armies is like trying to use a broom to sweep back a high tide." Moreover, the armies might become impregnated with the very Bolshevism they were sent to combat. The only way to take action against Bolshevism, Wilson said, was to eliminate its causes. "We hear the

---

[8] *Foreign Relations, Paris Peace Conference*, vol. IV, p. 380.

[9] Wilson MS diary (Callwell, *Wilson*, vol. II, p. 175).

[10] Minutes, Council of Four, Paris, 27 March 1919, 3:30 p.m.; Paul Mantoux, *Les délibérations du Conseil des Quatre (24 mars-28 juin 1919)*, Paris, 1955, vol. I, pp. 52-55.

expression, 'clean up Hungary,' " Wilson continued, "which in fact means to crush Hungarian Bolshevism." So far as he was concerned, however, "If this Bolshevism remains within its own frontiers, then it should be no concern of ours."[11] With such a formulation Lloyd George, of course, agreed (few countries needed a revolution so badly as Hungary, he contended). Surprisingly, so also did Clemenceau, the principal proponent of the *cordon sanitaire*; now, presumably, the *cordon* would simply be extended around Hungary as well.[12] But Foch, although he spoke of a barrier, had in mind nothing so stationary. Like Churchill's scheme, his would have entailed an active drive on Moscow, using Allied resources and, perhaps ultimately, Allied personnel. For that reason, even Clemenceau would not accept it. The "defensive barrier" was never constructed.[13]

❖

Less than a week later, on Wednesday, 2 April, *The Times'* Paris correspondent telegraphed to his editor:

It is unfortunately impossible . . . to overcome the impression that the members of the Council of Four are wasting time in a vain attempt to reconcile the pro-German and pro-Bolshevist proclivities of some of their number with the requirements for a firm and lasting peace.

Of these "pro-Bolshevist proclivities" he stated:

It is now generally known in Paris that the idea of a shameful "deal" with the Bolshevists on the basis of some sort of Allied and American recognition of the Lenin-Trotsky "government," in return for economic, commercial, and financial concessions very nearly found acceptance in influential quarters here last week.

The idea had not been definitely rejected, the report continued, but only temporarily set aside.[14]

Here was the other strand of Allied policy toward Russia. In the House of Commons that same day, Sir Samuel Hoare asked if a member of the American delegation named "William Bullet" had

---

[11] *Ibid.*, pp. 55-56. For a suggestive analysis of Woodrow Wilson's thinking about Bolshevism as a social illness, see Mayer, *Peacemaking*, pp. 21-22, 27.

[12] *Ibid.*, p. 57.

[13] For an exhaustive treatment of the Peace Conference's handling of the problem of Bela Kun's communist regime in Hungary, see Mayer, *Peacemaking*, chs. 17, 21, 24.

[14] *The Times*, 3 April 1919. A leader in the same issue of *The Times* intoned: "The Prinkipo policy, for all the ridicule it brought upon its authors and all the mischief it did the Associates, is not killed, but only scotched, and threatens to revive in some other form."

not just returned from Russia bringing a peace offer from Lenin. Hoare urged that the government should not even consider any offer from the Bolsheviks. Replying, Bonar Law said that he personally knew of no such peace offer. Moreover, he had just telephoned to the Prime Minister in Paris. Lloyd George also knew nothing about it.[15]

The House accepted Bonar Law's statement. On 5 April, however, the *Daily News* reported:

> There is now before the Peace Conference a definite, concrete proposal signed by Lenin. The greatest secrecy surrounds the document, but it is known that it offers a way to end hostilities between the Russian Government and the Entente that has favourably impressed some of the most important representatives of the British Government.

But, on the 7th, a government spokesman again assured the House that nothing was known of any Bolshevik offer.[16]

Yet the rumors in the press persisted. On the 9th, therefore, a Conservative member, Clement Edwards, raised the matter again, this time upon the motion to adjourn. Edwards stated what he thought were the facts of the situation: an American named "Bullit" had been sent to Russia and had had long talks with Lenin. He had brought back to Paris "a written document signed by Lenin himself," in which there were "certain terms for the recognition of the Bolshevik Government." All of the terms were not known, but one was that "the whole of the Russian people" were to be "recognised as subjects of the Bolshevik regime."[17] What followed Edwards' assertion was hardly a debate, for only one point of view was put forward: member after member rose and gave vent to unlimited indignation that anyone (meaning the Prime Minister) could conceive of coming to terms with the Bolsheviks.

They were fortified in their indignation by a White Paper published by the government only two days before. No matter how much one allows for the temper of the times, this paper, entitled *A Collection of Reports on Bolshevism in Russia*,[18] can only be described as a wildly hysterical piece of propaganda. Its eighty-eight pages were filled with two types of matter: eyewitness accounts (all

[15] 114 *H.C. Deb.*, cols. 1327-30 and 1333-34.
[16] *Ibid.*, col. 1648. The spokesman was Cecil Harmsworth, Under-Secretary of State for Foreign Affairs.
[17] *Ibid.*, col. 2142.
[18] Cmd. 8 (Russia No. 1 [1919]).

unsigned and undated) given by British residents of Russia who had been imprisoned by the Bolsheviks and then repatriated; and secondhand reports from British military and consular personnel in the various parts of Russia controlled by the Whites. The latter were based entirely upon information furnished by unnamed anti-Bolshevik Russians. Thus, General Poole, from Denikin's head-quarters at Ekaterinodar, reported the establishment by the Bolshevik regime of "commissariats of free love" which had decreed the "nationalisation of women." Poole also told of wholesale murder by specially imported gangs of Chinese executioners who practiced unique forms of oriental barbarism. In the category of eyewitness accounts by British residents were reports of the torture of aged priests and the conversion of churches into brothels.

The White Paper had its origins in a memorandum to the Cabinet the previous October by Sir Basil Thomson, the head of the "Special Branch," asserting that, as a result of successful Bolshevik propaganda in the United Kingdom, hostility to Bolshevism—so marked, he said, among the British people in the early days of the Soviet regime—was fast disappearing, and people were beginning to question the necessity of intervention in Russia. Thomson called upon the government to release to the press detailed accounts of Bolshevik "horrors." Accordingly, on 14 November the Cabinet decided that the Foreign Office should collect as much material as possible regarding the behavior of the Bolsheviks for "full and speedy publication."[19] The project aroused considerable enthusiasm within the government; in Curzon's papers there are many notes from his colleagues urging greater speed in readying the "Bolshevik atrocity bluebook." As Churchill wrote on 28 March, "In the absence of a true view about the Russian situation, I find a difficulty in supplying the necessary reinforcements for Archangel and Murmansk; public opinion is not sufficiently instructed."[20]

In the meantime, the newspapers were not uninstructed. F. R. Harris, the member of the Foreign Office Political Intelligence Department who seems to have been chiefly responsible for dealing with Russian matters, remarked in March 1919 that he found it "easy to get 'horrors' into the press." But he went on to note that "they are

[19] War Cabinet minutes W.C. 502, 14 November 1918, noon; Cab. 23/8. Thomson's memorandum was Cabinet paper G.T. 5986, 12 October; Cab. 24/66.
[20] Churchill to Curzon, 28 March 1919; Curzon MSS, box 65. The same box contains many similar letters from others.

doubly useful if properly authenticated."[21] Harris' comment was symptomatic of a widespread attitude: it was desirable that atrocity stories be verified—but not necessary. Thus Sir Charles Eliot's telegram in late January that most people in Omsk regarded the reports of the "nationalisation of women" as a hoax did not prevent their subsequent appearance in the bluebook.[22] In May, when previous reports of massacres by the Bolsheviks in Riga turned out to be untrue, E. H. Carr wrote that they were "an instance of the almost reckless character of most of the anti-Bolshevik propaganda which is being circulated." And he added: "The principle on which public opinion, and unfortunately also the Allied Governments, appears to act is that any story is good enough if told against the Bolsheviks."[23] During the winter and spring of 1919 there was much correspondence within the Foreign Office regarding the contents and distribution of *A Collection of Reports on Bolshevism in Russia*.[24] Yet, of all the minutes and memoranda, not a single one pointed out the obvious absurdity of much of its contents.

In the House of Commons on 9 April, speaker after speaker quoted chapter and verse from the newly published bluebook.[25] When one member (and he was the only one), the outspoken Liberal, Colonel Josiah Wedgwood, called the document "anonymous tittle tattle!," he was shouted down with cries of "Shame!"[26] The temper of the House was perhaps best expressed by Horatio Bottomley, who said:

> Is the British Government going to entertain for one moment these overtures? I venture to anticipate the statement from the Treasury Bench to be that our Prime Minister, who . . . is not a traitor to his country, is not coming back next week to face this House with such a moral crime upon his soul as would be the making of any treaty with these murderers and villains.[27]

The government made no statement during this debate. Edward Shortt, the Home Secretary, admitted that he knew nothing about

[21] Minute by F. R. Harris, 13 March 1919, in file 37041/91/38; F.O. 371/3958.
[22] Eliot (Omsk) to Curzon, telegram 91, 27 January 1919, file 608/4/1/2258; F.O. 608/203.
[23] Carr's minute, 28 May 1919, was in file 597/1/2/11006; F.O. 608/185.
[24] See especially file — /43654/38; F.O. 371/4001. The Foreign Office made great efforts to ensure that the several printings of the blueblook got widespread newsstand distribution at the lower-than-cost price of two pence.
[25] See the entire debate; 114 *H.C. Deb.*, cols. 2141-82.
[26] *Ibid.*, col. 2145.   [27] *Ibid.*, col. 2163.

what was going on in Paris, but promised that he would convey to the Prime Minister "the unanimous feeling of this House" in favor of a resolution, in the form of a draft telegram, which had been placed that evening on a table in the House lobby by Clement Edwards and another Conservative member, Kennedy Jones, Lord Northcliffe's principal journalistic partner. The resolution stated:

We, the undersigned, learn with great concern that there is a proposal before the Peace Conference to recognise the Bolshevist Government of Moscow, involving also the recognition of Russians as subjects of that Government, and urge the British plenipotentiaries to decline to agree to any such recognition.[28]

Before the night's adjournment, more than 200 members had affixed their signatures to the telegram, and on the following morning it was forwarded to Paris. Shortt congratulated his fellow members on "a useful and valuable Debate" which had "made clear to the whole world . . . the opinion of the British House of Commons."[29]

❖

Not quite a fortnight before this debate, on the morning of 28 March, the Prime Minister had entertained a most unusual guest at breakfast in his flat in the Rue Nitot. The guest was a twenty-eight-year-old American, William C. Bullitt, who had just returned from Moscow.

Bullitt was a State Department political intelligence officer attached to the American delegation in Paris. His principal assignment was to give daily briefings to the American commissioners, and he was especially close to Colonel House. He also had ties with some of the younger members of the British delegation, in particular, it seems, with Philip Kerr. According to Bullitt's testimony in September 1919 before the Senate Foreign Relations Committee,[30] during January and February he met frequently and informally with Kerr and others to pool information and to discuss problems of concern to both governments. Russia, especially, drew their attention.[31] At this time Colonel House conceived the notion that a fact-finding

---

[28] *The Times*, 10 April 1919.   [29] 114 *H.C. Deb.*, col. 2177.

[30] Bullitt's testimony was printed in *Hearings before the Senate Committee on Foreign Relations*, Senate Document 106, 66th Congress, 1st session (Washington, 1919). It was also published commercially as *The Bullitt Mission to Russia: Testimony before the Committee on Foreign Relations of the United States Senate*, New York, 1919, and it is to this version (henceforth called *Bullitt Testimony*) that references here apply.

[31] *Bullitt Testimony*, p. 34.

mission should go to Soviet Russia unofficially and secretly in order to gather firsthand information about the Bolshevik regime. House and Secretary of State Lansing issued Bullitt formal instructions for such a mission on 18 February, the day following the disastrous Supreme Council session at which Churchill presented his proposals.[32]

During the following few days, however, Bullitt's mission was made into more than simply an effort to gather information. After the 17th, Bullitt told the senators, both Lloyd George and House were determined that, despite French objections, the idea of a Russian peacemaking effort, such as the Prinkipo proposal, should be revived. Lloyd George was still in London, but Bullitt arranged a meeting between the Prime Minister and House for 24 February in order that they might plan a joint Anglo-American approach. On the 19th, however, Clemenceau was seriously wounded by an assassin's bullet, and on the following day Lloyd George telephoned Kerr to say that, so long as the French Premier lay injured, he held a veto over the acts of the Council; any measure he opposed would inevitably fall to the ground. Thus Lloyd George abandoned his effort to renew the Prinkipo proposal. Instead, Bullitt was given the task not only of gathering information, but of attempting to obtain from the Bolshevik leaders "an exact statement of the terms on which they were ready to stop fighting."[33] His mission would thus serve as a substitute for one of the intended functions of the Prinkipo conference.

Before setting out, Bullitt discussed his mission with Kerr and also with Sir Maurice Hankey, the secretary to the Cabinet who was in Paris as secretary to the British delegation. He asked Kerr to secure from Lloyd George and Balfour a general indication of the conditions of a Russian peace that would be acceptable to them. On 21 February, Kerr sent Bullitt a letter which began:

My Dear Bullitt: I enclose a note of the sort of conditions upon which I personally think it would be possible for the allied Governments to resume once more normal relations with Soviet Russia. You will understand, of course, that these have no official significance and merely represent suggestions of my own opinion.[34]

[32] *Ibid.*, p. 34. See the copy of Bullitt's orders on p. 4.
[33] *Ibid.*, p. 34.
[34] *Ibid.*, p. 36. Kerr himself described his relations with Bullitt, more than a little disingenuously, in a note in response to a query from the Foreign Office; Kerr (Paris) to Sir R. Graham, 11 July 1919, *British Documents*, vol. III, no. 308.

In Bullitt's mind there was no question that Kerr had cast his note in the form of a personal opinion only to avoid officially committing the British government, and that in fact the note represented the views of Lloyd George. Bullitt told the Senate Foreign Relations Committee that Kerr had discussed the matter with Lloyd George and with Balfour. This may have been true, but Lloyd George was, after all, in London at the time. It is more probable that Kerr's note was not framed in any close collaboration with the Prime Minister but, rather, was Kerr's personal statement of conditions which he thought would be acceptable to his chief.[35] And as for Balfour, a note from Kerr to House on 21 February indicated that the Foreign Secretary had certain reservations about Bullitt's mission, the principal one being that the enemies of the Bolsheviks should simultaneously be sounded out for their notion of acceptable terms.[36]

In any case, the terms Kerr sent to Bullitt were the following:

1. Hostilities to cease on all fronts.

2. All de facto governments to remain in full control of the territories which they at present occupy.

3. Railways and ports necessary to transportation between soviet Russia and the sea to be subject to the same regulations as international railways and ports in the rest of Europe.

4. Allied subjects to be given free right of entry and full security to enable them to enter soviet Russia and go about their business provided they do not interfere in politics.

5. Amnesty to all political prisoners on both sides: full liberty to all Russians who have fought with the Allies.

6. Trade relations to be restored between soviet Russia and the outside world under conditions which, while respecting the sovereignty of soviet Russia insure that allied supplies are made available on equal terms to all classes of the Russian people.

7. All other questions connected with Russia's debt to the Allies, etc., to be considered independently after peace has been established.

8. All allied troops to be withdrawn from Russia as soon as Russian armies above quota to be defined have been demobilized and their surplus arms surrendered or destroyed.[37]

Perhaps the most interesting of these conditions was the second. It

[35] This is also the conclusion reached by Thompson (*Versailles Peace*, pp. 154-55), whose account of the Bullitt Mission (chs. V and VII) is excellent. See, in addition, Mayer, *Peacemaking*, ch. 14.
[36] Kerr to House, 21 February 1919; House MSS.
[37] *Bullitt Testimony*, p. 37.

was a clear reflection of a motif which ran through Britain's Russian policy during 1919—the desire to break up the old Russian Empire and, by reducing it in size, to reduce the possibility that the restored Russia of the future (whether White or Red) would be a threat to British interests, either in Europe or in Asia. We will encounter many other examples of this motif.

Armed with Kerr's proposals and with the knowledge, from Colonel House, that his own government would agree to similar terms, Bullitt and three other Americans set out for Russia on 22 February. They travelled, of course, as unofficial emissaries, since House and Lansing were afraid that the Bolsheviks might make embarrassing propaganda of any official peace overtures. On 8 March the little party reached Petrograd, where they were met by Chicherin and Litvinov. Two days later, with their Soviet hosts, they left for Moscow.[38]

Because they had been instructed to return to Paris as soon as they could, Bullitt and his colleagues could remain in Russia only little over a week. But what they saw in Moscow and Petrograd profoundly impressed them. "The Soviet Government is firmly established," Bullitt reported on returning to Paris at the end of March. "Perhaps the most striking fact in Russia today," he continued, "is the general support which is given the government by the people in spite of their starvation."[39] In the existing Russian conditions, he felt, no other form of government would have been possible. Elaborating on this point, he said:

No government save a socialist government can be set up in Russia to-day except by foreign bayonets, and any governments so set up will fall the moment such support is withdrawn. The Lenin wing of the communist party is to-day as moderate as any socialist government which can control Russia.[40]

Bullitt developed a great respect for the Soviet leaders and found them "full of the sense of Russia's need for peace."[41] After several days of continuous conversation in Moscow with Chicherin and

[38] Bullitt (Petrograd) to Lansing and House, 10 March 1919 (transmitted from Helsingfors, 11 March); *Foreign Relations, 1919, Russia*, pp. 76-77.

[39] The text of Bullitt's report to President Wilson and the other American plenipotentiaries in Paris, dated 25 March, is printed in *ibid.*, pp. 85-95. The section here quoted is from p. 86.

[40] *Idem*, p. 88.

[41] *Bullitt Testimony*, p. 45.

Litvinov, followed by a long conference with Lenin, he was given a list of the minimum peace terms acceptable to the Soviet government.[42] The terms were more moderate than any which Moscow had put forward before. To a great extent, they duplicated the conditions which Philip Kerr had given Bullitt—a similarity which, undoubtedly, was not coincidental. In summary, they were:

1) All existing *de facto* governments on the territory of the former Russian Empire and Finland would remain in full control of the territories they occupied at the moment of the Armistice, the revision of frontiers to take place only by the self-determination of the inhabitants. Each government would agree not to use force against any of the others.

2) The blockade would be raised and normal trade relations reestablished between the Allies and the territories under control of the Soviet government.

3) The Soviet government would have the right of unhindered rail transit to the sea and the use of all former Russian and Finnish ports necessary for trade.

4) Soviet citizens would have the right of free entry into Allied countries and countries set up on former Russian territory, provided that they did not interfere in the domestic politics of those countries. These rights would be reciprocated.

5) All governments on former Russian territory would grant a general amnesty to all political opponents, offenders, and prisoners, and the Allied governments would do the same with all Russian political prisoners whom they held. All prisoners of war, including civil war prisoners on both sides, would fall in this category.

6) All foreign troops would be withdrawn from Russia, and foreign military assistance to anti-Soviet governments on the territory of the former Russian Empire would cease. At the same time, the Soviet government and all other governments on this territory would demobilize their armies and reduce their armaments to peacetime levels which would be agreed upon at the peace conference.

7) All governments set up on Russian territory would recognize

---

[42] The Russian text of the memorandum given Bullitt by the Soviet leaders, dated 12 March 1919, is printed in *Dokumenty vneshnei politiki*, vol. II, pp. 91-95. English translations are in *Bullitt Testimony*, pp. 39-44; Degras, *Soviet Documents*, pp. 147-50; and *Foreign Relations, 1919, Russia*, pp. 78-80.

In his report to the President, Bullitt noted his opinion that these were, in fact, not minimum terms, and that the Soviet government would be willing to compromise on many of them. (*Ibid.*, p. 88.)

their share in the responsibility for the debts of the former Russian Empire.

The Soviet government undertook to accept these terms provided that the Allies should put them forward no later than 10 April. Allied initiative was of critical importance: the Bolshevik leaders could scarcely propose such immense sacrifices of territory themselves. These territorial provisions were particularly significant. As Bullitt himself put it, writing years later:

> Lenin's proposal meant, therefore, that the Soviet government offered to give up, at least temporarily, the whole of Siberia, the Urals, the Caucasus, the Archangel and Murmansk areas, Finland, the Baltic States, a portion of White Russia, and most of the Ukraine.[43]

Thus, as at Brest-Litovsk, Lenin was once again prepared to trade territory for security: so much, presumably, did the Soviet leadership fear immediate military defeat at the hands of the Whites and their Allied sponsors—and look forward to ultimate revolutionary success. Bullitt himself, flushed with enthusiasm over his accomplishment, wrote in his memorandum to the President that the Soviet terms presented "an opportunity to make peace with the revolution on a just and reasonable basis—perhaps a unique opportunity." And he asserted: "No real peace can be established in Europe or the world until peace is made with the revolution."[44]

Bullitt received the Soviet terms from Lenin on 14 March, and on the 16th, as soon as he arrived at Helsingfors, he cabled them to Paris.[45] Two days later he telegraphed to Colonel House asking him to show the proposals and his own covering messages to Philip Kerr. And he urged House to work for Allied acceptance of the Soviet offer. "You must do your utmost for it," he pleaded, "for if you had seen the things I have seen during the past week and talked with the men I have talked with, I know that you would not rest until you had put through this peace."[46]

The young American emissary arrived back in Paris on the evening

[43] William C. Bullitt, "The Tragedy of Versailles," *Life*, vol. XVI, no. 13 (March 1944), 98-116.

[44] Bullitt's memorandum, prepared in transit back to Paris and submitted on his arrival, 25 March 1919, is in *Foreign Relations, 1919, Russia*, pp. 85-89.

[45] Bullitt (Helsingfors) to U.S. Commission (for Wilson, Lansing, and House only), telegram Bull 5, 16 March 1919; *ibid.*, pp. 77-80. See also Fischer, *Soviets in World Affairs*, vol. I, pp. 171-72.

[46] Bullitt (Helsingfors) to U.S. Commission (for House), telegram Bull 9, undated (received Paris 18 March 1919), *Foreign Relations, 1919, Russia*, p. 84.

of 25 March. That evening and the next day he spent discussing the Soviet proposals with House, Lansing, and the other American commissioners. He later told the Senate Foreign Relations Committee that they were all enthusiastic about the terms; in fact, only House was wholeheartedly behind them.[47] Bullitt never saw the President, who cancelled a scheduled interview on the 26th because of a headache.

Early on the morning of the 28th he went to breakfast with Lloyd George. For the Prime Minister the time was not propitious. During the preceding week his differences with Clemenceau and Foch over virtually every aspect of the treaty of peace with Germany had come to a head, and he and four of his most trusted advisers—Kerr, Hankey, Henry Wilson, and General Smuts (who was one of the British plenipotentiaries)—had retired for the weekend to the forest of Fontainebleau to write the famous memorandum which eloquently argued that too harsh treatment of the Germans would only drive them into the arms of the Bolsheviks. "The greatest danger that I see in the present situation," Lloyd George stated in the memorandum, "is that Germany may throw in her lot with Bolshevism and place her resources, her brains, her vast organising power at the disposal of the revolutionary fanatics whose dream it is to conquer the world for Bolshevism by force of arms."[48] This paper had gone to Clemenceau on the 26th, and Lloyd George anxiously awaited the French Premier's reaction. In arguing for more moderate treatment of Germany, he had invoked the image of an implacable, warlike Bolshevism intent on absorbing all of Europe. Just two days later, however, he had to breakfast with a young American fresh from Russia whose message was that the Bolsheviks were, in fact, willing to offer most favorable terms of peace. It is no wonder that Bullitt was disappointed by Lloyd George's reaction.

Bullitt's disappointment was all the greater because it was not immediate. According to his Senate testimony, Lloyd George's initial response was nearly all he could have hoped for. Also present at the breakfast meeting were Kerr, Hankey, and Smuts. Bullitt told the

[47] *Bullitt Testimony,* p. 65. But see Thompson, *Versailles Peace,* p. 234.

[48] The so-called Fontainebleau memorandum, headed "Some Considerations for the Peace Conference Before They Finally Draft Their Terms," was published in 1922 as Cmd. 1614, *Memorandum Circulated by the Prime Minister on March 25, 1919.* Lloyd George printed most of it, with some important omissions, in *Truth About the Treaties,* vol. I, pp. 404-16. Much of it, including Lloyd George's excisions, is in Mayer, *Peacemaking,* pp. 581-83.

senators that the Prime Minister only glanced at the papers he had brought, saying that he had read them when they were cabled from Finland. Lloyd George then handed the documents to Smuts, asserting (as Bullitt later recalled), "General, this is of the utmost importance and interest, and you ought to read it right away." Smuts read Bullitt's report and immediately declared that the Soviet offer should not be allowed to lapse.[49]

Then, Bullitt told the senators, Lloyd George held up a copy of the day's Paris edition of Lord Northcliffe's *Daily Mail* and, pointing to its leading editorial, stated: "As long as the British press is doing this kind of thing, how can you expect me to be sensible about Russia?" The leader, entitled "Peace with Honour," was written by Henry Wickham Steed, the newly named editor of *The Times*, who had been told of Bullitt's mission by Gordon Auchincloss, Colonel House's son-in-law and a member of the American delegation.[50] It was filled with dark forebodings about the possibility that the Allies might make peace with the Bolsheviks.[51]

According to Bullitt, Lloyd George said that he had no doubt that the information contained in the American's report was accurate, yet he could scarcely say so in public. Instead, the Allies would have to send to Russia "somebody who is known to the whole world as a complete conservative, in order to have the world believe that the report he brings out is not simply the utterance of a radical." Bullitt, as a young radical, was clearly unacceptable. The Prime Minister then set to musing on this problem. Bullitt recalled:

[49] *Bullitt Testimony*, p. 66.

[50] See Thompson, *Versailles Peace*, p. 237. Steed himself in his memoirs (*Through Thirty Years, 1892-1922, A Personal Narrative*, London, 1925, p. 302) indicates that information was leaked to him from within the American delegation, but he does not name the source. The leak from Auchincloss also gave rise to Steed's leader in the *Daily Mail* of 27 March, "The Intrigue that May be Revived" (excerpts in Noble, *Policies and Opinions at Paris*, p. 288); the "intrigue," of course, was Prinkipo.

[51] The leader, reprinted by Steed in his memoirs (*Thirty Years*, pp. 303-4), stated: "The issue is whether the Allied and Associated Governments shall, directly or indirectly, accredit an evil thing as Bolshevism. Prospects of lucrative commercial enterprise in Russia, of economic concessions, and of guarantees for debts are held out to them if they will only fall down and worship Lenin and Trotsky. . . .

"Who are the tempters that would dare to whisper into the ears of the Allied and Associated Governments? They are not far removed from the men who preached peace with profitable dishonour in July, 1914. They are akin to, if not identical with, the men who sent Trotsky and some scores of associate desperadoes to ruin the Russian revolution as a democratic, anti-German force in the spring of 1917. They are the spiritual authors of the Prinkipo policy, and they it is who, in reality, inspired the offer of Tchitcherin . . . to make economic and commercial concessions to the Allies in connexion with the Prinkipo Conference."

He then said, 'I wonder if we could get Lansdowne to go?' Then he immediately corrected himself and said, 'No; it would probably kill him.' Then he said, 'I wish I could send Bob Cecil, but we have to keep him for the league of nations.' And he said to Smuts, 'It would be splendid if you could go, but of course, you have got the other job,' which was going down to Hungary. Afterwards he said he thought the most desirable man to send was the Marquis of Salisbury, Lord Robert Cecil's brother; that he would be respectable enough and well known enough so that when he came back and made the same report it would go down with British public opinion.[52]

The breakfast meeting ended, Bullitt related, with Lloyd George urging that he make his report public.

❖

By 10 April, when the Prime Minister received the telegram sent by Edwards, Jones, and the other M.P.'s, neither he nor the President had even mentioned Bullitt's mission in the meetings of the Allied heads of government, much less made any public statements.[53] The telegram was not the first from Jones and his followers. There had been another on the 8th accusing Lloyd George of violating the Coalition's election pledges by advocating that the Germans should be asked only for what they could pay as reparations, and not for the complete cost of the war. These were the "pro-German proclivities" of which *The Times* had spoken. On the advice of Bonar Law, the Prime Minister decided to cross the Channel and face the House on both the Russian question and the reparations issue.[54]

He could not leave for London until the 14th. On the 11th, while he was still in Paris, the tension which hung over his forthcoming statement was considerably increased by a violently anti-Bolshevik speech made by Churchill at a luncheon of the Aldwych Club.[55] The Secretary of State for War told his audience:

---

[52] *Bullitt Testimony*, pp. 66-67. For Philip Kerr's own brief version of this meeting, see his note to the Foreign Office, 11 July 1919, cited above, n. 34.

[53] The President had a single-track mind; preoccupied with other problems, he never gave attention to Bullitt's report. Bullitt himself was thoroughly disillusioned. He soon resigned from the State Department and returned to the United States. In a letter which Wilson never even acknowledged, he recalled to the President the Sixth of his Fourteen Points: "Russia, 'the acid test of good will,' for me as for you, has not even been understood. . . . (See *Bullitt Testimony*, pp. 68, 73-74; his letter, dated 17 May 1919, is on pp. 96-97.)

[54] Lloyd George, *Truth about the Peace Treaties*, vol. I, pp. 563-64. See also Riddell, *Diary*, p. 50, entry for 11 April 1919.

[55] Churchill's speech was printed in *The Times*, 12 April 1919.

Of all the tyrannies in history, the Bolshevist tyranny is the worst, the most destructive, the most degrading. . . . The atrocities by Lenin and Trotsky are incomparably more hideous . . . than any for which the Kaiser himself is responsible. There is also to be remembered—whatever crimes the Germans have committed . . . at any rate they stuck to their allies. They misled them, they exploited them, but . . . they did not desert or betray them. It may have been honour among thieves, but that is better than honour among murderers.

Churchill warmed to his theme:

Every British and French soldier lost last year was really done to death by Lenin and Trotsky, not in fair way but by the treacherous desertion of an ally without parallel in the history of the world.

There were, he admitted, necessary limitations on British assistance to the White Russian armies:

We are helping them with arms and munitions, with instructors and technical experts who volunteered for service. It would not be right to send out armies raised on a compulsory basis to Russia. If Russia is to be saved, it must be by Russian manhood.

There was another way to assist them, however:

A way of atonement is open to Germany. By combatting Bolshevism, by being the bulwark against it, Germany may take the first step toward ultimate reunion with the civilised world.

In Paris that same evening, Lloyd George, Bonar Law, and Riddell were dining together. The Prime Minister had evidently learned of Churchill's speech by telephone, and he was obviously disturbed by it. Turning to his dinner partners, he reportedly said: "In certain moods he is dangerous. He has Bolshevism on the brain. Now he wants to make a treaty with the Germans to fight the Bolsheviks. He wants to employ German troops, and he is mad for operations in Russia."[56]

Lloyd George decided to address the House on the 16th, after a day of preparations in Downing Street. It was the last sitting before the Easter recess. The Prime Minister moved the adjournment shortly before noon and spoke on the motion for over an hour. Much of his speech dealt with Russia. He did not mention the Bullitt mission or the Soviet peace proposal which Bullitt had brought to Paris. But

[56] Riddell, *Diary*, p. 50, entry for 11 April 1919.

from the outset he stated that there was "no question of recognition." It had "never been discussed" and "it was never put forward." The Bolshevik regime, he said, had committed such crimes against Allied subjects as to have made it impossible for the Allies to recognize it, "even if it were a civilised Government." Furthermore, the Bolsheviks were at that very moment attacking Britain's friends in Russia. Apart, he said, from all questions about whether the Soviet government could be recognized in any circumstances, it could not be recognized as the *de facto* government of Russia because there was no such thing. In fact, there was no longer even an entity which could accurately be called "Russia"; that was what made the task of the Peace Conference so complicated. It was impossible to know from one day to another which of the many different authorities in Russia was in control of a given piece of territory. Therefore, Lloyd George said, the Allies could only treat the country as a volcano "still in fierce eruption." The best they could do was "to provide security for those who are dwelling on its remotest and most accessible slopes, and arrest the devastating flow of lava, so that it shall not scorch other lands."[57]

What, the Prime Minister asked, were the alternatives to recognition? Military intervention, he thought, was impossible. It ran counter to "the fundamental principle of all [British] foreign policy"—never to interfere in the internal affairs of another country, no matter how badly it was governed. According to this principle, "Whether Russia is Menshevik or Bolshevik, whether it is reactionary or revolutionary, whether it follows one set of men or another, that is a matter for the Russian people themselves." He was sure, he stated, that every member of the House disagreed completely and fundamentally with all the principles upon which the "present Russian experiment" was based, and that they all deplored its consequences of starvation, bloodshed, ruin, and horror. But this disapproval, however strong, did not justify committing Great Britain to a gigantic military enterprise.

The Prime Minister reiterated what he had said time and again before, that it was easy to get into Russia but very difficult to get out. The Germans, he recalled, had had to keep a million men in the Russian morass even after the peace of Brest-Litovsk. And what would Britain do once Russia was occupied? Had anyone

[57] 114 *H. C. Debs.*, cols. 2939-40.

reckoned what an army of occupation there would cost? More in one year, he thought, than Britain could spend on railroads and canals in a quarter of a century. It would be ruinous. And he stated:

I share the horror of all the Bolshevik teachings, but I would rather leave Russia Bolshevik until she sees her way out of it than see Britain bankrupt. And that is the surest road to Bolshevism in Britain. . . . [To] attempt military intervention in Russia would be the greatest act of stupidity that any Government could possibly commit.[58]

Granted that military intervention was out of the question, Lloyd George continued, why should the British government continue to "support General Denikin, Admiral Koltchak, and General Kharkoff" (*sic*)?[59] It would do so because the White armies had been created with Allied assistance to fight the Germans. To have said to them, as soon as they had served the purposes of the Allies and after they had taken all the risks, "Thank you; we are exceedingly obliged to you. You have served our purpose. We need you no longer. Now let the Bolshevists cut your throats," would have been wholly unworthy of any great nation. The British government, the Prime Minister declared, meant to stand by its friends. Elaborating, he said:

We are not sending troops, but we are supplying goods. Everyone who knows Russia knows that, if she is to be redeemed, she must be redeemed by her own sons. All that they ask is—seeing that the Bolsheviks secured the arsenals of Russia—that they should be supplied with the necessary arms to enable them to fight for their own protection and freedom in the land where the Bolsheviks are anti-pathetic to the feeling of the population.[60]

Another part of the government's program, he said, was "to arrest the flow of the lava . . . to prevent the forcible eruption of Bolshevism into Allied lands." To that end,

we are organising all the forces of the Allied countries bordering on Bolshevist territory from the Baltic to the Black Sea—Poland, Czechoslovakia,

---

[58] *Ibid.*, col. 2942.
[59] *Ibid.*, cols. 2942 and 2943. The "Kharkoff" slip (Lloyd George presumably meant Krasnov) and the question, "How many Members have ever heard of Teschen? I do not mind saying that I had never heard of it . . . ," are two of the most striking blunders Lloyd George ever made in debate, and they were both made in his speech of April 16 (Teschen, col. 2938). They furnished the right-wing press (never the left-wing) with ammunition used again and again in attempting to show that the Prime Minister was uneducated and ill-informed, and therefore unworthy of representing Great Britain at an international gathering.
[60] *Ibid.*, col. 2943.

and Roumania. . . . If Bolshevism attacks any of our allies, it is our business to defend them. For that reason, we are supplying all these countries with the necessary equipment to set up a real barrier against an invasion by force of arms.[61]

This promise to defend the border states was the last point regarding Russia that Lloyd George had planned to make. But then J. R. Clynes rose and asked whether the Prime Minister could "make any statement on the approaches at all, except what has appeared in the papers." Clynes pressed his point: "I put the question because it has been alleged that you have had them." The Prime Minister replied:

No, we have had no approaches at all. Of course, there are constantly men of all nationalities coming from and going to Russia always coming back with their own tales. . . . But we have had nothing authentic. We have had no approaches of any sort or kind. I have heard only of reports that others have got proposals which they assume have come from authentic quarters, but these have never been put before the Peace Conference by any member of that Conference. . . . I think I know to what the right hon. Gentleman refers. There was a suggestion that there was some young American who had come back. All I can say about that is that it is not for me to judge the value of these communications. But if the President of the United States had attached any value to them, he would have brought them before the Conference, and he certainly did not do so.[62]

Lloyd George's speech was, at best, an exercise in expediency. Only two months before, during the discussions about the Prinkipo proposal, he had repeatedly told the Supreme Council that he felt that the Bolsheviks were the dominant faction in Russia and that the Allies were virtually forced to come to terms with them. But on 16 April, the language of his speech, if not the tone, could scarcely have been distinguished from that of some of Churchill's speeches. One can only conclude that he feared that taking the same line in the House of Commons that he had taken in Paris would have prompted the Conservatives to leave the Coalition and so bring down his government. The token of this fear was his denial that he knew of Bullitt and the Soviet peace proposals. According to Bullitt, various members of the British mission in Paris called upon him on the following day to apologize for Lloyd George's statement.[63]

[61] *Ibid.*, cols. 2943-44.
[62] *Ibid.*, col. 2945.
[63] *Bullitt Testimony*, p. 93.

There is no way of knowing whether or not the Prime Minister's fears were justified. But it is certain that the Conservative majority in the House was considerably reassured by his statement on Russia. Clement Edwards, who had initiated the debate on 9 April which had brought about Lloyd George's trip to London, commented:

I am perfectly certain that his repudiation of the idea of any recognition of Bolshevism will give gratification among the law-respecting people in the whole of the civilized countries; and . . . his definite statement that there was going to be no attempt to abandon the loyal elements in Russia who have helped to fight, will also be welcomed, and will give considerable gladness to our Allies in that country.[64]

Another comment on Lloyd George's performance—not so much upon his speech as upon his disavowal of any knowledge of Bullitt —was made by H. Wilson Harris, the *Daily News'* correspondent in Paris, who wrote:

Even the most discerning critics would hardly have known that the young American in question was invited to breakfast with the Prime Minister as soon as he arrived in Paris, that the Prime Minister knows as much about the young American's report as does President Wilson, that like half a dozen statesmen here of whose opinions I have knowledge, he was profoundly impressed by the information the young American was able to supply, and that the value attaching to the information had, at the time the speech was made, been demonstrated by the letter published to-day—which Mr. Lloyd George had signed before he left Paris last Monday—signifying approval of the scheme for the revictualing of Russia.[65]

The letter to which Harris referred was the Supreme Council's reply to the so-called Nansen proposal for supplying emergency food relief to Russia, particularly to the Bolshevik areas, where the need was most critical. Although the proposal has always been associated with the name of Fridtjof Nansen, the Norwegian explorer and humanitarian, it actually came from Herbert Hoover, who was then director of relief for the Supreme Economic Council and head of the American Relief Administration which had so efficiently supplied food to the German-occupied areas of Belgium and France. On 28 March, Hoover wrote to President Wilson suggesting that "some neutral of international reputation for probity and ability

<hr />

[64] 114 *H.C. Deb.*, cols. 2960-61.   [65] *Daily News*, 19 April 1919.

should be allowed to create a second Belgian Relief Commission for Russia."[66]

In making this proposal, however, Hoover was not motivated solely by humanitarian concerns. Under his plan the Allies would supply relief only if the Bolsheviks gave assurances that they would "cease all militant action across certain defined boundaries and cease their subsidizing of disturbances abroad." Such an arrangement, Hoover thought, might provide a period of rest and stability for the emergent states of Eastern Europe and might also give the Russian people a start in the direction of moderation. It would not, he made clear, involve any Allied recognition of, or relationship with, the "Bolshevik murderers"; and at the same time it would "at least test out" whether or not Bolshevism was "a militant force engrossed upon world domination."

The President welcomed the plan—in part, Hoover suggests in his memoirs, because "it would keep the Allied debating organizations in Paris busy talking for some time, and while it was pending it would keep Churchill's and the militarists' pressures on the United States in the background."[67] Nansen, however, was not so easy to persuade (he feared involvement in a scheme which so obviously mixed political with humanitarian considerations),[68] and not until a week later was Hoover able to send to each member of the Council of Four a note which he, Colonel House, and several subordinate members of the American mission had drafted and Nansen had signed, urging the establishment of a commission of neutral nations for the provisioning of Russia with foodstuffs and medicines.[69]

Not only did Hoover take the leading part in the drafting of Nan-

---

[66] Excerpts from the "Nansen proposal" are printed in the following volumes, each containing certain passages which the others omit: *Foreign Relations, 1919, Russia*, pp. 100-102; Herbert Hoover, *The Ordeal of Woodrow Wilson*, New York, 1958, pp. 117-19; Herbert Hoover, *Memoirs*, vol. I: *Years of Adventure 1874-1920*, New York, 1951, pp. 412-14. Virtually all of it is printed, along with a penetrating analysis of Hoover's assumptions, in Mayer, *Peacemaking*, pp. 24-28. For a discussion in detail of the background to Hoover's proposal (the idea seems to have originated, not with Hoover, but with his associate Vance McCormick, chairman of the U.S. War Trade Board), see Thompson, *Versailles Peace*, pp. 230-32.

[67] Hoover, *Memoirs*, vol. I, p. 414. This volume contains a more complete account than does Hoover's *Ordeal of Woodrow Wilson*.

[68] Hoover, *Memoirs*, vol. I, pp. 414-15. Nansen does not mention his fears in his *Russia and Peace*, London, 1923, which is not at all informative regarding these weeks.

[69] Nansen to President Wilson, 3 April 1919; *Foreign Relations, 1919, Russia*, p. 102—also in Hoover, *Memoirs*, vol. I, pp. 414-15.

sen's proposal, but he was also responsible for the Supreme Council's reply.[70] Signed by the members of the Council on 17 April and published two days later, this reply welcomed Nansen's proposal on humanitarian grounds and stated that the Four Powers would be glad to cooperate, "without thought of political, military or financial advantage." But it then proceeded to lay down some markedly political conditions. Distribution of foodstuffs and medical supplies, said the note, "should be solely under the control of the people of Russia themselves." This meant the "people in each locality," not the central Soviet government, although the Moscow government would (presumably out of gratitude!) pay the cost of the supplies and the expenses of shipping them to Russia. Equally far-reaching conditions were put forward in the following terms:

> That such a course would involve cessation of all hostilities within definite lines in the territory of Russia is obvious. And the cessation of hostilities would, necessarily, involve a complete suspension of the transfer of troops and military material of all sorts to end within Russian territory. Indeed, a relief to Russia which did not mean a return to a state of peace would be futile, and would be impossible to consider.

Similar conditions, it will be remembered, had been rejected by the Bolsheviks as part of the Prinkipo proposals.

Hoover immediately arranged to have the Council's reply, together with the original proposal and a covering note addressed to Lenin over Nansen's signature, transmitted to Moscow by the Eiffel Tower radio station. Unknown to Hoover, however, and despite the fact that Clemenceau had given his agreement to the whole scheme, officials within the French government (apparently with the support of Foreign Minister Pichon) prevented the message from being broadcast. As time passed, and no reply was received from the Bolsheviks, Hoover became suspicious and finally had the message transmitted from Holland.[71] Thus the Soviet government did not learn of it until 4 May.[72] On the same day the Supreme Council re-

---

[70] *Ibid.*, p. 416. For the circumstances of the drafting of this note by members of the American mission, see George F. Kennan, *Russia and the West under Lenin and Stalin*, Boston, 1961, p. 140, and Thompson, *Versailles Peace*, pp. 251-60. The text of the note (Orlando, Lloyd George, Wilson, and Clemenceau to Nansen, 17 April 1919) is in *Foreign Relations, 1919, Russia*, pp. 108-9.

[71] Hoover, *Memoirs*, vol. I, pp. 417-18.

[72] According to an editorial note in *Dokumenty vneshnei politiki*, vol. II, p. 159. The text of Nansen's message to Lenin is on pp. 159-60; its English version (the language in which it was sent) is in *Foreign Relations, 1919, Russia*, p. 111.

ceived a note from the Russian Political Conference in Paris, representing all the White governments, strongly urging that precautions be taken to keep relief supplies out of the hands of the Soviet authorities for fear that they would use them only to strengthen the Bolshevik regime. A similar request came from the Finnish government.[73]

The Soviet reply—a note from Chicherin to Nansen—was broadcast by Moscow Radio on 7 May. But once again, the Eiffel Tower station refused to pass it on, and the Council learned of it only through its reception on the 14th by a Swedish station.[74] Chicherin thanked Nansen for the generous spirit in which his original offer was conceived but charged that his "benevolent intentions" had been seized upon by the Allied Powers for political purposes. Any demand for the cessation of hostilities, he said, was a political act, for it would prevent the Bolsheviks, who had every reason to expect success, from achieving it. The Foreign Commissar then proceeded to list all of the overtures for peace the Soviet government had made, and he then went through a long, bitterly phrased recitation of White atrocities which had been made possible by Allied assistance. For these reasons, Chicherin concluded,

we are in a position to discuss the cessation of hostilities only if we discuss the whole problem of our relations to our adversaries, that is, in the first place, to the Allied governments. That means to discuss peace and to open real negotiations bearing upon the true reasons for the war waged against us and upon those conditions which can bring us lasting peace.[75]

When this Soviet reply finally reached the Supreme Council, on 19 May, it was discussed with almost academic detachment and then dismissed. Lloyd George spoke for all his colleagues when he commented that Chicherin's statement was "another instance of the extraordinary difficulty in eliciting facts." It implied that the Soviet government was refusing Nansen's offer for fear that it would compromise the prospects of a Bolshevik military victory, when all the

[73] The Russian Political Conference's statement, signed by Prince Lvov, Sazanov, Chaikovsky, and Maklakov, 4 May 1919, is in *ibid.*, p. 110. The Finnish protest was delivered to the Allied embassies in Stockholm and summarized by the U.S. Minister in telegram 269, 3 May 1919; *ibid.*, p. 109.

[74] Hoover, *Memoirs*, vol. I, p. 418.

[75] Radiogram, Chicherin to Nansen, 7 May 1919; *Dokumenty vneshnei politiki*, vol. II, pp. 154-59. A slightly inaccurate translation is in *Foreign Relations, 1919, Russia*, pp. 111-15.

information reaching the West now indicated that the Bolsheviks were on the verge of a military collapse.[76]

Lloyd George was correct: in mid-May 1919 it suddenly seemed as if the Russian problem would solve itself by means of a victory for the anti-Bolshevik forces. Both Kolchak and Denikin, after a winter of frustration and failure, now seemed bent upon success. In March, Kolchak had launched an offensive which, except for a long Bolshevik salient with its point at Orenburg (now Chkalov), had by the end of April regained most of the ground lost since the Czech advance to the Volga in August 1918. Now he planned a two-pronged advance, with one force moving down toward Tsaritsyn (later Stalingrad, now Volgograd) to make contact with Denikin and another aiming northwest in the hopes of effecting a junction with Ironside's forces in North Russia. Denikin, also, was moving forward. On 9 May cavalry units of the Volunteer Army had decisively defeated the Tenth Red Army, capturing large quantities of equipment and initiating the hoped-for drive up the Volga toward Tsaritsyn.[77]

Thus, to the heads of government gathered in Paris, the fall of Moscow—and therefore of the Soviet regime—seemed not unlikely. The problem now, Lloyd George emphasized to the other members of the Four on 7 May, was to decide upon measures which would lead the successors to the Bolsheviks to pursue policies agreeable to the Allies. The time had come, he said, for the Allies to impose upon Kolchak and Denikin definite conditions which they would have to fulfill in order to receive continued Allied support. Thus far, the two had given the Allies precious little in the way of guarantees. Their purportedly liberal programs were of the type which reactionaries always put forward when they want to give an appearance of liberalism. They said, for example, "there must be land reform," but they gave no indication about how land reform might be achieved.[78]

By suggesting that the Allies place conditions on their future support, Lloyd George was stressing one strand of a two-strand pro-

[76] Minutes, Council of Three (Orlando was absent), 19 May 1919, 11:30 a.m.; *Foreign Relations, Paris Peace Conference*, vol. V, p. 706, and Mantoux, *Conseil des Quatre*, vol. II, p. 109.

[77] Denikin, *Ocherki russkoi smuty*, vol. V, pp. 81-84.

[78] Minutes, Council of Four, 7 May 1919, 11 a.m.; *Foreign Relations, Paris Peace Conference*, vol. V, pp. 497-98, and Mantoux, *Conseil des Quatre*, vol. I, pp. 505-6. Mantoux's first-person notes are more revealing than Hankey's third-person version.

posal which had attracted considerable support within the British government during the preceding few weeks. The other strand was the according of some sort of "recognition" to Kolchak, whose primacy was acknowledged by all of the other anti-Bolshevik leaders. Sir Charles Eliot initiated the discussion by telegraphing from Vladivostok on 5 April that, in his opinion, the time had come to consider recognizing Kolchak's regime as a "Provisional Government for Siberia." During the preceding two months, Eliot said, although the Omsk government's authority was still only tenuous in the Far East, it had grown considerably more popular in western Siberia, where there was no alternative government remotely in sight. Recognition would lend it prestige and authority, which would make it more effective in keeping law and order, and also in conducting the military operations scheduled to begin in May. But, should the Allies accord Kolchak recognition, Eliot suggested, they should also insist upon his fulfilling certain conditions which they might lay down.[79]

Eliot's proposal of recognition for Kolchak received strong support from the General Staff,[80] and also from Curzon. In a long despatch to Balfour in Paris on 15 April, the Acting Foreign Secretary asserted that then, if ever, was the moment to recognize Kolchak's government. (He also specified, as neither Eliot nor the General Staff had done, that he had in mind recognition as the Provisional Government of *Siberia*—and not, as the others may have hoped, of all Russia.) The Admiral was in need of encouragement, Curzon said; the abortive Prinkipo proposal had badly hurt the morale of the anti-Bolshevik forces. Recognition would do much to enhance his position. Curzon went on to emphasize (as Eliot had, but the General Staff had not) that it was imperative that Kolchak work toward the creation of "conditions in which the will of the Russian people regarding their future form of government can be freely expressed." Recent debates in Parliament, he said, had shown that British public opinion would support any organized movement to crush Bolshevism that was not acting "in the interests either of a

[79] Eliot (Vladivostok) to Curzon, telegram 338, 5 April 1919, file 598/2/1/7649; F.O. 608/188. Eliot also put the same arguments in a private letter to Curzon, 10 April; Curzon MSS, box 65.

[80] "General Staff Memorandum for Secretary of State in connection with Sir C. Eliot's telegram No. 338 of 5th April, 1919," circulated by Churchill on 15 April as Cabinet paper G.T. 7117; Cab. 24/78.

monarchical restoration or of the extinction of the new states which have come into being as a result of the Russian revolution." Whether or not it would be feasible to attach specific conditions to the recognition of Kolchak's government was a matter, Curzon said, on which Eliot must give advice. "But public opinion in this country would hardly be satisfied with any less assurance, and indeed it would probably be necessary to add that should Admiral Kolchak by his actions show any tendency to disregard these conditions, support of him would be immediately withdrawn."[81]

Both strands of Sir Charles Eliot's proposal—the desirability of according recognition to Kolchak and of attaching conditions to that recognition—were endorsed by the War Cabinet on 29 April. Lloyd George was in Paris, but the Cabinet instructed Bonar Law, who presided, to call his attention to its views.[82] The result was the Prime Minister's statement in the Council of Four on 7 May. Yet on this occasion he did not mention recognition; he talked only of the need to secure promises from Kolchak regarding his future behavior. Presumably he felt that the case for recognition was not yet conclusive enough, despite the inclinations of the Cabinet in London. There was no further discussion of Kolchak among the Four on the 7th, however: that afternoon they were to hand to the Germans the text of the Versailles treaty, and there were still many arrangements to make. Two days later, when they again turned to Russian problems, President Wilson asserted flatly that he had no confidence in the Admiral. The Allies might obtain promises from him, but could they force him to honor them? His own position, the President said, remained what it had always been—that the only proper policy for the Allies was to clear out of Russia and allow the Russians to fight out their differences among themselves.[83]

Lloyd George replied. He was more optimistic than before—a reaction, perhaps, to Wilson's pessimism. The Allies could, he thought, make Kolchak live up to his promises. The fact that Bolshevism would have failed because it had met with the opposition of the whole world would surely be a lesson for Kolchak. Besides, the Admiral would be to a much greater extent in the hands of the Allies

[81] Curzon to Balfour (Paris), despatch 2285, 15 April 1919, file 598/2/1/7649; F.O. 608/188.
[82] War Cabinet minutes W.C. 560, 29 April 1919, noon; Cab. 23/10.
[83] Minutes, Council of Four, 9 May 1919, 4 p.m.; *Foreign Relations, Paris Peace Conference*, vol. V, pp. 528-29, and Mantoux, *Conseil des Quatre*, vol. II, pp. 16-17.

than the Bolsheviks had been. The Bolsheviks had bled Russia white; Kolchak would be dependent upon the Allies for the goods, such as the locomotives and rolling stock, by which Russia would be restored. Moreover, Lloyd George said, he had gotten a very favorable impression of Kolchak from Russians in Paris (he mentioned P. L. Bark, the Minister of Finance in the Tsar's last government!). Not only was Kolchak a man in whom the Allies could place their confidence, but he was "surrounded by young men who, before the Revolution and in its initial stages, had taken a progressive position."[84] (Here, if ever, was a tragic piece of misinformation; Kolchak himself was undoubtedly an honorable man, but his fatal flaw was that he allowed himself to be surrounded, as he sadly complained in a letter to his wife, by "moral decay, cowardice, greed and treachery"—an opinion which was shared by virtually all non-Russian visitors to his headquarters.)[85] Lloyd George was sure, he told his colleagues, that the Allies could impose conditions upon Kolchak if they acted immediately.

The optimism of these remarks contrasts strikingly with the doubt and hesitation with which—even as recently as two days before—the Prime Minister had previously approached the Russian problem. It was as if he had convinced himself that Kolchak was indeed the solution to the problem which had caused him such anguish. His original feeling that the Allies must somehow come to terms with the Bolsheviks had caused serious unrest among the French and had nearly provoked a rebellion in the House of Commons. Now, in May, when a solution suddenly seemed near at hand, he was not only willing (as he had told the House on 16 April) to give full support to the anti-Bolshevik forces, but he was willing to go one step further and involve British troops in serious offensive operations. In the Council of Four on 9 May, following his remarks about Kolchak, he said: "We shall have to take another decision: should our troops at Archangel march to meet Kolchak?"

President Wilson, who, under Lloyd George's urging, had just reluctantly agreed that American troops might remain in Siberia until a definite Allied policy was decided upon, answered: "The American troops at Archangel certainly shall not." The exchange continued:

[84] *Ibid.*, pp. 17-18. Here again, Mantoux's version is the more revealing.
[85] See Fleming, *Kolchak*, p. 136.

LLOYD GEORGE: If Admiral Kolchak is able to join us, that would be the end of Bolshevism; that would demonstrate its irremediable weakness, and the further we advance towards the south, the greater will be the number of Russians who will rally to us. If Kolchak is on the verge of success, then now is the moment to impose our conditions upon him and to treat with him.

PRESIDENT WILSON: It is always dangerous to meddle in foreign revolutions.

LLOYD GEORGE: Here it is the Russians who are acting. All we shall do is second them.[86]

The argument was not pursued further. Lloyd George must have been aware, however, that any drive south or west from Archangel would have to be executed almost entirely by Allied troops; local contingents were both too few and too unreliable. Such an operation would hardly have been simply "seconding" the Russians. Furthermore, the Prime Minister, in his enthusiasm, had resorted to an argument whose basic premise had been contradicted by all the evidence of the previous autumn: that the farther the Allied troops advanced in North Russia, the more Russians would rally to their colors.

The Americans had already stated that they would withdraw their troops from North Russia as soon as the weather conditions permitted.[87] Therefore, Lloyd George was not so much concerned with securing American participation in extended military operations in the North as he was in getting President Wilson's agreement to any policy which the Allies might adopt regarding Kolchak. The Prime Minister's basic task was to convince the President—as he himself had evidently been convinced—that Kolchak was not a reactionary. To this end, Lloyd George urged that the Council should interview Chaikovsky, who was then in Paris as a member of the Russian Political Conference and for whom, the Prime Minister said, he had the greatest respect.[88]

The four heads of government interviewed Chaikovsky on 10 May. Had there been present any of the other ministers of the Archangel government who, only eight months before, had accompanied him on the journey, forced upon him by monarchist officers, to Solovetski

[86] Mantoux, *Conseil des Quatre*, vol. II, p. 19.

[87] Such an assurance had been given by the American Secretary of War to the chairmen of the Senate and House Military Affairs Committees on 18 February 1919; see *Foreign Relations, 1919, Russia*, p. 617.

[88] See Lloyd George's remarks in the Council's session of 7 May, 11 a.m., *Foreign Relations, Paris Peace Conference*, vol. V, p. 497.

Island in the White Sea,[89] they would surely have judged the old man's performance to be remarkable. He pronounced himself absolutely confident that Kolchak, although necessarily a dictator, had derived his power from the essentially democratic and liberal population of Siberia, and that he would never use it to promote reaction. He was equally sure about Denikin, although he admitted that the fact that South Russia was an area of large estates, rather than the small holdings characteristic of Siberia, would make it more difficult for Denikin to follow an enlightened course than for Kolchak. He pointed, however, to a strikingly liberal declaration which Denikin had just made. In any case, he said, Denikin was unimportant compared to Kolchak, for the latter controlled much greater resources and more populous regions.

When Lloyd George stated that the Allies felt that it was of vital importance that a constituent assembly be summoned, Chaikovsky replied that Kolchak had promised to resign his dictatorship as soon as it should become possible to summon such an assembly. No one, Chaikovsky said, could ask for more. Kolchak, he emphasized, had not wanted to be dictator but had had the role forced upon him by those who had carried out the coup at Omsk. To another of Lloyd George's questions—whether or not Kolchak would agree to the national independence of the border states—Chaikovsky could not unequivocally reply. He himself felt that the great pressure for independence was due to the overcentralization which the Tsars had fostered, and that the border regions were economically too weak for absolute separation from Russia. He favored instead a federal solution, with complete equality among the members of the federation.[90]

The Council made no attempt to reach a decision; for the following week they were occupied almost entirely with the terms of the treaty of peace with Austria, and Russia was hardly mentioned. On 20 May, however, the Four again raised the problem of Kolchak. It was generally agreed that, in exchange for their continued support, the Allies could and should exact from Kolchak definite pledges to establish a government on a democratic basis and to accept Russian frontiers which should be laid down by the League of Nations.

[89] See Volume I, pp. 246-47.
[90] Minutes, Council of Four, 10 May 1919, 12 noon; *Foreign Relations, Paris Peace Conference*, vol. V, pp. 544-51, and Mantoux, *Conseil des Quatre*, vol. II, pp. 27-31.

Accordingly, Philip Kerr was called into the Council chamber and directed to draft a note to Kolchak along those lines.[91]

Over the next week successive drafts of the note were prepared and discussed. The Council's deliberations were given special urgency by the rumor, noted on 23 May and confirmed the following day by Viscount Chinda himself, that the Japanese government proposed unilaterally to recognize Kolchak's government as the Provisional Government of all Russia. Chinda, Japan's Ambassador in London and one of her two plenipotentiaries at Paris, told the astonished members of the Council of Four that his government believed that official recognition would be materially conducive to the restoration of orderly and efficient government in Russia, and therefore they proposed to recognize Kolchak. Since both Denikin and the North Russian government recognized the supreme authority of Omsk, the Japanese saw no reason why Omsk should not be recognized as the government of all Russia.[92]

This was a surprising proposal. Not only did it go much further than the Allies had considered going (despite British inclinations toward some sort of recognition, the Council had not even discussed recognition of Omsk as the government of Siberia, much less as that of all Russia), but it was a complete departure from past Japanese policy, which had seemed to be directed at hamstringing Kolchak's efforts to build a strong, unified government. Seen at the distance of half a century, Tokyo's sudden *démarche* is just as mystifying as it must have seemed to the statesmen in Paris in May 1919; one can only speculate that the *démarche* was made primarily to force the other Powers to realize that, when it came to matters with Asian ramifications, Japan was always to be consulted.[93]

---

[91] Minutes, Council of Four, 20 May 1919, 11 a.m.; *Foreign Relations, Paris Peace Conference*, vol. V, pp. 735-37, and Mantoux, *Conseil des Quatre*, vol. II, pp. 127-29. It should be noted that, almost invariably, the only participants in all of these conversations about Kolchak were Lloyd George and President Wilson. Clemenceau would signify his assent from time to time, but infrequently would he add anything of substance to the discussion. Orlando seldom even bothered to signify his agreement.

[92] Minutes, Council of Four, 24 May 1919, 4 p.m.; *Foreign Relations, Paris Peace Conference*, vol. VI (Washington, 1946), pp. 15-16, and Mantoux, *Conseil des Quatre*, vol. II, pp. 201-2. For the rumor, see minutes, 23 May, 11 a.m.; *ibid.*, p. 179, and *Foreign Relations, Paris Peace Conference*, vol. V, p. 861.

[93] Explanations in Tokyo were no more clarifying. See the British military attaché's report of an interview on 16 May with the minister of war, who said that the Japanese Cabinet had preferred to await developments but had decided that Kolchak was the authority most likely to restore law and order in Siberia, and that therefore

Whether or not this was the case, the Japanese quickly retreated from their position. Philip Kerr's draft note made no mention of recognition but only stated the conditions upon which assistance to Kolchak would be continued. Chinda told the Council of Four that his government wished to go further, but, since the Allied note was at least a preliminary step toward eventual recognition, Tokyo would rest content with it.[94] In the subsequent discussion, Chinda insisted upon only minor changes in the wording of the note.

As finally adopted by the Council, the note said that the Allied governments were disposed

to assist the Government of Admiral Kolchak and his Associates with munitions, supplies, and food, to establish themselves as the government of all Russia, provided they receive from them definite guarantees that their policy has the same objects in view as that of the Allied and Associated Powers.[95]

Most of the conditions attached to this Allied support were straightforward. Kolchak's government was to agree:

1) To summon, as soon as it reached Moscow, a constituent assembly elected by free and secret franchise, or to reconvene the 1917 assembly until elections for a new one could be held.

2) To permit the holding of free elections for local government in all areas.

3) To countenance no attempt to revive the former system of class privileges or land ownership, and to support a program of civil and religious liberties for all Russian citizens.

4) To recognize the independence of Finland and Poland, leaving questions of frontier adjustment to the League of Nations.

5) To permit League of Nations consultation in the solution of the problems of relations with the three Baltic states, the Caucasus, and the Transcaspian territories, if a settlement should not otherwise be speedily reached, and to recognize the *de facto* governments of these areas until a settlement was made.

---

recognition was called for. He also said that Japan would cut off all its aid to Semenov unless he put himself entirely under Kolchak's authority. (Report no. XXVIII, 18 May 1919, forwarded by Ambassador Greene in his despatch 206, 20 May, file 598/2/1/15381; F.O. 608/188.)

[94] Minutes, Council of Four, 24 May 1919, 4 p.m.; *Foreign Relations, Paris Peace Conference*, vol. VI, pp. 16-19, and Mantoux, *Conseil des Quatre*, vol. II, pp. 202-3.

[95] The text of the note finally sent to Kolchak is appended to the minutes of the Council of Four, 27 May 1919, 4 p.m.; *Foreign Relations, Paris Peace Conference*, vol. VI, pp. 73-75.

6) To join the League of Nations as soon as a democratic government had been established, and to cooperate with other nations in matters of limitation of armaments and military organizations.

7) To abide by previously made pledges to recognize all Russian debts except those contracted by the Bolsheviks.[96]

Little substantive change was made in these conditions during their discussion by the Council of Four. Lloyd George pressed for a clause limiting conscription in Russia; he feared, he said, a 6,000,000-man Russian army in league with a rearmed Germany. Clemenceau was adamantly opposed to such a clause, probably because he desired a large Russian army as a check on Germany and because he was afraid it would lead to pressure for the abolition of conscription in France. Condition 6 was the result; conscription was not specifically banned.[97]

The note to Kolchak was despatched on 27 May. Though too late to have any effect on its terms, a strongly worded telegram came from Sir Charles Eliot at Vladivostok advising that Kolchak be asked to give an assurance that arrests would be made in the future only upon definite charges, and that the persons arrested would be guaranteed a speedy and public trial. People in eastern Siberia had had a surfeit of liberal proclamations, Eliot said; what they wanted were actual reforms.[98]

Kolchak—with assistance from General Knox—replied immediately to the Allied note.[99] Not surprisingly, he agreed to all of the named conditions. He would not retain power, he promised, one day longer than the interest of the country required. His first thoughts, after the final defeat of Bolshevism, would be to fix a date for elections for a constituent assembly. His only reservations were about the border states: the rather vague language of his note indicated that he was much more ready to grant them autonomy

---

[96] On 27 November 1918, shortly after he came to power, Kolchak issued a proclamation accepting the obligations of the former Russian governments and promising to begin payment as soon as the unity of Russia was again achieved. The text of the proclamation is printed in minutes, Council of Four, 24 May 1919, 4 p.m.; *Foreign Relations, Paris Peace Conference*, vol. VI, pp. 16-17.

[97] Minutes, Council of Four, 23 May 1919, 4 p.m.; *Foreign Relations, Paris Peace Conference*, vol. V, pp. 901-3, and Mantoux, *Conseil des Quatre*, vol. II, pp. 190-92.

[98] Eliot (Vladivostok) to Curzon, telegram 485, 26 May 1919 (received 1 June); *British Documents*, vol. III, no. 225.

[99] Kolchak's reply, sent as a telegram from the French chargé d'affaires at Omsk to Paris, 4 June 1919, is appended to the minutes of the Council of Four, 11 June, 5:45 p.m.; *Foreign Relations, Paris Peace Conference*, vol. VI, pp. 321-23.

than full independence. Taken as a whole, Kolchak's reply was a statement of commendably liberal intentions. But what else could the Allies have expected, controlling as they did the aid which was the lifeblood of the anti-Bolshevik movement?

In the last fortnight of May, when the Four were meeting to determine the text of their note to Kolchak, the Supreme Ruler's armies had penetrated well beyond the Urals. The towns of Ufa and Perm were 70 miles behind his front lines, and Kazan lay less than that distance ahead of them. On 24 May, after the Allied note had been drafted, Lloyd George looked ahead confidently and told his colleagues that they would next have to decide whether they should confine their efforts to rendering assistance to Kolchak, or whether they should recognize his regime as the government of Siberia—or even as that of all Russia.[100]

The Council was never faced with such a decision, for the end of May marked the limit of Kolchak's success. The Bolsheviks were somehow aware that the Allies were on the verge of according him recognition. As Trotsky telegraphed from his field headquarters on 1 June, once the Allies had made such a formal commitment to Kolchak, they would "go on and on" and flood Siberia with men and supplies. "The only way to prevent this," he said, "is by treating the Eastern Front as the most important one." The Red Army would assume the offensive, "since any hesitation, let alone withdrawal on our part on the Eastern Front would create conditions favorable to the recognition of Kolchak."[101]

The Red Army succeeded. On 9 June, four days after Kolchak's reply was received in Paris, it recaptured Ufa. By the 12th, when the Supreme Council met to acknowledge the Admiral's note and to assure him on continued support,[102] his forces were in full retreat —a retreat that six months later would lead to his surrender and execution in the wastes of the Siberian Far East.

[100] Minutes, Council of Four, 24 May 1919, 4 p.m.; *ibid.*, pp. 19-20.
[101] Trotsky (Kantemirovka) to Council of Defense (Moscow), telegram 92/s, 1 June 1919; printed in Meijer, *Trotsky Papers*, vol. I, no. 271.
[102] Minutes, Council of Four, 12 June 1919, 4 p.m.; *Foreign Relations, Paris Peace Conference*, vol. VI, p. 348. The note is printed on p. 356. See also Mantoux, *Conseil des Quatre*, vol. II, p. 395.

CHAPTER V

~~~~~~

THE END OF INTERVENTION:
WITHDRAWAL FROM NORTH RUSSIA

I have the feeling that if one advances into the middle of Russia it is
much as if one were pushing one's hand into a great sticky pudding
and one has the fear that eventually one will be engulfed and will
never be able to extricate oneself.

> —*Entry in the diary of Major-General
> Edmund Ironside, Archangel, 9 January
> 1919*

~~~~~~

THE decisions which resulted in the Supreme Council's expression
of support for Kolchak were the last of any importance regarding
Russia at the Paris Peace Conference. A month later, after the signature of the Treaty of Versailles with Germany, the senior statesmen
departed to their respective capitals, transforming the Council of
Heads of Governments into the Council of Heads of Delegations,
concerned principally with working out the details of the treaties
of peace with the remaining members of the Central Powers. For
all problems, not only that posed by Russia, the locus of decision-
making and policy formulation increasingly became the national
capitals, rather than the Conference machinery in Paris.

Even before the departure of the heads of governments, however,
the Conference had proved its inability to concert Allied policy toward Russia at any but the verbal level. Despite the existence of the
Conference machinery and the pious commitment of all of the
Powers to employ it, the actual conduct of military operations in
Russia had in practice remained largely a matter for unilateral decision on the part of the national government most deeply involved
in any given sector. When the British government decided early in
1919 to remove General Malleson's British-Indian force from
Transcaspia, it did not bother to consult or even to inform its fellow

Allies.[1] Although the French went through the motions of consulting the Supreme Council before they withdrew from Odessa early
in April, they made clear that they would allow their troops to
remain only if significant support from the other Allies was forthcoming.[2] The action (or lack of action) of American and Japanese
units in Siberia never came under the supervision of any controlling
Allied body. North Russia, the only theater in which substantial
numbers of British troops were fighting, was no different: when the
Cabinet decided, on 4 March, that they should be withdrawn, it did
not even go through the motions of consultation.[3]

The decision to withdraw British forces from North Russia during
the summer of 1919 (President Wilson had already announced that
American troops, the only others present there in large numbers,
would be removed as soon as the spring thaw came) in no sense implied an acknowledgment that the Bolsheviks were destined to be
victorious in the Russian Civil War. Rather, it resulted from the fact
that North Russia was viewed as relatively unimportant, compared
with Siberia and the South, as a theater of operations, and from the
belief that the British public would not easily accept the retention of
a sizable British force in the Arctic snows for yet another winter.
The civil war as a whole, however, was viewed as anything but lost.
On the contrary, as we have seen, the spring of 1919 saw the fortunes of Admiral Kolchak rise steadily to the point where many observers took his ultimate success almost for granted. Similarly, in the
summer, when Kolchak faltered and drew back, Denikin began an
advance that carried his forces by October to within little more than
100 miles of Moscow. Only after his failure, and the simultaneous
failure of General Nikolai N. Yudenich to capture Petrograd, did
the "White cause" (*Beloe delo*—the title, incidentally, of a leading
anti-Bolshevik periodical published during the 1920's in Berlin) seem
to be lost.

The remainder of this volume will trace the processes by which
the British government, by far the leading foreign participant in the
Russian Civil War, disengaged itself from all assistance of any importance to the anti-Bolshevik side. The story is complex and con-

[1] See Volume I, pp. 327-28.
[2] See Marshal Foch's remarks to the Council of Four, 25 March 1919, 3:30 p.m.;
Mantoux, *Conseil des Quatre*, vol. I, pp. 22-23. For the actual military operations involved, see above, pp. 47-48.
[3] For this decision, see above, pp. 134-35.

fusing. In order to make it less so, I have elected to concentrate in this and the following two chapters primarily on the several theaters of warfare, and to focus only afterward on events in London. The reader must therefore be aware as he proceeds that he is being shown only part of a larger canvas. He would do well to wait until he has seen it all before he attempts to draw any firm conclusions about British intervention in the Russian Civil War—or about the difficulties and dilemmas faced by any Power intervening in, and then disengaging from, a bitter civil war fought far from its own soil.

❖

Because this chapter and the two which follow concentrate on the military forces and political movements opposing the Bolsheviks, they will pay relatively little attention to conditions existing within Soviet-controlled territory. This lack of attention parallels that of the British government in London: the Soviet regime was almost totally isolated from the outside world, and in the absence of information the attention of outsiders tended instead to focus on events on the periphery of the Bolshevik camp. Before turning our own attention to these events, however, it is useful at the outset to make some observations about the British government's knowledge (or lack of knowledge) of Soviet internal conditions and about the ways in which this information figured in the making of policy.

Throughout the period covered by this volume—indeed, from the departure of Bruce Lockhart from Russia at the end of September 1918 until the arrival in Moscow of the first British mission following the signature of the Anglo-Soviet Trade Agreement in March 1921—London had no overt official source of information about conditions within the territory controlled by the Soviet regime. There were, of course, covert sources—agents working through Sir Basil Thomson's Directorate of Intelligence and perhaps other services as well—but there is no evidence in the archives that much was made of the information they provided. Thomson passed on to the Foreign Office (with precautionary measures to protect his sources) those reports which he thought of interest to the Russia Department, and they may now be seen in the Foreign Office files. With few exceptions they were of a trivial, gossipy nature, devoting inordinate attention to accounts of personal rivalries within the upper circles of the Bolshevik leadership. These were, we know now, either unfounded or else grossly exaggerated. As minutes written on them make clear, they gained relatively little credence within the Foreign Office and probably played a minor part in the formation of images of Soviet conditions in the minds of those who dealt with Russian problems. They were not considered sufficiently important for circulation to the Cabinet.

The Cabinet, instead, received a series of memoranda prepared by the Political Intelligence Department of the Foreign Office. Information acquired by covert means undoubtedly went into these papers, but again one gets the impression that this was not an important element. One of these memoranda, entitled "Conflicting Reports on Conditions in Soviet Russia," dealt directly with the problem of information.[4] Dated 16 October 1919, it began flatly: "No authoritative statement has ever been made about conditions in Soviet Russia and there is no question upon which people differ more widely." It then went on to distinguish four categories of information sources.

First were Bolshevik sources, chiefly the press and radio; these it dismissed as propaganda, useful for elucidating Soviet policy toward the outside world but of no value in revealing internal conditions. Second were reports from British subjects, of which there were three sorts: a) the writings of pro-Soviet journalists (the only sort allowed in), such as Arthur Ransome;[5] b) the reports of secret agents such as Paul Dukes, who had been chief of British intelligence in Russia in 1918-19 (and who, after his return from Russia in 1919, was allowed to serialize his observations in *The Times*);[6] and c) reports by British residents of Russia or prisoners of war who had been

[4] Russia/027, 16 October 1919, Cabinet paper G.T. 8399; Cab. 24/90. Other memoranda in this series, with very few exceptions, were unimpressive productions. One exception was "Memorandum on the Aims and Strategy of Bolshevism," Russia/023, 12 April 1919, Cabinet paper G.T. 7128, Cab. 24/78, which discussed Lenin's use of "peace in the face of *force majeure*" as the principal element in his defensive strategy.

[5] Ransome, who knew Russia well, visited Petrograd and Moscow in February and March 1919 and wrote about his experiences in *Six Weeks in Russia in 1919*, London, 1919.

[6] Dukes wrote a series of a dozen articles, with the overall title of "Bolshevism at Close Quarters," which ran in *The Times* on 14, 15, 16, 17, 21, 30, and 31 October, and 1, 3, 4, 11, and 12 November 1919. In them he described—from a pronouncedly anti-Soviet position—nearly every aspect of life under Bolshevik rule. A number of articles followed in 1920 as well. Although only three of Dukes's articles had appeared at the time of the writing of the Political Intelligence Department memorandum under discussion here, advance texts of the whole series must surely have been circulated within government departments dealing with Russia.

permitted by the Soviet government to leave. In the third broad category were Russian sources, either White intelligence services or Russians who had escaped from Soviet-controlled territory. According to the memorandum, reports from these Russian sources confirmed those of the "reliable" Britons—that the Soviet regime was on its last legs, that it had no support among the Russian population, and that its practices were vicious and barbaric almost beyond description. Fourth were American sources, chiefly Bullitt and those who accompanied him on his mission. They were comparable to the pro-Soviet British journalists; they drew their information from the same Soviet spokesmen, and their use of the materials they obtained was equally uncritical.

The memorandum then concluded with a "General Review of the Situation in Soviet Russia"—here, presumably, was an approach to the provision of the "authoritative statement" whose absence it had decried. In summary, conditions were poor. The secret police (the Cheka) were running the country in collaboration with Trotsky and Zinoviev. Lenin had tried, but failed, to moderate their excesses. Yet, at the same time, the whole Bolshevik structure was crumbling. Nothing had been built. No "constructive" land policies had been implemented. Despite its optimistic propaganda, the Soviet regime could not prevent the "general breaking up of the forces" upon which it had hitherto relied.

It is scarcely necessary to comment on the inadequate and superficial nature of this sort of analysis, although it should be noted in mitigation that 16 October 1919 was precisely the zenith of the civil war—the moment of maximum advance for both Denikin from the South and Yudenich along the Baltic, and hardly a time likely to give rise to predictions of permanence for Bolshevik rule. Yet the memorandum is worth noting here because its conclusions were not untypical and because—unlike other papers—it included a detailed discussion of the sources of information about Soviet Russia which were utilized by the British government during 1919. This is not to say that other sources were unavailable. The Bolshevik leaders would have been only too happy to receive other missions such as Bullitt's. For obvious reasons, given the temper of the Conservative majority in the House of Commons during the spring of 1919, none was sent by Lloyd George. Similarly, in March 1919 the Prime Minister seems to have rejected without explanation and without even bring-

ing to the Cabinet for discussion a request from the Labour party
that Ramsey Macdonald and Charles Roden Buxton be given passports so that they might go to Russia as part of a commission of enquiry being organized by the Second International at Berne.[7]

In the absence of better sources of information than the ones cited
in the Political Intelligence Department's memorandum, members of
"action" departments of the Foreign Office, or of other government
departments, were free to draw their own conclusions about Soviet
internal conditions. Thus, in late July 1919, O. C. Harvey of the
Russia Department wrote a paper, arguing as follows:

The Bolshevik Government has now held power for over eighteen
months. A gentleman who has recently returned from Moscow testifies to
the general orderliness of that city. The Bolshevik forces have proved
themselves efficient soldiers, and their artillery practice is admittedly
good. The considerable success which they have won in Siberia and in
North East and North West Russia postulates efficient work both on the
lines of communication and in the munition factories. We know that German engineers and technical experts have been given high posts in the
administration. It is impossible to account for the stability of the Bolshevik
Government by terrorism alone. A handful of violent men may terrorise
a city, or a small and compact country, but they cannot infuse ardour into
farflung armies or hold down millions. When the Bolshevik fortunes
seemed to be at the lowest ebb, a most vigorous offensive was launched
before which the Kolchak forces are still in retreat. Not terrorism, not
even long-suffering acquiescence, but something approaching enthusiasm
is necessary for this. We must admit the fact then that the present Russian Government is accepted by the bulk of the Russian people.[8]

Hindsight, of course, tells us that Harvey was much nearer a correct assessment than were his colleagues who postulated the imminent collapse of the Bolshevik regime. Yet only his comment on the
"orderliness" of Moscow and his (inaccurate) report of the employment of German experts in high positions show dependence in any
degree on "inside" information. The rest of his remarks might just as

---

[7] On 27 February 1919, Buxton wrote to Philip Kerr asking whether he might be
given a passport. Kerr sent the letter to the Foreign Office for advice. According
to minutes of 20 and 24 March, however, the passport office of the Foreign Office
received instructions (presumably from the Prime Minister's office) to deny the
request. (Entries 36879 and 41664 in file – /91/38; F.O. 371/3958.) The matter is not
mentioned in the Cabinet's minutes. The *Daily News* on 13 March reported the
refusal of passports to Buxton and Macdonald.

[8] "Allied Policy in Russia," 28 July 1919; *British Documents*, vol. III, no. 342.

well have been made on the basis of the sort of circumstantial evidence available to any external observer. So far as British policy was concerned, however, it made very little difference what sorts of analyses of Soviet internal conditions were turned out, or upon what sorts of information they were based. As we shall see, decisions within the Cabinet concerning the extent to which the government should support the anti-Bolshevik side were based upon estimates of the domestic British political and economic costs, and the likely military effects, of additional increments of support. In the formulation of such estimates, appraisals of conditions within the camp of the enemy were of minor importance. For this reason, it mattered little that information was imperfect or, indeed, altogether lacking.

By contrast, information would have been of great importance had the British government aimed, not at a military solution, but at negotiations with the Bolsheviks for some kind of political settlement. In that case, the achievement of an optimal negotiating position would have required as accurate as possible an appraisal not only of the strengths and weaknesses of the Soviet regime—of the resources at its disposal and of the degree to which it had managed to obtain both the active and the passive support of the populations it claimed to rule—but also of the images which the Bolshevik leaders themselves had of their domestic and international situations. Yet, after the failure of the Prinkipo proposal and the near rebellion of the Conservative backbench members of the Coalition majority, the British government gave no further serious consideration to the possibility of negotiations with the Bolsheviks. Lloyd George never put forward the idea for discussion within the Cabinet. His estimate of the strength of his own political base made it necessary for the civil war in Russia to run its course first; only after the Bolsheviks had demonstrated their mastery over the field of battle could the notion of negotiations with them even be mooted. At that point, of course, negotiations could only have resulted in an implicit recognition of their mastery. The time for achieving some balance of opposing forces within the territory of the former Russian Empire had passed. One may well ask, of course, whether such a time ever existed. Given the scant information about Soviet conditions at its disposal, the British government was in a poor condition during 1919 to supply a considered answer to such a question.

The End of Intervention

❖

The War Cabinet's decision on 4 March that British troops should be withdrawn from North Russia early in the following summer was a good example of the sort of decision which had its roots in estimates of domestic British economic and political costs and local North Russian military effects, and not in wider considerations. Withdrawal would take place because both General Sir Henry Wilson and the Cabinet considered the provision of the large-scale reinforcements that would have been necessary to put significant pressure on Moscow from North Russia to be out of the question: the C.I.G.S. saw more pressing uses for the limited British military manpower available, while the Cabinet was well aware (as Wilson was, too) of the unpopularity of the combat operations in North Russia, both with the conscript troops still on the scene awaiting demobilization, who were doing the bulk of the fighting, and also with the public—especially the working classes—at home.

In deciding that British forces should be withdrawn from North Russia early in the coming summer, the War Cabinet authorized Winston Churchill to make whatever preliminary arrangements he judged necessary to bring about a safe evacuation.[9] Four days later, on 8 March, Churchill met with Lloyd George to discuss the details of the operation. In order that there should be no misunderstanding, Churchill summarized their conclusions in a letter to the Prime Minister which, with the latter's approval, was then circulated to the Cabinet. They agreed on two principal points. The first was that any Russians who felt that they would subsequently be exposed to danger by virtue of their having worked with the British forces in North Russia would be evacuated to a place of refuge. The second was that, if the War Office judged that reinforcements would be required to cover the extrication of the British forces and Russian refugees, they could be taken from volunteers reenlisting for Army service. "It will be made clear to these men," Churchill wrote, "that they are only going to extricate their comrades and not for a long occupation of Northern Russia."[10]

By the end of the month another decision was reached—for the

---

[9] See above, p. 135.

[10] Churchill to Lloyd George, 8 March 1919. The only copy of this letter I have found is in the Austen Chamberlain Papers in the Library of the University of Birmingham (AC 24/1/27). Although it was circulated to the Cabinet (on 3 April, with a covering note from Churchill), it was evidently not classified as a "Cabinet paper."

present, at least, not to inform the Provisional Government of the Northern Region, at Archangel, of the forthcoming withdrawal. Here was a course of action directly contrary to the advice of F. O. Lindley, the British Commissioner in North Russia, who felt that London had a moral obligation to inform the Archangel government of its intentions immediately. Curzon, however, thought otherwise, and on 25 March he presented his view in a memorandum that was given tacit approval by the Cabinet six days later.[11] There could be no question, Curzon wrote, "that such a notification conveyed at the present time would have effects which would react far beyond Archangel itself." The Soviet government would be certain to regard it "as a sign that the Allied Governments had definitely decided to abandon to their fate those Russian groups with whom they have hitherto been co-operating"; by the same token, the anti-Bolshevik forces throughout Russia would be correspondingly discouraged—Lindley himself had previously telegraphed that "the whole Russian situation depends on morale."[12] Therefore, Curzon concluded, given the Cabinet's intention to provide for the safety of all Russians who felt endangered, "there would seem to be no reason why notification should not be deferred at least until the relief force was on the point of arrival." That would furnish a delay of several months; "events may by then have taken a course which would render the effect of the evacuation of Northern Russia less objectionable."

Indeed, at that very moment events seemed to be taking such a course. Toward the end of March a volunteer detachment consisting of one British officer, ten British and five French soldiers, and a civilian representative of the Archangel government succeeded in making their way to the Pechora River, just West of the Urals some 400 miles east of Archangel. There they came into contact with advance contingents of Kolchak's northern army. The importance of the junction was obvious. If a summer campaign could forge a firm link between the Siberian and the North Russian fronts, British forces could withdraw from North Russia without automatically turning the region over to the Bolsheviks. "Even if it did not result

[11] "The Evacuation of North Russia," Cabinet paper G.T. 7035, 25 March 1919; Cab. 24/77. For its treatment by the Cabinet, see War Cabinet minutes W.C. 552, 31 March, noon; Cab. 23/9. The memorandum repeated arguments made by Walford H. Selby of the Foreign Office in a long minute dated 21 March (file 42889/3669/38; F.O. 371/3993).

[12] Lindley (Archangel) to Curzon, telegram 157, 17 March 1919, file 42889/3669/38; F.O. 371/3993.

in an internal upheaval which would overthrow the Bolshevik régime," said a subsequent telegram from the War Office to General Knox in Siberia, "it would place us in a far better position to make peace with them than at the present time, when any offer of negotiations would have all the appearance of a confession of failure owing to military reverses."[13] General Ironside, at Archangel, planned to effect the union not only with British troops but with locally recruited Russians. At last the conscription measures of the Archangel government were succeeding: by the end of March it had under arms nearly 13,500 Russians, and April saw the addition of 1,500 more.[14]

On 4 April, Churchill circulated to his Cabinet colleagues the text of a message he had just received from Lloyd George, stating: "I do not wish any interference with any arrangements you may have made for making the evacuation of troops and those associated with them in Northern Russia perfectly safe."[15] On that same day *The Times* published a War Office statement to the effect that the military situation in North Russia had become very critical, and that British forces there were in grave danger. This was untrue. The military situation had reached a crisis in late January, but British and American troops had successfully broken the Bolshevik attack.[16] There were no subsequent attacks of any significance, and by April the thaw had begun, turning the ground into a quagmire. Ironside later learned that deliberately exaggerated accounts of his danger had been planted in the press in order to prepare public opinion for the despatch of reinforcements to him.[17] The same issue of *The Times* carried a leading article, "The Military Situation in Russia,"—presumably inspired by the same source—which stated:

A campaign against Petrograd or towards Moscow would have to be judged on its political merits or demerits; but from the purely military

[13] Director of Military Operations to Knox (Omsk), telegram 79014, 18 June 1919; W.O. 33/967, no. 2261. For reports of the initial contacts on the Pechora River, see Ironside (Archangel) to Director of Military Intelligence, telegrams T.H. 280 and T.H. 286, 26 and 31 March, and E. 114/G. to War Office, 30 March; W.O. 33/966, nos. 1436, 1469, and 1462.

[14] Ironside MS diary, entries for 31 March, 20 April, and 1 May 1919.

[15] A copy of Churchill's memorandum is in the Austen Chamberlain Papers (AC 24/1/26). Note that it was circulated only a day after his circulation of his letter to Lloyd George of 8 March, cited above, n. 10. Like the latter, I have not run across it elsewhere.

[16] Ironside, *Archangel*, pp. 95-104, 121-23.

[17] *Ibid.*, p. 106.

point of view it might be the best, perhaps the only effectual, means of assisting the Army at Archangel. The greater the danger of our Army at Archangel, the more unreal becomes the distinction between defensive and offensive operations in Russia. The offence may be the truest defence.

Five days later the press carried a War Office recruiting appeal for a North Russian relief force.[18] Two brigades, each of 4,000 men, were to be raised. Enlistment was open only to fully trained troops in excellent physical condition, who would be given service at the same rank at which they were demobilized. They would, the War Office stated, be used to relieve some of the worn-out, physically inferior conscripts who still made up the bulk of the British forces in North Russia. Furthermore, they would be used for the defense of existing positions, not for offensive operations. The recruiting appeal came at a time when newly demobilized soldiers were having particular difficulty finding civilian jobs. In a matter of a few days, both brigades were filled. They were soon to enter a fierce little war in which no quarter was given. The opposing sides were evenly armed except in the air, where the Royal Air Force quickly established supremacy over the few older and slower Soviet aircraft which ventured into the skies; the British were therefore able to use aircraft in support of their land and river operations, while the Bolsheviks were not.[19] The British also used gas. On 29 May this practice was defended with some vigor in the House of Commons by Churchill, who claimed the enemy was doing the same. "I do not understand why, if they use poison gas, they should object to having it used against them," he said in response to a question from the Labour benches. "It is a very right and proper thing to employ poison gas against them."[20] The available records do not support Churchill's statement, however; they contain reports of the use of gas by British forces but no mention of its use by the Bolsheviks.[21]

[18] *The Times*, 9 April 1919.
[19] Ironside, *Archangel*, pp. 157 and 180.
[20] 116 *H.C. Deb.*, col. 1522.
[21] Ironside mentioned the use of gas by his forces at several points in his diary; he was not much impressed with its efficacy as a weapon because, except when wind conditions were exactly right, it could only be employed behind enemy lines by having it dropped from aircraft (MS diary, entries for 31 March and 3, 27, and 29 August 1919; also his Final Report, enclosed in his diary following 27 September 1919).
In W.O. 33/966 there is extensive telegraphic correspondence between Ironside and the War Office concerning a new type of gas being supplied to Ironside (see nos. 1052A, 1066, 1149B, 1441, and 1483). The War Office cautioned Ironside (tele-

Less than a week after the publication of the recruiting appeal, the War Office despatched to Ironside a long General Staff memorandum on "Future Policy and Proposals for Action."[22] Although it contained no definite orders, it proposed that British troops be used to undertake an advance up the Dvina River toward Kotlas in order to make the junction with Kolchak's forces secure. The memorandum frankly admitted that the use of the reinforcements then being sent out for such a purpose would lay the government open to the accusation of breaking faith, "on the grounds that these troops were provided and despatched to rescue our beleagured [*sic*] garrison, and not to undertake offensive operations against the Bolsheviks." On the other hand, "quite apart from any political considerations," it would certainly be necessary to act offensively to a certain extent in order to carry out the "delicate and difficult operation of withdrawal." The memorandum continued:

If this is conceded it is impossible to tie down General Ironside as regards the details of his operations or to forbid him to advance beyond a certain line. All military experience, and in particular the history of our present operations in North Russia, teaches the impossibility of setting a definite limit to operations once they have been undertaken. Therefore, provided it is made quite clear to General Ironside that all British and non-Russian units must be withdrawn before the winter, it is considered he should be left a free hand to achieve his object in the most effective manner possible.

In such terms did the War Office justify to itself the employment of

---

gram 76529, 27 March 1919, no. 1441): "The invention is very secret and, of course, once used the secret would be divulged. It is only intended that this weapon should be used if specially necessary." Ironside did not use it himself, but it was employed under General Lord Rawlinson, who came out in the late summer to supervise the evacuation of British forces (see below, p. 196). Rawlinson reported to the War Office on 7 September: "New gas seems to make men temporarily incapable of fighting, judging from cases amongst enemy troops in hospital; there have been no deaths. . . . Success of these operations [he described some in which small British units easily overcame larger Bolshevik forces] is mainly attributed to new gas; this has been extensively used by dropping bombs from aeroplanes and appears to have had very demoralizing effect on enemy." (Telegram G.C. 121; W.O. 33/975, no. 3408.)

Neither in Ironside's diary nor in his Final Report, nor in any of the War Office materials available in the Public Records Office, is there any mention of the use of gas by the Bolsheviks. A telegram from the British military mission at Narva (no. S. 152/15, 8 September 1919; W.O. 33/975, no. 3416) states that General Yudenich's forces marching on Petrograd had captured some gas shells from Soviet forces, but that as yet none had been used.

[22] This memorandum is part II of the General Staff's "The Situation in North Russia," Cabinet paper P. 114, 15 April 1919; Cab. 29/2. It is printed as an appendix to Ironside, *Archangel*, pp. 202-11.

British volunteer troops for a purpose quite different from the one for which they had volunteered. For Churchill, the arrangements were as satisfactory as any for which he might reasonably have hoped. In late April he wrote a jubilant note to Curzon, stating:

> You will see that, owing to Koltchak's victories, the improvement in the morale and increase in numbers of the Russian troops in North Russia, and the fact that we have at our disposal a compact body of highly disciplined volunteers, there is now a prospect, for the first time, of our getting clear from North Russia without humiliation to ourselves and disaster to all who have trusted in us.[23]

However, there remained the necessity for Cabinet approval. Churchill had been given broad authority to bring about the evacuation of British troops, but the planned operations, although they would ultimately end in the stipulated departure, could not easily be described merely as a withdrawal. On 1 May, Lloyd George gave his tentative agreement. Following a dinner alone in Paris with the Prime Minister and Bonar Law, Henry Wilson noted in his diary: "We had a long talk about Russia. After great struggles, LG agreed to my proposition to let Ironside join Gaida [the Czech general commanding Kolchak's northern army] at Kotlas."[24] Churchill could now approach the rest of the Cabinet. First, however, he needed to be certain that Kolchak would agree. The plans being made in London would require a significant effort from the Siberian as well as the North Russian side, yet thus far Kolchak had not been consulted. On 30 April, the day preceding his conference with Lloyd George and Bonar Law, Wilson sent a long telegram to General Knox at Omsk asking him to transmit its contents to Kolchak in any manner he felt advisable.[25] Public opinion in Britain and in the other Allied countries demanded that all Allied troops be withdrawn from North Russia before the winter, Wilson stated. He then went on to sketch out what he called "Ironside's plan for a hard blow to reach Kotlas." The British offensive, however, would be "governed by and contingent upon the degree of cooperation he gets from

[23] Churchill to Curzon, 28 April 1919; Curzon MSS, box 65.
[24] Wilson MS diary, entry for 1 May 1919 (Callwell, *Wilson*, vol. II, p. 186). Gajda, it will be remembered, had in late 1918 resigned his command of the Czech Corps and offered his services to Kolchak.
[25] Wilson to General Blair (Vladivostok) for relaying to Knox (Omsk), telegram 77536, 30 April 1919, marked "Very Secret. To be deciphered by a senior staff officer," W.O. 33/966, no. 1735.

Kolchak," which in turn would depend upon Kolchak's own plan of operations.

From London's viewpoint, Wilson said, a junction between the two forces seemed highly desirable, for it would assure the "permanent stability" of the North Russian government after the withdrawal of British forces. On the other hand, he did not want to impose on Kolchak a plan of operations which the Admiral might consider unwise. "We recognise," the C.I.G.S. continued, "that Kolchak is the paramount factor in the military situation in Russia as a whole, and that his operations must be designed to further the cause of Russia and not be unduly biassed by the special or local interests of Allied Governments." In Wilson's view there were three possibilities open to Kolchak. First, he could move southwest to try to effect a junction with Denikin. This seemed unpromising, however. The distances were vast, transportation was difficult, and strong concentrations of Bolshevik forces lay in the way. Moreover, the likely rewards did not seem to Wilson as great as those from either of the other two operations. Of those, one would be a move directly upon Moscow, at the same time reaching out on both flanks toward the White and Black Seas. If Kolchak was strong enough, this plan would have the quickest, most decisive results. Finally— the third plan—Kolchak could move northwest toward Viatka and Vologda, securing direct access to Archangel and the White Sea. The great advantage of this plan, to Wilson, was that, once a junction in the north were effectively made, Kolchak would be in a strong position to bide his time and strike toward Moscow and Petrograd as circumstances permitted. Therefore, he told Knox, if Kolchak found it possible to reconcile a "northern movement" with his main plan, he should state what support he would require. "Until we know that he considers the Northern operation feasible and under what conditions he is prepared to adopt it, we cannot lay the project before the Cabinet," Wilson said. "But armed with a sound plan we would do our best to obtain sanction and whatever we promise will certainly be carried out."

Kolchak's reply to this proposal did not reach London until the middle of May. Knox telegraphed simply that the Admiral had agreed.[26] There is no indication, however, that Kolchak put forward

[26] Knox (Omsk) to Wilson, telegram N.R. 2635, 6 May 1919 (but not relayed

any plan of his own, or that he laid down any of the requirements for support which Wilson had requested from him. Nevertheless, Churchill now felt that he was in a position to put his proposal before the Cabinet, and he did so on 11 June—a fortnight following the arrival at Archangel of the first relief brigade and a week following the arrival of the second.[27] He needed his colleagues' approval, he explained, "as for the first time we proposed to depart from our present defensive policy and embark upon definite aggressive action against the Bolsheviks." Both Churchill and Wilson emphasized that the British troops involved would not be placed in serious danger. Ideally, they would effect a firm junction with Kolchak's forces and then retire. If that proved impossible, they would secure the town of Kotlas for local North Russian troops so as to deny that important Dvina River port to the Bolsheviks for the winter and still have time to withdraw before the White Sea froze.

These arguments aroused little discussion, and Churchill received the permission he sought. But, immediately after the meeting, news reached London that Kolchak's forces had suffered a serious setback, and Curzon (who had presided over the Cabinet in Lloyd George's absence), Austen Chamberlain, and Edwin Montagu all insisted that the Cabinet should have another chance to examine the situation before Ironside actually began his attack.[28] Churchill agreed. "The news from the Siberian front is disappointing but not necessarily fatal," he wrote to Curzon on 12 June. "There is no question of any move on our part before the 1st of July, and it would be possible to stop the operations up to the very last moment, when the whole situation must be re-surveyed in the light of the then existing facts."[29]

There were, in fact, two reexaminations. At the first, on 18 June, Curzon asserted that he had been in favor of a "forward policy," but not one "that might launch our men on an expedition into Central Russia that was doomed to failure." He did not want the War Office's plans to develop so far that Ironside would be able to say that he was no longer dependent upon Kolchak, and that

---

on from Vladivostok until 13 May), marked "Very Secret. Private and C.I.G.S. Personal." File 611/2/3/11854, F.O. 608/205.

[27] War Cabinet minutes 578A, 11 June 1919, 6:30 p.m.; Cab. 23/15.

[28] So Curzon told the Cabinet on 18 June 1919, noon, War Cabinet minutes (headed "advance copy"—no other version is available) W.C. 580A; Cab. 23/15.

[29] Churchill to Curzon, 12 June 1919; Curzon MSS, box 68.

he was going forward on his own. Bonar Law then interjected that, when he and the Prime Minister had approved Sir Henry Wilson's plan in Paris, the C.I.G.S. had left them with the clear impression that the operation would not be undertaken unless there was a possibility of joining forces with Kolchak. The meeting was inconclusive; a final decision would be made on 27 June, when Wilson would be able to attend himself. Meanwhile, Ironside was to be allowed to proceed with his preparations.[30]

It is notable that the Prime Minister had taken no part in these deliberations. Nor did he on the 27th. The Peace Conference in Paris was in its climactic stage—the Treaty of Versailles was signed on the 28th—and Lloyd George was completely absorbed in the great controversy with Clemenceau and Woodrow Wilson over the last minute modifications of the Treaty. Thus, Curzon again presided over the Cabinet.[31] Since it now seemed most unlikely that Ironside would be able to join Kolchak, he said, there remained only two real possibilities: either Ironside would succeed in reaching Kotlas and in destroying the docks and wharves used by the Bolshevik river flotilla, or he would not. In the first case, he would merely have to withdraw, with a consequent diminution of British prestige. The second case—failure to reach Kotlas—would come as a result of a military disaster. Neither alternative appealed to Curzon.

Churchill and Wilson countered these arguments. The latter outcome—failure to reach Kotlas—seemed to Wilson, as the government's principal military adviser, highly unlikely. Churchill justified the former. By taking Kotlas the British would leave the North Russian government—the "most democratic" of all the anti-Bolshevik administrations, he called it—in a very good position to defend itself after their withdrawal. In such circumstances British prestige would not be injured, as Curzon feared. Then Churchill broadened his focus to the whole effort of intervention. The Soviet regime was far from stable, he said, and its armed forces were unreliable. The wars all over Russia were "wars of the weak." He did not foresee an early collapse of Bolshevik power, but he hoped that the White armies would be fully self-supporting by 1920. By that time there would be need to reconsider all of British policy: "it would be a great mistake for us to break our political necks for Rus-

[30] Minutes cited above, n. 21.
[31] War Cabinet "draft minutes" (no other version is available) W.C. 585B, 27 June 1919, noon; Cab. 23/15.

sia by maintaining indefinitely a kind of equipoise warfare." His aim was to disentangle from North Russia and wind up affairs there in such a way that no dishonor would attach to the British departure. But his policy could only be successful "if our military advisers were allowed to carry out their carefully made plans for the withdrawal of our troops." Thus did Churchill argue for allowing Ironside to launch his attack.

Curzon then tried a different tack. He had invited to the meeting Sir David Shackleton, a former trade-union leader and Labour member of Parliament, now the Permanent Under-Secretary in the Ministry of Labour. At Curzon's request, Shackleton somberly described the rising feelings within the labor movement against intervention in Russia. Only the previous day, the Labour Party, at its annual conference, had passed a strong resolution denouncing intervention in all its forms and instructing the party's National Executive to consult the Parliamentary Committee of the Trades Union Congress "with the view to effective action being taken to enforce these demands by the unreserved use of their political and industrial power."[32]

Here, in the threat of a general strike—a threat echoed in more strident tones by the Triple Industrial Alliance of the Miners' Federation, the National Union of Railwaymen, and the Transport Workers' Federation—was the implication of a departure from the Labour party's tradition of reserving industrial action only for industrial, and not political, goals. In the end, as it turned out, tradition was too strong.[33] Sir Basil Thomson had been right, earlier in the spring, in predicting that, at a time of rising unemployment, Russia was not the sort of issue which would lead the British labor movement across the brink of "Direct Action."[34] But Shackleton was also right in warning the Cabinet on 27 June that the moderate members of the movement would have an increasingly difficult time in restraining the "more ardent spirits" so long as intervention in Russia continued. Men of all classes, he said, were coming to support Labour's view that the Soviet government ought to be given a fair chance. There was "bound to be trouble," he predicted, if the

[32] Labour Party, *Report of the Nineteenth Annual Conference*, London, 1919, p. 156. See Graubard, *British Labour and the Russian Revolution*, pp. 73-74.
[33] *Ibid.*, pp. 74-82, and Alan Bullock, *The Life and Times of Ernest Bevin*, vol. I, London, 1960, pp. 101-7.
[34] See above, p. 133.

annual Trades Union Congress in September were to follow on the heels of a casualty list of "British soldiers killed in Russia while fighting to suppress a Soviet Government."

Churchill protested. He was not expecting large casualty lists from the North Russian operations; otherwise, he would not have made the recommendations he did. The Bolsheviks would offer little resistance. All experience thus far, he said, showed "that the Bolsheviks had never been able to screw up enough courage to offer any prolonged resistance." No one challenged this generalization. Instead, Henry Wilson argued forcefully that the alternative to the present plans—withdrawal from North Russia without first striking a blow at the Bolsheviks—would expose British forces to greater danger than the short, sharp offensive which Ironside had planned. Wilson's argument was by its nature irrefutable. A Cabinet of civilians could not easily challenge his contention that the planned operation would *save* British lives. Ironside got the signal to begin.

At the time of this Cabinet decision, Churchill, if not his colleagues, still clung to the hope that the scheme for effecting a junction between North Russia and Siberia might yet be realized. For this purpose he turned once more to the Czechoslovak Corps, which was still guarding the western sections of the Trans-Siberian Railway. Like other plans during the preceding eighteen months involving the Czechs in Siberia, the one Churchill produced originated in a misunderstanding.[35] In a conversation with Lloyd George in Paris on 22 June, Eduard Beneš, the Czech Foreign Minister, had expressed his disappointment that not enough Allied shipping was available at Vladivostok for the early repatriation of the 60,000 or so members of the Corps. Perhaps, Beneš had said, it might be possible to ship them through Archangel instead.

Lloyd George told Churchill of this interview. Immediately, the latter's fertile imagination set to work. After a brief meeting with Beneš, he drafted an elaborate scheme whereby the Allies would take responsibility for the repatriation of the Czechs if, in turn, 30,000 of them would fight their way through to Kotlas to effect the junction with Ironside's force. After the Czechs had cleared the way, Kolchak's forces would follow. In effect, Churchill's plan meant that the Czechs would do a job which the White forces could not do for themselves, and, as the Secretary of State for War

---

[35] See Volume I, pp. 154 and 170.

admitted, they would probably have to fight for every one of the 500 miles to Kotlas. Once they had succeeded, they would make their way down the Dvina to Archangel and embark for home; their colleagues who had remained in Siberia would be repatriated through Vladivostok.[36]

Churchill's memorandum was put before the Council of Four on 25 June and immediately referred to the military representatives of the Supreme War Council.[37] In the meantime, however, Beneš had become worried that he had not made himself clear in his original conversation with Lloyd George, and he sent the Prime Minister a letter stating that public opinion in Czechoslovakia would hardly stand for more fighting against the Bolsheviks, especially if it were in support of Kolchak. Would it not be possible, he asked, for the Corps to travel to Archangel as neutrals?[38] Expressing his disappointment, Lloyd George showed Beneš' letter to the Council of Four on the 26th.[39] Somehow, the objections of the Czech Foreign Minister were disregarded; on the 28th the Council approved the text of a telegram to Kolchak asking for the Supreme Ruler's approval of the military operations which Churchill had proposed.[40]

In all of these discussions, no one had ever bothered to ascertain the attitude of the leaders of the Czech Corps. Early in July, when reports of the proposed plan finally reached General Janin, the French commander of the Corps, he flatly refused to permit his troops to fight their way out through Archangel and insisted that they should be evacuated by way of Vladivostok.[41] With Janin's refusal,

[36] Churchill's plan is set forth in a memorandum, dated 24 June 1919, printed as an appendix to minutes, Council of Four, 25 June, 4 p.m.; *Foreign Relations, Paris Peace Conference*, vol. VI, pp. 684-86.

[37] Minutes, Council of Four, 25 June 1919, 4 p.m.; *ibid.*, p. 674, and Mantoux, *Conseil des Quatre*, vol. II, p. 515. The military representatives discussed the matter inconclusively at their 73rd and 74th meetings, Versailles, 30 June and 1 July, minutes S.W.C. 433 and 434; Cab. 25/125.

[38] Beneš' letter, written 23 June 1919 but not sent to Lloyd George until the 26th, is printed as an appendix to minutes, Council of Four, 26 June, 11 a.m.; *Foreign Relations, Paris Peace Conference*, vol. VI, pp. 708-9. It is from this letter and from Lloyd George's remarks in the Council of Four, 23 June, 4 p.m. (Mantoux, *Conseil des Quatre*, vol. II, pp. 491-92), that we know of the original conversation on the 22nd between Beneš and Lloyd George.

[39] Minutes, Council of Four, 26 June 1919, 11 a.m.; *ibid.*, pp. 525-26.

[40] Minutes, Council of Four, 28 June 1919; *Foreign Relations, Paris Peace Conference*, vol. VI, pp. 743. The telegram to Kolchak, sent 2 July, is appended, pp. 744-45.

[41] Eliot (Omsk) to Curzon, 5 July 1919, through Vladivostok as telegram 608, 10 July, file 595/5/1/15970; F.O. 608/182. Also Steveni (Omsk) to British Mission, Vladivostok, telegram 186, 6 July (to War Office on 13th); W.O. 33/967, no. 2615.

the matter was effectively closed. The Czechs would give Kolchak no help. Without their assistance, the long-sought junction of anti-Bolshevik forces in North Russia and Siberia became a military impossibility.

❖

Meanwhile, in Archangel, Ironside had reached conclusions even more pessimistic than those of his superiors in London, who at least supposed that his forces would have no difficulty in reaching Kotlas. The water level in the Dvina River, the principal line of communication, had dropped, he wrote in his diary, to the lowest point in fifty years, "where it is more a series of pools and sandbanks than a river."[42] If it continued to drop, the naval monitors and gunboats on which he had counted for heavy artillery support—and for the rapid withdrawal of his forces once they had taken Kotlas—would lack room to maneuver; some stretches might even become impassable. The weather was hot. The mid-summer Arctic sun never set, making sleep difficult for the troops. On 26 June, the day preceding the Cabinet's decision to allow Ironside to begin his offensive, he wrote in his diary that, with the river still falling and no prospect of enough rain in the Urals to make a difference, "all hope of any operations to Kotlas is over."

These remarks, however, Ironside reserved for his diary. To London he betrayed no such pessimism. In his diary on 19 June, he explained why: "I do not think for a minute that I can get to Kotlas but I do not want to be left wiring for permission to do things just when I want to be doing them." This was not recklessness. Rather, it was the desire of a field commander at the end of a long and imperfect line of communications to be in a position to make decisions rapidly for himself. "We do not want to lose a single man," he wrote in his diary, and he continued, echoing arguments made by Edwin Montagu and Austen Chamberlain within the Cabinet: "One might well hear an M.P. getting up and saying in the House that all Russia was not worth the bones of one British grenadier."[43] On 27 June, when he learned of the Cabinet's decision, he noted: "That means they are giving me a free hand and I cannot ask for better than that."

Ironside was convinced, as was Henry Wilson, that in order to

[42] Ironside ms diary, entries for 13 and 23 June 1919.
[43] *Ibid.*, entry for 15 June 1919.

facilitate the evacuation of British forces from North Russia it would first be necessary to strike the Bolsheviks a stunning blow. "I must do something to relieve the situation before I begin to clear off down the river," he wrote. "One cannot simply begin to walk off with a man kicking one up behind all the time."[44] But he did not feel that for this purpose he necessarily had to capture Kotlas. Implicitly he drew a distinction between the evacuation of British forces and the placing of the Archangel government in a position where it could carry on the war against the Bolsheviks alone. Unlike Churchill, Ironside had little faith in the ultimate success of the anti-Bolshevik cause, because he had only contempt for the social class from which the White officers came. As entry after entry in his diary makes clear, he felt that the Russian officers in Archangel were effete, reactionary, and feckless, with none of the rapport with their men which makes for effective fighting units. Given its leadership, Ironside felt, the anti-Bolshevik cause could never become a genuine national movement. "I cannot go and put my head right into the middle of Russia with no prospect of the movement becoming a national one," he wrote on 11 June. And a week later: "Kolchak, I feel in my bones, is a broken reed. Please goodness he doesn't collapse so completely that they can all turn on me."[45]

Ironside kept his pessimism to himself, for he feared the demoralizing effect it would have on both the British and the Russian troops under his command. His aim was to win a decisive victory over the Bolsheviks and then establish the North Russian forces in positions which they could hold through the following winter. Only then would he announce the forthcoming British departure. Otherwise, if the spirit of the Russian forces were destroyed, the British withdrawal would become a much more risky operation. Ironside was enormously grateful for his two relief brigades; the morale of the British conscript troops who had spent the winter in the North was so low that earlier in the year some had refused to turn out of their quarters for a trip to the front. In fact, instances of insubordination among these troops, who had been forced to fight on in Russia months after the end of the European war for which they had been conscripted, were very few.[46] From the Russian troops,

[44] *Ibid.*, entry for 11 June 1919.
[45] *Ibid.*, entries for 3 April and 11 and 19 June 1919. For other expressions of Ironside's views on the Russian officer class, see above, p. 22.
[46] See "A Note on British Mutinies in North Russia," at the end of this chapter.

however, Ironside experienced full-scale mutiny. In mid-May, at Pinega, 80 miles east of Archangel, two companies rioted and killed two of their officers over the North Russian government's inefficiency in meeting their demands for pay. Ironside personally went to take charge of the situation, and he reacted harshly. "I regret to report that I had to shoot 15," he telegraphed to the War Office, "but the companies are back at duty."[47]

In July there were two even more serious mutinies. The first involved a Russian battalion with a mixed complement of British and Russian officers. Composed chiefly of deserters and prisoners from the Bolshevik side, it had been created by the British as an experiment in regeneration, instead of allowing valuable manpower to waste in prison. The experiment failed: early on the morning of 7 July, eight members of the battalion shot their sleeping officers, killing eight Britons (including three orderlies) and four Russians, and led more than ninety of their comrades over to the Bolsheviks.[48] Ironside reported the execution of eleven men against whom there was "direct evidence of complicity" by a loyal Russian machine gun company.[49] The second mutiny came on 20 July, when an entire Russian regiment, guarding the line of communication which stretched from Onega, on the southernmost bay of the White Sea, to a point some 50 miles up the Onega River, went over to the Bolsheviks. On this occasion there were no accomplices left behind to execute. During the following days minor incidents occurred in many Russian units. Ironside felt that the situation had come close to one of general

[47] Ironside (Archangel) to War Office, telegram E. 1362/E. 1, 18 May 1919; W.O. 33/966, no. 1918.

[48] Ironside to War Office, telegram E. 1532/E. 1, 8 July 1919; W.O. 33/967, no. 2530. Also Ironside MS diary, entry for 7 July, and *Archangel*, pp. 157-59.

[49] In such circumstances, whom—if anyone—does a commanding officer have executed? The telegrams here are revealing. Ironside reported to the War Office on 16 July: "Eight men who engineered the mutiny have escaped, but I am having about 20 executed." (Telegram E. 1553/E. 1; W.O. 93/967, no. 2672.) The War Office reply, on the 18th, was sharply critical: "The execution of so large a number of men as twenty cannot be approved unless the circumstances are such that you are unable to maintain your authority without having recourse to such drastic measures. It is thought that it should suffice to shoot but a small number as examples, and unless the evidence against the remainder is such as to render them liable to conviction for murder, the number executed should not exceed the number who lost their lives as a direct result of the mutiny. Please telegraph action taken." (Telegram 79829; W.O. 33/967, no. 2689.) Ironside then replied on the 19th: "Eleven men, against whom direct evidence of complicity, have been shot. Varying terms of imprisonment have been given to remainder. The number of deaths of British and Russian officers is greater by one than the number of executions. There were several deaths of other ranks." (Telegram 1562/G.; W.O. 33/967, no. 2694.)

mutiny.[50] According to General V. V. Marushevsky, who commanded the Russian forces at Archangel (under Ironside, who was "Allied Commander-in-Chief"), the British general lost all of his usual buoyant enthusiasm and became gloomy and aloof. "It was clear," Marushevsky later wrote, "that for British policy in the North, an altogether new era had begun."[51]

Indeed it had, although neither Marushevsky nor General E.L.K. Miller, the head of the Archangel government, was aware just how drastically the mutinies had affected Ironside. They had convinced him, he wrote in his diary on 23 July, that the White forces could not hold out on their own and that, therefore, there was no reason to delay the British departure. That same day, in London, news of the Onega mutiny produced a precisely similar reaction from the Cabinet. Austen Chamberlain asserted that he and some of his colleagues had from the very outset viewed the plans for an offensive in North Russia with the gravest misgivings. They had never been convinced, he said, that the possible political advantages were worth the costs involved, but they had yielded before "strong pressure from the military authorities." Now that all of the arguments had been proved invalid, British troops should not remain in North Russia a day longer than the minimum time necessary for their safe evacuation. Chamberlain's statement was received with silent agreement.[52]

Not only did Ironside favor a rapid withdrawal, but he also felt that he now had to be prepared to disarm the local Russian forces: there was a distinct, if remote, possibility that they would suddenly join the Bolsheviks and turn their guns on the British. In any event, even if the worst did not occur, Ironside was persuaded that he could not, as he had previously planned, leave to the Russians the military equipment his forces had brought with them, for fear that it would simply fall into the hands of the Bolsheviks. He expressed his dilemma in his diary:

I shall have to think out very careful plans for this, for I cannot allow the Russians to catch even an inkling that I am contemplating doing away with the Army that I practically forced them to mobilise. It is a wretched

[50] Ironside (Archangel) to War Office, telegrams B.C. 33 and 34/E. 1, 22 July 1919; W.O. 33/967, nos. 2734 and 2729. ms diary entries, 20-23 July. *Archangel*, pp. 161-64.
[51] General V. V. Marushevsky, "God na severe" (A Year in the North), *Beloe delo* (The White Cause), vol. III, Berlin, 1927, p. 41.
[52] War Cabinet minutes W.C. 598, 23 July 1919, noon; Cab. 23/11.

situation if there ever was one. Miller will never admit that he cannot hold out after I go and I shall have to pretend to give him all the assistance that I can and at the same time I must be careful not to give him stores which will fall into the Bolshevik hand immediately after we go. With Denikin doing so well [in South Russia] it would be a pity if we just turned the scale against the people we are backing. I am quite sure in my own mind that the mobilised Reg[imen]ts will behave exactly as the S.B.L. [i.e., the Slavo-British Legion—the battalion which mutinied on 7 July] have. We may be able to stave off the mutiny by our presence, but the very minute we go it must come off.[53]

At last, on 27 July, Ironside and R. H. Hoare, who had replaced F. O. Lindley as chief British diplomatic representative in North Russia, met with the members of the Provisional Government to give them definite word of the coming evacuation. Until then, Miller had been under the impression that a British force would be left in Archangel over the coming winter. Without it, he asserted, further resistance to the Bolsheviks would be useless. Ironside did not dare reveal to the Russians the timetable of the final offensive he planned to make in order to prepare for the withdrawal, for fear that it might leak out. Nor did he feel that he could inform them of his decision that all Allied forces were to leave Archangel by 1 October; Miller, Ironside noted in his diary, was under the impression that they would remain until November.[54]

From the perspective of the larger framework of British policy, the evacuation itself presented nothing of unusual interest once the basic decisions had been made. The final decision came on 29 July, when the Cabinet considered the proposal, made separately by Hoare, Ironside, and General Maynard, commanding the Allied garrison at the northern outpost of Murmansk,[55] that some sort of arrangement

[53] Ironside MS diary, entry for 11 July 1919.

[54] *Ibid.*, entries for 27 and 31 July 1919. Ironside (Archangel) to War Office, telegrams E. 1575/-, 1576/-, and 1587/E. 1, 28 and 30 July; W.O. 33/967, nos. 2797, 2798, and 2818. Hoare (Archangel) to Curzon, telegrams 497 and 500, 28 July; *British Documents*, vol. III, nos. 339 and 341.

[55] Murmansk has not been discussed in this chapter because it lacked the policy significance of Archangel. Although Maynard's troops had been holding an enormous amount of territory, operating along the railway all the way from Murmansk to Lake Onega—nearly 500 miles—they met with relatively little opposition. There were never any plans for a British offensive down the railway to Petrograd—unlike the operations from Archangel aimed at reaching Kolchak—and the Bolsheviks made no serious moves northward. While Maynard's troops were involved in many skirmishes and patrol encounters, their actions never had the same significance

should be negotiated with the Bolsheviks under which the Allied forces would on their part agree to depart, and the Bolsheviks would agree not to interfere with the evacuation and not to take reprisals upon the Russians who had collaborated with the Allies. Hoare proposed that, in agreement with the Bolsheviks, there should be established in Archangel an interim governmental authority which could keep order and maintain municipal services during the evacuation and the transition to Soviet control. The alternative, Hoare said, was to conduct the evacuation as a purely military operation, which might result in needless destruction and leave the local population open to Bolshevik reprisals.[56]

These suggestions aroused no enthusiasm in the Cabinet. "It would be most disastrous for any British Government to ask the Bolsheviks to grant an armistice," Churchill stated. He could not conceive that the present government could "sink so low." Moreover, he said, "an armistice would open up the whole question of our relations with the Bolsheviks throughout Russia, and surely we could not take such a step without consulting our Allies." Churchill's last contention was disputed by Lloyd George; the British government was under no obligation to consult anyone else regarding such matters, he said. But neither did the Prime Minister favor negotiations for a withdrawal. "We could not trust the Bolsheviks not to indulge in massacres," he said. The only course would be to conduct the evacuation as a military operation and to offer asylum to all the local Russians who wished it. This was agreed to by the Cabinet.

Orders went out to Ironside authorizing him to assume, from the date which he felt desirable, the position of "Military Dictator of the Archangel Region." On no account was he to negotiate a truce of arms with the Bolsheviks, "as this would have the worst possible effects on other fronts and compromise the political situation." Back in March, when he had first been informed about the Cabinet's decision to withdraw from North Russia in the autumn, Ironside had been ordered to "work on the assumption that all stores, including arms and equipment not necessary during the evacuation, will be

---

as those of Ironside's Archangel force. See Major-General Sir C. Maynard, *The Murmansk Venture*, London, 1928, pp. 193-300.

[56] Hoare (Archangel) to Curzon, telegram 497, 28 July 1919; *British Documents*, vol. III, no. 339. Ironside (Archangel) to War Office, telegram B.C. 56/E. 1, 27 July, and Maynard (Kem) to War Office, telegram M. 4179/G., 28 July; W.O. 33/967, nos. 2788 and 2795.

left for the Russian troops who will remain to defend Archangel."
Now this order was rescinded. Instead, he was to make preparations
to destroy all stores which could not be removed and which were
likely to be of any military value to the enemy. Only foodstuffs were
to be left behind.[57]

As a military operation the evacuation was complicated indeed.
Churchill hinted at its complexity before the House of Commons
on 29 July, when he said:

There is no more difficult and delicate operation than the withdrawal of
troops in the face of an enemy who must necessarily be elated . . . and
when those troops are mixed up with local troops, a very large proportion
of whom are going to remain behind and have to make some arrangement for their future life with those in whose power they will be, the operation becomes fraught with all sorts of complications and anxieties.

Accordingly, he had given the commanders on the spot absolute
freedom of action regarding their local operations:

If reinforcements are needed, reinforcements will be sent to them; if they
wish to manoeuvre in this direction or that . . . so as to secure the best and
safest possible circumstances for embarkation, they shall have the fullest
liberty to do so, and so far as I am concerned I am not prepared to give any
forecast or detail of the method or manner in which this operation, of
which we make no concealment . . . is to be carried out.[58]

Because Sir Henry Wilson did not feel that the War Office could
exercise sufficient supervision over the "simultaneous and almost
interdependent operations" of evacuating both Archangel and
Murmansk, General Sir Henry Rawlinson (created Baron Rawlinson of Trent while in North Russia) was sent out as supreme commander with some additional contingents of British troops.[59] Before
Rawlinson arrived, on 10 August, Ironside launched his final assault
against the Red Army's positions astride the Dvina River. His purpose was twofold: primarily to inflict a really decisive defeat upon

[57] War Cabinet minutes W.C. 601, 29 July 1919, 10:30 a.m.; Cab. 23/11. The
earlier orders to Ironside were in War Office telegram 75978 CIGS, 7 March; W.O.
33/966, no. 1278A. The revised orders were in telegram 80136, 31 July; W.O.
33/967, no. 2836.
[58] 118 *H.C. Deb.,* cols. 1990-91.
[59] For the reasoning behind Rawlinson's appointment, see Henry Wilson's letter
to Churchill, 26 July 1918, in Cmd. 818, Army, *The Evacuation of North Russia,*
London, 1920. With Rawlinson were sent two battalions of infantry, one of marines,
two machine gun companies, one of engineers, and five tanks (Maynard, *Murmansk,*
p. 295).

the enemy so that the British evacuation could proceed in safety, but also to help the White forces, both by bolstering their morale and by establishing firm positions from which they could—if they wished—fight on after the British had left.[60]

Ironside's attack was a complete success. His force of about 3,000 British and 1,000 Russians entirely outflanked the enemy defenses and killed, wounded, or captured over 6,000 Bolshevik troops. The British forces, which bore the brunt of the attack, lost only 145 killed and wounded. Their advance ended with the occupation of the villages of Puchega and Borok, some 20 miles from their starting point and a bit more than half the distance up the Dvina between Archangel and Kotlas. There were no other Soviet contingents on the river as far as Kotlas, so the safety of the British evacuation was assured. As the attackers withdrew, they left the river heavily mined.[61]

The events which followed were gloomy ones. Rawlinson tried to persuade General Miller to evacuate his Russian forces to Murmansk, a region both easier to defend and more easily accessible to supplies from England. Miller refused; his soldiers were, after all, defending their own homes and families, and in any case Kolchak had ordered him to stay at Archangel.[62] Relations between British and Russians during the last month were courteous, but severely strained. When Miller could not be persuaded to move to Murmansk, Rawlinson came to the conclusion—as Ironside earlier had done—that the Whites at Archangel were inevitably doomed. Therefore, he endorsed Ironside's earlier decision not to give them the war material which the British had to leave behind and thus risk its falling into Bolshevik hands.[63] While the Russians grimly watched, the British destroyed or dumped into the Dvina guns, motor lorries, and millions of rounds of ammunition. Miller sent frantic telegrams to Chaikovsky, Nabokov, and other White representatives abroad, urging them to beg the Allied governments that this destruction be stopped and the equipment handed over. Other telegrams pleaded

---

[60] Ironside, *Archangel*, p. 164. See Hoare (Archangel) to Curzon, telegram 503, 30 July 1919, setting forth the North Russian government's request that the British make a decisive attack before withdrawing: *British Documents*, vol. III, no. 346.

[61] Ironside, *Archangel*, pp. 167-68; Churchill, *Aftermath*, pp. 242-44.

[62] Ironside, *Archangel*, pp. 171-72; Maynard, *Murmansk*, pp. 296-98; Major-General Sir Frederick Maurice, *The Life of Lord Rawlinson of Trent From His Journals and Letters*, London, 1928, p. 264.

[63] *Ibid.*, p. 265 (Rawlinson's diary entry for 16 August 1919).

that the British remain for one more month and leave at the end of October instead of September. These requests were later reduced to desperate appeals for just one more week and, finally, to pleas that a few British volunteers be left behind. They were all rejected. But the Russians were given all remaining food supplies.[64]

The process of British evacuation formally began on 1 September, and thenceforth Rawlinson was in absolute control. On the 10th the British troops at Archangel left their advance positions and started the phased withdrawal into the port. On the 15th Maynard launched his final offensive at Murmansk, and a week later he started his own withdrawal.[65] Meanwhile, Churchill had announced on the 11th that the government considered it to be its duty to offer a means of escape to all Russians who had compromised themselves by help-ing the Allied forces since the beginning of the Northern interven-tion.[66] Although Ironside expected that he would get over 18,000 applications for evacuation, only 5,596 were forthcoming from Arch-angel—911 military men and 4,685 civilians—while Murmansk added only a few hundred more. Rawlinson reported that, although every facility was given to Russian civilians at Archangel, "the poorer classes did not come forward in the numbers expected," pre-ferring instead to take their chances with the Bolsheviks. More than three-quarters of those who did accept passage were removed to the Baltic states, with the remainder going to the Black Sea. A few—192 civilians—went to England.[67]

By 27 September the last British troops had left Archangel; on 12 October, exactly as planned, the evacuation of Murmansk was com-pleted.[68] Thus the British government had extricated itself from that

[64] See the telegrams between Miller in Archangel and Nabokov and Sablin (Lon-don) and Sazanov, Maklakov, and Chaikovsky (Paris), 12 August-27 September 1919, in I. Mints, compiler, "Interventsiya i severnaya kontr-revoliutsiya" (Inter-vention and Northern Counter-Revolution), *Krasnyi Arkhiv*, vols. 51-52, 1932 (nos. 1-2), pp. 100-111. For the destruction of military equipment, see Miller's tele-gram to Sazanov and Chaikovsky, 28 September, in N. Prokopenko, compiler, "K istorii interventsii na severe" (Towards the History of the Intervention in the North), *Krasnyi Arkhiv*, vol. 98, 1940 (no. 1), p. 134. See also Ironside, *Archangel*, p. 181, and Strakhovsky, *Intervention at Archangel*, p. 228.

[65] Ironside, *Archangel*, p. 172; Maynard, *Murmansk*, pp. 301-10.

[66] *The Times*, 12 September 1919.

[67] Rawlinson (Murmansk) to War Office, telegram G.C. 189, 4 October 1919; W.O. 33/975.

[68] Behind them at Archangel, however, the British left a military liaison officer who remained almost until the entry of the Red Army in February 1920. His telegrams to London may be found in W.O. 33/975 and W.O. 33/996. They also organized an intelligence service to run secret agents in and out of North Russia

area of Russia in which British men and resources were the most heavily committed. It is impossible to state how much this commitment had cost the British Empire, either in lives or in money. Churchill announced on 6 May 1919 that, to that date, 460 British Empire soldiers had lost their lives in North Russia.[69] A year later he stated that, during the period between the Armistice with Germany and the final evacuation in October 1919, the casualty figures in North Russia were 179 dead, 405 wounded and 95 missing (of whom 78 were subsequently exchanged as prisoners).[70] There is no way of telling how many of the 179 dead were included in the figure of 460 dead before 6 May and how many were killed in the heavy fighting following that date. So far as financial cost of the North Russian operations is concerned, the available figures cover only the period from the Armistice to the evacuation: the total cost for this period was officially listed as £18,219,000.[71]

On 1 December 1919, Sir Henry Wilson, in a memorandum to the Cabinet, commented that there was "one great lesson to be learned" from the history of intervention in North Russia. He continued:

It began with the landing of 150 marines at Murmansk in April, 1918. These were reinforced by 370 more at the end of May, which were in turn reinforced by 600 infantry and machine-gunners on 23rd June. From that time onwards demands for reinforcements followed each other without intermission and our commitments steadily grew without our being able to resist them, until the British contingent numbered 18,400....

I think the moral of this is easy to point. It is that once a military force is involved in operations on land it is almost impossible to limit the magnitude of its commitments.

The C.I.G.S. urged the government to bear this lesson in mind; in succeeding years, given the existing chaos of the world, it could expect to receive "continual appeals for troops, 'even a company or two,' from every part of three continents." Those troops should not

---

from Finland to provide information and to maintain contact with anti-Bolshevik elements. There are many telegrams relating to this effort in W.O. 33/975.

[69] 115 *H.C. Deb.*, col. 773.

[70] 131 *H.C. Deb.*, cols. 2131-32.

[71] From Cmd. 772, Army, *Statement of Expenditure on Naval and Military Operations in Russia, from the Date of the Armistice to the 31st of March 1920*, 1920. For this White Paper, see the Appendix to this volume.

be sent, Wilson said, without the most careful consideration of "the larger obligations" which their despatch involved.[72]

But Wilson himself, in concentrating on what he believed to be the "one great lesson" of the Northern intervention, did not in fact consider all of the "larger obligations" involved. Curzon, however, hinted at the most immediate of these obligations in a message to Chicherin on 20 February 1920. By then the Red Army had decisively defeated the White forces in the North and the Provisional Government was about to surrender. Curzon's message to Chicherin came in response to a desperate appeal from General Miller asking the British government to use its influence to prevent the Soviet government from taking reprisals against the North Russian troops and civilian population.[73] In his message Curzon stated:

You will readily understand that as His Majesty's Government were for over a year in a large measure responsible for the feeding and general well being of the population of the Northern Region it would make a peculiarly painful impression in this country if serious disorders occurred or severe reprisals were exercised by the Soviet authorities against the population which had resisted them for so many months.[74]

Curzon's appeal had been drafted by J. D. Gregory, the head of the Foreign Office Russia Department. Along with his draft telegram, Gregory sent to Curzon a minute suggesting that, since the British government was, in fact, now powerless to affect Soviet behavior in North Russia, "it would be wiser not to accompany our request with either bribes or threats." Gregory continued:

It will not of course be overlooked that this step will to a certain degree constitute an experiment in negotiation with the Soviet Government. . . . If the Soviet Government on their part really give some proof of good behaviour, we shall have indubitably made some advance from the era of savagery and intransigence which has hitherto rendered attempts at conciliation impossible.[75]

Gregory did not reckon, however, with the possibility that the

---

[72] Wilson's memorandum is printed in Cmd. 818. The fact that it was made public is revealing.

[73] Miller's message, dated 17 February 1920 and received by the Foreign Office on the 19th, is in *British Documents*, vol. III, no. 688.

[74] Curzon's message to Chicherin, transmitted through the British mission in Reval as telegram 61, 20 February 1920, is in *ibid.*, no. 695.

[75] Gregory's minute, dated 19 February 1920, is in file 180271/3669/38; F.O. 371/3994.

Soviet government's capabilities might not match its intentions. Chicherin replied to Curzon's message as soon as he had received it: he willingly agreed that the lives of those who surrendered would be spared.[76] But Moscow was a long way from Archangel, and its authority was imperfect. By the time Chicherin had sent his reply to Curzon, Miller and a few of his aides had fled Archangel on an icebreaker and the Red Army had entered the town. Simultaneously, a revolution occurred in Murmansk. For a year and a half the civil war in these two northern outposts had been frozen into latency by the fact of British occupation. Now, with the locus of power transformed, there were scores to be settled. From its beginnings, the civil war in the North was marked by extraordinary brutality on both sides; in their moment of victory the Red Army and the Bolshevik partisans within the towns showed no more mercy than had been shown them by their opponents, or than they themselves had shown in the past.[77] These were circumstances scarcely propitious for an "experiment in negotiation."

[76] Chicherin's reply, by wireless on 21 February 1920, is printed in *Dokumenty vneshnei politiki*, vol. II, pp. 384-85; a translation is in *British Documents*, vol. III, no. 696.

[77] Reports coming to the Foreign Office from various sources indicated that the bulk of the excesses in Archangel were committed, not by the Red Army, but by civilian irregulars and partisans: file –/3669/38; F.O. 371/3994.

A NOTE ON BRITISH MUTINIES
IN NORTH RUSSIA

The circumstances surrounding the mutiny or mutinies of British troops in North Russia are not clear. Ironside reported to the War Office (telegram E. 1088/E. 1, 8 March 1919; W.O. 33/966) an incident in late February in which a service battalion which had just made the overland journey from Murmansk refused to go to the front. Two sergeants, the "ringleaders," were court-martialled and sentenced to death. However, in accordance with secret orders from the King that no death sentences were to be inflicted upon British personnel after the Armistice, Ironside commuted their sentences to life imprisonment. (See Ironside, *Archangel*, pp. 112-13.)

The War Office telegrams from North Russia in the Public Records Office refer to no other such incidents. Neither do Ironside's diary nor his book. Major-General Sir C.C.M. Maynard, commanding at Murmansk, mentions no instances of mutinous behavior in his book, *The Murmansk Venture*, London, n.d. (circa 1928). In August 1919, General Lord Rawlinson came out to Archangel to assume overall command of both North Russian theaters during the evacuation. I was able to look briefly through his extensive diaries in the Library of Churchill College, Cambridge, but found no mention of mutinies. Nor are any referred to in his biography (Major-General Sir Frederick Maurice, *The Life of General Lord Rawlinson of Trent, from His Journals and Letters*, London, 1928).

However, speaking in the House of Commons on 22 December 1919, Walter Long, the First Lord of the Admiralty, indicated that a more serious mutiny had in fact taken place at one point during the North Russian operations, but he did not specify the date or place. Some ninety men, Royal Marines on duty with the Army, Long said, were found guilty of insubordination and refusal to obey orders while engaged in active operations. Long stated that of thirteen condemned to death—commuted by the General Officer Commanding-in-Chief (whether this was Ironside, Maynard, or Rawlinson is unclear, as each might have been so described) to five years in prison—twelve were to be released after one year, one after two years. Of twenty men given five years of imprisonment and fifty-one given two years' hard labor, all had their sentences reduced to six months. (123 *H.C. Deb.*, cols. 1018-19.)

No such incidents were mentioned in the press. Reports from North Russia, however, were subject to military censorship.

Finally, there is the somewhat different case of Lieutenant-Colonel John Sherwood-Kelly, who had won the Victoria Cross, the D.S.O., and the C.M.G. for bravery on the Western Front. He had volunteered for duty with the relief forces, and had been given command of a battalion. Immediately upon arriving in Archangel, he was involved in a number of small incidents involving what was later described as unsoldierly behavior in base camp. In mid-June, however, he seemingly lost his nerve and withdrew his battalion from a combined offensive operation with Russian forces. Ironside thereupon deprived him of his command and sent him back to Archangel for garrison duties. There he allegedly compromised security by including details of the forthcoming evacuation of British forces in letters home. At this second lapse Ironside initially threatened a court-martial but, on account of Sherwood-Kelly's splendid war record, relented and sent him home on the condition that he would request immediate demobilization and, as Ironside put in his diary, "quietly disappear."

Instead, soon after Sherwood-Kelly reached England, he sent a letter to the *Daily Express* (printed on 6 September 1919) in order to make known "certain facts which otherwise might never come to light." He had responded to the appeal for volunteers in April, he said, "in the sincere belief that relief was urgently needed in order to make possible the withdrawal of low category troops, in the last stages of exhaustion, due to the fierce fighting amid the rigours of an Arctic winter." Immediately upon reaching Archangel, however, he "received the impression that the policy of the authorities was not what it was stated to be." In the weeks which followed, he was "reluctantly but inevitably" driven to the following conclusion: "The troops of the Relief Forces which we were told had been sent out purely for defensive purposes, were being used for offensive purposes, on a large scale and far in the interior, in furtherance of some ambitious plan of campaign the nature of which we were not allowed to know." Sherwood-Kelly also formed the opinion that "the puppet-Government set up by us in Archangel rested on no basis of public confidence and support, and would fall to pieces the moment the protection of British bayonets was withdrawn."

From an officer with such distinguished credentials, these were indeed damaging statements. For his courage in making them, according to the *Daily Herald* (9 September 1919), Sherwood-Kelly was loudly applauded by the Trades Union Congress which was meeting in Glasgow on the day his letter appeared. Two months later, he was tried by court-martial and forced to resign from the Army (proceedings in *The Times*, 29 October 1919). Sir Basil Thomson, in his weekly reports on "Revolutionary Organisations in the United Kingdom," noted that Sherwood-Kelly's letter had "brought the question of intervention once again into prominence"; his "correspondents" reported "that in Liverpool, Newcastle, Nottingham and Glasgow the outburst of resentment has been remarkable." (Reports nos. 20 and 21, 11 and 18 September, Cabinet papers G.T. 8144 and 8192; Cab. 24/87.)

Ironside, meanwhile and subsequently, remained silent. Only from his diary, and not from his book (where he described the incident at the front without mentioning Sherwood-Kelly's name: *Archangel*, pp. 152-53), can one discover that Sherwood-Kelly, in writing to the *Express*, may have acted from motives that were other than personally disinterested. (Ironside MS diary, entries for 22 and 23 June, 28 July, and 12 and 23 August 1919; also Rawlinson [Archangel] to War Office, telegram G.C. 155, 18 September 1919; W.O. 33/975, no. 3523.) Sherwood-Kelly's letter to the *Daily Express*, together with his message to the Trades Union Congress, may also be found in W. P. Coates and Zelda K. Coates, *Armed Intervention in Russia, 1918-1922*, London, 1935, pp. 169-72.

CHAPTER VI

THE END OF INTERVENTION:
THE FAILURE OF
KOLCHAK AND DENIKIN

Mundir angliiskii,
Sapog yaponskii,
Shtik frantsuzskii,
Pravitel omskii . . . .

(Uniforms from England,
Boots from Japan,
Bayonets from France,
Dictator from Omsk . . . .)

—a Siberian song from the
time of intervention

In the total context of the Russian Civil War, the military operations in North Russia were of minor importance—a "sideshow," as even the fiercest peripheral encounters of two world wars came to be called. The troops from both sides who fought in the swamps and snows of North Russia numbered no more than a few tens of thousands. They contested for the control of territory which, although vast, was sparsely settled and difficult to traverse. By contrast, the battles in the South and in Siberia involved armies numbering in the hundreds of thousands, based upon regions rich both in population and resources. These were the decisive theaters. From them would come the blows which threatened Soviet power in Moscow. The only way in which such a threat might ever have come from North Russia would have been by means of a vast increase in the number of troops coming there from abroad. Since massive reinforcements were never even a remote possibility, North Russia remained a sideshow, important for our account because it was the only theater in which sizable numbers of British soldiers entered into combat

Winston Churchill and David Lloyd
George at Paris during the Peace Conference. PRINCETON UNIVERSITY LIBRARY

Wilson, Clemenceau, Balfour, and Sonnino during the Peace Conference. RADIO TIMES HULTON PICTURE LIBRARY

General V. V. Marushevsky, commander of Russian forces, and Major-General Edmund Ironside, Allied commander, inspect newly formed Russian civilian guards at Archangel, April 1919. NATIONAL ARCHIVES

An Allied blockhouse in North Russia, winter 1918-19. NATIONAL
ARCHIVES

An R.A.F. Sopwith "Camel" preparing for takeoff in North Russia,
March 1919. NATIONAL ARCHIVES

General Lord Rawlinson (second from left), who came out to North
Russia to assume overall command during the evacuation, September
1919, and General Ironside (in dark greatcoat) interrogate a Bolshevik
prisoner. IMPERIAL WAR MUSEUM

A 3.7 inch mountain howitzer and gun crew in North Russia, summer 1919. IMPERIAL WAR MUSEUM

A British Lewis gun post guarding a railway bridge during the evacuation of North Russia, September 1919. IMPERIAL WAR MUSEUM

General Ironside and British and Russian officers review troops at Archangel, spring 1919. Note the wooden road surfaces which were universally employed in North Russia as a means of combating freezing conditions. IMPERIAL WAR MUSEUM

Priests at Ekaterinburg blessing the standards of a Russian regiment
bound for the front, November 1918. NATIONAL ARCHIVES

A Czech armored train in Siberia. NATIONAL ARCHIVES

Naval guns mounted on an armored train, Vladivostok. NATIONAL
ARCHIVES

A British armored train, North Russia. NATIONAL ARCHIVES

Bolshevik prisoners, Siberia. NATIONAL ARCHIVES

General Rudolf Gaida, the Czech leader of an abortive movement to overthrow Admiral Kolchak. NATIONAL ARCHIVES

Bayonet drill at the training school run by the British military mission on an island in the bay off Vladivostok. NATIONAL ARCHIVES

Sir Charles Eliot, British High Commissioner for Siberia, at his desk, Vladivostok. NATIONAL ARCHIVES

A battalion of the Hampshire Regiment marches through Vladivostok
before entraining for Omsk, November 1918. NATIONAL ARCHIVES

with the Bolsheviks, but never a zone from which would come the answer to the overriding political question: Who would rule Russia —the Bolsheviks or their enemies?

In late May 1919, when the Supreme Council in Paris sent Admiral Kolchak its note implying a willingness to recognize soon his claim to be "Supreme Ruler of All Russia"[1] and promising him continued Allied assistance, the answer to this question seemed clear. Kolchak's forces had crossed the Urals and penetrated deep into European Russia. At the same time, in the South, Denikin's Volunteer Army was pressing towards Odessa, Kharkov, and Tsaritsyn (later called Stalingrad, now Volgograd). Scarcely had the Supreme Council's note reached Kolchak, however, when his advance was not only stopped but turned around. Within a fortnight Ufa had fallen, within another Perm. On 14 July the Red Army took Ekaterinburg, on the 27th Chelyabinsk. By the first week in August, Kolchak's forces had been driven back another 200 miles to a point east of the Tobol River more than half of the distance from the Urals to Omsk.[2] In the face of these defeats Kolchak impulsively dismissed the Czech general, Gajda, perhaps his most able field commander, for "excessive ambition"—but also for having views too sympathetic to the Socialist-Revolutionaries and other left-wing but anti-Bolshevik groups.

To British observers in Siberia, both military and diplomatic, this action was a symptom of the dominance over Kolchak of the corrupt and reactionary officers who formed the "Stavka," his staff. Gajda, they thought, was the only leader who could inspire any feelings of loyalty from the Siberian peasants who comprised the bulk of Kolchak's armies.[3] Nearly all of the other officers, in the words

---

[1] The following exchange between Curzon and Walford Selby, of the Foreign Office, is revealing. On 18 June 1919, Selby minuted on a draft of an outgoing telegram: "The Allied Governments have not 'recognised' Admiral Koltchak's Government. They have only agreed to continue their support on certain conditions which he has accepted." Curzon then scrawled: "Very well. But if we have not recognised him I don't know what it all means. Everyone knows that it is recognition." (File 89561/91/38; F.O. 371/3959.)

[2] For these events: Blair (Ekaterinburg) to Knox (Omsk), telegram 253, 30 June 1919; Britmis [i.e., British Mission] (Vladivostok) to War Office, telegram 4277, 24 July; Knox (Vladivostok) to War Office, telegram 4455, 3 August: W.O. 33/967, nos. 2499, 2755, and 2882.

[3] For Gajda's dismissal and British reactions to it: Blair (Ekaterinburg) to Knox (Vladivostok), telegram 215, 23 June 1919, and Steveni (Omsk) to Britmis (Vladivostok), telegram 174, 29 June, W.O. 33/967, nos. 2436 and 2523; Eliot (Omsk) to Curzon, unnumbered, undated telegram through Jordan (Peking), 14 July,

of a report from Omsk, were "hangers on of Cossack officer type who believe men provided they are beaten and flogged enough will fight for present Government."[4] A constant theme running through reports to the War Office by General Knox and other officers—who themselves had enthusiastically greeted Kolchak's accession to power the previous November and who still respected the Admiral himself, although not his entourage—was that the White officers had (in Knox's words) "learned nothing from the war and less from the revolution."[5] Sir Charles Eliot, the High Commissioner, telegraphed on 29 July that even Kolchak showed "no sign of understanding" that his task was to provide an administration which people would find preferable to Bolshevism.[6]

Kolchak's British material did him little good. Valuable equipment was often issued to units hundreds of miles behind the lines while troops at the front went without it. Sometimes it simply lay unused in storage depots. One member of the British mission later wrote that the Bolsheviks captured enough British uniforms at Perm to clothe a division. "More frequently," he wrote, "the uniforms walked over to the Reds, thousands at a time, with the Whites inside them." Supplies issued at Omsk in the morning sometimes were on sale in the town bazaar before evening. By the end of 1919, a quarter of the Soviet troops fighting in Siberia wore British uniforms.[7] In mid-July, Knox telegraphed that the "few measures of ordinary common sense" he had persuaded Kolchak to adopt had come about only by virtue of the leverage the British mission had as the source of the Admiral's supplies; for this reason, despite the wastage, he felt the flow was worth continuing. But by the end of the month Knox had changed his mind. "It would be like pouring money into a sieve to give further equipment without adequate con-

---

file 611/2/1/15939, F.O. 608/205; Eliot (Omsk) to Curzon, telegram 12, 29 July, *British Documents*, vol. III, no. 343; Eliot (Omsk) to Curzon, despatch 25, 17 July, file 142512/11/57, F.O. 371/4097. The last item encloses what is purportedly a stenographic transcript of the final interview between Gajda and Kolchak on 7 July in Kolchak's railway wagon; it reached Eliot through Gajda's representatives. See also Fleming, *Kolchak*, pp. 158-59.

[4] Quoted in O'Reilly (Vladivostok) to Curzon, telegram 727, 16 August 1919; *British Documents*, vol. III, no. 382.

[5] Knox (Vladivostok) to War Office, telegram 4069, 14 July 1919; W.O. 33/967, no. 2644.

[6] Eliot's telegram 12, cited above, n. 3.

[7] Captain Francis McCullagh, *A Prisoner of the Reds: The Story of a British Officer Captured in Siberia*, London, 1921, pp. 67-69.

trol," he telegraphed. The support of anti-Bolshevism in Siberia, Knox stated, should be left to the United States and Japan which, unlike Great Britain, had economic interests in the region.[8]

The same conclusion had already been reached in London. When Curzon learned of the fall of Chelyabinsk he scrawled in blue pencil across the message: "A lost cause."[9] On 24 July, Churchill circulated to the Cabinet a General Staff paper urging that the two British battalions then in Siberia be brought home as soon as shipping conditions would allow, that General Knox's military mission be reduced to a minimum size, and that all British efforts be concentrated on aiding Denikin, whose forces continued to press forward as Kolchak's fell back. These recommendations received the Cabinet's approval.[10] To Knox the War Office telegraphed:

We can only make an adequate effort in one theatre and under these circumstances it would be an act of the greatest folly to dissipate our resources between two theatres. The choice is between Siberia and South Russia and there can be no question on which it falls.

Knox had already pointed out that shipping times to the Far East were so long that no supplies still to be shipped could arrive in time to affect the outcome of Kolchak's autumn campaigns. Now he was told to use his own judgment concerning when he should inform Kolchak of the decision to concentrate on Denikin; in the view of the War Office, however, "it would not seem wise to do so under present circumstances."[11]

The government's decision met with the full approval of Sir Charles Eliot, who, like Knox, felt that Siberia should be left to the United States and Japan which were so much closer. But Eliot telegraphed Curzon asking what would become of the office of British High Commissioner. His own feeling, he said, was that the recent decision should not be interpreted as an abandonment of Kolchak, but simply as an indication that, given the limited amount of material assistance which Britain could supply to the anti-Bolshevik move-

[8] Knox's telegram 4069, 14 July 1919, cited above, n. 5, and Knox (Omsk) to War Office (as telegram 9005 from Vladivostok), 1 August; W.O. 33/967, no. 2899.

[9] Curzon's minute, 1 August 1919, is in file 110398/11/57; F.O. 371/4096.

[10] General Staff, "The Military Situation in Russia. July, 1919," Cabinet paper G.T. 7785; Cab. 24/84. War Cabinet minutes W.C. 599 and 601, 25 July 1919, 11:30 a.m., and 29 July, 10:30 a.m.; Cab. 23/11.

[11] War Office to Britmis (Vladivostok) for Knox, telegram 80251, 5 August 1919; W.O. 33/967, no. 2926. Knox remarked on shipping times in telegram 4069, cited above, n. 5.

ment—of which Kolchak was, after all, still the acknowledged head —the government thought it better to concentrate it all on Denikin. Eliot added that he had learned that the French also intended to cease sending supplies to Kolchak.[12]

Curzon's reply, on 20 August, stated that Eliot's interpretation of the British government's views was correct and that there should be no changes in the office and functions of High Commissioner.[13] Curzon referred, undoubtedly, to the High Commissioner's formal role, which was simply to represent the British government in all political questions: no matter how great the reductions in British material assistance, there was no reason why Eliot, or his successors, could not continue to exercise this formal role. But they were to discover that, without the inducement of British aid, their representations and advice—punctuated as they were by the withdrawal on 8 September and 1 November of the two British battalions— would fall on even less attentive ears.

Not surprisingly, the sharp reversal in Kolchak's fortunes during the early summer of 1919 produced pressures within the British government for a reexamination of policy. They were largely resisted, however. The principal dissidents, who expressed themselves at a series of Cabinet meetings in late July and early August,[14] were H.A.L. Fisher, the Liberal former academic, now President of the Board of Education; George Barnes, who had broken with the Labour Party he had once led over his support of the Coalition in the election of the previous December (he was then a member of the War Cabinet) and who now served as Minister without Portfolio; Christopher Addison, the Minister of Health; and Austen Chamberlain, the Chancellor of the Exchequer.

Fisher, Barnes, and Addison all argued variations on the same theme: the Soviet regime had apparently moderated its behavior and was attracting a certain amount of popular support within Russia— support which grew greater to the degree that the Bolsheviks could represent themselves as leading a national movement against foreign

---

[12] Eliot (Omsk) to Curzon, telegram 24, 14 August 1919; *British Documents,* vol. III, no. 369.

[13] Curzon to Eliot (Omsk), telegram 522, 20 August 1919; *ibid.,* no. 375.

[14] Aside from the meetings of 25 and 29 July 1919, cited above, n. 10, these were on 1 August, 11:30 a.m., and 12 August, 11:30 a.m. (War Cabinet minutes 605 and 612; Cab. 23/11).

invaders; Kolchak, by contrast, was a reactionary, dependent upon Allied assistance for his very existence; and the British people, in turn, were growing increasingly antagonistic toward their own government whose policies in Russia they failed to understand. Barnes put it most strongly: he did not, he said, "see how the Government could pursue any policy which the people of the United Kingdom thought was directed against a people's representative Government."[15]

The reply came from Lloyd George. It was a mistake, he said, to treat the present military operations in Russia as a campaign against Bolshevism. If the Allies had decided to "defeat Bolshevism," great armies would have been required, in contrast to the small forces that were sent. Although "one member of the Cabinet" consistently urged this policy, he himself had "always protested against it," and the Cabinet had accepted the view that it was "not our business to interfere in the internal affairs of Russia." If Russia preferred a Tsarist government, or any other sort of government, including a Bolshevik government, that was her business. Personally, he did "not admire any of the Russian Governments." Massacres of the Jews under the Tsars had been as terrible as any of the deeds of the Bolsheviks. Therefore, Lloyd George said, he objected to the British government's present involvement being considered a campaign against Bolshevism. It had begun as part of the war against Germany, and had been continued because of the supposition that the Russian people would rise to aid Kolchak and Denikin against Bolshevik tyranny. In the case of Kolchak, the supposition was apparently incorrect, and therefore Great Britain should cease to support him. But Denikin's situation was different; the "people" seemed to be with him, and British support should continue. There was no need to send troops, however. Enough trained Russian manpower existed. Nor could the British government go on supporting Denikin indefinitely; it was "entitled to give him his chance," but it could not "help to maintain civil war in Russia for ever." "If Denikin really had the people behind him," the Prime Minister asserted, "the Bolsheviks could never overcome him."[16]

This argument, portraying the British role in Russia as half participant, half spectator, was scarcely new for Lloyd George. He had used it since the previous autumn to silence both those who wanted more

[15] Meeting of 25 July. [16] Meeting of 29 July.

intervention and those who wanted less, and on this occasion, although in fact it avoided rather than answered their objections, it was enough to silence critics like Barnes, Fisher, and Addison. Barnes even stated, as Lloyd George obviously wished him to, that he would agree to British support going thenceforth *only* to Denikin.

Austen Chamberlain's objections were of a different sort. As Chancellor of the Exchequer he did not feel that intervention was producing results in any way commensurate with its costs. Churchill, the head of the department which was spending the money, replied. The achievements of intervention already had been enormous, he said, and they were particularly extraordinary considering the small size of the forces employed. Yet he could only cite one specific achievement, and even it was disputable, although no one chose to dispute it: "If we had not intervened in Russia the little States in which the League of Nations took so much interest would have been overpowered by now, and we should certainly have been forced to support the cordon sanitaire"—the implication, presumably, being that whatever Churchill meant by *cordon sanitaire* would have cost the British Treasury more. Instead, it turned out that Churchill still had his mind on future achievements. Denikin was confident of success, he said, and Kolchak might yet be able to retrieve his position.[17] He put the thought more picturesquely in a note to Curzon:

> The Kolchak and Denikin operations, taken as a whole, are still approaching their climax. . . . I do not believe the Siberian army is finished. At any rate it is drawing 120,000 Bolsheviks (1/4 of their whole force) into a very unsound strategic situation. The Siberian forces can retreat to Omsk, or if necessary to Irkutsk, & if at any time their pursuers cease to totter after them, they will be able to totter back in their turn. It is more than likely that both America and Japan will make exertions to save the situation in this part of the world. Meanwhile Denikin's successes continue.[18]

During the winter and spring of 1919, Churchill had said very little about the actual costs of the British involvement in Russia. The minutes of the Cabinet record nothing more than passing, imprecise references to costs. Indeed, Churchill was pressed regarding them, not by the Cabinet, but by the House of Commons, where he met repeated requests for figures. Each time, however, he responded that

[17] Meeting of 29 July.
[18] Churchill to Curzon, 14 August 1919; Curzon MSS, box 65.

the task of gathering figures would demand too great an effort from his already hard-pressed department. But he also sought, in a general way, to minimize the importance of the costs. Thus, on 6 June, he told the House that the bulk of the munitions being sent to Russia were surplus stocks—so-called non-marketable stores—left over from the War. "They are on our hands," he said. "What are we to do with them?" When Sir Donald Maclean, the leader of the Opposition Liberals, interjected, "Can we not have the figure?," Churchill replied: "If you take as a basis what these munitions cost to make, no doubt the figure would be a considerable one. More than £20,000,000 of munitions on that basis have been sent."[19] On 29 July he admitted that this sum might well be £30 million, but he observed that, had the War Office instead chosen to preserve and store these munitions for some future war, the costs would have been great.[20]

Only a fortnight later—and probably to the surprise of many members, given Churchill's previous reticence—the War Office published a White Paper itemizing British expenditure on Russian operations from the Armistice to 31 July.[21] In his statements in the House, Churchill had given the impression that the bulk of the costs had been in the category of "non-marketable stores" (listed, apparently, at purchase price, and so-called because no buyer could readily be found), but the White Paper revealed that the total for cash outlay and marketable stores, £35.9 million, was some £2.5 million higher. The most striking figure was the sum of £19.2 million worth of non-marketable stores which *already* had been sent to Denikin, more than three times as much as to any other sector of operations. Under the category of cash and marketable stores, aid to Kolchak, at £8.3 million, was £1.5 million higher than aid to Denikin. As for military operations by the British armed services, by far the highest item was £12.1 million for North Russia, while the Royal Navy's operations in the Black and Baltic Seas had cost some £5.2 million. Summed up, the total cost of intervention since the Armistice, including both marketable and non-marketable stores, was listed as £69,285,000.

The publication of the White Paper coincided with a proposal in the Cabinet by Churchill, primarily in response to Chamberlain's entreaties, that a "final packet" of non-marketable munitions and

---

[19] 116 *H.C. Deb.*, col. 2467.   [20] 118 *H.C. Deb.*, col. 1992.
[21] Cmd. 307, Army, *Expenditures on Military and Naval Operations in Russia from the Date of the Armistice to July 31, 1919*, published 14 August 1919. See the appendix to this volume.

about four or five million pounds worth of marketable supplies be sent to Denikin along with a message stating that Great Britain could do no more for him. Churchill hoped that these supplies would be sufficient to see Denikin through a victorious campaign. "If, on the other hand, an equipoise was maintained between the conflicting forces," Churchill told the Cabinet, then Great Britain "should try and get Lenin's Government and the anti-Bolshevists to come to terms"—a startling proposal for Churchill, but one which aroused no comment. The principle of a "final packet" was accepted; Churchill was told to prepare a precise estimate of its size.[22] Early in October the Cabinet approved his resulting memorandum. Marketable stores in the final contribution were not to exceed £3 million.[23]

Figures like these are abstract and largely meaningless. The magnitude of British assistance to Denikin is better grasped from a listing of the more important supplies furnished. According to the final report to the War Office by Major-General H. C. Holman, who commanded the British military mission in South Russia, these supplies during the period between March 1919 and 27 March 1920, when Denikin's forces were driven from the mainland to a refuge in the Crimea, included more than 1,200 guns and nearly 2 million shells, 6,100 machine guns, 200,000 rifles, 500 million rounds of small-arms ammunition, more than half a million complete uniforms, 629 trucks and ambulances, 279 motorcycles, 74 tanks, 6 armored cars, 100 aircraft, 12 500-bed general hospitals, 25 field hospitals, and large amounts of communications and engineering equipment.[24] Nearly all came from the vast dumps which had grown up during the War at Salonika, Alexandria, and other ports on the Mediterranean. With the exception of the aircraft, little was shipped from Great Britain, and the aircraft themselves were in ready supply.[25] A large proportion of this material, therefore, undoubtedly fell under Churchill's category of "non-marketable stores."

[22] War Cabinet minutes W.C. 612, 12 August 1919, cited above, n. 14.

[23] War Cabinet minutes W.C. 628, 7 October 1919, 4 p.m.; Cab. 23/12. Churchill's memorandum, "Final Contribution to General Denikin," Cabinet paper G.T. 8224, 25 September, requested £11 million in "surplus non-marketable" stores, £2.25 million in "surplus marketable" stores, £200,000 in non-surplus stores, and £550,000 for transportation; Cab. 24/89.

[24] "Major-General Sir H. C. Holman's Final Report of the British Military Mission, South Russia" (undated, but prepared in April 1920), para. 200, file N 3724/3724/38; F.O. 371/5448.

[25] In a memorandum of 21 February 1919, Churchill referred to "an enormous

Between the arrival of this equipment at Novorossiisk (Denikin's principal port) and its appearance at the front, however, stood all of the disorganization and chaos of South Russia. Initially, British supplies were furnished under an arrangement whereby they were turned over to the Russians as soon as they were landed. This effectively deprived the British military mission of any means of ensuring that the vast stocks of supplies were efficiently allocated and utilized. Moreover, it allowed Denikin to use British supplies as a factor in the politics of South Russia, holding them back from forces such as the Don Cossacks, with whose separatist political aims he did not sympathize. As a result, valuable equipment piled up in rear depots, while British officers at the front were powerless to requisition it for the units to which they were attached. Theft, waste, spoilage, and nonmaintenance were common. Not infrequently, equipment simply rotted on the quays. Poorly guarded ammunition dumps were blown up by saboteurs. One British observer reported that nearly every petty official and bureaucrat in South Russia wore a British uniform, while at the front, although the supply of uniforms far exceeded the number of Denikin's troops, only twenty-five percent of the troops wore them. Officers often drew a double issue of clothing and sold the surplus at lucrative prices. Among the British hospital supplies were 1,500 nurses' uniforms; this same observer never saw one on a Russian nurse, but he saw "girls who were emphatically not nurses, walking the streets of Novorossisk wearing regulation British hospital skirts and stockings." Hospital beds and bedding were appropriated by officers and officials for their own homes. During the battle in which the Red Army captured Kharkov in November 1919, British anti-freeze fluid was sold across the bar of the Hotel Métropole while lorries and tanks froze for lack of it.[26] These practices drove the British military mission nearly to despair. General Holman continually pleaded with Denikin to put an end to them, but with little result. On 3 September, after a tour of the

---

surplus [of aircraft] in this country," and stated that he was shipping 100 of them to Denikin; Cabinet paper G.T. 6867; Cab. 24/75.

[26] John Ernest Hodgson, *With Denikin's Armies. Being a Description of the Cossack Counter-Revolution in South Russia, 1918-1920*, London, 1934, pp. 180-87. Hodgson, a journalist, wrote his book in 1922 but withheld it from publication until he felt that emotions surrounding the civil war and intervention had abated. He was extremely partial to the White cause and had no sympathies with Bolshevism.

front, Holman called on Denikin and left a blunt *aide mémoire* stating:

At a time when between 150,000 and 200,000 complete sets of clothing and equipment had been issued to your supply service and armies, I found not a single Russian soldier with a complete set of British equipment; soldiers barefooted and in rags, fighting on cold nights without greatcoat, blanket, or waterproof sheets, and on hot days without a water-bottle; sick and wounded lying on the ground in their filthy rags without the first necessities of treatment, while a rich store of British medical equipment lay at the base [at Novorossiisk]; British guns without buffer or lubricating oil, or the necessary tools or spare parts, all of which had been delivered at the base. . . . I do not wish to weary you with the details of all I have seen, but I should be guilty of the gravest dereliction of duty if I failed to state clearly that this state of affairs, if continued, can only lead to disaster. Against all this is the proof positive of what can be done by the proper use of the material which His Majesty's Government is so glad to put at your disposal.[27]

Eventually, Holman was able to get from Denikin an army order which left British material in the hands of the British mission until it had arrived at the fighting unit for which it was intended.[28] But this measure came too late. In his final report to the War Office, Holman bitterly commented: "the incompetence and corruption of the administrative services and departments could not be overcome by any scheme."[29]

That Holman's appeals found little response is not surprising. Denikin had few pressing reasons, during the summer and early autumn of 1919, to institute discomfiting reforms. Holman's warning on 3 September of impending disaster came at a time of flooding success. Indeed, the British decision to cease supporting Kolchak and to concentrate all available resources on Denikin can only be understood against the background of Denikin's amazing progress. His advance began in late May—exactly when Kolchak's was finally checked. On 25 June the western corps of the Volunteer Army took Kharkov; a week later, on the eastern flank, after terribly bitter fighting, Tsaritsyn fell to General Baron P. N. Wrangel's forces; between the two the Don Cossacks advanced steadily towards

[27] From Holman's interim report, I.F. 2182, 8 October 1919, section 16, Cabinet paper C.P. 219; Cab. 24/94.
[28] *Idem.*
[29] From Holman's final report (cited above, n. 24), para. 108.

Tambov; behind them, by the end of June, the Volunteer Corps of the Crimea finally succeeded in occupying the entire peninsula.[30]

At Tsaritsyn, on 3 July, Denikin met with his commanders to plan the march on Moscow. Against the judgment of Wrangel and others, he ordered a three-pronged attack on a vast front nearly 1,000 miles wide. The Red Army was caught off-guard, and Denikin's plan met with spectacular success. By mid-September, Kiev, Kursk, and Voronezh had all fallen to the steady advance of the Volunteers. On 13 October, a week after the British Cabinet had agreed on its "final packet" of assistance for Denikin, his forces took Orel, 250 miles south of Moscow.[31]

In this offensive a British tank battalion and two squadrons of the Royal Air Force played important roles. Attached to Holman's military mission, their assignment from London was to serve only as instructors. But it took time to train tank crews, even more time to train airmen, and the need of the White forces for air and armored support was urgent. British tank instructors soon took to leading their pupils into combat on the pretense of giving them battle instruction. Holman reported to the War Office that the rolling grass plains of South Russia were ideal for tank operations, which were successful "beyond all expectations" against the Bolsheviks, who had no such weapons.[32] The R.A.F. officers at first adopted the same practice, but soon they dropped even this pretense and the two squadrons functioned directly as autonomous fighting units. Holman reported that their skillful low flying was especially effective in disrupting Soviet cavalry formations. They also repeatedly attacked the river craft of the Bolshevik Volga flotilla, inflicting heavy losses.[33] One target was denied them: Moscow. The War Office telegraphed Holman in late September that at least for the present the bombing

---

[30] Denikin, *Ocherki russkoi smuty*, vol. V, pp. 104-16.

[31] *Ibid.*, pp. 120-23, 230-32. For a good discussion of Denikin's strategy, see George A. Brinkley, *The Volunteer Army and Allied Intervention in South Russia, 1917-1921: A Study in the Politics and Diplomacy of the Russian Civil War*, Notre Dame, Indiana, 1966, pp. 185-94.

[32] Holman (with Denikin's field headquarters, place unspecified) to War Office, telegram Q. 823, 11 June 1919; W.O. 33/967, no. 2334. Also Denmiss [*i.e.*, Denikin Mission] (Taganrog) to War Office, telegram 1981, 25 September; *ibid.*, no. 3620.

[33] From Holman's final report (cited above, n. 24) para. 52. Hodgson, *With Denikin's Armies*, pp. 141-44, discusses British air and tank operations. For a vivid firsthand account by an R.A.F. officer who flew in South Russia, see Captain Marion Aten and Arthur Orrmont, *Last Train Over Rostov Bridge*, New York, 1961, *passim*.

of the capital was not to be allowed, as there was "no military value in this operation."[34]

❖

The nearer Denikin came to Moscow during the course of his six months' offensive, the more acute became two sets of problems which had always been implicit, if not immediate, in the relationship between the Allied governments and the anti-Bolshevik movement. These concerned the nature of the political order to be instituted by the government which the Whites would install once the Soviet regime had fallen, and the policies this government would pursue regarding the border nationalities which had taken advantage of the dissolution of the Tsarist Empire to declare their complete independence. Because of Britain's leading role among the Powers involved in intervention against the Bolsheviks, these problems were felt more acutely in London than in any other capital.

Within the Cabinet and the Foreign Office there had been anxieties from the very outset of intervention that British support of the anti-Bolshevik movement would result only in the restoration of the oppressive, discredited monarchical regime which for so many generations had been considered as the antithesis to the Englishman's conception of liberty. For this reason the British government, and indeed the Supreme Council as a whole, had been reluctant to grant full recognition to Kolchak; recognition, it was thought, should be held in reserve as a lever with which to move the White Russian leadership in democratic directions. These anxieties were not much eased by Kolchak's reply to the Supreme Council's note of 27 May, despite its liberal tone: it was known only too well that General Knox, on Churchill's instructions, had coached Kolchak in the expression of properly liberal sentiments.[35] Thus, on 18 June, Walford Selby, the deputy head of the Foreign Office's Russia Department, wrote in a minute to Curzon that a friend of his, an officer just returned from service with the military mission at Omsk, had told him that Kolchak and his entourage seemed to think that the British government had an absolutely free hand to support the anti-Bolshevik cause, and that Knox did not sufficiently impress upon the Admiral the importance of public opinion in the United Kingdom.

[34] War Office to Denmiss (Taganrog), telegram 81290, 19 September 1919; W.O. 33/967, no. 3551.
[35] See Sir Charles Eliot's annoyed private letter to Curzon, 30 May 1919; Curzon MSS, box 65.

With Denikin, Selby observed, the situation was even worse: he was personally more reactionary than Kolchak, and his proclamations were "frequently such as to create grave difficulties" for the British government from its domestic critics. "I think it is of the utmost importance," Selby wrote, "that the Russian groups whom we are supporting should fully realise the trend of opinion in this country and the issues which are involved."[36]

Along with this minute Selby enclosed a draft of a telegram which, after minor modifications by Curzon, was despatched on 21 June to Sir Charles Eliot. "There is a considerable section of opinion in this country," the message stated, which is intensely suspicious of British support of Kolchak "on the ground that the Allies are supporting the extreme reactionary elements in Russia who stand for no smaller programme than the restoration of Russia on the basis of 1914." Eliot should make Kolchak appreciate fully that every act which tended to confirm that view was used within the United Kingdom as an argument against the government's policy. "While we are satisfied that [Kolchak] himself stands for principles which accord with the traditional policy of this country," the telegram continued —conceding a point which was by no means clear—"and that we are accordingly justified in supporting him in spite of the criticism which is directed against us, it is desirable that he should lose no opportunity of impressing upon his entourage the momentous issues involved in the positions which they may assume, and should warn them that the continued assistance of Great Britain . . . is involved. It would be impossible for any Government in this country to continue for long a policy which had not public opinion behind it."[37]

Telegrams of this sort went to Siberia, and not to South Russia, because of Kolchak's position as the acknowledged head of the anti-Bolshevik movement. Denikin, by contrast, saw himself as simply a military figure, a general fighting a war. To Kolchak he would leave all decisions regarding the future government of Russia. During nearly the entire period of Denikin's advance and retreat, no British political officer was attached to him. Although the Cabinet decided on 29 July that such an officer should be sent to South Russia, the matter was considered so lacking in urgency that the man selected, the noted geographer and Unionist M.P., Halford J. Mac-

[36] Selby's minute is in file 89561/91/38; F.O. 371/3959.
[37] Curzon to Eliot (Omsk), telegram 430, 21 June 1919; *British Documents*, vol. III, no. 271.

kinder, was not offered the position until 23 October, and he did not arrive at Denikin's headquarters to assume his duties as British High Commissioner until 10 January 1920. By that time there was little he could do besides arrange for the evacuation of the Volunteer Army to the Crimea.[38]

Although Denikin did not acquire Kolchak's political preeminence, the circumstance of his advance at a time when Kolchak was retreating made the behavior of the troops under his command necessarily a matter of greater concern for the British government than the conduct of those under Kolchak. One aspect in particular aroused anxiety: the pogroms which often accompanied the capture of a town from the Bolsheviks. These campaigns against the Jews had been one of the most reprehensible features of the Tsarist regime, particularly in the Ukraine. During the civil war, partly because the Jews came to be identified with Bolshevism, but also because of the general increase of violence and lawlessness, many Jews were wantonly robbed and killed. When Denikin's forces entered the Ukraine in September 1919, these outrages took place to a hitherto unprecedented degree. They were extremely distressing to Western opinion, and they certainly did the White cause considerable harm.[39]

Although there was a certain reluctance among some of the senior officials of the Foreign Office to become involved in questions as complex and as laden with emotion as the pogroms, their attitude was not shared by Churchill, who sent a stream of telegrams to the British military mission with Denikin, and to Denikin himself, urging that every measure be taken to prevent the outbreak of further excesses.[40] Denikin claims in his memoirs that he did not approve

[38] The lengthy correspondence between Curzon and Mackinder concerning the latter's appointment, together with other materials relating to Mackinder's commission, are gathered together as F.O. 800/251, "Private Papers of Sir H. J. Mackinder relating to his Mission to South Russia." The Cabinet meeting of 29 July is cited above, n. 10.

[39] See William Henry Chamberlin, *The Russian Revolution, 1917-1921*, New York, 1935, vol. II, pp. 226-31. Chamberlin's account is based upon a wide range of authoritative material, as is the discussion in Walter Z. Laqueur, *Russia and Germany*, London, 1965, pp. 87-88.

[40] See Churchill's quotations from his telegrams to Denikin in his *Aftermath*, p. 255, and the War Office's telegrams 81138, 81273, and 81903 to the British mission with Denikin, 11 and 18 September and 25 October 1919; W.O. 33/975, nos. 3461, 3538, and 4023. Also the War Office telegrams 78694 and 78695 to Generals Gough (Helsingfors) and Knox (Vladivostok), 6 June 1919, asking them "tactfully, but strongly" to warn Yudenich and Kolchak (respectively) against ex-

of the pogroms—they had demoralizing effects upon his troops[41]—but there was little he could do to prevent them. The officers through whom he had to enforce his wishes were often pronounced anti-Semites themselves; they could scarcely have been expected to take firm measures against their men. Similarly, both officers and men often turned a blind eye to acts committed by the inhabitants of the towns they occupied. The pogroms continued.

If the British government could do nothing to prevent the pogroms, it could and did intervene to forestall the outbreak of war between the Volunteer Army and the republic of Georgia. The actual dispute between the Georgians and Denikin was over the control of the districts of Tuapse, Sochi, and Sukhumi, lying on the Black Sea coast between Novorossiisk and Batum; each side claimed that the inhabitants of these districts looked to it for protection against the other.[42] But the real issue at stake was the independence of the states of the Caucasus as opposed to Denikin's goal of a united Great Russia occupying as much as possible of the territory of the former Tsarist Empire. Denikin's attitude was accurately described by a British intelligence officer who visited him at his headquarters in September 1919, when the Volunteer Army was in the midst of its march towards Moscow:

> As regards the Caucasus, there appears to be only one point of view, namely, that they were an integral part of Russia; for the present they could stay as they were but as soon as the time came, they had got to come back to Russia, peaceably if possible, but if not, force would be used. The "time" appeared to be merely when General Denikin had sufficient troops available to deal with them should they prove obstinate.[43]

---

cesses that "will alienate sympathies of British nation and render continuance of support most difficult"; W.O. 33/966, nos. 2120 and 2121.

Foreign Office attitudes are reflected in two minutes by Sir Eyre Crowe, Assistant Under-Secretary of State. The first, on 1 August 1919, commented on a memorandum on Ukrainian pogroms from Chaim Weizmann, the Zionist leader: "It is to be remembered that what may appear to Mr. Weizmann to be outrages against Jews, may in the eyes of the Ukrainians be retaliation against the horrors committed by the Bolsheviks who are all organised and directed by the Jews." The second, on 1 October, rejected a proposal from Weizmann that the British government provide facilities for a small Jewish mission to visit Denikin: "I do not at all like the proposal. I am most reluctant to take up the question of Jews in Russia." (Files 602/2/1/16783 and—/19325; F.O. 608/196.)

[41] Denikin, *Ocherki russkoi smuty,* vol. V, pp. 146-50.

[42] See Brinkley, *Volunteer Army,* pp. 146-56.

[43] Report by Major L. H. Torin (Batum) to General Staff "Intelligence" (Constantinople), 15 September 1919; *British Documents,* vol. III, no. 460. On this re-

Against him, in pursuing this policy, Denikin had the British government. Yet the British point of view was by no means clearly articulated. Given its importance, it is amazing that during 1919 the Cabinet never once addressed itself directly to the question of whether British policy should work toward a united or a dismembered Russia. The issue was simply too large and complicated; a full discussion would have required too much valuable Cabinet time. Instead, there were merely glancing blows. Thus, the Cabinet minutes for 25 July 1919, in the middle of a discussion of the nature of the British commitment to Denikin, state merely: "Although he did not wish to raise this large question of policy now, the Prime Minister said that personally he was very much afraid that a united Russia would be a great menace to us in the East."[44]

On this occasion no further remarks were recorded. Two months later, however, following a discussion focused on the Baltic area, Lloyd George specifically raised the question of what should be "the ultimate aim" of British policy regarding Russia.[45] Here the minutes record him as saying:

The question was would it be in the interests of the British Empire to aim at a [united][46] Russia under any government, whether it was Bolshevist or anti-Bolshevist, or of any other tendencies, however good it might be. It would be inevitable that such a government would have a natural inclination to creep forward and, as Lord Beaconsfield had pointed out in connection with the situation in the past, such a government would, he thought, result in a peril not only to the British Empire but to the peace of the world. The other alternative was to aim at having certain independent states such as the Ukraine, and possibly Turkestan. The population of the Ukraine was different to that of the rest of Russia and consisted principally of peasant proprietors. The Cossacks were also different in their characteristics from the people of North and Central Russia. The future of the British Empire might depend on how the Russian situation developed, and he personally did not view with equanimity the thought of a powerful united Russia of 130,000,000 inhabitants.

The only reply came from Churchill. The question was very deli-

---

port Lord Hardinge minuted: "We shall have lots of trouble soon with the supporters of the 'All United Russia' policy." Curzon added: "A Frankenstein"—referring, presumably, to the monster and not to its creator.

[44] War Cabinet minutes W.C. 599, 25 July 1919, 11:30 a.m.; Cab. 23/11.

[45] War Cabinet minutes W.C. 624 A, 25 September 1919, 11 a.m.; Cab. 23/15.

[46] The minutes here used the word "limited," which surely is an error, as it completely contradicts the sense of Lloyd George's statement.

cate, he said. Russia had been Britain's ally in the War. Was it not "a bit cold-blooded" to suggest now that the British government wanted Russia "limited" in the future? The minutes continue: "Whatever we did, he did not think the choice was open to us and that within a few years we should see a united Russia and that from then on the Russians would never cease to claim any territories that might now be lopped off what was the old Russian Empire." He only hoped, Churchill added, that Britain would be on good terms with that future Russia.

Churchill was the only Cabinet-level advocate of the "Great Russian" position, and he urged it consistently throughout 1919. His basic premise (as he told the so-called Inter-Departmental Conference on Middle Eastern Affairs—the successor to the wartime Eastern Committee—on 6 March) was that Britain had no vital interests at stake in the border states of the Caucasus or, indeed, in any of "the other Small States" as well, and that, no matter how much to be desired was the abstract goal of self-determination, there was no doubt that, eventually, owing to their weakness, all of them would be reabsorbed into Russia. Therefore, the issue was not one for which it was worth incurring the future hostility of anti-Bolshevik leaders like Denikin and Kolchak when they succeeded in establishing a government in Moscow. Britain would one day depend upon a restored Russia as a balance against Germany; to clash with Denikin and Kolchak over the border states would only drive them toward Germany.[47]

Churchill was by no means insensitive to the demands of the "small states" for independence, however. "The duty of the Allies," he wrote in a memorandum in mid-September, "should be to try to reconcile the two conflicting points of view." Why, he asked, should this be thought impossible? He continued—suggesting, however, not a method, but a goal:

The conception of a Russia consisting of a number of autonomous States, grouped together on a federal basis into a Russian union, is one within which all legitimate aspirations may be comprised. Such a Russian empire would be less of a menace to the future peace of the world tha[n] the vast

[47] Inter-Departmental Conference on Middle Eastern Affairs, 11th minutes, 6 March 1919; F.O. General/216. The "conference"—which remained known as the "Eastern Committee"—was under the direction of the Foreign Office. Curzon remained chairman, while the other members were either ministers or high-ranking civil and service officers.

centralized empire of Czarism. And this is the moment when the critical situation of all the Russian parties and forces should make it possible, by a wise exercise of Allied policy, to give such a turn to events. A policy of the partition or dismemberment of Russia, although it might be for the moment successful, cannot have permanent results and could only open up an indefinite succession of wars, out of which, in the end, under Bolshevik or reactionary standards, a united militarist Russia would arise. Every effort should therefore be made to guide affairs into the channel which leads into a federalized Russia, without prejudice either to local autonomy or the principle of general unity.[48]

Such for Churchill was the ideal. But in the absence of the ideal, he left no doubt that he preferred the "principle of general unity." Writing to Curzon on 5 October, when Denikin was nearing the limit of his forward progress, he argued that, much as the British government might wish to uphold the principle of independence for the states of the Caucasus, if it came to a choice, London's weight should be thrown unambiguously behind Denikin. He urged:

I do suggest to you most earnestly that the possibility of the advance of Denikin to Moscow and the fall or flight of the Bolshevik régime, and of the reconstitution of a National Russia, should be our main pre-occupation at this moment. I do not think we could any longer stop it if we chose. All we can do is, by quarrelling with Denikin in the moment of success, harassing his flanks and cutting off his supplies, to exclude ourselves from any share in the fruits of a victory which our past exertions have helped to gain. I hope that the true proportion of events will be preserved and that the gigantic issues involved will not suffer on account of very small passing interests of a subsidiary character.[49]

The Bolsheviks were falling, Churchill said, and their end might come much more quickly than was generally imagined: "they may pass like a heap of snow melts under a hot sun, leaving behind only the dirt which it had gathered."[50] It was not unlikely that in the very near future "Russia may assume her position as a Great Power restored to sanity and civilisation." Therefore, he warned, "on our attitude in these fateful months depends the vital question whether

---

[48] "Russian Policy. Memorandum by the Secretary of State for War," 16 September 1919, circulated as Cabinet paper G.T. 8207, 22 September; Cab. 24/89. Excerpts, including this paragraph, are in Churchill, *Aftermath*, pp. 251-53.

[49] Churchill to Curzon, 5 October 1919, file 137299/91/38; F.O. 371/3961.

[50] Churchill credited this image to John Picton Bagge, formerly Acting Consul-General in Odessa, then a member of the Foreign Office's Department of Overseas Trade.

it is to Germany or to Great Britain that her new rulers will turn."

Here, then, was the argument that attempting to preserve the independence of the border states would ultimately fail in this immediate objective and would only serve to drive a reconstituted anti-Bolshevik Russia into the orbit of Germany. Its obverse was that a *dismembered* Russia also would fall easily under German influence. This variation was vigorously stated by Brigadier-General Terence H. Keyes, the chief political officer in the British military mission at Denikin's headquarters, in a letter to Sir Eyre Crowe of the Foreign Office on 2 February 1919. Keyes wrote:

> In Transcaucasia itself we are laying up another Balkan question in just as inflammable a region. These "republics" can never carry on even among themselves without a strong superior power, and from our Indian frontier experience we know that the Moslem tribes of the Caucasus can never be kept in order unless one power holds both ends of the passes. . . .
>
> If we permit the disintegration of Russia to begin in Transcaucasia, nothing will stop it at the waterparting. The tribes of the Northern slopes and the Cossacks of the Kuban and Terek will go too. The Don must follow, and then there will be no hope of keeping the Ukraina in any form of federation with Great Russia. The Baltic provinces would then certainly split off definitely and Central Russia would remain a helpless mass with no exit to the sea—an inevitable prey to the new Germany. It would be the irony of fate that a republican Germany should fall heir to the results of this scheme of Imperial Germany, and that the old "Asia" party should be avenged on us by leaving an open sore on the borders of Asia.[51]

Keyes was a rarity: an Indian Army officer who urged the Great Russian position—an anomaly due, perhaps, to his having served in varying liaison capacities with the Russian army in Rumania since 1917. Most Indian Army officers took a different line: Russia had for generations been the source of greatest danger to the British Empire in the East. Now a group of small buffer states were in the process of formation between Russia and the approaches to the Indian Empire. These could be permeated with British influence and thus serve as needed bulwarks against future Russian strength. Their independence should at all costs be protected.

This "Indian Army position" had important practical implications for British policy. During November and December 1918, it will be remembered, Transcaucasia had come under occupation by two

---

[51] Keyes (temporarily at Bucharest) to Crowe, 2 February 1919, file 602/1/4/3027; F.O. 608/196.

British divisions. One, under Major-General W. M. Thomson, had come from Mesopotamia and northern Persia (Thomson was previously commander of the so-called North Persian Force) to Baku; it was an Indian Army formation nearly all of whose officers were from the Indian Army. The other came from the British base at Salonika to Batum. Its commander, Major-General G. T. Forestier-Walker, and nearly all of its officers had fought in the European war. Some had had service with the Russian army. The differences between these two forces, the former occupying Azerbaijan, with its headquarters at Baku and outposts stretching up to Petrovsk on the Caspian coast of Daghestan, the latter occupying Georgia, with its headquarters at Tiflis, were later described in a Foreign Office memorandum:

These two British divisions occupying Transcaucasia had, therefore, very distinct predilections and antipathies. The Salonika division disliked Moslems, preferred Christians, and sympathised with all and any Russian reactionary movement; the Mesopotamian division were said to adore Moslems, despise Eastern Christians, and to have the traditional Anglo-Indian suspicion of everything pertaining to Russian imperialism. Between these two opposing lines of sympathy held by the British military authorities, and to some extent affecting their actions, the peoples of Transcaucasia could discover no definite British policy. Georgians found the British in Georgian territory sympathetic enough, but also strangely sympathetic towards every reactionary Russian party, whether of Koltchak, Denikin or Yudenitch, to all of which the Georgian people were fiercely opposed. The Tatars of Azerbaijan, on the other hand, found the British steeped in Moslem sympathies, and regarding reactionary Russians with almost as much hostility as did the Tatars themselves.[52]

Of these two positions, the latter was dominant. Forestier-Walker had to return to England early in the spring of 1919 owing to poor health, and Thomson was left at the head of British forces throughout Transcaucasia. Moreover, General Sir George Milne at Constantinople, under whose Black Sea command the two divisions in Transcaucasia fell, tended to sympathize with the cause of independence for the new states of the region.[53] Throughout 1919 there was a

[52] From "Outline of Events in Transcaucasia from the Beginning of the Russian Revolution in the Summer of 1917 to April 1921," by W. J. Childs and A.E.R. McDonnell, 31 May 1921, file E 8378/8378/58; F.O. 371/6280.

[53] See, e.g., Milne (Constantinople) to War Office, telegrams C.H. 10 and G.C. 630, 2 and 28 April 1919; W.O. 33/965, nos. 4045 and 4298.

real danger that Denikin would attack both Georgia and Azerbaijan in order to seize supplies which the two states denied him and also to fill what he considered to be vacuums of power into which Bolshevik forces might slip, thus endangering his rear. In June the British command in Transcaucasia, on the instructions of the War Office, intervened and drew a demarcation line which Denikin was not to cross. Sochi was included in his territory, but Daghestan, which the Volunteer Army had invaded in May, was declared outside it. Denikin simply disregarded that portion of the line, however, and continued moving his forces into Daghestan.[54]

From Constantinople General Milne cabled London protesting that Holman, the head of the British mission with Denikin (and, incidentally, directly under the orders of the War Office rather than, like Thomson, under Milne), had encouraged Denikin to disregard the line.[55] The War Office decided to bow to a *fait accompli,* however. On 17 July it telegraphed to Holman and to Milne laying down a new line which included Daghestan in Denikin's zone. But Holman was to make Denikin understand that upon his observance of this line depended continued British support. At the same time, the states of the Caucasus were to be told that they must not attack Denikin and that, unless they cooperated with him at least to the extent of supplying him with petroleum and denying it to the Bolsheviks, the British government could not insist that he stay north of the line.[56] For the next few months an uneasy truce prevailed. Churchill underlined its fragility in a note to Curzon in September: "If we are not careful we shall have battles taking place with British officers on both sides, stirring up their particular gamecock to fight."[57]

The War Office's reluctance to challenge Denikin over the movement of his forces into Daghestan undoubtedly reflected Churchill's commitment to the White Russian (and therefore Great Russian) cause, but it also reflected the basic weakness of the British military position in Transcaucasia. Curzon's success in the Eastern Committee

[54] War Office to Milne (Constantinople), telegram 78690, 6 June 1919; W.O. 33/974, no. 4657. See also Denikin, *Ocherki russkoi smuty,* vol. IV, pp. 132-34; Kazemzadeh, *Struggle for Transcaucasia,* p. 245; and Brinkley, *Volunteer Army,* pp. 162-63.

[55] Milne (Constantinople) to War Office, telegram I. 6319, 24 June 1919; W.O. 33/974, no. 4781.

[56] War Office to Milne (Constantinople), telegram 79816, 17 July 1919; W.O. 33/974, no. 4907. See also Denikin, *Ocherki russkoi smuty,* vol. IV, p. 134.

[57] Churchill to Curzon, private letter, 10 September 1919; Curzon MSS, box 65.

the previous December, when he had led his colleagues to agree to the employment of British troops for "holding Batum at one end, Tiflis at the centre, and most of all Baku at the eastern end" of the railway and pipeline through the region, was ephemeral. As early as 30 January 1919, Lloyd George warned the Supreme Council at Paris not to expect these forces to remain indefinitely; he did not think, he said, that the British government had "the slightest intention of being mandatories even for the oil-wells of Baku," although some Power had to be in the region in order to protect the Armenians.[58] Scarcely a month later, on 6 March, the War Office succeeded in reversing completely the earlier decision. The Inter-Departmental Conference on Middle Eastern Affairs, to which the Cabinet had delegated authority, decided that the withdrawal of British military forces from the Caucasus and of naval units from the Caspian Sea should begin immediately.[59]

At this meeting, and at several preceding it in February when the discussion was begun, even Curzon expressed concern about the growth of the British commitment in the Caucasus far beyond his original expectations. On 17 February he stated:

We originally went to the Caucasus in order to expel the enemy [i.e., the Turks and Germans] and hold the line to the Caspian. Operations were gradually extended, and it now appeared that we were running, or attempting to run, everything. The men on the spot had found it necessary to go much further than our policy had ever intended that they should, and, in consequence our credit was being deeply committed.[60]

And on 6 March:

Our commitments in the Caucasus had grown insensibly and without the knowledge of the Eastern Committee. . . . We now found that though, broadly speaking, our policy had been to prevent these States from flying at one another's throats and to encourage them in establishing their independence, in practice, we had set up Governments, or at any rate military Governorships, in all these States, and instead of being looked upon as benefactors and friends, we appeared to be generally unpopular and to be regarded with grave suspicion throughout the Caucasus.[61]

[58] Minutes, Council of Ten, 30 January 1919, 3:30 p.m.; *Foreign Relations, Paris Peace Conference*, vol. III, p. 806.

[59] The Conference minutes for 6 March are cited above, n. 47.

[60] Inter-Departmental Conference on Middle Eastern Affairs, 7th minutes, 17 February 1919, 5 p.m.; F.O. General/216. See also 6th minutes, 13 February, 3 p.m.

[61] Minutes for 6 March, cited above, n. 47.

In these developments Curzon noted two distressing paradoxes. First, "the result of our attempts to establish the independence of these States seemed to be that we had a military Governor in every State." And second (in fact, a corollary of the first), "it was a remarkable fact that though . . . we were the saviours of the situation, we appeared to be disliked by all parties."[62]

Since Curzon had been by far the most vociferous advocate of the initial commitment to send troops to the Caucasus, Churchill and Henry Wilson now had no trouble in securing the withdrawal they both desired. Wilson encapsulated his own view in a letter to a friend:

. . . my whole energies are now being bent to getting our troops out of Europe and Russia, and concentrating all our strength in *our* coming storm centres, viz. England, Ireland, Egypt and India. . . . Since the statesmen (?) can't and won't lay down a policy, I am going to look after and safeguard our own immediate interests, so that when all the hot air now blowing about Leagues of Nations, Small States, Mandatories, turns to the icy cold wind of hard fact, the British Empire will be well clothed and well defended against all the bangs and curses of the future.[63]

Although Wilson was a leading force behind the decision for withdrawal, he was scarcely happy with it. But the choice, he felt, was either to remain in Transcaucasia until the small republics were able to defend themselves, which would require the commitment of at least two divisions for as long as fifteen years, or to face the virtual certainty of bloody warfare among the republics, and the eventual taking over of the whole region by Denikin. The former was impossible, given the Army's other responsibilities; the latter was merely disagreeable.[64]

In an effort to find a solution, the British government turned to a suggestion that General Smuts had put forward briefly during the Eastern Committee's deliberations the previous December—that the mandate for the Caucasus be given to Italy. To the Italians, who had long eyed the oil deposits and other mineral resources of the Caucasus and who felt, in any case, that they had not received a rightful share of the spoils of war, the idea was immediately appeal-

[62] *Idem.*
[63] Wilson to Rear-Admiral Sir Walter Cowan, 11 April 1919; excerpt in Callwell, *Wilson*, vol. II, p. 182.
[64] Wilson MS diary, entry for 20 March 1919.

ing. To their allies, the idea was attractive for precisely the same reason: it offered a possible solution to the whole thorny question of Italian claims, which threatened to rip apart even the thinnest veneer of Allied cooperation and unity at the Peace Conference. On 21 March, in Paris, Balfour secured the agreement of Italian Foreign Minister Sonnino to the proposal that his government assume responsibility for Transcaucasia, and three days later Wilson and the Italian Chief of Staff, General Diaz, worked out preliminary plans for Italian troops to take over the British positions. The C.I.G.S. did so with distaste; "a most disgraceful and cynical arrangement," he wrote in his diary.[65] Curzon found the notion more than distasteful, however. Previously, he had dismissed it as a "chimera."[66] Now he wrote privately to Balfour:

With all respect, this seems to me absolute madness, and the Italians can have very little idea of what they are in for, if they lightheartedly accept such a burden. They have no knowledge of that part of the world; it has no connections with their national interests or their political ambitions; they will not carry the smallest weight or respect among the Caucasian peoples; they will be confronted there, when we retire, with a situation with which they will be wholly unable to cope; and the result, I take leave to warn you, will be disorder, bloodshed, and anarchy of a most shocking description.[67]

Yet if Curzon ever suggested any other alternative—if he even seriously urged that British troops should remain, as opposed to bitterly regretting the circumstances which made necessary their departure —the present writer has come across no record of it. On 9 April the Supreme War Council formally approved the transfer of responsibility from Britain to Italy.[68]

Something of the ambivalent attitude with which the British government agreed to this transfer was shown in a meeting of Lloyd George, Clemenceau, and President Wilson on 5 May. Orlando, the remaining member of the Four, was not present: the Italian delegation had withdrawn from the Peace Conference in protest against the attitude of the others—especially President Wilson—to

[65] Wilson MS diary, entry for 24 March 1919.
[66] In the Inter-Departmental Conference on 13 February, 3 p.m.: 6th minutes, F.O. General/216.
[67] Curzon to Balfour (Paris), 25 March 1919; Curzon MS, box 65.
[68] Noted in a letter from Hankey to the secretary of the Italian delegation at the Peace Conference, 26 May 1919; *British Documents*, vol. III, no. 229.

Italy's Adriatic claims, and they had not yet returned. As a result, anti-Italian feelings were high. The President had somehow only just learned of the Anglo-Italian agreement regarding the Caucasus, and he announced himself to be strongly opposed to it: to allow the Italians into the Caucasus, he said, would seriously threaten the peace of the world. Instead of protesting, Lloyd George agreed that Italian presence would have "as bad an effect as possible," but he was nevertheless quick to support Henry Wilson (who had come in for this part of the discussion) in his contention that British forces could not remain, and that "some civilised Power"—meaning even Italy—would have to be in occupation, or else "there would be the most terrible massacres." Perhaps, Lloyd George suggested, some of the British troops to be withdrawn from the Caucasus might remain for the present in Constantinople, "in order to have them ready to counter any move by the Italians."[69]

The Prime Minister did not indicate what kind of move he supposed the Italians might make, but three days later, despite the American President's stated desire that he wished to reserve his opinion on the matter, Henry Wilson called on Baron Sonnino and told him that British forces would begin to withdraw from the Caucasus on 15 June. The Italians, Wilson said, should prepare not only to move in their own troops, but also to take over the Caspian fleet, which was still in British hands.[70] On 10 May, the British command in the Caucasus notified the governments of both Georgia and Azerbaijan of the forthcoming transfer of power.[71]

These plans would have been carried to completion had the government of Orlando and Sonnino remained in power in Italy. On 19 June, when Francesco Nitti became Premier, he found that a military expedition had already been prepared: a "considerable number of divisions" were ready, as were the ships that would transport them to the Caucasus. Nitti was shocked to learn that not only the former government but "intelligent financiers and men of very advanced ideas" were convinced supporters of the expedition. The new Premier, however, was certain that it could only prove to be a

---

[69] Minutes, Council of Four, 5 May 1919, 11 a.m.; *Foreign Relations, Paris Peace Conference*, vol. V, pp. 467-68. See also Mantoux, *Conseil des Quatre*, vol. I, p. 487.

[70] Wilson MS diary, 8 May 1919 (Callwell, *Wilson*, vol. II, p. 191). For the previous history of the Caspian fleet, see Volume I, p. 320.

[71] Avalishvili, *Independence of Georgia*, p. 201; Kazemzadeh, *Struggle for Transcaucasia*, p. 227.

difficult and expensive military adventure; against much opposition, he ordered the whole project cancelled.[72]

Unofficial word of this Italian decision began to reach London early in July; on the 6th Balfour telegraphed Curzon from Paris that the government should base its policies on the assumption that the Italians would not go into the Caucasus.[73] This was the information which caused the War Office to modify in Denikin's favor the demarcation line it had laid down between his forces and the Transcaucasian republics: unless Allied troops were to remain, there would be little means of enforcing such a demarcation.[74]

Official confirmation of the Italian decision came on 1 August.[75] During the following two weeks the British government seemed suddenly to become aware of the potential seriousness of the situation. On the 9th Balfour wrote to Lloyd George from Paris:

Evidence is reaching us from every quarter that the withdrawal of British troops will be followed by the most appalling massacre of the Armenians and general bloodshed throughout the Caucasus. . . . I do not like to look forward to the day when it will be said that . . . the British precipitated a massacre of Armenians by deliberately withdrawing their troops in the face of the advice of all local authorities as to the probable consequences. Coming on the top of the withdrawal from Archangel I do not think it will make a very pretty story.

The only solution which Balfour could see was for the Americans to take the mandate.[76]

Balfour sent a copy of his letter to Curzon, who replied on the 12th.[77] He had seen the American ambassador, who, as expected, had said that an American mandate was out of the question.[78] Moreover, he had again appealed to Sir Henry Wilson. The C.I.G.S. had told him that a postponement of the evacuation was impossible: the British troops in the Caucasus were men overdue for demobilization who long before had been assured that they were about to come

---

[72] Francesco S. Nitti, *Peaceless Europe*, London, 1922, pp. 147-48.

[73] Balfour (Paris) to Curzon, telegram 1126, 6 July 1919; *British Documents*, vol. III, no. 296.

[74] See above, p. 225.

[75] The confirmation came in response to a request from Curzon for a definite statement of Italian intentions. See *British Documents*, vol. III, no. 330, n. 2.

[76] Balfour (Paris) to Lloyd George, 9 August 1919; *ibid.*, no. 364. This letter was circulated as Cabinet paper G.T. 7949; Cab. 24/86.

[77] Curzon to Balfour (Paris), unnumbered letter, 12 August 1919; *ibid.*, no. 367.

[78] Curzon described his interview with the American ambassador in his despatch 459 to the British chargé d'affaires in Washington, 11 August 1919; *ibid.*, no. 366.

home; in any case, the bulk of their military equipment had been removed and the shipping program for the withdrawal was already in operation. Curzon told Balfour that the matter had been put before the Cabinet that morning, and, in view of what the American ambassador and the C.I.G.S. had said, "it was deemed impossible to take any responsibility such as that involved in a reversal of policy now."[79]

Curzon's letter was filled with recriminations. From the very outset, he said, he had pointed out that it was "incredible" that the government should even consider relying upon the Italians to take responsibility for the Caucasus. And he continued:

Nothing, indeed, can prevent the anticipated outbreaks now, except the retention in the country of the forces we are about to remove. This policy I have consistently advocated for the last nine months; and you may perhaps remember my expounding it at length at meetings of the Eastern Committee, which you, among others, attended.[80] At that date I proposed that we should remain in occupation of the Caucasus for a limited time: a year or more, as might be required, until the local Republics were able to stand on their own legs. But I obtained no sympathy or support for this idea. . . .

I see, therefore, no adequate or satisfactory solution of the present problems, nor any means of averting the disasters which you anticipate.

In the event, Curzon's fears were proved to be exaggerated. Except for a garrison force of two battalions left at Batum until the completion, in the summer of 1920, of the Turkish peace settlement, British troops had left the Caucasus by mid-October 1919. Their departure was followed by border incidents among the several Transcaucasian republics, but the predicted massacres did not take place. In January 1920, however, Allied statesmen were to turn once more to the problems of the Caucasus. Central among those problems was one which, at the time of Denikin's advance during the summer and autumn, had indeed seemed remote: the danger that the region might be overrun by the Red Army.[81]

❖

The withdrawal of British troops from the Caucasus coincided, roughly speaking, with the evacuation of North Russia and also,

---

[79] For the Cabinet decision, see minutes for 12 August, cited above, n. 14.
[80] For these Eastern Committee discussions, see above, ch. II.
[81] See below, pp. 321-25, 330-38.

as the following chapter will show, with the British government's decision to inform the newly independent Baltic republics that it could take no responsibility for protecting them against their Russian enemies. Here were the reductions in military commitments for which Sir Henry Wilson and Churchill, too, argued so strongly. Yet this period—September and October 1919—saw as well the apogee of Denikin's advance toward Moscow and (as Chapter VII will also show) of Yudenich's advance toward Petrograd. Hopes for the downfall of Bolshevism were high. Even Kolchak seemed to share in success. In mid-September his forces halted their retreat and launched a counter-offensive which drove the Red Army back across the Tobol River to a point more than half the distance from Omsk to the Urals. This was no inconsiderable event, for Kolchak was still recognized by the other anti-Bolshevik leaders as the Supreme Ruler of All Russia. Yet at just this moment he himself was in danger of deposition at the hands of an anti-Bolshevik but liberal and democratic movement which had formed in the Siberian Far East. The movement's leaders enjoyed the sympathy of the British government's representatives at Vladivostok, both civil and military, and the bitter hostility of their counterparts at Omsk. Between these two sets of British officers there arose an anguished debate about ends and means which is not only of great fascination in itself, but of relevance to other civil-war situations in which a foreign Power has found itself supporting a faction which has not managed to gain the support of the population.

By the autumn of 1919, Sir Charles Eliot had left Siberia to become Ambassador in Japan. As High Commissioner he had divided his time between Kolchak's headquarters at Omsk and Vladivostok, where the Allies had agreed to locate their principal offices. After his departure his duties themselves were divided. To Vladivostok, as Acting High Commissioner, came William E. O'Reilly, a forty-six-year-old diplomat whose previous service had been primarily in the Balkans, Iberia, and Latin America, as well as in the Foreign Office itself. At Omsk was Robert MacLeod Hodgson, a year younger, who had served since 1906 in the British Consulate at Vladivostok, first as Vice-Consul, than as Consul. In April 1919 he went to Omsk where, during Eliot's periodic visits to Vladivostok, he was chief political representative. After Eliot's departure Hodgson retained this assignment. With him at Omsk was General Knox, who himself had served in Russia continuously since 1911, when he became military attaché at St. Petersburg. Although the headquarters of the British military mission were at Vladivostok, Knox preferred to remain at Omsk in order to be near Kolchak. While there, he left the Vladivostok mission in the charge of his deputy, Brigadier-General J. M. Blair. Like O'Reilly, Blair had not seen previous service in Russia. But he had arrived in the late summer of 1918 when the military mission was first established, and during the intervening year he had travelled all over the vast territory under Kolchak's formal control.

It is important to distinguish here between formal control and actual control. Kolchak's authority formally ran the 3,000 miles from Omsk to Vladivostok. But the Maritime Provinces and Vladivostok itself were more nearly under the control of the Japanese (who still maintained more than 30,000 troops there) and their agents, the brutal Cossack atamans Gregorii Semenov and Ivan Kalmykov, whom Kolchak never felt strong enough to discipline effectively. Between the Maritime Provinces and Omsk, particularly in the region around Lake Baikal, the principal source of order was the Czechoslovak Corps, which still guarded the railway. At Vladivostok, too, was a sizable contingent of Czech soldiers, while in the immediate vicinity of the town were nearly all of the 7,000 American troops who had come with the first waves of intervention in August 1918. Finally, various towns along the railway were in fact controlled by bands of armed "partisans," whose political allegiances ran along the left end of the spectrum from Menshevik through Socialist-Revolutionary to Anarchist. These partisans held little love for the Bolsheviks, but they had far less for Kolchak.

All these circumstances meant that the world—and the Russian Civil War—appeared very different from Vladivostok than from the seat of Kolchak's dictatorship at Omsk. In particular, Kolchak's regime itself seemed weaker, more inefficient, and far more reactionary to observers at Vladivostok than it did to those at Omsk. This difference in perspective divided not only the British, but the American and French missions, both civil and military, as well. One member of the French military mission later wrote: "There were, in effect, two sharply separated politics: the *ancien régime* politics of Omsk, and the democratic politics of Vladivostok."[82] In the case of the British government's observers during the late summer and autumn of 1919, the difference in perspective between Omsk and Vladivostok was reinforced by the very different backgrounds and experiences of O'Reilly and Blair, as compared with Hodgson and Knox. Thus it is hardly surprising that, when an opposition movement directed against Kolchak arose in Vladivostok, these two sets of British officers should have come sharply into conflict both over their assessments of the movement and over their prescriptions for British policy regarding it.

The movement which crystallized these divisions was formed during late August and early September 1919. It was composed principally of left-wing democratic politicians, mostly Socialist-Revolutionaries (S-R's), under the leadership of I. A. Yakushev, who had been President of the so-called Siberian Regional Duma which had met briefly at Tomsk in January 1918 before being broken up by local Bolsheviks. A number of these men—enemies of Kolchak as well as of Lenin—made their way to Vladivostok during the following eighteen months. Drawing support from the dock workers and other workers' associations, they became the most important Russian political grouping in the town. Without military support, however, they could scarcely become an effective opposition in the Siberia of 1919, and thus the catalyzing element which made them a movement worthy of attention was the arrival in late August of the young Czech general, Rudolf Gajda, freshly dismissed from his command of Kolchak's northern army.[83]

[82] Commandant Joseph Lasies, *La tragédie sibérienne*, Paris, 1920, p. 137. Indeed, the whole of Lasies' book focuses on the conflicts between the Russians and the Allied representatives at Omsk, on the one hand, and Vladivostok on the other. So does the account of the chief of the American military mission, Major-General William S. Graves, *America's Siberian Adventure, 1918-1920*, New York, 1931. Most unusual was the case of Roland S. Morris, U.S. Ambassador to Japan, who was on special assignment in Siberia. While Morris was at Omsk he was enthusiastically behind Kolchak; when he travelled to Vladivostok, his enthusiasm changed to hostility. See the annoyed telegram 386 from Ernest L. Harris, U.S. political representative at Omsk, to Secretary of State, 19 September 1919, *Foreign Relations, 1919, Russia*, pp. 427-30, and Knox's telegram of 15 September, cited below, n. 88.

[83] The account presented here of the formation of the anti-Kolchak movement at Vladivostok is based principally upon that in S. P. Melgunov, *Tragediya Admirala Kolchaka*, part III, vol. II, Belgrade, 1931, pp. 3-16. This work by a leading Russian historian draws from a wide range of source materials. For an account less partial to Kolchak (but more impressionistic), see Boris Soldovnikov, *Sibirskiya avantiury i General Gaida (iz zapisok ruskago revoliutsionera)* (Siberian Adventures and

Gajda had been stripped of his command but not of his prerogatives: he journeyed from Omsk to Vladivostok (apparently with the original intention of sailing from there to Europe) in a train of his own, with a small staff and a guard of soldiers. His journey was unhurried. At many towns along the way, he later wrote, "leaders of various political movements came to me in my train to request that I not leave Siberia . . . and said that all Siberia had followed my quarrels with Kolchak and had taken my side."[84] At Irkutsk, the location of the greatest concentration of Czech legionaries, Gajda received a particularly warm reception. There he apparently made his peace with the Czech high command with whom he had broken in late 1918 when he left their ranks in order to join Kolchak.

Soon after Gajda's arrival at Vladivostok, Yakushev and other S-R's called upon him. They agreed, Gajda later recounted, that the situation at Omsk was "catastrophic." But having talked, they separated: at the time it was still Gajda's intention to sail for Europe. Then, however, he was "struck by completely unexpected news." In a local newspaper he read that Kolchak had deprived him of his rank of lieutenant-general, and he thereupon decided to remain in Vladivostok until he had received "satisfaction" for this affront to his honor.[85] Thus Yakushev and his fellow politicians received a promise of the military support they needed in order to make actual the movement they had been planning. Thereafter Gajda's railway carriage resting at a siding near the Vladivostok station became the scene of active plotting for the overthrow of Kolchak's dictatorship.

Early in September the movement came to the attention of O'Reilly, the British Acting High Commissioner. Previously, in mid-August, he had telegraphed that there were "unusually persistent rumours of an impending movement here in favour of more democratic internal policy," but he had not then been able to ascertain whether it aimed at overthrowing or reforming the Kolchak regime. His own opinion was that it would be worth paying a considerable

General Gaida. [Notes of a Russian Revolutionary]), Prague, n.d., pp. 5-48. See also the briefer account by I. A. Yakushev himself, "Komitet sodeistviya sozyvu Zemskogo Sobora" ("Committee for the Furthering of the Convocation of the Zemsky Sobor"), *Sibirskii Arkhiv*, Prague, 1929 (no. 2), pp. 73-80.

[84] R. Gajda, *Moje paměti. Československá anabase; zpět na Urál proti bolševikům; Admirál Kolčak* (My Memoirs. Czechoslovak Anabasis; the Return to the Urals against the Bolsheviks; Admiral Kolchak), Prague, 1920, as quoted in Melgunov, *Tragediya Admirala Kolchaka*, p. 6.

[85] Gajda, as quoted in Melgunov, *Tragediya Admirala Kolchaka*, p. 9.

military price—even a disruption of the anti-Bolshevik forces so severe as to drive them all the way back to Irkutsk—in order to bring about "a popular and therefore intrinsically stable Siberian Government," for the long-run chances for success of such a government would be much greater than those of the existing Omsk regime.[86] With this attitude—and with the conviction, expressed still earlier in August, that the British government had "treated Siberia mainly as a military problem and ... failed," and that "we have now to begin again and build on a sounder foundation"[87]—O'Reilly telegraphed on 6 September that the movement at Vladivostok had "taken definite shape" around the idea of convening a congress—the so-called Zemsky Sobor—of representatives of Siberian municipal councils and rural "Zemstvo" organizations. "If it could be arranged that Koltchak should adopt Assembly into his régime all would be for the best," he said, "but difficulties on both sides seem insuperable." O'Reilly reported that the movement had the "full sympathy" of the Czechs, who had "sufficient local forces to protect Assembly from interference without embarrassing other Allies by request for intervention"; they were, he said, "incensed" by Kolchak's treatment of Gajda. But Gajda himself, O'Reilly asserted, was saying that he intended "to do nothing against Koltchak" except justify himself.[88]

Five days later O'Reilly had his first meeting with the leaders of the movement. They told him that, besides their directing committee in Vladivostok, they had an organization extending throughout Siberia, and that they expected to supersede the Kolchak government "practically without resistance whenever word was given them by their adherents at Omsk." Then they would convene their congress of municipal and Zemstvo representatives, either at Vladivostok or at Irkutsk, in order to choose a provisional government which would take measures aimed at reforming internal administration, holding the line at the front, and preparing for the election of a Siberian constituent assembly. They were confident of success, O'Reilly reported, because they expected "ample support" from all ranks of the army. They also hoped to establish close relations with

[86] O'Reilly (Vladivostok) to Curzon, telegram 726, 16 August 1919; *British Documents*, vol. III, no. 381.
[87] O'Reilly (Vladivostok) to Curzon, telegram 711, 9 August 1919; *ibid.*, no. 362.
[88] O'Reilly (Vladivostok) to Curzon, telegram 767, 6 September 1919; excerpts in *ibid.*, no. 416, n. 1. The political program of those calling for the assembly (the "Zemsky Sobor") is discussed in Yakushev's article, cited above, n. 83.

Denikin; he would, they felt sure, recognize that the Kolchak dictatorship had failed, and would himself draw a lesson from it. They were only anxious for Allied support once they had established themselves.

"I replied," O'Reilly telegraphed Curzon, "that object of Allies was to help Russian people to liberty, self-government and peace and that we sympathized with all Russians who had that object at heart." The Allies had supported the Kolchak government, he said, because it seemed to be the only "organization" through which they could effectively assist the Russian people. He had himself hoped that the proposed municipal and Zemstvo assembly could "be made compatible with Koltchak's leadership," but he now "regretfully" had been forced to conclude that such a partnership would be impossible, and that the Allies would have to choose between Kolchak and the movement which sought to replace him, judging each on its merits. Such a judgment, O'Reilly asserted, would scarcely be up to him.[89]

O'Reilly's listeners had been the civilian leaders of the movement. Three days later, on the evening of 14 September, General Blair interviewed Gajda, who could scarcely have been more frank. Until the present, he told Blair, he had "never moved a finger" against Kolchak, but now he intended to do all in his power to overthrow the Admiral and his government. Reporting his conversation to Knox at Omsk and to the War Office, Blair commented that now the anti-Kolchak movement had acquired the leadership it previously lacked. Gajda told Blair that, unlike the civilian participants, or Colonel Butenko, the commandant of the fortress at Vladivostok, who was sympathetic to the plotters, he did not believe that a change of regimes could be accomplished without bloodshed. But he stated that he had already managed to obtain promises of support from many senior commanders at the front, and that those who opposed the coup would be "removed."

Blair reported—as O'Reilly also had—that the American Ambassador to Japan, Roland S. Morris, who was then completing a long inspection visit to Siberia, had expressed warm sympathy toward the leaders of the insurrectionary movement and had implied that he was prepared to recommend that, if they succeeded in seizing

[89] O'Reilly (Vladivostok) to Curzon, telegram 772, 11 September 1919; *British Documents*, vol. III. no. 416.

power, Washington should offer them strong support. The Czechs, too, would give active assistance, Blair said. Given these circumstances, he asked Knox, was he still to use the British battalion at Vladivostok to put down anti-Kolchak disturbances there? His presumption, he said, was that he should not, and he explained: "It is now more than ever essential that Allied representatives should show a united front both as regards political and military action."[90]

Just as Blair did not want to involve British troops, so he also did not want to involve the Russian commissioned and non-commissioned officers whom the British were training at Vladivostok. On 18 September General S. N. Rozanov, Kolchak's Governor-General for the Far East, told Blair that he anticipated an uprising in the near future and asked for his views regarding the employment of troops from the British school. Blair replied that the British mission would prefer that the school's troops not be used but that, as they were Russian, the decision must be up to Rozanov. Reporting the conversation to Knox, he commented that Rozanov had little force on which he could rely beyond that represented by the school; he was, however, in the process of concentrating near Vladivostok whatever units he could find. The dominant factor in the situation, Rozanov told Blair, would be the position taken by the Czechs. There were then 8,000 in Vladivostok, and their number was constantly increasing. Were they Allies or not, Rozanov asked? If they were, they were pledged not to interfere in internal affairs. If they did support the anti-Kolchak movement, what would be the attitude of the other Allies toward them? Blair's report on this interview does not indicate that he attempted to answer these questions.

In his telegram to Knox and the War Office, Blair went on to deprecate the timing of the planned rising, since it would nullify the recent gains at the front, but he explained: "The leaders of the anti-Government movement state that they cannot delay in case the people, now thoroughly dissatisfied, throw in their lot with the Bolsheviks." He himself was far from optimistic; "it would appear possible for civil war to start in the army itself," he said. Even if this did not occur and the rebels were able easily to achieve power, the

[90] Blair (Vladivostok) to Knox (Omsk) and War Office, telegram 5122, 15 September 1919; W.O. 33/975, no. 3486. See also O'Reilly (Vladivostok) to Curzon, telegram 775, 14 September, reporting on his talks with Morris and the Czechs, and Blair's with Gajda; *British Documents*, vol. III, no. 424.

ultimate success of their government would depend upon whether or not it could give the people what Kolchak had failed to give. Blair continued:

It can only do this if in a position to afford economic and financial relief. This is obviously impossible without Allied assistance, so that it will be looked upon with the same disfavour as the Kolchak Government within a few months of its coming into existence.

Having tried the Kolchak Government and the new one, and being dissatisfied with both, the people will most certainly turn to Bolsheviks as a last resource, as they have never felt the real horrors of its régime.[91]

Thus far we have focused only on Vladivostok. Now we should widen our account. When these messages reached Omsk, they produced a reaction of limitless outrage. Even before Knox and Hodgson had received Blair's report of his talk with Gajda, both had sent strong telegrams protesting against O'Reilly's actions in granting an interview to Yakushev and his civilian colleagues, whose avowed object was the overthrow of Kolchak's government. The rebels would find no support whatsoever in western Siberia, Knox told the War Office. "Vladivostok is not Russian, and I contend that no one from there has a right [of] misleading the Foreign Office," he said. Through his inexperience of Russian conditions, O'Reilly had become the victim of "his own false deductions and local tittle tattle." Knox continued: "The movement is not well intentioned for all its leaders are men who have a personal grievance. In military circles it has no real support though any movement is capable of breaking up an army which is tried as ours is now." No other government which Siberia could produce, he said, could do one-tenth as well against the Bolsheviks as that of Kolchak. The French government had already sent instructions that none of its representatives should have anything to do with the anti-Kolchak movement; Knox urged that London should do the same.

When Knox learned that not only O'Reilly but also Blair, his own deputy, had been involved, his rage was compounded. "Warn [Gajda] for me that in my opinion he will serve no one but the Bolsheviks if he starts any movement and he will forfeit all sympathy in England," he telegraphed to Blair. And he issued other instructions: the British battalion was to be used in accordance with the

[91] Blair (Vladivostok) to Knox (Omsk) and War Office, telegram 5183, 18 September 1919; W.O. 33/975, no. 3531.

wishes of the majority of the council of Allied military representatives, and in that council Blair was to vote "for supporting the Kolchak Government's authority." In addition, he was to place the British training school at the "entire disposal of loyal Russian authorities." In the event of an uprising, Knox said, the Russian personnel of the school would "just make the difference," for he could not believe the Czechs would actually support the rebels. As Allies, they would be bound, as were the British, by the decisions of the Allied council. He and Hodgson agreed completely, Knox said, that "if persisted in, this movement might easily break up the army, but it would not be able to replace it by a new army, and all Siberia would lapse to Bolshevism."[92]

In London, Winston Churchill's reaction to these developments was much the same. "Koltchak's battle is going well," he wrote to Curzon on 17 September, referring to the counter-offensive which the Admiral's forces had launched, "but I am greatly alarmed at the way in which our representatives are lending themselves to discussing his being undermined by revolution at Vladivostok." He hoped that Curzon would issue "explicit instructions" for British diplomatic agents to continue to support Kolchak and not give any encouragement to those who would displace him.[93] At the Foreign Office, Sir John Tilley, the Acting Under-Secretary of State, agreed. "I venture to think we should stick to Koltchak so long as he remains in power & should do nothing to contribute to his fall," he wrote in a minute to Curzon on the same day, and added: "Mr. O'Reilly's flaw comes of trying to ride two horses." Moreover, he said, it should be remembered that Kolchak and Denikin were "still one"; while Kolchak's position in Siberia might be weak, "his" position in South Russia was strong.[94] Tilley enclosed the draft of a telegram to O'Reilly, which Curzon ordered sent without amendment. It stated:

You should do nothing in any way to weaken position of Koltchak to

[92] Knox (Omsk) to Blair (Vladivostok) and War Office, telegrams 9083, 9086, 9094, and 9207 on 15, 16, 18, and 21 September 1919; W.O. 33/975, nos. 3559, 3560, 3534, and 3629. There was an average delay of five days between Knox's despatch of these telegrams from Omsk and Blair's relaying them to the War Office; presumably Blair relayed them as soon as they arrived at Vladivostok. I have not been able to find Hodgson's telegrams to O'Reilly protesting against the latter's actions; perhaps O'Reilly never forwarded them on to London. Knox, however, cites them in his own telegrams.

[93] Churchill to Curzon, 17 September 1919; Curzon MSS, box 65.

[94] Tilley's minute, 17 September 1919, is in file 129878/11/57; F.O. 371/4096.

whom the Allies accorded their support, who is still the only figure who represents a possible Russian Government and whom Denikin recognizes as his Chief. You should not give encouragement to Czechs or other rivals or allow them to suppose that we are prepared to accept them as an alternative to Kolchak.[95]

To this admonition O'Reilly replied that he had, in fact, informed the Omsk government's diplomatic representative at Vladivostok about his dealings with the anti-Kolchak movement. In doing so he had stated that he would always be ready to "fight battles" for the Admiral so long as Omsk kept him supplied with "ammunition," such as a recent decree promising, albeit vaguely, to summon an advisory assembly of Zemstvo representatives. But he had also told the Omsk representative, O'Reilly reported, that it was by no means easy to support Kolchak when he did things such as appointing to a provincial governorship "brigands like Kalmykov," who lately had been guilty of yet one more atrocity—the execution without trial of ten men at Khabarovsk.[96] In early August, before he had even known of the existence of the opposition movement, O'Reilly had stated to Curzon what he thought should be the British government's basic premise in dealing with the Kolchak regime: "We must continue to do our best for them but there is no reason to accept their view of what is best."[97] Now, reacting to the Foreign Office's criticism, he reiterated his position. He respectfully submitted, he said, that the line he had taken was in the "best interests" of Kolchak and "calculated to strengthen his hand." By allowing the Omsk government to think that it would receive British support regardless of its behavior, it would only be encouraged to continue the pursuit of policies which would inevitably lead to its discredit and destruction.[98] Three weeks later, angered by a telegram from Curzon to Washington appealing for greater American support for Kolchak on the grounds that "all our authorities agree that his fall would involve extension of Bolshevism throughout Siberia."[99] O'Reilly was driven to an even sharper restatement. He hoped, he telegraphed to Curzon, that the phrase "all our authorities" would not

[95] Curzon to O'Reilly (Vladivostok), telegram 558, 18 September 1919; *British Documents*, vol. III, no. 432.

[96] O'Reilly (Vladivostok) to Curzon, telegram 786, 24 September 1919; *ibid.*, no. 443.

[97] O'Reilly (Vladivostok) to Curzon, telegram 711, 9 August 1919; *ibid.*, no. 362.

[98] Telegram 786, cited above, n. 96.

[99] Curzon to Grey (Washington), telegram 1847 (repeated to Vladivostok), 10 October 1919; *ibid.*, no. 466.

be interpreted so as to include him, as the Americans in Siberia were fully aware that he disagreed. He continued: "The dilemma 'Koltchak or Bolshevism' is a bogey by which we have been scared for too long and until we show that we have seen its falseness we shall be unable to give advice at Omsk with any effect because it will be thought that in last resort we would always do anything rather than allow Koltchak to fall."[100]

The line dividing O'Reilly's view—which was shared by Blair—from one of outright neutrality between Kolchak and those who were trying to unseat him was perhaps more fine than O'Reilly was willing to recognize, a fact that was underlined by a crisis which arose in Vladivostok late in September. During the week following his conversation with Blair on 18 September about the use of troops from the British school, Rozanov moved into the town large numbers of other troops, principally drawn from Kalmykov's Cossack squadrons, in order to forestall the uprising he expected. These newly arrived troops reportedly behaved in a particularly lawless manner. On one occasion they kidnapped in broad daylight a Russian colonel who had been openly critical of Kalmykov's atrocities; his mutilated body was later found in an outlying suburb. Other incidents resulted in the deaths of an American and a Czech soldier at the hands of Cossack officers.

In response to this situation, the council of Allied military representatives decided unanimously on 26 September to serve Rozanov with an ultimatum: by moving troops into Vladivostok he had violated the previously reached arrangement whereby the Allies would take responsibility for keeping order in the town, while the Russians would keep their troops out. He was therefore to remove them all by noon on the 29th.[101] The *démarche* was singularly clumsy. Kolchak, of course, viewed it as a violation of Russian sovereignty and a direct challenge to what little power he possessed. To Rozanov he telegraphed orders directing him to leave his troops in place.[102]

[100] O'Reilly (Vladivostok) to Curzon, telegram 846 (repeated "to save time" to Washington), 15 October 1919; *ibid.*, no. 475.
[101] Blair (Vladivostok) to Knox (Omsk), telegram 5339, 27 September 1919; W.O. 33/975, no. 3642. The text of the note to Rozanov was transmitted in Vladivostok telegram 5502 to Knox, 4 October; *ibid.*, no. 3723. See also Graves (Vladivostok) to the Adjutant General (Washington), telegram 481, 27 September; and Caldwell (U.S. Consul, Vladivostok) to Secretary of State, telegram 529, 30 September; *Foreign Relations, 1919, Russia*, pp. 521-23.
[102] The text of Kolchak's telegraphic order to Rozanov, and also of the exchanges between Rozanov and the Allied command, is in G. K. Guins, *Sibir,*

Knox—no less angered—reacted by removing Blair from his command. On 29 September he telegraphed:

> British troops are on no account to be used to enforce this ultimatum.
>
> You will at once protest to the council of Allied military representatives on my behalf against this ultimatum which, whatever the provocation, can only be regarded as an infringement of Russia's sovereign rights. The proper method was to lodge any complaint ... at Omsk.
>
> I consider you have disobeyed ... in voting for this ultimatum. You will, therefore, hand over command of the base to the next senior officer pending inquiry.[103]

Given Knox's (and Kolchak's) position, the council had no choice but to withdraw its ultimatum. The puzzling aspect of the whole affair is why it was issued in the first place. That the Czechs and the Americans supported it is understandable. Their relations with Rozanov, Kalmykov, and Semenov, the three pillars (albeit tenuous ones) of Kolchak's authority in the Far East, were strained almost to the point of open hostilities. Relations between the Americans and the Japanese, who, in fact, were subsidizing Kalmykov and Semenov, and perhaps Rozanov as well, were nearly as strained. Thus, even though the Japanese declared that, unlike the other Allies, they would not be willing to support the ultimatum with force, it is surprising to find them voting with the Americans against Rozanov. Equally unexplained is French acceptance of the ultimatum, given French policy (like British policy) of support for Kolchak against his opponents. Here, perhaps, was another example of the difference of perspective between Vladivostok and Omsk. In any case, Rozanov's troops remained in Vladivostok, and the uprising against Kolchak was put off.[104]

O'Reilly's tour at Vladivostok lasted only a few weeks longer than

---

soyuzniki i Kolchak. Povorotnyi moment russkoi istorii, 1918-1920 gg. (*Vpechatleniya i mysli chlena Omskago pravitelstva*) (Siberia, the Allies and Kolchak. The Turning Point of Russian History, 1918-1920. [Impressions and Thoughts of a Member of the Omsk Government]), Peking, 1921, vol. II, pp. 336-40. The Omsk regime's note of protest, given to the American representative there on 30 September, is in *Foreign Relations, 1919, Russia,* pp. 523-24.

[103] Knox (Omsk) to Blair (Vladivostok), unnumbered telegram, 29 September 1919; W.O. 33/975, no. 3706.

[104] See the Omsk government's note to the State Department, 13 October 1919; *ibid.,* pp. 530-31. Also Melgunov, *Tragediya Admirala Kolchaka,* part III, vol. II, pp. 19-20. For a sustained indictment of the behavior of the Japanese and their relations with the Cossack atamans, see Graves, *America's Siberian Adventure, passim,* but esp. pp. 248-74.

Blair's. Although there was no little anger within the Foreign Office about the intemperate language which Knox consistently employed in commenting on O'Reilly's actions[105]—just as there was concern over the extent to which Knox himself had (in the words of one departmental minute) "completely associated himself with the reactionaries"[106]—there was also dismay over what Curzon called the "maladroit energies" of O'Reilly.[107] The last straw seems to have been a long telegram on 4 October commending to Curzon's attention a series of twenty numbered propositions, which might be summarized as follows: Although it was "desirable that Bolshevism should be defeated preferably by a Government headed by Admiral Koltchak," the fact was that his government was likely to fall unless either the prevailing discontent could be allayed or the Allies were to use force against the anti-Kolchak movement. However, since the movement was not Bolshevik, the Allies could not "consistently with their principles use force against it." Moreover, Kolchak was unlikely to allay the discontent; he had recently announced a number of vague reforms, such as the future convening of an advisory assembly of Zemstvo representatives, but these were merely subterfuges aimed at avoiding real reforms. To O'Reilly, the only solution was the adoption by Kolchak of measures so basic as to bring him the support of the movement now arrayed against him, or else acquiescence in his replacement. The Allies, he said, should be prepared to extend recognition and support to a really democratized Siberian regime, whether it be headed by Kolchak or by his opponents.[108] Despite Kolchak's glaring weaknesses, however, such a notion was still essentially unpalatable in London. When O'Reilly's telegram reached the Foreign Office, Lord Hardinge commented on it: "This telegram is in reality a series of platitudes and an absolute waste of money. We need a better representative in Vladivostok."[109]

---

[105] Characteristic of many was a minute by P. V. Emrys-Evans, of the Russia Department, on 23 September. "It is monstrous that Gen. Knox should be allowed to use such language about the Acting High Commissioner. . . . In common with many of his profession, Gen. Knox suffers from the illusion that he is as capable of conducting diplomacy as he is of commanding a battalion." (File 132631/11/57; F.O. 371/4096.)

[106] Emrys-Evans in file 138188/11/57, 8 October 1919; F.O. 371/4096.

[107] Curzon in file 138730/11/57, 13 October 1919; F.O. 371/4096.

[108] O'Reilly (Vladivostok) to Curzon, telegram 814, 4 October 1919; *British Documents*, vol. III, no. 458.

[109] Hardinge in file 138219/11/57; F.O. 371/4096. O'Reilly's talents were judged

O'Reilly's twenty propositions arrived at just the moment when the British government was screwing itself up to take a step it had declined to take the previous spring at the time of Kolchak's greatest military successes: accordance to the Admiral's regime of some sort of definite recognition. Recognition, of course, had long been urged by Knox. When it had failed to come in the wake of the Supreme Council's declaration of support and Kolchak's reply, in late May and early June, he had telegraphed angrily to the War Office:

Kolchak has been put severely through his democratic paces and his reward is long over due. . . . I know this hesitation is not the fault of the War Office, but it delays rapid success. We are not faint-hearted and we will stick it out, though no one loves Siberia, but we have an uneasy feeling that the whole Great Adventure may be called off any day owing to some scurrilous article from the pen of an American Jew.[110]

Now, in the autumn, despite Kolchak's military reverses, Knox continued to urge recognition. Such a step, he telegraphed on 19 September, would restore the Omsk government's financial position; it could then get commercial credit with which to purchase needed supplies on the world market. More important, it would effectively stop "the harmful manoeuvres of place-hunters"—Knox's scornful designation of the opposition movement at Vladivostok.[111] Ten days later Knox approvingly called the War Office's attention to an additional argument, one originating with his civilian colleague at Omsk, Hodgson. "Recognition should be accorded," Hodgson said in a telegram addressed to O'Reilly, "not when its concession can be no longer of any utility to a thoroughly established régime, but when it can be of some help towards strengthening a cause with whose triumph we have identified ourselves."[112]

Hodgson's argument was accordingly reflected in a formal note from the War Office to the Foreign Office on 3 October. The Army

---

sufficient for the Bolivians, however. He was promoted—and exiled to La Paz as Envoy Extraordinary and Minister Plenipotentiary. In a last, bitter telegram to Curzon from Vladivostok he expressed his disappointment that his actions had been so misunderstood; he had been slow in defending himself, he said, in expectation that Curzon would "understand and protect" him. (Telegram 877, 26 October 1919; *British Documents*, vol. III, no. 496.)

[110] Knox (Vladivostok) to War Office, telegram 3666, 28 June 1919; W.O. 33/967, no. 2392.

[111] Knox (Omsk) to War Office (relayed as Vladivostok telegram 9097), 19 September 1919; W.O. 33/975, no. 3604.

[112] Knox (Omsk) to War Office, telegram 9235, 1 October 1919; W.O. 33/975, no. 3684.

council, the note said, recommended the early recognition of Kolchak, if necessary by the British government acting independently of its Allies, as the only means of preventing a further deterioration of the Omsk regime's position. Previous Allied behavior could only have led Kolchak to believe that, while the Powers were willing to recognize him if he were victorious, they were not prepared to risk anything beforehand to help bring about his victory. The British government, the note implied, should prove to Kolchak that this impression was erroneous.[113]

Although the Foreign Office did not get around to considering this War Office proposal for nearly a fortnight, the ensuing debate, recorded in a series of minutes, elucidated many of the premises underlying British intervention in the Russian Civil War, and it is therefore worth following in detail. J. D. Gregory, the head of the Russia Department, initiated the discussion with a long minute written on 14 October.[114] At the outset he flatly dismissed the suggestion that Great Britain should take some sort of unilateral action to recognize Kolchak. In this, and in the contention that, if Kolchak's regime were accorded any sort of recognition, it should be as a *de facto* All-Russian government, rather than, as the War Office proposal implied, a Siberian government, there was unanimity within the Foreign Office. The question at issue, Gregory noted, was whether or not the British government should try to press recognition upon its Allies. "We seem to be entering on a new phase in contemporary Russian history," he wrote, "possibly reaching a crisis." Denikin seemed on the verge of a decisive victory. He was only twelve miles from Orel.[115] Its capture might easily mean the fall of Moscow before the end of the current campaigning season. On the other hand, the Bolsheviks were pouring in reinforcements. If they could hold Denikin another month, they might succeed in securing themselves indefinitely. Nevertheless, Gregory said, "we have got now to reckon with the chances of Denikin getting to Moscow in the near future being fairly high." Thus the British government faced the following dilemma:

Denikin and Kolchak are one for political purposes. The merits of recognising Kolchak should therefore be tested by the military prospects of

[113] Secretary, Army Council, to Under-Secretary, Foreign Office, 3 October 1919, file 138755/11/57; F.O. 371/4096.
[114] In file 138755/11/57; F.O. 371/4096.
[115] In fact, as we have seen, Orel had already fallen to Denikin.

Denikin. We do not want an eleventh hour recognition: it would look bad. But it is also risky to commit ourselves to an act from which we might have to withdraw—and we might have to do so (a) because the main figure or figure-head (Kolchak) was in the meantime overthrown (b) because we found we had alienated all the moderate parties. Denikin and Kolchak (or their entourages—which is virtually the same thing) are notoriously reactionary. Even if Denikin gets to Moscow, the Russian problem is not solved.

Confronting this dilemma, Gregory himself came down cautiously on the side of recognition. He continued:

Nevertheless, we are pledged to see Denikin through now. It is no good adopting half-measures. It is no good the Foreign Office having one policy and the War Office another. So we had better use every weapon at our disposal to help the Kolchak-Denikin combination to attain its objective, and if recognition is going to help, perhaps it would be better to employ it. At least we might put the arguments for and against before the Allied Governments in Paris and ask them whether they consider that the military developments in South Russia and possibly even on the Siberian front justify the recognition of a Government which, if it does not command universal support, even among the non-Bolshevist Russians, is the only one in the field and therefore the only one at present capable of introducing an orderly régime into Russia generally.

Two days later a somewhat similar argument was advanced, in stronger terms, by R. A. Leeper of the Political Intelligence Department.[116] Leeper argued for Allied recognition of "the Denikin-Kolchak Government" and the early despatch of a British high commissioner as political adviser to Denikin. He was more confident than Gregory that Denikin would have no trouble taking Moscow, and he also thought it likely that Yudenich would succeed in taking Petrograd. For him recognition was important chiefly as a means of adding emphasis and leverage to the advice which would be offered by the high commissioner and the staff of technical experts who would accompany him.[117] "I venture to submit that it would be

[116] In file 145297/91/38, 16 October 1919; F.O. 371/3961.
[117] Leeper suggested Sir Samuel Hoare, a Unionist M.P. prominently identified with the White Russian cause, for the position of High Commissioner. As we have seen, the appointment eventually went to Halford Mackinder. But if Denikin had taken Moscow, his political adviser might well have been Winston Churchill. On the very day Leeper wrote, Churchill told Henry Wilson that if Denikin were successful he himself would go out, "as a sort of Ambassador," to "help Denikin mould the new Russian Constitution." (Wilson MS diary, entry for 16 October 1919.)

wise for us to be on the spot before Moscow is taken and to exercise what influence we can in those directions we think most important," he said, and he continued: "For the moment Denikin's political views are of very little importance as far as Russian opinion is concerned. What is important is the question whether his administration can benefit the country more than that which is now disappearing as a result of the Bolshevik failure."

Thus Leeper was not so much troubled as Gregory by the prospect that in extending recognition to Kolchak (or to "Kolchak-Denikin") the British government would be recognizing a reactionary regime. The situation would be different if there were other possible governments from which to choose, but life rarely presented such luxuries. What mattered most in the present case was to ensure that British influence, of all foreign influences, would be paramount. With this argument Gregory was in accord, and he rephrased it himself the following day in blunter language:

I venture to agree with the above. Whatever view is taken of the future of Russia, the fundamental object of any policy is to prevent the Germans from getting a grip on her. At all costs and under all conditions we have got to forestall Germany. As far as we can see now, Denikin is about to come out on top. The German coup in the Baltic States is evidently timed to coincide with a Denikin victory: and if we don't look out, the Germans will get the credit of having helped to save Russia. We must be ready to prevent the Germans from scoring. If we get our influence established in time with Denikin, we shall stand to win.[118]

Gregory's "German coup" was an unsuccessful attempt by German *Freikorps* troops, in combination with a small Russian formation subsidized from Berlin, to capture the Latvian capital of Riga. It was—as we shall see in the following chapter—an event of minor importance, although, at the time Gregory wrote, its outcome was still uncertain. But the emphasis which he placed on "forestalling Germany" should be noted. British troops had first come to Russia as part of the war against Germany; then and in following years German capabilities to exploit Russia were exaggerated in London, and otherwise dubious policies were justified on the ground that they were necessary to constrain Germany. In this manner Gregory overcame his reservations about the reactionary character of a Kolchak-Denikin regime in Moscow.

[118] Gregory's minute, 17 October 1919, followed Leeper's (cited n. 116).

The case within the Foreign Office against the recognition of Kolchak was not so much substantive as procedural. Sir John Tilley advanced it on 16 October when he wrote that he was much concerned with the "reproach" that the British government, while quite ready to recognize a victorious Kolchak, was unwilling beforehand to take any risks. Nevertheless, he felt that, once the policy of non-recognition had been adopted, it should be adhered to until some event took place which would fully justify a change. Perhaps, he said, Denikin's victories constituted such an "event"; perhaps, as well, recognition would make Denikin "less ready to fall into the arms of the Germans." Nevertheless, Tilley concluded, he preferred to wait, rather than to move precipitously.[119]

Curzon took the same line, more pointedly. "We seem to be swinging round rather rapidly," he wrote on the 19th. "There is certainly nothing that succeeds like success." Only a fortnight previously he was reading "Mr. Gregory's confident predictions" of the failure of Kolchak and the impending collapse of Denikin. "And now I find him advocating the recognition of one and the hasty despatch of Commissioners right and left so as to catch the rays of the rising sun." At the same time, he found the British government encouraging the Baltic states to make peace with the Soviet government at whose funeral it was now proposed to assist. For Curzon it was a bit unsettling. He was not so much concerned with consistency, however, as he was that the British government "should not take a false step now." Although he was not averse to having the matter formally discussed at the Allied council at Paris, he also was inclined, as Tilley was, to wait.[120]

In reply, Gregory freely admitted that he had guessed wrongly; predictions regarding Russia were always dangerous, he wrote. It now seemed that the internal strength of the Bolshevik forces was far less than he and his colleagues had supposed, and that the Whites would indeed win the present war. Yet, although he favored —as, he said, he consistently had done—the recognition of the "Kolchak-Denikin combination," he was not particularly optimistic about it. He explained:

Personally, I am skeptical as to whether a Denikin victory is the best

[119] Tilley's minute, 16 October 1919, was in file 138755/11/57, and thus in direct response to Gregory's of 14 October (cited n. 114).
[120] Curzon's minute, 19 October 1919, followed Gregory's (cited n. 118).

means of killing Bolshevism and regenerating Russia. But we are necessarily bound to accept facts, and this particular fact seems to be nearing acceptance rather quicker than I had anticipated. If it is going to turn out like that, I feel it is no good our trying to qualify our acceptance. I said that in my memorandum, and I do hold most strongly that it is no good doing things by halves. We have only one cardinal point in Russian policy, and that is to forestall the Germans. To do this we must accept any and every situation that comes along—with no matter what lightning rapidity it upsets previous calculations—and turn it at once in an anti-German direction. That is the main thing that matters.[121]

Once again, Curzon rejected Gregory's appeal for action. "I do not feel at all clear about this," he wrote. "Apparently Denikin's successes are to be followed by the recognition of Kolchak. I would sooner that it were justified by Kolchak's successes." Still, Curzon said, he preferred to wait.[122] Thus, on 25 October, the Foreign Office formally replied to the War Office's note of the 3rd. Lord Curzon had carefully considered the Army council's views regarding recognition, the reply curtly stated, but he was "of the opinion that it is a matter which must be decided by the Allied Governments acting in concert, and that His Majesty's Government are precluded from taking any separate action." Carefully avoided was the most important question: whether or not Curzon was willing to press the Allies for recognition. But the omission made clear that he was not.[123]

✧

By the time this note reached the War Office, Denikin's forces were already in retreat. They managed to hold Orel for only one week. On 20 October the Red Army reentered the town and began the advance which took it, by the end of the year, to the Black Sea. Denikin's "Moscow campaign" had been a tragic error. Stretched across a vast front hundreds of miles from the source of their supplies, terribly fatigued by the forced pace of their advance, and demoralized by Bolshevik propaganda and the failure of the populations

---

[121] Gregory's minute, 20 October 1919, followed Curzon's (cited n. 119).

[122] Curzon's minute, 22 October 1919, followed Gregory's (cited n. 120).

[123] The Foreign Office's reply, sent by Gerald S. Spicer, the assistant secretary supervising the Russia Department, on 25 October 1919, is in file 145297/91/38; F.O. 371/3961. See the correspondence in *British Documents*, vol. III (nos. 527 and 536), relating to an appeal from the Russian Embassy in London for British recognition of Kolchak's government. Curzon made clear to the Russians, and to the French government, which had stated to London its willingness to follow the British lead, that recognition was wholly out of the question.

of the regions through which they passed to rally to their support, the White troops were no match for the fierce attacks which the Red Army suddenly unleashed upon them. When their forward progress was finally checked, they found behind them, not reserves and reinforcements, but chaos and confusion. Only in a few areas did the retreating Whites offer real resistance. From an army which once had seemed to menace Moscow, the Volunteers turned into a fleeing, disorganized rabble.[124] The question of recognition, so pressing in mid-October, by the end of the month had the urgency of a scholastic controversy.

The end of October brought the beginning of the end in Siberia as well. Hodgson reported from Omsk that the Red Army had recrossed the Tobol River and that Kolchak's forces, "exhausted and now outnumbered," were in retreat along the entire front. Whole detachments deserted to the Bolsheviks.[125] On 12 November the government abandoned Omsk and began the journey eastward to Irkutsk; three days later Soviet troops occupied the drab provincial town which once had been the seat of the "Supreme Ruler of All Russia."[126] For Kolchak himself the only brief trace of brightness in the entire dismal scene was the ignominious collapse of the opposition movement at Vladivostok. On the night of 17 November—exactly a year following the coup which had brought Kolchak to to power at Omsk—Gajda led his forces in an uprising from his railway-car headquarters near the station. The move was utterly foolhardy. The Allied military council had already decided that it would take a position of "full neutrality"—and not allow the insurgents into the town, where they hoped to find most of their working-class support. On the morning of the 17th, heavily armed Japanese detachments drew what was, in effect, a cordon between the railway yards and the main part of the town. Pinned as they were between the Japanese and the harbor, the rebels became easy targets for Rozanov's artillery. Gajda himself was captured and

---

[124] Denikin, *Ocherki russkoi smuty*, vol. V, pp. 230-38.

[125] Hodgson (Omsk) to Curzon, telegram 526, n.d. (relayed from Vladivostok, 3 November 1919); *British Documents*, vol. III, no. 512.

[126] Hodgson (Chita) to Curzon, n.d. (relayed from Vladivostok, 24 November 1919); *ibid.*, no. 557. Knox (Navonlikolaievsk) to War Office (through Britmis, Vladivostok, as telegram 4803), 21 November; W.O. 33/975, no. 4345. For a vivid account of the evacuation of Omsk, see entries for 1-14 November in L. E. Vining, *Held by the Bolsheviks; The Diary of a British Officer in Russia, 1919-20*, London, 1924, pp. 91-96.

beaten by Rozanov's troops before being allowed to leave on a departing steamship.[127]

Although the threat to Kolchak's authority seemed temporarily to have ended, Vladivostok was not the only focus of opposition. Five weeks later, on the day before Christmas, a coalition of S-R's and Mensheviks seized power at Irkutsk with the aid of a regiment which had gone over to their side. In so doing they swept aside the ministers of Kolchak's government who, after fleeing Omsk, had set themselves in "office" in an Irkutsk hotel. Kolchak at the time was still in the comparative safety of his armored train between Irkutsk and Omsk, but on 6 January 1920 he resigned his authority and placed himself in the hands of the Czechs. On the 14th they handed him over to the S-R and Menshevik coalition, which itself, six days later, lost control of Irkutsk, and of the fate of the distinguished prisoner in its jail, to a Bolshevik "Military Revolutionary Committee." On 6 February, fearing the loss of Kolchak to a small White force which had fought its way through with the intention of liberating him, the committee ordered his execution. Early the following morning the sentence was carried out, and the Admiral's body was shoved through a hole in the ice covering the Ushakovka River, a tiny tributary of the great Angara.[128]

A month previously M. W. Lampson, who had succeeded O'Reilly as Acting High Commissioner in Siberia, telegraphed from Chita that it would only be a matter of time before the Bolsheviks wiped out Semenov, the last White leader of any importance in Siberia. In addition, he asserted, the further presence of the Allies in Siberia could serve no useful purpose and might, indeed, be "actively harmful" in that it would retard the "natural development" of the Russian people. Even if that development were to lead to Bolshevism, Lampson said, the Allies were powerless to prevent it.[129]

[127] M. W. Lampson (Acting High Commissioner, Vladivostok) to Curzon, telegrams 938 and 942, 17 and 18 November 1919; *British Documents*, vol. III, nos. 547 and 548. See the account in Melgunov, *Tragediya Admirala Kolchaka*, part III, vol. II, pp. 27-35, and in Soldovnikov, *Sibirskiya avantiury*, pp. 54-71.

[128] See the masterly treatment of these events in Fleming, *Kolchak*, pp. 163-217. For his account of Kolchak's "trial" Fleming draws extensively from Elena Varneck and H. H. Fisher, eds., *The Testimony of Kolchak and Other Siberian Materials*, Stanford University, 1935, *passim*.

[129] Lampson (Chita) to Curzon, unnumbered telegram, 11 January 1920; *British Documents*, vol. III, no. 642. Regarding Semenov, Lampson's prediction was incorrect; early in 1920 he fled to Manchuria from where, under the protection of the Japanese, he operated as a kind of bandit-governor for the next quarter-century;

The Failure of Kolchak and Denikin

British involvement in Siberia did not long survive Kolchak. In late February and early March the military mission was withdrawn, and on 12 March Curzon telegraphed to Lampson: "Post of High Commissioner in Siberia has been abolished. You should arrange to close the mission." On the Foreign Office minutes which preceded the issue of this order, Lord Hardinge wrote: "So ends a not very creditable enterprise." Curzon, as a final comment, bracketed Hardinge's "not very" and substituted "highly dis."[130]

---

captured by the Red Army in 1945, he was executed in Moscow by a Soviet firing-squad in 1946.

[130] Curzon to Lampson (Peking), telegram 88, 12 March 1920; *British Documents*, vol. III, no. 698.

Although British involvement in Siberia came to an end in March 1920, that troubled territory had not seen the end of Allied intervention. American, Czech, and Japanese military forces remained. American and Czech withdrawal had started, however; the last American contingents left Vladivostok on 1 April 1920, while the Czechs were gradually repatriated over the following summer months.

But the Japanese, instead of withdrawing, considerably increased the size of their garrisons and firmly established their control over the entire Maritime Province. This is not the place to discuss the subsequent events of Japanese occupation, ending with the withdrawal at the end of 1922. Nor is it the place to discuss the curious Soviet bourgeois puppet state, the Far Eastern Republic, which was established in the western part of the Transbaikal province during the period from March 1920 until the Japanese withdrawal, especially to attract Western sympathies and thus to serve as a means of levering out the Japanese. Only after the Japanese left was the Far Eastern Republic absorbed into the rest of Soviet Russia. For these developments, see John Albert White, *The Siberian Intervention*, Princeton, 1950, pp. 350-406; Unterberger, *America's Siberian Expedition*, pp. 184-229; and Stewart, *White Armies*, pp. 392-413.

CHAPTER VII

THE END OF INTERVENTION:
THE BALTIC REGION

In consequence of this, General Gough decided to form a Russian Government . . . .

—*from a report to the Foreign Office by the Acting British Commissioner in Reval, 18 August 1919*

THE date 20 October 1919 was undoubtedly the most decisive in the Russian Civil War. On this day Denikin's forces were driven from Orel, barely 200 miles from Moscow, and compelled to begin a retreat which ended only at the sea. And on this same day, the troops of the North-Western Army, under General Nikolai N. Yudenich, found their way finally barred after they had penetrated into the very suburbs of Petrograd. Like the other White commanders, Yudenich received material assistance from the British government, but on a much less generous scale than any of the others. For British support of Yudenich was affected by a whole complex of events which took place in the Baltic region during 1919; these events must be taken into account before we can consider the reformulation of policy in London, at the end of 1919 and the beginning of 1920, which prepared the way for a wholly new relationship between Britain and the Soviet government.

The North-Western Army had its origins during the summer of 1918 in the plans of a group of extreme reactionary officers in the anti-Bolshevik underground at Petrograd to establish, behind German lines and with German support, an army with which they could march against the Bolsheviks. The Germans welcomed these plans as a means of freeing a large number of their own troops for service in the West and, also, as a means of establishing a Russian regime with close ties to Germany. The so-called Northern Corps which formally came into being on 10 October 1918 was located at

Pskov and composed of local Russians, officers smuggled out of Petrograd, and former prisoners of war repatriated from Germany. By the end of October it numbered some 3,500 men.[1]

Any hopes that the little army might receive the extensive support which the Germans had promised vanished at the time of the Armistice of 11 November. With Soviet forces moving toward Pskov, the commander of the Northern Corps entered into an agreement with the Estonian government—which was also sorely pressed by the Bolsheviks—under which the Corps would come under Estonian command and be paid and supplied from Estonian sources. The marriage was one of convenience; the officers of the Northern Corps were the most reactionary sort of Russians, dedicated to the ideal of a Great Russia in which there was little room for an independent Estonia. For the moment, however, the menace of Bolshevism was enough to assure satisfactory cooperation; but in the eyes of the Estonians the Corps was suspect both for its Great-Russianism and for its original connections with Germany.

By the spring of 1919 the position of both Estonia and the Northern Corps had become more secure. Although the Red Army had overrun most of Latvia, the Estonians had successfully defended their own territory and had liberated some of northern Latvia. The Northern Corps had steadily grown in size with the addition of deserters from the Red Army. In late April, Yudenich, who had made a brilliant name for himself fighting the Turks in the Caucasus, arrived from Helsingfors (Helsinki) and announced that Kolchak had appointed him commander-in-chief of the Northern Corps and of any other anti-Bolshevik Russian troops in the area. Yudenich brought with him a so-called Political Council, composed of prominent Russian *émigrés* from Helsingfors, which would comprise the civil government of the territory to be liberated by his troops. On 13 May, in conjunction with the Estonians, the Northern Corps began an offensive which succeeded, during the next few weeks, in driving the Bolsheviks from a substantial strip of territory east of Lake Peipus running from Narva, on the coast, to Pskov—an area

[1] For the background of the North-Western Army, see David J. Footman, *Civil War in the Baltic Area*, Part II: *The North Western Army*, St. Antony's College, Oxford, 1959 (mimeographed), pp. 1-3. See also Page, *Formation of the Baltic States*, pp. 128-29, and C. Jay Smith, Jr., *Finland and the Russian Revolution, 1917-1922*, Athens, Ga., 1958, pp. 134-35.

with a population of half a million. Whole Bolshevik detachments joined the ranks of the Northern Corps; by June it numbered some 25,000, and suddenly it had become a force to be reckoned with.[2]

Meanwhile, the situation in the Baltic states had been considerably complicated by the presence in southern Latvia of a sizable German force under the command of General Graf Rüdiger von der Goltz. Von der Goltz had arrived in Libau (Liepaya) on 1 February to take command of a small German garrison which had been left there after the Armistice ostensibly—as provided in Article 12 of the Armistice—to maintain order and to look after the liquidation of remaining German interests, Libau being at the time the only area of Latvia not in Bolshevik hands. Article 12 also provided that the Germans should withdraw whenever the Allies thought the moment suitable. Von der Goltz, however, had no intention of withdrawing. Instead, he sent for reinforcements. Immediately he set himself the task of driving the Bolsheviks from Latvia and establishing German predominance there and in the other Baltic states. Ultimately, he hoped to destroy Bolshevism in Russia and to replace it with a regime which would welcome German participation in the reconstruction of the Russian Empire.[3]

With his "Iron Division" and other *Freikorps* units, consisting mainly of volunteers sent out from Germany, von der Goltz launched an offensive which took Mitau (Yelgava) in early March and Riga on 22 May.[4] In these towns the conduct of his troops and of the so-called Baltic Landeswehr can only be described as organized vandalism; a Foreign Office memorandum written in July called their occupation of Riga "a veritable reign of terror."[5] Some three thousand inhabitants of Riga lost their lives.[6] The Allies, naturally, were quite concerned, but, since they were not prepared to send

[2] See the Foreign Office "Memorandum respecting the Situation in the South Baltic States," by O. C. Harvey, 11 July 1919; *British Documents*, vol. III, pp. 1-7. Also Footman, *North Western Army*, pp. 3-8, and Smith, *Finland*, p. 135.

[3] General Graf Rüdiger von der Goltz, *Meine Sendung in Finnland und im Baltikum*, Leipzig, 1920, p. 201. For the background to these events, see David J. Footman, *Civil War in the Baltic Area*, Part I: *Von der Goltz and Bermondt-Avalov*, St. Antony's College, Oxford, 1959 (mimeographed), pp. 1-12; and Robert G. L. Waite, *Vanguard of Nazism: The Free-Corps Movement in Postwar Germany, 1918-1923*, Cambridge, Mass., 1952, pp. 98-99, 109.

[4] Waite, *Vanguard of Nazism*, pp. 111-18.

[5] From the memorandum cited in n. 2.

[6] Tallents (Reval) to Curzon, telegram 2, 10 June 1919, file 599/2/4/13424; Alexander (Riga) to Curzon unnumbered despatch, 11 June, file —/12924; both in F.O. 608/190. Waite, *Vanguard of Nazism*, pp. 118-19.

their own troops, there was little they could do. In May there arrived an Allied military mission under Lieutenant-General Sir Hubert Gough who had commanded the British Fifth Army until the German offensive of March 1918. Along with Gough came Stephen Tallents, a Board of Trade official who had previously spent some time in the region looking after food relief, as British Commissioner for the Baltic provinces. Gough's responsibility was to supervise the withdrawal to Germany of von der Goltz's troops.[7]

Von der Goltz, however, refused to take orders from Gough and insisted that he would obey only the German government. But where Gough failed, the Estonian army succeeded. On 19 June the Iron Division began to advance against Estonian and Latvian troops in northern Latvia. Expecting an easy victory, von der Goltz met with a decisive defeat. An armistice was arranged by the Allied representatives; its terms included the immediate evacuation of Riga by the Germans and their complete withdrawal from Latvia "as soon as possible."[8] Through a combination of subterfuge and procrastination, however, von der Goltz's troops remained in Kurland throughout the rest of the summer and into the autumn.[9]

Stymied for the time being in his task of extending German influence over Latvia and virtually disavowed by the German government, which, in fact, was powerless to insist upon his immediate withdrawal, von der Goltz set about organizing a Russo-German army which would establish itself (and German influence) in Western Russia.[10] The Russians in this force were largely former prisoners of war. By the autumn, some 12,000 of them, sent from Germany, had been added to Goltz's 30,000 or so Germans.[11] At the head of this so-called Army of Western Russia, von der Goltz placed the Georgian adventurer and ardent Germanophile, Colonel P. M. Bermondt-Avalov. This effort by von der Goltz was also a failure. In October the force began what purported to be an advance toward Dvinsk from their base at Mitau; in fact, it was another at-

---

[7] See the Foreign Office memorandum cited in n. 2.

[8] Sir Stephen Tallents, *Man and Boy*, London, 1943, pp. 327-30. The terms of the Armistice of Strasdenhof, 3 July 1919, as laid down by General Gough, are in *British Documents*, vol. III, no. 8.

[9] See Waite, *Vanguard of Nazism*, p. 122.

[10] Von der Goltz, *Sendung*, p. 225; Footman, *Von der Goltz and Bermondt-Avalov*, pp. 18-19.

[11] Foreign Office memorandum, "Germany and the West Russian Government," by O. C. Harvey, 9 October 1919; *British Documents*, vol. III, no. 125.

tempt to seize Riga. But the Latvians, aided by the guns of British warships in Riga harbor, decisively defeated the ragged Russo-German force.[12]

Von der Goltz does not, of course, belong directly to the story of British intervention in the Russian Civil War. But he played an important role in the events of the Baltic region during 1919, and he was a source of immense concern to British military representatives there. Perhaps because of the presence of his force, the British government was particularly wary of any trace of "German influence" among other anti-Bolshevik elements in the Baltic. There was no surer way to damn a proposal than to say that it was German-inspired. Thus London resolutely refused to allow Yudenich's movement to receive any supplies from German sources. The government's attitude (and its exaggerated fear) was typified in the remark of a Foreign Office official in early October that "it would be better that Petrograd should not be captured at all than that it should be captured by the Germans."[13]

❖

One consequence of von der Goltz's unsuccessful offensive against Estonia in June 1919 was that through a combination of circumstances the Estonian government received the unwarranted impression that there was still a connection between the Germans and Yudenich's Northern Corps. As a result, the Estonians cut off their support of the Russians.[14] Yudenich turned for support to the Finnish army, under the command of General Mannerheim, Regent of Finland, thus introducing yet another factor into the complex situation existing in the Baltic region during the summer of 1919.

Dealing with the Finns was, for Yudenich, something of a last resort. Like Kolchak and Denikin and many of the White representatives at Paris, Yudenich still considered Finland to be a province of Russia—entitled, perhaps, to a large degree of internal autonomy, but certainly not to complete independence.[15] Above all, it was un-

[12] For a detailed account of this episode, based upon Admiralty records, see Bennett, *Cowan's War*, pp. 168-80; also Footman, *Von der Goltz and Bermondt-Avalov*, pp. 21-31.

[13] From Harvey's memorandum of 9 October 1919, cited in n. 11. Note the near coincidence of dates with J. D. Gregory's minute (cited in ch. VI, n. 118), advocating recognition of Kolchak's government in order to forestall German influence and referring to a German "coup" in the Baltic.

[14] Footman, *North Western Army*, p. 9.

[15] Kolchak, in his reply to the Supreme Council's note of 26 May, had said

thinkable that *Finland* should make territorial demands upon *Russia*. Yet Finnish nationalists had long been eyeing the Russian area of Eastern Karelia, whose sparse population was predominantly Finnish,[16] and there was little question that the Finns would demand recognition and territorial concessions as the price for the services of their army—the most efficient fighting force in the Baltic region. As early as March, one of Mannerheim's senior generals told an American representative that Finland would expect the Murman peninsula as a reward for taking Petrograd.[17]

Yudenich, of course, knew that Finnish support would not come cheaply; nevertheless, the circumstances of his Northern Corps were such that on 8 May he moved to open negotiations with Mannerheim.[18] On the 28th General Gough telegraphed to London that Mannerheim had told the Russians that Finnish troops would join in the attack on Petrograd only on condition that Finland be ceded Pechenga and the narrow strip connecting that Arctic port with Finnish territory; that the Baltic Sea be neutralized and Russian and Finnish fortresses destroyed; that the frontier between Finland and Russia be determined by plebiscites among the local populations; and that the Allies furnish the Finns with aircraft, tanks, and other war material and possibly extend financial support as well.[19]

Toward these Finnish-Russian negotiations the policy of the British government was, to say the least, ambiguous. Typical of the attitude which prevailed within the Foreign Office was a minute written by E. H. Carr in early April, stating:

It is most undesirable that General Yudenich should be in any way encouraged to interfere in Finland or Esthonia or to make either of these countries a base for offensive operations against Petrograd. Both Finns and Esthonians distrust him as a representative of the old Russian imperial-

---

that "the final solution of the Finnish question must belong to the Constituent Assembly." See above, p. 169. For a discussion of the White Russian attitude toward Finnish independence, see Smith, *Finland and the Russian Revolution*, pp. 135 and 144-45.

Britain, it will be remembered, extended *de facto* recognition to the government of Finland on 6 May 1919; see above, ch. I, n. 100.

[16] For the Eastern Karelia question, see Smith, *Finland and the Russian Revolution*, pp. 92-98.

[17] Reported by U.S. Vice-Consul at Viborg, 14 March 1919, in a telegram summarized in *Foreign Relations, 1919, Russia*, p. 674.

[18] Smith, *Finland and the Russian Revolution*, p. 145.

[19] Gough (Helsingfors) to War Office, telegram B.S. 11, 28 May 1919; excerpts in *British Documents*, vol. III, no. 282, n. 2.

ism and would, at best, fight with him very half-heartedly. The result of any such effort would probably be the sweeping of Esthonia, and possibly Finland, by Bolshevism.[20]

Curzon fully shared this view. Yudenich, he said on many occasions, was a thoroughgoing reactionary who undoubtedly aimed at recovering the border states for Russia. The mere possibility of his getting to Petrograd would be a powerful force for disruption in the Baltic region, just as, in Transcaucasia, an invasion by Denikin's troops would have the same effect there.[21] Throughout the Russian Civil War Curzon was but a lukewarm supporter of Kolchak and Denikin; he could not even summon that level of enthusiasm regarding Yudenich.

The obverse of the argument that Yudenich would appear threatening to the neighboring new republics was that, if by some chance he were to succeed in inducing the Finns to take Petrograd, Finland's ensuing territorial claims would be equally likely to lead eventually to conflict. Curzon took this line with General Gough in an interview in May just before Gough's departure to take up his duties as head of the British military mission to Finland and the Baltic provinces. He had sent for him, Curzon told Gough, because, although the general was under the orders of the War Office, he did not want Churchill's views to be his sole guide. In particular, he did not want Churchill's hostility to Bolshevism to lead Gough to actions contrary to the policy of the Foreign Office and the British government. This policy, in the Baltic region, was one of noninterference. Gough was to be especially careful not to give Mannerheim any encouragement to march on Petrograd. He was to make it quite clear to the Regent that the Finns could not expect British support or approval if they undertook such an operation. The Cabinet viewed with anxiety the enmity that might be aroused between Great Britain and a future Russian government, no matter what its nature, if Finnish troops occupied Petrograd with British support, be it physical, financial, or only moral.[22]

[20] Carr's minute, 7 April 1919, was in file 591/1/1/6611; F.O. 608/177. This file series (591/1/1/—) contains repeated overtures, made throughout the spring of 1919 by Yudenich or the White Russian representatives in Paris, for British support. Reaction within the Foreign Office, as expressed in minutes, was uniformly the same.
[21] See, e.g., Curzon's remarks in War Cabinet minutes W.C. 545A and 588A, 17 March 1919, noon, and 4 July, 11:30 a.m.; Cab. 23/15.
[22] General Sir Hubert Gough, *Soldiering On*, London, 1954, pp. 190-91.

After his talk with Curzon, Gough called at the War Office, where Churchill subjected him to views of a very different sort. Churchill did not share Curzon's reservations. As he was to tell the Cabinet early in July, in his opinion there would be no great harm done even if all of the parties which might possibly become involved—Yudenich, the Finns, the Estonians, and even the Germans—reached Petrograd at the same time. "Our own opportunity would then arrive," he said, adding: "We should have control of foodstuffs, and consequently could direct affairs."[23] In his interview with Gough in May, Churchill constantly paced the floor as he talked, pointing to a large wall map of Russia on which were marked the converging movements of Kolchak, Denikin, British forces in North Russia, and Yudenich's proposed advance on Petrograd. Churchill seemed absolutely convinced, Gough later wrote, that these forces would succeed in overthrowing the Soviet regime. When Gough remarked that he felt that the White movements were separated by vast distances and handicapped by inferior numbers, Churchill asserted that Bolshevik morale was so low that the advance of any of the encircling armies would bring about the disintegration of Soviet rule. For Churchill, Yudenich's campaign was a vital segment of the ring encircling Bolshevism.[24] A short time after his conversation with Gough, he promised Nabokov, the Russian Chargé d'Affaires in London, that he would persuade Mannerheim to join Yudenich in an offensive.[25]

In his memoirs, Gough claims that during his service as chief of the military mission he acted in strict accordance with the policy that Curzon outlined.[26] In fact, however, he had no choice but to comply with the instructions from the War Office. Thus, on 30 May, two days after he had seen Mannerheim and been told of the conditions under which the Regent would give Yudenich military support, Gough telegraphed to his superiors asking if he should continue simply trying politely to persuade Mannerheim to moderate his terri-

[23] War Cabinet minutes W.C. 588A, 4 July 1919; Cab. 23/15. Note Churchill's rhetorical questions in a letter to Balfour on 23 August: "Is it a bad thing for us or a good thing that the Germans should equip a corps of Russians collected from their Russian prisoners & use them to attack the Bolsheviks? No doubt they will increase their influence in the Baltic States by so doing, but is it not well worth while letting them do this if in fact the Lenin-Trotsky régime is struck at effectively?" (Balfour MSS.)

[24] Gough, *Soldiering On*, p. 191.

[25] Reported by Nabokov to Kolchak in a telegram of 13 June 1919; cited by Fischer, *Soviets in World Affairs*, vol. I, p. 200, from the Kolchak archives which he saw in Moscow.

[26] Gough, *Soldiering On*, p. 191.

torial demands, or if, perhaps, he should threaten economic or other sorts of pressure.[27] Such pressures, or even persuasion, it need hardly be pointed out, were scarcely in keeping with a policy of non-interference.

Nevertheless, whether Gough's official actions were in accord with the views of the Foreign Office or not, his private opinions seem to have been. In a personal letter to Curzon on 1 June, Gough expressed his own opinion that, while Finnish participation in a march upon Petrograd would be an undoubted military advantage, from a political point of view it would be extremely dangerous. There was considerable opposition within Finland to such an adventure, said Gough, and in any case the capture of Petrograd by the Finns would create a source of "great and lasting friction" between Russia and Finland.[28]

Curzon, of course, agreed with this analysis, and on 16 June he wrote to Balfour in Paris that, in his opinion, the British government could not countenance any advance upon Petrograd by Finnish forces unless the Finns would give a binding guarantee that they had no intention of establishing themselves in Russian territory, and unless such a guarantee were accompanied by a definite understanding between the Finnish government and Kolchak. Only if these conditions were fulfilled, said Curzon, should the British government even consider proposals for supporting the Finns with money, equipment, and food.[29] Balfour agreed with Curzon; to the Acting Foreign Secretary's conditions he added another—that the Finnish Diet should also approve the march upon Petrograd. In the extreme state of flux within Finland there often seemed to be little connection between Mannerheim's actions and public opinion.[30]

On 19 June, however, the War Office received word that the negotiations between Mannerheim and Yudenich had crystallized into an agreement which unconditionally recognized the independence of Finland, assigned to the populations of the disputed provinces of Olonets and Karelia the right to decide their future on the principles of self-determination, and provided for the possible future

[27] Gough to War Office, telegram B.S. 16, Helsingfors, 30 May 1919; summarized in a memorandum from the Director of Military Intelligence (Thwaites) to Under-Secretary of State for Foreign Affairs (Graham), 7 June; *British Documents*, vol. III, no. 262, pp. 382-83.
[28] Gough (Helsingfors) to Curzon, 1 June 1919; excerpts in *idem*, n. 4.
[29] Curzon to Balfour (Paris), despatch 3943, 16 June 1919; *idem*, p. 381.
[30] Balfour (Paris) to Curzon, despatch 1015, 19 June 1919; *ibid.*, no. 266.

neutralization of the Baltic Sea and Finland. As the British military mission pointed out, the agreement represented a significant decrease in the hitherto "exorbitant" Finnish demands.[31] The attack on Petrograd suddenly seemed very possible, and Balfour telegraphed Curzon to instruct Sir Charles Eliot, at Omsk, to get Kolchak's assent in writing.[32]

The time, it will be remembered, was a few weeks after Kolchak's forces had begun their retreat from their position west of the Urals. The Supreme Ruler was sorely in need of anything that would reduce the pressure on his front and enable him to advance once more, and it was therefore only natural that he should welcome an attack upon Petrograd. The idea seemed attractive to the War Office as well. Ironside was just beginning his offensive toward Kotlas; the project for a North Russian-Siberian junction had not yet been finally abandoned, but an advance from the Siberian side was vitally needed. On 23 June a telegram from Vladivostok informed the War Office that Kolchak had no objection to a Finnish occupation of Petrograd provided that Russian forces should participate in the operation and that Yudenich should take charge of the administration of the city. Relaying this news to Helsingfors, Sir Henry Wilson ordered Gough to make it clear both to the Finns and to Yudenich that the British government "strongly" supported Kolchak's views.[33] On 23 June, Kolchak himself telegraphed to Mannerheim, begging him to attack Petrograd.[34] He also appealed to the Allied Powers to use their influence with the Finnish government toward the same end. But this appeal (a formal statement from Kolchak's foreign office at Omsk) contained a reservation which evidently Henry Wilson had not noticed. It stated:

Kolchak desires to be known that the active assistance of Finland and its eventual advances into this [i.e., Petrograd] or any other part of Russian territory could not in the future be considered as a claim to any political aspirations. Omsk Government believes all outstanding questions between

[31] The terms of the agreement, provided by the British military mission in the Baltic, was telegraphed by the War Office to Balfour in Paris, 19 June 1919; printed in *ibid.*, no. 272, n. 1.

[32] Balfour (Paris) to Curzon, telegram 1072, 21 June 1919; *ibid.*, no. 272.

[33] C.I.G.S. (Paris) to Gough (Helsingfors), sent by Balfour as telegram 3, 23 June 1919; *ibid.*, no. 273.

[34] For Kolchak's appeal to Mannerheim, see Subbotovsky, *Soyuzniki, russkie reaktsionery i interventsiia*, pp. 245-46.

Finland and Russia may be peacefully settled with the assistance of the League of Nations.[35]

Whether or not reservations of this sort were noticed in London, they obviously were in Finland. Gough telegraphed the War Office on 28 June that the policy of the new Finnish Cabinet (which had been formed in late April) was one of peace and constitutional reform, and that, on the strength of the agreement with Yudenich alone, Mannerheim certainly could not convince either the government or the Diet that a war of aggression should take place. Gough thought that the Diet would agree to an advance upon Petrograd only if they could be convinced that it would mean the death of Bolshevism and the end of tension on Finland's borders, if they knew that any Russo-Finnish agreement would be guaranteed by the Allies, and if the Allies were to promise assistance in the form of money and munitions. Gough concluded:

If Finland marches and the venture is a failure allies alone will be blamed and the Yudenitch-Mannerheim combination will be entirely discredited. Therefore it is essential that the allies ensure success of operation if allies wish Finland to advance. . . . Matter for decision appears to be (A) Are we to support the M-Y combination who are without the consent of the present cabinet undoubtedly planning operations or (B) Are we to support the present cabinet who require allied assurances and participation or (C) Are we to stand aside and give no assistance, allow Mannerheim and his government to settle their own differences and say we have no objection to Finns advancing on Petrograd?[36]

As Gough had indicated, the Finnish attack upon Petrograd would come about only as the result of decisive pressure from the Allies. But instead of choosing any positive action, Churchill (bowing, presumably, to more cautious colleagues like Curzon) chose Gough's course (C)—merely indicating that the British government had no objections to the Finnish advance, but making no real offers of support. His reply to Gough, on 1 July, stated:

The British Government have not sought to initiate the project for the capture of Petrograd. We were told that Mannerheim wanted to advance his own account. We have obtained from Admiral Koltchak Russian ap-

[35] U.S. Consul-General (Omsk) to Acting Secretary of State, 24 June 1919 (quoted in telegram 2445 to Paris, 27 June); *Foreign Relations, 1919, Russia*, p. 681.
[36] Gough (Helsingfors) to War Office, telegram B.S. 97, 28 June 1919; excerpts in *British Documents*, vol. III, no. 286, n. 1.

proval of Mannerheim's advance subject to Judenitch advancing in concert, and other conditions which you know, but direct responsibility for this operation or for inviting the Finnish Government or General Mannerheim to undertake it was never assumed by us. We should be glad to see it done, and, if it succeeds, arrangements have been made to supply a certain amount of food for the population. We cannot promise the assistance in arms and munitions asked for by the Finns. You are therefore limited to your alternative "C". . . . The difficulties of your Mission are fully recognized by us . . . but it is really safer to remove all ambiguity or illusions from the minds of the various parties with whom you are in touch.[37]

An identical approach was taken by the Supreme Council in Paris. Meeting on 7 July, it adopted without discussion the policy recommended by the Commission on Baltic Affairs (one of the working committees of the Peace Conference). The Commission felt that the Allied governments should not take the responsibility of involving the Finns in military operations whose chances of success it was impossible to predict. But it also felt that the Finns had not acted against the Bolsheviks in the past because they did not know how their actions would be viewed by the Allies. Therefore, the Commission advised that, in order to remove any doubts, the Supreme Council should tell the Finns "that in case they felt able to grant the request to act made to them by Admiral Koltchak, the Allied Governments, without bringing any pressure on the Finnish Government, would have no objection to that operation."[38] A telegram to this effect was despatched to Helsingfors; Mannerheim later described it as "a somewhat Platonic declaration which, needless to say, produced no results."[39] As Gough telegraphed on 14 July, it was "absolutely certain" that the Finns would not march against Petrograd unless they had a guarantee of positive Allied support.[40]

By this time the fighting strength of the North-Western Army (as the Northern Corps had been renamed) was about 21,000 men, with 70 guns. They were, moreover, very short of military supplies, particularly ammunition, uniforms, and medical equipment. The

[37] War Office to Gough (Helsingfors), telegram 79361, 1 July 1919, *ibid.*, no. 291, n. 1. Churchill indicated in the Cabinet (War Cabinet minutes W.C. 588A, 4 July 1919; Cab. 23/15) that the telegram was his.
[38] Minutes, Council of Heads of Delegations, 7 July 1919, 3:30 p.m.; *British Documents*, vol. I, London, 1947, no. 4, pp. 29-30. The report of the Commission on Baltic Affairs is printed (undated) with these minutes.
[39] Mannerheim, *Memoirs*, p. 221.
[40] Gough (Helsingfors) to Balfour (Paris), telegram G78, 14 July 1919; *British Documents*, vol. III, no. 310.

British mission had promised to make up these defects, but the shipments had been delayed in England and no supplies had yet arrived. Gough and V.H.C. Bosanquet, the British Consul-General at the Estonian capital of Reval (Tallinn), both warned the government, in late July, that the need of the Russians for material assistance was so acute that they would take it from any source, even from Germany.[41]

To the undoubted relief of the British representatives, the first shipload of supplies arrived on 2 August. Gough took advantage of the arrival, however, to write a strong letter to Yudenich. There had been talk among some of Yudenich's officers, Gough said, that the British equipment was too meager and too late, and that the Russians could have had much more from the Germans. On the contrary, Gough said, he was amazed that the British government had been able to send so much so quickly, in view of all it was doing for the White forces in other parts of Russia. He warned Yudenich that some of his officers were showing reactionary tendencies ill-suited to the democratic Russia of the future. Now that the North-Western Army had begun to receive its British equipment, Gough said, he expected to see the beginning of the attack upon Petrograd in the near future.[42]

Gough realized, however, that equipment was not enough, since Yudenich's force was clearly too small to capture Petrograd. With Finnish support apparently out of the question, Gough turned to the Estonians. On 8 August he arrived in Reval from Helsingfors and immediately convoked, on board the British light cruiser H.M.S. *Galatea,* a conference of Allied representatives and leading members of the Estonian government. Gough put forward a request for close cooperation between the Estonian and North-Western armies. The Estonians asked for some time to consider this demand. They were afraid, they said, that any reconstructed Russia would deny Estonia's right to national independence. Thus far they had received no satisfactory assurances from any authoritative group of pro-Ally Russians that Estonian independence would be respected. On

[41] Gough (Helsingfors) to Balfour (Paris), telegram G. 105, 23 July 1919; *ibid.,* no. 331. Bosanquet (Reval) to Curzon, telegram 166, 27 July 1919; *ibid.,* 338.

[42] Gough's letter to Yudenich, dated Helsingfors, 4 August 1919, is printed in the compilation of documents, "Obrazovanie severo-zapadnago pravitelstva" (The Formation of the North-West Government), *Arkhiv Russkoi Revolyutsii* (Archive of the Russian Revolution), vol. I, Berlin, 1922, pp. 306-8.

the other hand, the Soviet government had offered to recognize the independence of Estonia provided only that the Estonians cease all cooperation with the North-Western Army. Gough pointed out that Yudenich was willing personally to guarantee that he would respect Estonia's independence, but the Estonians replied that such a guarantee was insufficient: they required one from a regularly constituted Russian government.[43]

"In consequence," wrote Harry Pirie-Gordon who, in Tallents' absence, was Acting British Commissioner for the Baltic provinces and who took part in the conversations with the Estonians, "General Gough decided to form a Russian Government. . . ."[44] On this day, 8 August, most of the members of Yudenich's Political Council were in Helsingfors. An urgent telephone call from their colleague, S. G. Lianozov, brought them to the Estonian capital. Immediately upon their arrival on the 10th, they were taken to the British Consulate. Gough himself had gone back to Helsingfors, but he had left his assistant, Brigadier-General Frank G. Marsh, to act in his place. With Marsh at the Consulate were British, French, American, and Estonian officers, John Pollock, a correspondent for *The Times,* and the other members of Yudenich's Political Council. Yudenich himself was absent on military duties.[45]

The time was 6:15 p.m. Marsh made a short speech in Russian, which he spoke fluently. The situation of the North-Western Russian Army, he said, was "catastrophic." Without Estonian help an advance against Petrograd would be impossible. But the Estonians demanded Russian recognition. There was no time to seek such assurances from Kolchak, and in any case the Estonians looked upon Kolchak with suspicion. Therefore, Marsh said, it was up to the Russians in the room to form a government which could conclude an

[43] These events and those which followed were described in Pirie-Gordon (Reval) to Curzon, despatch D.C. 132, 18 August 1919; *British Documents,* vol. III, no. 385.

[44] *Idem.*

[45] The formation of the North-West Russian government has been described in three separate accounts, each by members of the Political Council who participated in all of the "discussions" with General Marsh, each agreeing both in substance and in detail with the others: A. V. Kartashev, V. D. Kuzmin-Karavayev, and General M. N. Suvorov in "Obrazovanie severo-zapadnago pravitelstva," cited above, n. 42, pp. 297-301; M. S. Margulies, *God interventsii* (A Year of the Intervention), Berlin, 1923, vol. II, pp. 202-7; and V. Gorn, *Grazhdanskaya voina na severo-zapade Rossii* (The Civil War in North-West Russia), Berlin, 1923, pp. 106-8. The last was reprinted in entirety in the Soviet anthology, *Yudenich pod Petrogradom—iz belyikh memuarov* (Yudenich before Petrograd—from White Memoirs), Leningrad, 1927, pp. 9-162.

agreement with the Estonian government. Russians loved to talk and quarrel, he said; now it was time to stop talking and act. It was then 6:20. If they had not formed a government by 7 o'clock they would receive no further Allied assistance. Marsh's exact words, according to one report, were: "We will throw you aside." (*My vas budem brosat.*)[46] Since it was essential that the new government include all men of ability, some would find themselves working with men whose political opinions differed considerably from their own. Upon their "earnest and single-minded efforts now" would depend the future existence of an anti-Bolshevik North-West Russia in which they could live. With these remarks, Marsh handed over the text of an agreement to be signed with the Estonians and a list of the Russians he thought should be included in the government. Then, with the other Allied representatives and the Estonians, he left the room.[47]

The task of forming a government, even for *émigré* Russians shut in a room with a time limit imposed upon them, was more difficult than Marsh had imagined. Although the Russians did emerge by 7 o'clock having appointed three plenipotentiaries empowered to act for them,[48] it was not until 14 August that Pirie-Gordon could telegraph Curzon: "After negotiations lasting for four days during which pressure was constantly exerted by British Military and Diplomatic Missions and Representatives of France and United States, a North-West Russian Government for Provinces of Pskoff, Novgorod and Petrograd has been formed."[49]

The final list of ministers did not correspond exactly with Marsh's suggestions, although some of the portfolios were allocated as he asked.[50] S. G. Lianozov ("a well-known and respected Moscow

---

[46] "Obrazovanie severo-zapadnago pravitelstva," p. 297.

[47] *Ibid.*, pp. 297-98. Marsh's draft agreement with the Estonians is on pp. 301-2, and his suggested composition of the government is on p. 302. Pirie-Gordon transmitted his own summary of Marsh's speech, "Conference 6-15 p.m. August 1919, at the Headquarters of the British Military Mission, Reval," as an appendix to his despatch D.C. 132 which was not, however, printed with the despatch (cited in n. 43). The appendix may be found in file 122010/116696/38; F.O. 371/4027. It agrees in all essentials—save harshness of language—with the version in "Obrazovanie severo-zapadnago pravitelstva." The present account draws on both versions.

[48] "Obrazovanie severo-zapadnago pravitelstva," p. 298.

[49] Pirie-Gordon (Reval) to Curzon, telegram D.C. 11, 14 August 1919; *British Documents*, vol. III, no. 372.

[50] The composition of the government is in *idem.*

financier," according to *The Times*)[51] became Prime Minister, while Yudenich was Minister of War and Commander-in-Chief. Nor had any agreement been signed with the Estonians. The Estonian government had also been going through a reorganization (not, however, inspired by the Allies), and there was no time for a formal agreement before 14 August, when Marsh left for Helsingfors. He took back with him only a "preliminary declaration" by the North-West government, recognizing the independence of Estonia and expressing confidence that "the All-Russian government of Admiral Kolchak" would arrive at a similar appreciation of the situation.[52] Marsh had to use pressure to extract even this "preliminary declaration" of recognition; when told that there was some question whether or not Yudenich would sign, Marsh is reported to have said, "We have another Commander-in-Chief all ready."[53] In leaving for Helsingfors, he apologized for any offense which might have been caused by his brisk manner. He was, he said, simply a soldier who had to get things done. There was no time for formalities.[54]

In his relations with the Estonians, too, Marsh had little time for formalities. On 13 August he wrote a letter to Poska, the Foreign Minister, which concluded: ". . . although I recognise that you will not have had time . . . to give me a formal reply, I beg you to realize that I expect a favourable agreement to be arrived at between you and the Russian Government at a very early date."[55]

With Marsh back in Finland, however, the Estonians had time to consider what had happened and to ponder the worth of a guarantee of recognition from a Russian government which (as Pirie-Gordon reported on the 14th)[56] was making its headquarters at

[51] *The Times*, 16 August 1919 (in a despatch from Reval, 12 August, by the correspondent who took part in the negotiations).
[52] A Russian text of the declaration—evidently a first draft—is in "Obrazovanie severo-zapadnago pravitelstva," pp. 302-3. A translation of a considerably longer, and presumably final, version is printed as Appendix L to Pirie-Gordon's despatch D.C. 132 of 18 August 1919; *British Documents*, vol. III, no. 385.
[53] "Obrazovanie severo-zapadnago pravitelstva," p. 299; Gorn, *Grazhdanskaya voina*, p. 113. There is no indication as to whom Marsh had in mind for this role; perhaps (see below) it was Bermondt-Avalov!
[54] "Obrazovanie severo-zapadnago pravitelstva," p. 300.
[55] Marsh's letter, written on behalf of Gough, 13 August 1919, is printed as Appendix N to Pirie-Gordon's despatch D.C. 132 of 18 August; *British Documents*, vol. III, no. 385.
[56] Pirie-Gordon (Reval) to Curzon, telegram D.C. 14, 14 August 1919; *ibid.*, no. 373.

Reval because the majority of its members feared that their lives would be in danger if they were to venture into the territory which they claimed to govern. Therefore, the Estonian government, instead of agreeing to participate in the attack on Petrograd—and it should be remembered that the sole purpose for the formation of the North-West Russian government was to achieve this end—decided to raise its price and demand full *de jure* recognition from the Allies.[57] Gough, when he learned of this new demand, telegraphed that the Allies must comply with it, otherwise "disaster" was to be expected.[58]

By this time, news of these occurrences in Reval had started to arrive in London. Except for Pirie-Gordon's brief initial telegram,[59] the first information which reached the Foreign Office about the formation of the new Russian government was a completely distorted account in *The Times* of 16 August.[60] On the following day, when Curzon received one message from Pirie-Gordon requesting that he inform the Russian Political Conference in Paris that the North-West government had been formed as a result of Allied pressure (and hence was not to be regarded as a challenge to the authority of Kolchak), and another saying that Pirie-Gordon had given the Russians permission to buy certain supplies in Germany,[61] his initial surprise at what he later termed "the Ruritanian experiment which General Gough and his Merry Men have been making in Esthonia"[62] turned to angry incredulity. To Balfour in Paris he telegraphed that the British officers in Reval had acted not only with-

---

[57] Poska to Marsh (Reval), 16 August 1919; *ibid.*, no. 385, appendix P.

The British government accorded *de facto* recognition to the Estonian government during the first days of May 1919, as Balfour made clear during a session of the Council of Foreign Ministers in Paris on 9 May. Neither the French nor the American governments had taken a similar step, however, for such a step would have meant acknowledging the dissection of Russia. Both governments, nevertheless, carried on unofficial dealings with Estonian representatives as though there had been *de facto* recognition. (Minutes, Council of Foreign Ministers, 9 May 1919, 3 p.m.; *Foreign Relations, Paris Peace Conference*, vol. IV, pp. 687-88.)

[58] Gough (Helsingfors) to Balfour (Paris), telegram G. 174, 17 August 1919; *British Documents*, vol. III, no. 383.

[59] Cited above, n. 49. Telegraphic transmission from Reval at this time was irregular; while some messages arrived overnight, others required three or four days.

[60] Although John Pollock, *The Times'* correspondent, was fully aware of the circumstances in which the new government was formed, his article was, roughly, a description of British officers in attendance at the birth of a new democracy, with fulsome praise to all concerned.

[61] These messages were Pirie-Gordon (Reval) to Curzon, telegrams D.C. 20 and 21, 15 and 16 August 1919; *British Documents*, vol. III, nos. 378 and 379.

[62] In a letter to Balfour (Paris), 20 August 1919; Balfour MSS.

out London's authority but even without London's knowledge. They should be informed, Curzon said, that they had acted *ultra vires*.[63]

Balfour, too, found the news an absolute surprise. The Americans and the French knew even less, he telegraphed in reply on the 19th, and he himself did not profess to understand the affair, which read rather like the "prospectus of a bubble company." The procedures followed by the British officers certainly seemed most irregular, he said, but nevertheless he was reluctant to put a stop "summarily" to a scheme which seemed to have the warm approval of all the Allied representatives on the spot. He therefore urged that the government should withhold final judgment until it had more information.[64]

Additional information was embarrassingly quick in arriving. On that same day an indignant Nabokov came to the Foreign Office and characterized the whole affair as "most objectionable." He was certain, he said, that Kolchak would never confirm the agreement contemplated between the North-West government and Estonia.[65] And the Cabinet, meeting at noon (before Balfour's telegram had even reached London), decided to repudiate Gough's "most irregular" action and to direct him to desist from any action "which could justify the Russian North-West Government in subsequently reproaching the Allies for not giving them support." On the following day, 20 August, the Cabinet went even further, deciding that all the British officers involved should be formally reprimanded and told that London could not assent to any of their proposals regarding recognition of either the North-West Russian or the Estonian governments, or the purchase of supplies in Germany.[66] Gough, who specifically stated that the new government had been formed at his instigation,[67] was recalled, as was Pirie-Gordon.[68] The Foreign

---

[63] Curzon to Balfour (Paris), telegram 1096, 18 August 1919; *British Documents*, vol. III, no. 384.

[64] Balfour (Paris) to Curzon, telegram 1285, 19 August 1919; *ibid.*, no. 391.

[65] "Note by Mr. Gregory of a conversation with M. Nabokoff," 19 August 1919; *ibid.*, no. 390.

[66] War Cabinet minutes W.C. 617 and 619, 19 August 1919, noon, and 20 August, 11 a.m.; Cab. 23/12.

[67] In his telegram G. 174, 17 August 1919; cited in n. 58.

[68] "Why is not Pirie-Gordon withdrawn?" Curzon asked in a minute on 22 August. "I have no idea who he is or who appointed him. But he appears to be a dangerous splasher who would be better employed in some other & quieter pool." (In file 119142/116696/38; F.O. 371/4027.) Pirie-Gordon was duly replaced.

Office's final conclusion on the episode was expressed in weighty prose:

We cannot too strongly express our sense of the unauthorised and unwarrantable character of these proceedings. The officers concerned, both military and political, appear to have acted with a precipitancy, a levity, and a lack of responsibility for which it is difficult to find a parallel. They have not shrunk from committing not merely their Governments, but the good names of their respective countries to a venture, which, whatever its chances of success—and they appear to be but slight—has left altogether out of consideration both the limited nature of their own legitimate functions, and the immense issues that are involved.[69]

In his own defense, Gough submitted a paper arguing that the North-West government, far from being "a fresh factor which has suddenly arisen," was in fact "nothing more than the administration of General Judenitch put on an organised basis"—"a Russian Government created by Russians" in order to provide "proper civilian administration" in a region previously ruled only by scattered military commanders.[70] But, on 30 August, Yudenich himself telegraphed to Nabokov severely condemning the interference of the British military mission "in the internal affairs of the Army." Marsh, said Yudenich, had foisted upon him a government of "men of doubtful character"; the conditions under which it had been formed were "deeply humiliating" to him personally and had made its recognition of Estonian independence "utterly worthless."[71] On 9 Octo-

---

[69] Curzon to Balfour (Paris), despatch 5574, 21 August 1919, file 607/4/1/18209; F.O. 608/200. The file copy was signed, and probably drafted, by G. S. Spicer, the assistant secretary then supervising the Russia Department.

[70] Gough's undated paper, submitted soon after his return to England on 27 August 1919, was circulated by Churchill on 3 September as Cabinet paper G. T. 8101; Cab. 24/88. A curious light on Gough's own attitude toward these events is reflected in a letter he wrote on 31 August to Asquith, a close friend, stating:

"I am just home from a very interesting but difficult time in the Baltic. I am not certain if I go back, as if I do I must have the support of the Government, and that is doubtful. . . .

"I would like to tell you my impressions of the Russian situation—Personally I think we are backing the wrong horse! All the émigré class of Russians are inefficient and untrustworthy and I do not think they will or could ever govern Russia again. They are, in spite of the help we have given them, quite ready to sell us to the Germans, and there is a vast Russo-German plot brewing." (Asquith Papers, Bodleian Library, Oxford, box 4.)

For additional light on Gough's attitude—and that of Marsh—see below, pp. 344-45.

[71] Nabokov left a copy of Yudenich's telegram at the Foreign Office on 2 September 1919; it is printed in *British Documents*, vol. III, no. 403, n. 2.

ber, Marsh—still on the scene despite Curzon's displeasure[72]—provided a final ludicrous touch to the unhappy episode by urgently advising Sir Coleridge Kennard, the British Chargé d'Affaires at Helsingfors, that the North-West Russian government should immediately be dissolved, presumably because it was tainted with German influence.[73]

Regardless of its shabby pedigree, the new government existed, but without a guarantee of Estonian assistance the North-Western Army was in no better position than it had been before the government had been formed. Yudenich had, however, received some spectacular assistance from the British naval squadron operating in the Baltic Sea. At 2 a.m. on 18 August, while R.A.F. aircraft created a diversion by bombing the island fortress and naval base of Kronstadt guarding Petrograd, seven motor-torpedo boats passed through the minefields and other defenses at the entrance of its harbor and sank two battleships, a destroyer, and a submarine depot ship. The action was the most successful of several similar raids during the summer.[74] Another notable success was the sinking, on 18 June, of a Soviet cruiser in the same harbor.[75] For Yudenich, however, these were only moral victories. British naval superiority in

[72] Curzon made several attempts to have General Marsh removed. These attempts annoyed Henry Wilson and other high Army officers. After a talk with Wilson on 11 October 1919, Churchill wrote to Curzon to explain why:
"I found the C.I.G.S. rather upset about your wish to recall Marsh, and he has since sent me a minute complaining that military officers have been placed in a false position because the Foreign Office have not been able to give them that guidance in policy to which they were entitled, and that in consequence they are unjustly blamed. Of course I know that any complaint we may make against the Foreign Office can be passed on by you to Paris, from which no effective policy has been obtained. But at the same time I think you ought to know that there is a strong feeling in the War Office that the Gough Mission has been unjustly judged." (File 142122/116696/38; F.O. 371/4027.)

[73] Kennard (Helsingfors) to Curzon, telegram 528, 9 October 1919; *British Documents*, vol. III, no. 463.

[74] These activities by British coastal motor boats and R.A.F. units based at Biorko Sound in Finland form the subject of Captain Augustus W. S. Agar's *Baltic Episode: A Classic of Secret Service in Russian Waters*, London, 1963, esp. pp. 152-79. See also Bennett, *Cowan's War*, pp. 145-60. Rear-Admiral Sir Walter Cowan, commanding the Baltic squadron, described the year's operations in Baltic Letter no. 580 to the Admiralty and Commander-in-Chief, Atlantic Fleet, 31 December 1919, circulated as Cabinet paper C.P. 469 (Cab. 24/96), and also in his final despatch printed in the Fifth Supplement to the *London Gazette* of Tuesday, 6 April 1920, pp. 4232-44. Because the two Soviet battleships were sunk at their moorings, they were later raised, but their repair required many months.

[75] Agar, *Baltic Episode*, pp. 80-97 (Agar, who led this raid, won the Victoria Cross for it); Bennett, *Cowan's War*, pp. 122-27.

the Baltic was absolute—there was never any serious question that the Bolshevik fleet would venture out of the protection of its mine-fields. Moreover, these successes were not without their price: 128 British officers, seamen, and airmen were killed, while 17 vessels (in-cluding one light cruiser and two destroyers) and 37 aircraft were lost.[76]

Meanwhile, in Paris, the Estonian request for *de jure* recognition was brought before the Supreme Council by Balfour on 20 August. The Estonians, he said, were virtually holding a pistol at the Coun-cil's head; if the Allies would not recognize them and assist them with money and arms, they would make peace with the Bolsheviks, thus ending all hopes of effectively fighting Bolshevism in that area. It was blackmail. Philippe Berthelot, of the Quai d'Orsay, pointed out—and Balfour agreed—that Kolchak would never recog-nize the independence of Estonia. Therefore, the Council could do nothing; although it was generally agreed that the Baltic states de-served recognition, such an action was judged to be incompatible with the Allied policy of support for Kolchak and Denikin.[77]

The Baltic states were thus left in a very unsatisfactory position. Their principal aim was to remain independent. If they were to join the proposed attack upon Petrograd without the security of Allied guarantees of recognition and assistance, the chances were—depend-ing upon the outcome of the campaign—that they would end up either under the domination of the Bolsheviks or under the equally odious control of the Great Russians. Since the White leaders would never have recognized their independence, the only logical course open to them was to conclude with the Bolsheviks a peace based upon such recognition. On 31 August the Soviet government made a formal peace proposal to Estonia.[78] Similar proposals, addressed to the governments of Latvia, Lithuania, and Finland, followed on 11 September.[79] On 14 and 15 September, representatives from the three Baltic states and Finland met at Reval and decided that all four governments, acting jointly, would begin talks with the Bolsheviks.

---

[76] See Appendix A, "The Price of Admiralty," to Bennett, *Cowan's War*.

[77] Minutes, Council of Heads of Delegations, Paris, 20 August 1920, 3:30 p.m.; *British Documents*, vol. I, no. 38, pp. 446-49.

[78] The proposal of peace to Estonia, signed by Chicherin and broadcast by radio on 31 August 1919, is in *Dokumenty vneshnei politiki*, vol. II, pp. 242-43.

[79] These proposals are in *ibid.*, pp. 244-45.

They arranged to meet at Dorpat (Tartu) ten days later to decide upon the conditions of peace which they would accept.[80]

They were an anxious ten days for all parties concerned. On the 16th, Curzon ordered the British missions at Reval and Riga to make immediate representations to the Estonian and Latvian Governments not to make peace. The British government, Curzon said, "would deplore individual action being taken by them" and trusted that they would, as heretofore, "conduct their foreign policy only as part of a concerted plan with the Allied Governments." The government would be happy, Curzon continued, to listen to any suggestions which the Baltic governments might make, and to tender such advice as it could.[81] Conspicuously absent in Curzon's message was any reference to what Britain might offer besides advice in exchange for the risks the Baltic states would run in adhering to the "concerted plan" of the Allies. Churchill tried to fill the void. He was delighted, he wrote to Curzon on the 17th, to see his message urging the Baltic states not to make a separate peace with the Bolsheviks. "With regard to any of these little Baltic states," he continued, "I can easily give them a consignment of weapons, if that makes the difference to their carrying on and if you ask me for them. This will give you a lever behind your telegram."[82]

Initially, it seemed as if no lever might be needed. Poska, the Estonian Foreign Minister, assured Pirie-Gordon (who still was on the scene because his replacement had not yet arrived) in an interview on 18 September that his government had unanimously decided not to make peace without British permission. It would enter into negotiations with the Bolsheviks only to satisfy public opinion, but it had no intention of carrying the negotiations through to the actual conclusion of peace. Pirie-Gordon thought that Poska was in earnest. It was generally felt in Estonia, he reported to Curzon, that peace with Moscow would be the prelude to a Bolshevik insurrection.[83]

Only three days later, however, in a formal note, Poska admitted

[80] Tallents (Reval) to Curzon, telegram 106, 15 September 1919; *British Documents*, vol. III, no. 425. See also the excerpts from Tallents' telegram 107, same date; *idem*, n. 3.

[81] Curzon to British missions at Reval and Riga, repeated to Helsingfors, 16 September 1919; *ibid.*, no. 426.

[82] Churchill to Curzon, 17 September 1919; Curzon MSS, box 65.

[83] Pirie-Gordon (Reval) to Curzon, telegram 49, 18 September 1919; *British Documents*, vol. III, no. 433.

that his government might, in fact, be prepared to conclude peace with the Bolsheviks. Soviet troops had left Estonia, and Moscow had offered to recognize Estonian independence, said the note. Such circumstances left the Estonian government "no valid reason which it could place before the people and army for sanctioning further bloodshed and economic sacrifices." At the same time, the Russian forces which aimed at overthrowing Bolshevik rule—with the sole exception of the North-West Russian government—were set "tooth and nail" against recognizing Estonian independence. The Estonian government indeed wished to follow the "concerted plan" of the Allied Powers, but they had to confess a certain difficulty in perceiving what that plan was. The note concluded by asking what role Estonia was expected to play in the plan, and by stating once more that, if that role were one of armed intervention in Russia, both *de jure* recognition and extensive material assistance would be required.[84]

The Finnish government took a similarly ambivalent line. On 14 September, Sir Coleridge Kennard reported that Holsti, the Finnish Foreign Minister, had told him that Finland would agree, if pressed, to intervene in Russia—in exchange for a loan, military equipment, and a pledge that the Powers would obtain from the future Russian government a guarantee of Finnish independence. But Holsti also said that he did not see how Finland could take active measures against the Bolsheviks in the immediate future.[85] Four days later, the Finnish Prime Minister and Foreign Minister both assured Kennard that they were prepared to decide their policy toward Soviet Russia in absolute accordance with the wishes of the British government. But they also stated that, failing some intimation in the near future of what was required of them, they would assume that London was no longer interested in their attitude toward Russia.[86] From Riga came the same sort of message. The Latvian government would continue fighting the Bolsheviks provided the Allies accorded Latvia *de jure* recognition, supplied military equipment for

---

[84] The text of the Estonian note was sent to Curzon by Pirie-Gordon (Reval) as telegram 56, 21 September 1919; *ibid.*, no. 437.

[85] Kennard (Helsingfors) to Curzon, despatch 111, 14 September 1919; *ibid.*, no. 88.

[86] Kennard (Helsingfors) to Curzon, telegram 471, 18 September 1919; *ibid.*, no. 434.

an army of 75-100,000 men, and granted a long term loan of £ 15 million.[87]

Curzon brought all these messages with him to the Cabinet on 24 September. The effect of the demands they contained was to call forth a major restatement of British policy. Unfortunately, the Cabinet minutes for 24 September are silent regarding the nature of the discussions which took place. They state only that, "after prolonged discussion," the Cabinet agreed that Curzon should prepare a draft note to the several Baltic governments, based on the following principles. The question of recognizing the independence of Estonia, Latvia, and Lithuania was one for decision by the Peace Conference or the League of Nations, and not for independent decision by the British government. Although the Allies would, of course, secure the complete evacuation of German forces still in the region, the British government could not undertake to furnish any additional military supplies to the Baltic provinces. Nor could it provide the financial support which had been asked of it. And, finally, the responsibility for deciding whether or not the Baltic provinces should make peace with the Bolsheviks must rest solely with their own governments.[88]

Curzon prepared the requested draft note for the following morning's session of the Cabinet. But both he and Churchill felt it necessary to present at the same time memoranda criticizing these conclusions.[89] Curzon called his an "Appreciation" of the situation, and it was simply that. Since the British government had decided not to grant the Baltic states the *de jure* recognition or the material assistance which they wanted, he presumed that they would now proceed to negotiate with the Bolsheviks. After all, he said, British recognition of the mere autonomy of the three states meant nothing to them: any Russian government would go that far. Only *de jure* recognition would supply them with a sufficient reason to continue fighting the Bolsheviks. If the Baltic states made peace, Curzon continued, both Finland and Poland would inevitably follow: the Finns would otherwise be left isolated in the north, while public

---

[87] Tallents (Riga) to Curzon, telegram 131, 22 September 1919; *ibid.*, no. 438.
[88] War Cabinet minutes W.C. 623, 24 September 1919, 4 p.m.; Cab. 23/12.
[89] Both Curzon's "Appreciation" and Churchill's "Notes by the Secretary of State for War," 25 September 1919, are printed as appendices to War Cabinet minutes W.C. 624, 25 September, 11 a.m.; Cab. 23/12.

opinion in Poland was strongly in favor of establishing a stable frontier with Russia so that Polish forces could be moved westward to defend against possible German incursions. Thus, if the northern states made peace with the Bolsheviks, Poland would have difficulty in not following.[90] Therefore, Curzon wrote, the British government must prepare itself for the collapse of the whole western front against the Bolsheviks as far south as the Ukraine, and the brunt of the Bolshevik attack would fall entirely upon Denikin. Moreover, it would not be surprising if the Baltic states turned to Germany for the assistance which Britain had denied them.

Curzon suggested no solutions; he urged only "accepting with good grace a situation for which we should have been partially responsible," and attempting to maintain as cordial relations as possible with the governments involved. Churchill's tone was sharper. "It is worth noting," he wrote, "that every one of these steps, necessary as some of them are, helps the Bolshevists, with whom on other parts of the front we are at war." Briefly, he summarized the consequences he foresaw. The Baltic states would come to terms with the Bolsheviks, as would in all probability Finland and Poland. The North-Western Army might be wiped out, or else it would turn to Germany, and the population of Petrograd, which previously had been encouraged to expect delivery from Bolshevism, would be reduced to despair. Any hopes which the Russians at Archangel and Murmansk may have had of holding out after the imminent British departure would be dashed. And the 97,000 Bolshevik troops thus liberated in all these sectors would immediately be "hurled" upon Denikin. In this manner, "the death-knell will have been struck of British influence in these regions, and the episode will be, rightly or wrongly, regarded by Russia as a supreme act of indifference and abandonment." Churchill's conclusion followed:

It would be much simpler, much safer, and, in the long run, much cheaper to continue to make war upon the Bolsheviks by every means in our power (which do not involve the employment of British troops or the expenditure of large sums of money), with a coherent plan on all fronts at once, until such time as either a definite victory is won, or it is decided to make a general peace in which all parties would be included.

[90] The question of Poland's role in the climactic phases of the Russian Civil War, and of British policy regarding it, will be examined in the first chapter of Volume III of the present work.

Churchill's argument was not illogical: at the time he made it, Denikin's armies were still approaching Moscow, and the outcome of the civil war was by no means foreseeable. But it did contain an implied contradiction. In order to keep the Baltic states from initiating peace negotiations, it would (if Curzon's argument were accepted) be necessary to recognize them *de jure*. This, too, would be regarded by "Russia"—Churchill meant Kolchak and Denikin—as "indifference and abandonment," and Churchill, of course, was well aware of it. Two days later, he sent urgent telegrams to Knox and Holman requesting that they tell Kolchak and Denikin that the Bolsheviks had offered to recognize the "absolute independence" of the three Baltic states; unless an equally satisfactory guarantee could be given by Kolchak and Denikin, and supported by the Allies, the three states would—understandably—make peace, thus gravely imperiling Yudenich's army and, eventually, Kolchak and Denikin as well.[91]

The replies to Churchill's entreaties were entirely predictable: firm refusals. Holman telegraphed on 30 September that Denikin was fully aware of the gravity of the situation. Subject to revision by a future Russian government, he was prepared to recognize the right of the Baltic provinces, and of all other regions which desired it, to "liberal autonomy." Beyond this he would not go. In particular, Russia must not be cut off from access to the sea. "Denikin will not [bend] the fraction of an inch from his sole aim, the restoration of a united Russia," Holman reported, and he continued: "He is [a] far-seeing patriot and cannot be deflected from his object, neither will he make promises, the fulfillment of which he cannot guarantee, nor stoop in order to gain a temporary advantage." Instead, Holman said, Denikin would gamble on an all-out effort to get to Moscow before the Bolsheviks were able to bring to bear against him the troops which would be freed if Yudenich's front collapsed because of the Baltic states' acceptance of peace.[92]

Knox's reply, on 6 October, was bitter and petulant. He had seen Kolchak, who had nothing to add to the message he sent in response to the Supreme Council's note of 27 May: as temporary ruler of Russia, he could not make decisions on matters which obviously

[91] War Office to Britmiss (Vladivostok) and Denmiss (Taganrog), telegram 81449, 27 September 1919; W.O. 33/975, no. 3646.

[92] Denmiss (Taganrog) to War Office, telegram N. 280, 30 September 1919; W.O. 33/975, no. 3671.

must be left to a constituent assembly. Knox agreed. He really did not see what London expected Kolchak to say, he telegraphed, adding: "We cannot expect him to enter a bidding competition with the Soviet Government, and even if he were to outdo the Bolsheviks I do not believe that these Baltic States would fight at all." Russians felt, Knox said, that the Great Powers had at least as much at stake as they did: if the Baltic states made peace, they would soon succumb to Bolshevism, and thus "the disease will creep nearer Western civilisation." And Russians wondered—rightly, Knox said—whether Allied control over the supply of foodstuffs and manufactures to the Baltic states did not provide even more leverage than Kolchak had over their decision to make peace or continue at war.[93]

In trying to persuade Kolchak and Denikin to recognize the independence of the Baltic states, Churchill had acted on his own, without reference to the Foreign Office, in an effort to create sufficient grounds to reverse the Cabinet's decision of 24 September.[94] That decision was embodied in Curzon's draft telegram to British representatives in the Baltic states and Finland, containing the text of a note to the governments involved, which received Cabinet approval on the 25th. Identical telegrams went out immediately.[95] They dealt first with the matter of recognition. The British government had already accorded *de facto* recognition to the Baltic governments, they said.[96] *De jure* recognition was not a question for decision by Britain alone; it could only be decided upon by the Peace Conference or the League of Nations sitting in sequel to the Peace Conference.[97] But the Baltic states might rest assured that Britain would do everything possible to secure the satisfaction of their "legitimate aspirations" so far as might be "consistent with a final and peaceful settlement in North-East Europe."

There was scant comfort for the Baltic statesmen in this assurance;

[93] Knox (Omsk) to War Office, 6 October 1919, sent as Britmiss (Vladivostok) telegram 9255, 10 October; W.O. 33/975, no. 3812.
[94] Noted in file 142203/116696/38; F.O. 371/4027.
[95] Curzon to British missions in Reval, Riga, and Kovno (repeated to Helsingfors), 25 September 1919; *British Documents*, vol. III, no. 445.
[96] London accorded *de facto* recognition to the Lithuanian provisional government on 23 September 1919, thus (as Curzon told Tallents [Riga], telegram 59, 23 September) placing the Lithuanians on an equal footing with the Estonian and Latvian governments; *ibid.*, no. 441.
[97] This was a novel doctrine. Obviously the British government could have accorded *de jure* recognition unilaterally—as it did in 1924 regarding the Soviet government.

they found little more when the telegrams turned to their requests for material and financial assistance. The depletion of available stocks and the shortage of shipping, they said, made continued British contributions of military supplies impossible. Neither could London assume any new financial responsibilities. Yet it must not be thought that Britain had abandoned the Baltic states. Should they be invaded by Bolshevik forces, "His Majesty's Government might be prepared to make the sacrifices, which are not justified by present conditions, and to reconsider their decision as to the supply of war material."

The Baltic governments could not have based their policy on a pledge as vague as that, and Curzon was well aware of it. Thus, the conclusion of the telegrams embodied a significant change in British policy. It read as follows:

In these circumstances His Majesty's Government feel that they are not entitled to exercise any pressure upon the free initiative of the Baltic States and that their Governments must be at liberty to decide upon such action as may be most conducive to the preservation of their own national existence. It is for them to determine with unfettered judgement whether they should make any arrangement, and if so of what nature, with the Soviet authorities; and if, as seems to be in contemplation, they decide to act in unison, the effective control of the situation should be within their power.

This British declaration reached the Baltic governments just before the conference at Dorpat at the end of September. As Tallents afterward reported, it had "a very good effect" in removing the impression that the British government, "while giving inadequate military and no financial support," expected the Baltic states to remain at war with the Bolsheviks.[98] At Dorpat, the Estonian, Latvian, and Lithuanian governments decided to inform the Soviet government that they would begin preliminary peace talks no later than 25 October.[99]

✧

Meanwhile, Yudenich continued making preparations for his attack upon Petrograd. For a brief period, he entered into negotiations

[98] Tallents (Reval) to Curzon, telegram 273, 2 October 1919; excerpts in *British Documents*, vol. III, no. 445, n. 2.
[99] So Chicherin was informed in a note from Poska, 4 October 1919; *Dokumenty vneshnei politiki*, vol. II, p. 255.

with Bermondt-Avalov for a combined offensive including some detachments from the "Army of Western Russia" raised by the latter and von der Goltz. This appears to have been fostered, in part, by General Marsh, who in late August arranged a meeting at Riga between Bermondt and some of Yudenich's representatives.[100] Marsh himself was much taken with Bermondt, whom he considered to be a man of "more character and decision" than Yudenich and "more likely to develop a serious situation eastward . . . and . . . therefore more worthy of support in men and supplies."[101] This opinion, it should be noted, was not shared by other British representatives who had met Bermondt.[102]

Enamored of the idea of a joint offensive by Bermondt's and Yudenich's forces, Marsh appears to have given Bermondt permission once more to revive the flow of military supplies and Russian prisoners of war from Germany[103]—an action which had been forbidden earlier in the summer by the Allied governments, and thus "another grave case of improper action on the part of General Marsh."[104] In any case, the negotiations between Bermondt and Yudenich soon proved fruitless—Bermondt's combination of megalomania and sheer incompetence made it difficult for anyone to reach an agreement with him. In October, after Bermondt's forces started their move toward Riga, Yudenich denounced him as a traitor to Russia.[105]

It is doubtful whether Yudenich ever really expected cooperation from Bermondt, but he was counting on help from the Estonians. The conference which Marsh convoked at Riga at the end of August was also attended by representatives of the Estonian army, and plans were made for an offensive beginning on 15 September in which Estonian detachments were to play an important part. Therefore, the Estonian government's decision to make peace with Moscow came as a severe blow to Yudenich, so severe, indeed, that

---

[100] See Tallents (Riga) to Curzon, despatch 38, 1 September 1919; *British Documents*, vol. III, no. 76.

[101] Marsh (Helsingfors) to War Office, telegram G. 209, 29 August 1919; *ibid.*, no. 72.

[102] See Tallents' caustic description of Bermondt in his despatch 38 (cited in n. 100) and in his memoirs (*Man and Boy*, pp. 362-63).

[103] Tallents (Riga) to Curzon, despatch 44, 9 September 1919; *British Documents*, III, no. 85.

[104] Lord Hardinge's comment, in a letter to the Director of Military Intelligence (General Thwaites), 30 September 1919; *idem.*, n. 3.

[105] Footman, *Von der Goltz and Bermondt-Avalov*, p. 30.

within the British War Office there was a strong feeling that his offensive should be called off. A General Staff paper of 3 October recommended that the North-Western Army be transferred to Denikin's front—shipped by sea from Reval to Danzig, and then by rail from Danzig to Kiev. Otherwise, the paper said, if Yudenich persisted in his plan to attack Petrograd, "a valuable anti-Bolshevik force, equipped almost entirely by ourselves at considerable expense, will then be lost."[106]

Before any action could be taken on these recommendations—the Foreign Office viewed the matter as one for the Supreme Council in Paris—Yudenich began his offensive, starting with a series of minor engagements during the first week of October.[107] At this time the North-Western Army had a strength of approximately 17,000 combatants, armed with 57 heavy guns, some 700 light guns and machine guns, and 2 armored trains. Fighting with it were 6 British tanks manned by British crews.[108] Opposing this force was a Bolshe-

[106] The paper, dated 3 October 1919, was sent to the Foreign Office on the 7th, with a note drawing Curzon's attention "to the critical situation in which the Russian North-Western Army is placed owing to the fact that the Baltic States have entered into Peace negotiations with the Bolsheviks." Curzon sent the paper to Sir Eyre Crowe in Paris (despatch 7027) on the 14th, with instructions for Crowe to place the matter before the Supreme Council. Before Crowe did so, Yudenich began his offensive. (File 138182/116696/38; F.O. 371/4027).

[107] Although the War Office wished to call off Yudenich's offensive, General Marsh, at Yudenich's headquarters, seems to have urged him forward. According to Yudenich's chief of staff, Colonel Krusenstiern, Marsh insisted that the North-Western Army begin its attack even without the hoped-for aid of the Estonians and threatened to deprive the force of its British equipment if it did not attack. So Krusenstiern alleged in a report, "History of the Petrograd Campaign of the North-Western Russian Army, October-November 1919," written at the request of the American Commissioner for the Baltic provinces, John A. Gade, and transmitted on 27 November to Washington; U.S. National Archives, State Department file 861.00/6012.

[108] The six tanks had originally been intended for Murmansk but were diverted to the North-Western Army by decision of a General Staff conference, 9 July 1919, 11 a.m., at the War Office, on the grounds that they would make a greater contribution on Yudenich's front (minutes in file 606/5/2/15158; F.O. 608/200). Based at Narva, the British tank crews at first functioned as instructors, but, as on Denikin's front, they abandoned this role for active combat participation. (See British mission [Helsingfors] to War Office, telegrams G. 280, 289, and 332, 28 September and 2 and 15 October 1919; W.O. 33/975, nos. 3650, 3689, 3864.)

The employment of these crews in combat at a time when British public opinion was becoming increasingly restive about intervention resulted in the following telegram from the War Office on 28 October:

"Difficult questions are being asked as to British personnel with tanks. It should be made quite clear that unless they specifically volunteer no British personnel should be asked actually to take part in operations.

"Secretary of State wishes you to ensure that British personnel are not sub-

vik force that initially was no larger, but which was reinforced until, eventually, it far outnumbered the attackers.[109] Yudenich launched his main offensive on 12 October, his troops advancing on a wide front. Quickly they recaptured Pskov and took Yamburg (now Kingisepp). But the fighting around Yamburg resulted in the destruction of the bridge over the Luga River, rendering useless Yudenich's trains and his British tanks. Nevertheless, his rapid progress continued. On the 16th, while some of his detachments entered Gatchina, 35 miles south of Petrograd, others were landed, under the covering guns of the British Baltic squadron, near the coastal fortress of Krasnaya Gorka, some 25 miles from the former capital. Ahead of these forces the raw Soviet Seventh Army retreated in disarray; by 20 October, White troops were fighting in the industrial works on the outskirts of Petrograd.[110] Here, however, under Trotsky's personal leadership, the Soviet forces made a determined stand.[111] Yudenich's lieutenants had failed to cut all of the rail connections to the city, and the Bolsheviks were able to move up heavy reinforcements. In this situation, with his initial advance checked, Yudenich had little hope of capturing Petrograd without foreign help.

Once again, Yudenich looked toward Finland. In Paris, Sazonov told Finnish representatives that, should Finland intervene, Kolchak would be ready to recognize Finnish independence and to appoint a diplomatic representative to Helsingfors. Otherwise, Sazonov said, Finland would "lose an exceptional opportunity for establishing satisfactory relations with Russia."[112] To Sazonov's voice was added that of Mannerheim, who had lost the election for his country's presidency in late July and who was then in Paris. The

---

jected to unnecessary hardship or undue strain, and that everything possible is done for their comfort." (Telegram 81949 to British mission, Reval; W.O. 33/975, no. 4059.)

[109] For the strengths of both sides in these operations, see Gorn, *Grazhdanskaya voina*, pp. 280-90.

[110] See Imbrie (U.S. Vice-Consul at Viborg, Finland) to Secretary of State, telegrams 115, 116 and 122—14, 16, and 20 October 1919; *Foreign Relations, 1919, Russia*, pp. 722, 724-25. Also Bennett, *Cowan's War*, pp. 181-85.

[111] Trotsky played a leading part in the defense of Petrograd, planning all the operations himself and personally rallying the faltering defenders. See I. Deutscher, *The Prophet Armed: Trotsky, 1879-1921*, London, 1954, pp. 443-46.

[112] Related in a telegram from Sazonov to Sablin (Russian Chargé d'Affaires in London), 28 October 1919 (handed by Sablin to the Foreign Office, 29 October); *British Documents*, vol. III, no. 504.

fall of the Soviet regime was only a matter of time, he advised in an open letter to the man who had defeated him. By coming to Yudenich's assistance Finland would have, as Sazonov had said, a unique opportunity to build against the future.[113] In Helsingfors these appeals were firmly rejected. Finland could not mount an expedition against Petrograd without extensive foreign assistance, Holsti, the Foreign Minister, said. And, even if this assistance were forthcoming, the Finns would require from both the White Russians and the Allies not only more concrete guarantees of Finland's independence, but recognition of its territorial claims (principally in Eastern Karelia) as well.[114] In London the British government responded with merely a brief acknowledgment to a request from Sazonov that the Russian gold, given to the Germans by the Bolsheviks under the Treaty of Brest-Litovsk and since turned over by the Germans to the Allies, should be used to subsidize Finnish intervention.[115]

Thus, Yudenich received no assistance; in the face of superior Soviet forces, the North-Western Army retired from Gatchina on 3 November, from Gdov on the 7th, and from Yamburg on the 14th. In the midst of this retreat they were struck by a terrible epidemic of spotted typhus. On 25 November, the acting assistant British commissioner at Reval reported that the North-Western Army might "be said to have ceased to exist."[116]

Trotsky had wanted the Red Army to follow the surviving members of Yudenich's force across the frontier into Estonia, but Chicherin thought that such an action would only "rouse the English Liberals and moderate Tories against us" and "save a tottering Churchill." Lenin supported Chicherin, and the pursuing Soviet forces stopped at the frontier, demanding only that the White troops be disarmed.[117] The Estonians complied; all Russians crossing the border were disarmed and interned, and the ministers of the mori-

[113] Mannerheim's telegram to President Stahlberg, 29 October 1919, is printed in his *Memoirs*, pp. 234-35.

[114] Gorn, *Grazhdanskaya voina*, pp. 314-21. See Smith, *Finland and the Russian Revolution*, pp. 168-72, for a thorough discussion of these events.

[115] Memorandum from the Russian Embassy, Paris, to the Allied Powers, 3 November 1919; *British Documents*, vol. III, no. 515. The British acknowledgment, 12 November, is quoted in n. 2.

[116] Smythies (Reval) to Curzon, despatch 15, 25 November 1919; *ibid.*, no. 559. Tallents, *Man and Boy*, p. 364. Gorn, *Grazhdanskaya voina*, pp. 324-30.

[117] See the correspondence between Chicherin, Trotsky, and Lenin in Meijer, *Trotsky Papers*, vol. I, nos. 397, 399, 403, and 409-12.

bund North-West government were given a fortnight in which to leave Estonia.[118] The last White threat to Petrograd was at an end.

The way was now open for Estonia to come to terms with the Soviet government. Since the Baltic states had already been informed that the British government could offer them no advice, the Foreign Office made no official comment on the conferences which took place at Dorpat during December. Curzon did, however, instruct Tallents to use his influence to prolong the Soviet-Estonian negotiations as long as possible, in order to allow the Estonians to escape the humiliating terms the Russians first put forward. But he told the British commissioner to avoid giving the impression that Britain would furnish any material assistance. And he added:

Estonians must as we have previously said be only judges of their true interests and we do not wish to become responsible for their action in this crisis or expose ourselves to any justifiable reproach should their decision whatever form it takes have disastrous consequences.[119]

The Soviet government refused to enter into joint negotiations with all three Baltic states. Therefore, on 31 December 1919, the Estonians consented to a separate armistice, and, on 2 February 1920, the Treaty of Tartu (Dorpat) formally brought peace between Soviet Russia and Estonia. Moscow signed similar treaties with Lithuania, Latvia, and Finland during the following summer and autumn.[120]

Within the Foreign Office these events in the Baltic had, at least, a clarifying and simplifying quality, in contrast to those bizarre moments in August 1919 when British officers had brought into existence the North-West Russian Government. Curzon even went so far, early in January 1920, to observe that he welcomed the disappearance from the scene of Yudenich's army. From Churchill, in a private letter, came a stinging rejoinder.[121] Whatever the defects of the North-Western Army, it had managed for months, at practically no cost to the Allies other than a few shipments of

---

[118] Smythies' despatch 15, 25 November 1919, cited above, n. 116.

[119] Curzon to Tallents (Riga), telegram 167, 19 December 1919; *British Documents*, vol. III, no. 610.

[120] The dates of these treaties were: Estonia, 2 February 1920; Lithuania, 12 July 1920; Latvia, 11 August 1920; and Finland, 14 October 1920. Their texts may be found in *Dokumenty vneshnei politiki*, vol. II, pp. 339-54, and vol. III, pp. 28-42, 101-16, and 265-82, respectively.

[121] Churchill to Curzon, 5 January 1920, Curzon MSS, box 22.

munitions, to tie down 30-50,000 Bolshevik soldiers which otherwise, transferred to the southern front, would have made Denikin's lot even more difficult. Churchill continued:

The disappearance of the North-West Russian Army which you welcome will undoubtedly achieve that result now. Considering that we have spent large sums of money and are employing 2,000 officers and men in aiding General Denikin, and that this policy has hitherto commanded your full approval, I do not understand how it is that you can at the same time consistently welcome the disappearance of a force which, although operating in a different geographical theatre, is in fact an integral part of the anti-Bolshevik Russian forces.

Churchill's conclusion was an epitaph on the whole intervention and on the failure of his own efforts to provide it with direction. He wrote:

It is just this idea of war in compartments and sections that has been fatal to the military situation. The whole front is one, and withdrawal of pressure from any part increases the difficulties of any other part. To welcome the disappearance of the North-West Russian Army is in fact to welcome the disappearance of General Denikin's and Admiral Kolchak's armies. It seems to me that you are likely in the near future to have further causes of satisfaction of this character accorded you.

The Baltic area was the region most affected by one other aspect of Allied intervention in Russia during 1919—the blockade—which we must discuss before turning to the reassessment of British policy produced by the collapse of the anti-Bolshevik forces.

Between the Armistice with Germany in November 1918 and the ratification by Germany of the Treaty of Versailles the following July, the ports of Soviet Russia—notably Petrograd, but also the Black Sea ports when they were in Bolshevik hands—were blockaded under the war powers of the various Allied governments, which justified the measures as constituting part of their efforts to ensure that Germany would sign and ratify the Treaty. This was patently a pretext, however, for after the Armistice there was little chance that German weapons might pass to the Bolsheviks or, conversely, that Russian foodstuffs might be shipped to Germany. The Allies still rigidly blockaded Germany's own coasts, and a Poland hostile both to Germany and to Russia lay between them. Yet, pretext though it was, it nevertheless served to justify the blockade of Russia under international law.

As a report on 7 June to the Council of Four from the Supreme Economic Council pointed out, this justification would no longer obtain once peace formally came. Moreover, the coming of peace would bring the expiration of the agreements made by the various neutrals not to trade with states under Allied blockade. The result was a dilemma. While the Powers could prevent their own citizens, and ships registered under their own flags, from trading with the Bolsheviks, they could not, under international law, legally forbid such intercourse to citizens or ships of states which did not choose to comply with their wishes. Moreover, the report pointed out, even restrictions on Allied citizens by their own governments would require special legislation; given the ambivalent feelings in nearly all the Allied countries regarding Russia, such legislation would not be easy to achieve. And while restrictions on Allied citizens would deprive the Bolsheviks of certain resources, they would also serve simply to throw the bulk of the Russian trade to states like Germany and the neutrals, whose governments probably had no intention of preventing their citizens from trading at Soviet ports.[122]

Lloyd George emphasized this dilemma when the Council of Four met on 17 June to consider the Supreme Economic Council's report. He was hardly eager to see trade go to Germany simply because the Allies adhered to a principle. Yet neither Lloyd George nor any of the other statesmen present expressed a definite opinion on whether or not he *wanted* to permit trade with the Bolsheviks. The only definite position was the one taken on wholly legalistic grounds by President Wilson: since none of the Powers was formally at war with the Soviet government, there was no legal basis for a blockade. Therefore, traders would have to be allowed to trade, although, obviously, at their own risk. The Four finally decided to adopt as a temporary measure, subject to future revision, the solution recommended by the Economic Council: to cease interfering with trade, although not to announce either that the blockade had been lifted or that trade with Soviet Russia might take place.[123]

[122] The Supreme Economic Council's report, 7 June 1919, is in *Foreign Relations, 1919, Russia*, pp. 149-51.
[123] Minutes, Council of Four, 17 June 1919, 4 p.m., *Foreign Relations, Paris Peace Conference*, vol. VI, pp. 530-32, and Mantoux, *Conseil des Quatre*, vol. II, pp. 452-55.

This was hardly a satisfactory solution. Had the blockade machinery actually been removed, its absence would surely have been rapidly discovered. But the British government, whose warships, in effect, comprised the blockade machinery, had no intention of removing it. As we have seen, during the summer of 1919 the Royal Navy was engaged in active warfare in the Baltic against both the Bolsheviks and the *Freikorps* units of von der Goltz. Despite its daring torpedo boat raid into Kronstadt harbor on 18 June, the Navy still felt that it was not given enough scope for its operations. Thus, on 27 June, Admiral R. E. Wemyss, the First Sea Lord, wrote in a memorandum circulated to the Cabinet that the Admiralty "labours under a great disadvantage" in having to conduct a "minor war" without definite knowledge of the wishes and intentions of the government. This lack of knowledge, Wemyss said, damaged the morale of the officers of the Baltic force, because they could not feel certain that their actions would meet with London's approval. "The Admiralty would therefore welcome a decision that it is the desire of H. M. Government that the Bolshevik Naval Forces should be suppressed," Wemyss wrote, and he continued, in language that would be echoed by other commanders in other wars: "It is not fair to the Navy to employ it in the present fettered fashion."[124]

The unusual combination of pressure from the Admiralty and President Wilson's insistence, as described by Lloyd George, that no legal state of war existed between the Allies and the Bolsheviks because there had been no declarations of war, caused the Cabinet to decide on 4 July that

(a) In fact, a state of war did exist between Great Britain and the Bolshevist Government of Russia;
(b) In consequence of (a), our Naval forces in Russian waters should be authorised to engage enemy forces by land and sea, when necessary.[125]

These were meaningless decisions. The latter gave the Navy no clearer a directive concerning its conduct than it had had since the previous winter. And the former, because it was *not* accompanied by a declaration of war, or even by a public announcement of the British government's position, failed altogether to meet Woodrow Wilson's contention that under the existing circumstances a

---

[124] Cabinet paper G. T. 7578, "Trend of Events in the Baltic," 27 June 1919; Cab. 24/82.
[125] War Cabinet minutes W.C. 588A, 4 July 1919; Cab. 23/15.

blockade of Russia—desirable as it might be—could not legally be maintained. Here again, the Cabinet's minutes record only the decisions and not the arguments which led to them. Thus we do not know the Cabinet's intentions, but the decisions themselves could have had little effect on the Navy's sense of frustration, and none at all on the confusion which surrounded the blockade.

On 9 July, five days after this Cabinet meeting, peace formally came when the Reichstag ratified the Treaty of Versailles and it was signed by the German President and Premier. When the Supreme Council met again in Paris to consider the blockade, on the 15th, the problem was no longer hypothetical: the Swedish government was already insisting upon the right of its citizens to trade at Petrograd.[126] Before the Council was a memorandum by Sir William Mitchell-Thomson, Director of Restriction of Enemy Supplies, suggesting that physical controls over shipping in the Gulf of Finland might be continued because of the existence there of active hostilities; they might be "regularised" by an announcement that "under existing circumstances traffic into and out of ports in the Gulf of Finland can only be conducted under permit from the Allied Naval Command there."[127]

Supporting this British memorandum before the Council, Arthur Balfour argued that the fact that the waters of the Gulf were mined, and the need for secrecy in the zone of operations, made an informal blockade essential.[128] He did not suggest that trading vessels be subject to capture, sunk, or proceeded against in prize courts, but only that they be turned back to their point of origin; otherwise, it would be impossible to carry on naval warfare in such narrow waters. Balfour met with agreement from the French and the

---

[126] The Swedish government's position was noted in the minutes, Council of Heads of Delegations, 15 July 1919, 3:30 p.m.; *British Documents*, vol. I, no. 11, pp. 89-91. On 1 July, Sir Coleridge Kennard, then Acting Chargé d'Affaires in Stockholm, reported that the foreign minister had sent for him and asked him directly whether or not Great Britain was at war with Soviet Russia. He replied, Kennard said, "by stating that an actual state of war did not exist between Great Britain and Soviet Russia, and a state of peace did not exist either. . . . His Majesty's Government had not recognised Soviet Government. It was therefore out of the question for H. M. Government to be formally at war with them. We considered the Bolsheviks in Soviet Russia as a band of brigands against whom measures such as are generally employed against brigands had out of necessity been taken." Kennard noted that this explanation did not satisfy the Swedes, "as no Blockade of Russia had been officially notified to them." (Telegram 1085, file 592/2/3/17277; F.O. 608/181.)

[127] Mitchell-Thomson's memorandum, 11 July 1919, is appended to the Council minutes cited in n. 126 (*British Documents*, vol. I, pp. 99-100).

[128] The Council's minutes for this session are cited in n. 126.

Italian representatives, who argued that it was absurd to make war on the Bolsheviks in one sphere while allowing trade with them in another. But the Americans, Henry White and John Foster Dulles, once again emphasized their government's insistence on the scrupulous observance of legal forms. To President Wilson, the principle of freedom of the seas was too important to be compromised. So the seemingly endless discussions continued throughout the summer. On 25 July, Balfour drafted an urgent telegram to the President asking him to reconsider because of the special gravity of a situation in which British and White Russian troops were being killed.[129] The President replied that, while he was fully sympathetic with the aims of the proposed blockade, he could not constitutionally prosecute an act of war, such as a blockade affecting neutrals, unless Congress had declared war against the blockaded nation. He felt, however, that if the neutral governments were approached with the Allied case, they would themselves take measures to prevent their nationals from trading with the Bolsheviks.[130]

Discouraged by Wilson's insistence, Balfour reluctantly abandoned his efforts to work out a formula whereby Allied warships could stop neutral shipping and set out to find a policy acceptable to America.[131] But while the Council debated, the blockade continued—legally or not. The Powers, including the United States, refused to grant export licenses or clearance papers for cargoes or ships of their nationals bound for Soviet ports. And most of the few neutral or German ships which did brave the minefields in the Finnish Gulf were forced to turn back by British or French warships. Several times, in making their legal case, the Americans stated that, so far as they were concerned, the Allies could continue the blockade themselves.[132] During 1919, as during 1918, the volume of Soviet Russia's foreign trade was almost insignificant.[133]

Finally, on 29 September, after much wrangling, a note was

[129] Balfour's draft telegram is in *ibid.*, no. 18, Appendix D, pp. 202-3. Its text as sent in the name of the Allied Powers on 27 July is in *Foreign Relations, 1919, Russia*, pp. 154-55.

[130] The President's reply, sent as telegram 2714 from Secretary of State to American delegation (Paris), 2 August 1919; *ibid.*, pp. 155-57.

[131] Minutes, Council of Heads of Delegations, 8 August 1919, 3:30 p.m.; *British Documents*, vol. I, no. 31, p. 381.

[132] Henry White, head of the American delegation, made this statement as early as 25 July. (Council of Heads of Delegations, 25 July 1919, 3:30 p.m., *ibid.*, no. 17, p. 189.)

[133] See the report of the Commissariat of Trade and Industry to the Seventh Congress of Soviets, December 1919, in *Dokumenty vneshnei politiki*, vol. II, pp. 621-29.

drafted which met with the acceptance of all the Powers. Addressed to the neutral governments and to Germany, it requested (a) that clearance papers be refused to vessels intending to proceed to Soviet ports, (b) that an equivalent embargo be placed upon goods intended to be transmitted by land to Russian destination, (c) that passports be refused to individuals desirous of traveling to or from Bolshevik Russia, (d) that banks be prohibited from dealing with the affairs of, or transacting business with, Bolshevik Russia, and (e) that mails and telegraphic communications destined for, or coming from, Bolshevik Russia, so far as possible be denied transmission. These measures, the neutrals were told, were already in effect in the Allied countries.[134] Early in October this note was given to the neutrals. Curiously enough, weeks passed and no replies were received. Apparently the neutrals never did reply.[135] The German government, replying on 30 October, stated that, while it was anxious to combat Bolshevism, it nevertheless felt that restrictions on trade would only drive the remaining democratic elements in Russia into the Soviet camp and therefore serve to strengthen just those groups which such measures were designed to cripple.[136]

By this time, however, the whole issue was becoming largely hypothetical in any case. The Gulf of Finland was beginning to clog with ice. On 31 October the Cabinet decided that the British Baltic fleet should be withdrawn, leaving behind only a small nucleus "to show the flag."[137] On 20 November the Cabinet turned to the block-

[134] Minutes, Council of Heads of Delegations, 29 September 1919, 10:30 a.m.; British Documents, vol. I, no. 67, pp. 824-26. For the note, see Appendix G, p. 830.

[135] On 28 October, Cecil Harmsworth, the Parliamentary Under-Secretary of State for Foreign Affairs, told the House of Commons: "No answers have yet been received to the Note addressed to the neutral Governments and the German Government by the Peace Conference. The Allied naval forces have instructions to turn back ships sailing to Russian Baltic ports. These measures do not constitute a blockade in the legal sense of the word, and no notification has been addressed to neutral Governments other than that of which the terms have already been made public." (120 *H.C. Deb.*, col. 446.)

[136] *Manchester Guardian*, 31 October 1919. The text of the German note is in file 592/2/3/20081; F.O. 608/181.

[137] Conference of Ministers, 31 October 1919, noon; minutes appended to those of Cabinet 2 (19), Cab. 23/18. NOTE: At the end of October 1919, Lloyd George abandoned the War Cabinet format (its practices had long since been abandoned) and substituted for it a system of "regular" Cabinet meetings and "special" conferences of ministers, often hurriedly assembled to deal with one or two specific matters; the composition of conference meetings and Cabinet meetings were often (but not necessarily) identical, and conferences were usually (but not always) endowed with full decision-making authority. As in the present case, conference minutes were usually attached to a proximate set of Cabinet minutes (often those of a Cabinet at which similar matters were discussed). Under the new system, moreover, the records of both Cabinet meetings and ministerial conferences were

ade itself in order to meet a number of questions that had been put down in the House of Commons. Within the government, too, the blockade had few supporters despite the fact—as the Cabinet learned—that the only ships actually being turned back were those carrying military supplies. Now even these measures, because they rested on such shaky legal foundations, were abandoned: the Cabinet agreed that, after the ice melted in the spring, the blockade would not be reinstated unless the situation had drastically changed.[138] That afternoon Lloyd George told the House that "this problem" was "being solved by natural courses as with the formation of ice, both the ships which might have traded with Petrograd and the Allied war ships which might have turned them back, must go elsewhere." And he added: "It is not proposed that the British Fleet should undertake the patrol of the Baltic in the spring."[139]

The blockade was by no means the only barrier to trade between Soviet Russia and the rest of the world. There remained constrictions of all sorts, from license requirements to credit limitations to uncertainties about the legal title to Soviet goods. These would not be easily dismantled.[140] The mere removal of the blockade was of little but symbolic importance.

For our purposes, however, the blockade is important, not for the relatively slight effect it had on Soviet commerce, but for the light it sheds on the mentality of the Allied Powers which aimed at the destruction of Bolshevism. Never could the Allies fully admit that they were at war with the Soviet government. Instead, they allowed the rigid categories of international law, which were not intended to function in the shadowy area between war and peace, to impede for months their efforts to apply the sanctions they thought necessary. Always, at the back of their minds, Allied statesmen entertained a fear that, just possibly, the Bolsheviks did command the loyalty of significant parts of the Russian population. Were they to confront the enemy with naked force, instead of with force shielded by a façade of shabby legality, they would have nourished the doubts which, by the autumn of 1919, had begun to grow in more than one Allied capital.

---

formally referred to as "conclusions," and often, but not always, they were little more than that. In general, they reveal much less about the nature of the Cabinet-level discussions than did War Cabinet minutes.

[138] Cabinet conclusions 8 (19), 20 November 1919; 11:30 a.m.; Cab. 23/18.

[139] 121 *H.C. Deb.*, col. 1106.

[140] The process of doing so is one of the principal subjects of Volume III of the present work.

CHAPTER VIII

THE END OF INTERVENTION:
POLICIES AND POLITICS

Instead of plunging into a new war with Russia, it was decided to buy some butter from her and to sell her some cotton goods. And very good sense, too.

—*Manchester Guardian, 19 January 1920*

Peace is but a drop of water falling constantly on a stone; it makes at last a hole there.

—*Maxim Litvinov, 5 January 1920*

IT is tempting to view the course of British intervention in Russia during the year following the Armistice of November 1918 as a contest between the two greatest figures in British politics of the twentieth century, David Lloyd George and Winston Churchill. Certainly the record makes it appear so. In the Cabinet deliberations in London during November and December, in the debates in Paris and London in February 1919, in the decisions of the summer regarding withdrawal from North Russia and assistance to Kolchak, Denikin, and Yudenich, and in the reexamination of policy that took place in the autumn, the leading protagonists of opposing positions were Lloyd George and Churchill. So it also seemed to observers outside the government. Colonel Josiah Wedgwood, one of the most persistent critics of the government's Russian policy, wryly told the House of Commons on 5 November: "Our real difficulty on these benches is that we have against us a composite Government, a coalition between the Prime Minister and the right hon. Gentleman, the Secretary of War."[1]

There was much that was valid in such a view, but there was even more that was misleading. What appeared to be a contest was no contest at all: Churchill's influence never approached that of

[1] 120 *H.C. Deb.*, cols. 1554-55.

[294]

Lloyd George. Whenever their views came directly into conflict, Churchill's lost. Moreover, within the Coalition government Churchill occupied a position of near-isolation. The Cabinet's minutes are sufficiently sketchy so that it is impossible to tell always who may have shared Churchill's yearning for a large-scale, coordinated military effort against the Soviet regime, but it is easy enough to tell who did not. His fellow Liberals—Addison, Fisher, and Montagu, with the possible exception of Edward Shortt, the Home Secretary—did not. Neither, of course, did George Barnes, the Cabinet's working man. Yet on a question like intervention (or, indeed, on any other question) these men mattered little: as minority members of a Conservative-dominated Coalition, they had no place to go but into opposition.

What counted in the politics of the Coalition were the views of the Conservatives. As 1922 was to demonstrate, they indeed had some place to go. And among the Conservatives, those who counted most were Bonar Law, Chamberlain, Curzon, and Balfour (in that order). These four held differing views regarding Russia. All of them opposed Bolshevism as a doctrine with a vehemence close to that of Churchill. But regarding British policy, all of them, with the possible exception of Curzon, were more nearly in accord with the Prime Minister than with the Secretary of State for War. Chamberlain, as Chancellor of the Exchequer, was convinced the country could not afford intervention. More than any of his colleagues he was daily brought up against the gap between British commitments and the resources which could be obtained from a war-tired people and economy, and within the Cabinet he argued consistently for the reduction of British commitments. Bonar Law did not much concern himself with international affairs. But he was generally distrustful of foreign adventures and felt that they cost governments dearly in domestic popularity—1922 was to demonstrate this, too. Balfour's views on Russia are less easy to make out. Like most of his colleagues, he was not averse to a modest effort at intervention. But operations on the scale which Churchill suggested he viewed as politically and economically imprudent. In any case, he was in Paris as head of the British delegation throughout much of the summer and autumn of 1919 and took almost no part in the deliberations of the Cabinet in London. Nor did he bother, except regarding one or two quite specific matters, to submit his views on Russian problems in writing. Balfour was older by more than a decade than any of the other three. By the summer of 1919 he was exhausted. Although he retained the formal title of Foreign Secretary, all of the duties of the office fell to Curzon. Finally, on 29 October, the two switched titles (Balfour becoming Lord President of the Council) but not roles. For Curzon, with his Asian and imperial preoccupations, the great boon of the Bolshevik upheaval was that it seemed to eliminate Russia as a rival to the British Empire along thousands of miles of once contested frontier; the great defect of Churchill's policies was precisely that they threatened to re-create a Great Russia.

The only figure in the government who seemed consistently to share Churchill's views was Walter Long, the First Lord of the Admiralty. Long played a far from minor role within the ranks of the leading Conservatives, but in 1919 his influence was declining, along with his health. Milner, Churchill's predecessor at the War Office and Colonial Secretary during 1919, probably also shared his successor's policy preferences regarding Russia. Neither from the Cabinet's minutes, nor from Milner's own collected papers, however, can one be sure. In any case, Milner had little political importance. The same cannot be said, in 1919, of F. E. Smith, who, as Lord Birkenhead, became Lord Chancellor early in the year. But his views on Russia are largely unknown. He was a friend of Churchill and shared much of Churchill's temperament; but the record does not indicate that he also shared his interventionist policies. One could go on to consider other names—Shortt, the Geddes brothers, Sir Robert Horne—but to little purpose. Their views on intervention are obscure, and, even if they were in complete accord with Churchill, their political positions were such as to have enabled them to lend him little real support.

Where Churchill could have received perhaps his most useful support—from the professional military establishment within his own department—he was relatively unsuccessful. Field-Marshal Sir Henry Wilson (he received his baton in July 1919), the C.I.G.S., favored armed action against the Bolsheviks, provided the arms were not on British shoulders. We have already seen something of Wilson's rigidly held priorities. Soldiers were scarce. They were desperately needed in India, in Egypt, and most important—in Ireland and at home. Given the political climate of 1919, it would be impossible to recruit a number sufficient for the large-scale intervention which,

alone, could have been effective in Russia; to squander lesser numbers there, given the government's needs elsewhere, would have been
sheer folly, and Wilson never refrained from saying so, sharply. If
other high-ranking officers disagreed, they lacked the facilities for
making their views known. Wilson's position was strategic: he, not
Churchill, spoke for the professional military establishment within
the Cabinet, and his political connections were remarkably good—
probably as good as those of his Secretary of State.

To say that Churchill had no influential allies within the Cabinet
is not to say that support was lacking for intervention itself, provided that its scale was limited. At the time of the Armistice, the
arguments of Milner, Balfour, and Churchill were persuasive: the
British government owed a "debt of honor" to the Russians who had
remained loyal to the Allied cause. Moreover, those British military
formations already in Russia could not, in any case, be easily removed until the coming spring and summer. Why should they,
meanwhile, be either idle or neutral? Subsequent commitments were
not so much of manpower as of matériel, most of it surplus left
over from the vast stocks of wartime. What better use for it than
against the Bolsheviks? In these measures Churchill had many allies
—virtually the whole of the Coalition ranks in the House of Commons. Here, indeed, was the main source of his strength, the reason
he could for so long continue to advocate a Russian policy that so
little accorded with that of his Prime Minister. From the Coalition
backbenches came the cry, early in 1919, for the publication of what
became known as the "Bolshevik atrocity bluebook." From these
backbenches, from the Conservatives in particular, came the two
hundred signatures on the telegram to Lloyd George in Paris insisting that he deny the rumors that he was contemplating a compromise peace with Lenin.[2] On the Russian question Churchill was
closer to these two hundred backbenchers than he was to most
of his Cabinet colleagues. Although a firm alliance was impossible
—as a convert to Liberalism and as a principal author of the Darda-
nelles disaster, he was too much distrusted—the combination of
Churchill and these Coalition backbenchers worked to strengthen
the War Secretary's position within the Cabinet and to infuse Lloyd
George with a healthy sense of caution. The Prime Minister was
fond of making speeches about the dangers of interfering in other

[2] See above, ch. IV.

people's revolutions, but for the six months following the near-revolt among the Conservatives in April 1919 he made his noninterventionist speeches in private.[3] Lord Robert Cecil had in mind not only the rest of the government but Lloyd George as well when he stated, in February 1920:

> Whenever the anti-Bolshevists were successful, then there was a considerable reversion to what I may call the Churchillian policy. As soon as they were driven back there was a great movement towards non-intervention.[4]

Cecil was unfair to Churchill. The policies he ascribed to the government were interventionist, but they were not "Churchillian": Churchill's policies were never tried. Over the course of the year 1919, in a series of letters to the Prime Minister and to Curzon and in memoranda to the Cabinet, he made clear what the differences were between existing and "Churchillian" policies. One thread runs through them all. The Allies were pursuing no concerted policy. Even the British government had no clear sense of priorities; too often it undid with its left hand what it had done with its right. British assistance to the anti-Bolshevik side was on a scale large enough to constitute a serious drain on the Empire's resources, yet it was not sufficient, nor was it vigorously enough pursued, to lead to any definite result. "There is no 'will to win' behind any of these ventures," he wrote to Lloyd George on 27 February. "At every point we fall short of what is necessary to obtain real success."[5]

These were the constants in Churchill's equation. The variables were the manpower commitments he asked of the Allies. From the outset he embraced Marshal Foch's scheme for a massive campaign against Bolshevism marked, however, by a technological division of labor. The border states on Russia's western frontier would furnish large infantry armies. They would be equipped and supplied by the Great Powers and bolstered by "modern" aviation and armored formations of Western volunteer specialists. And the whole effort

---

[3] Thus, after a long talk with the Prime Minister regarding intervention on 10 July 1919, Henry Wilson noted in his diary: "It is clear L.G. wants to cut our connection with it altogether even to stopping supplies & munitions to Denikin & to Kolchak." And the following day, after another talk: "It is clear that LG's instinct is to make a clean cut." (Wilson MS diary.)

[4] 125 *H.C. Deb.*, col. 282 (12 February 1920).

[5] Churchill to Lloyd George, 27 February 1919; excerpts in Churchill, *Aftermath*, pp. 176-77.

would be led by an Allied general staff to which would be delegated considerable authority.

As we have seen, this scheme was rejected in February 1919 both by the British government and by the Supreme Council in Paris, and Churchill was enough of a realist not to return to it. In any case, with the White Russian successes of the spring and summer, such an enterprise no longer seemed of critical importance. Instead, he increasingly emphasized the need for coordination and a clear sense of priority among British policies. Thus, he strongly opposed efforts to make peace between the Bolsheviks and any of their national opponents—the Baltic states, Finland, and Poland in particular—which would liberate Soviet troops to fight against the Whites. And, in general, he urged that a clear choice be made between support of the White leaders, with their insistence on the reconstitution of a united Great Russia, and support of the aspirations for national independence of the peoples of the Baltic region and of Transcaucasia. For Churchill there was no question that the correct choice was the former, regardless of the sympathies which he, with many Englishmen, felt for the "small states."[6]

To a greater degree than any of his colleagues, Churchill had well developed notions, or alternate sets of notions, of what the future course of world politics would be. Germany and Japan would play inimical roles; their interests would almost invariably conflict with those of Great Britain, France, and the United States. Most to be avoided, therefore, was the creation of conditions which would bring about an alliance of Germany with Russia—"that very Russo-German alliance which, whether on a Bolshevik or anti-Bolshevik basis, constitutes the greatest danger that threatens us in the future"—to which Japan might adhere as well. Thus would arise a "new triplice" which would create "an antagonism of hostile forces as dangerously balanced as were those which preceded the outbreak of the Great War," confronting the democracies with "perils as great as those from which they have emerged."[7] In a memorandum written on 16 September 1919, Churchill set down his conception of the German-Russian relationship:

[6] We have seen many instances of Churchill's views of this sort. Perhaps their fullest expression came in a long memorandum he wrote on 16 September 1919 and circulated on the 22nd as Cabinet paper G.T. 8207; Cab. 24/89. Excerpts, but by no means the bulk of it, are in his *Aftermath*, pp. 251-53.

[7] From the memorandum cited in n. 6.

Generally speaking, it may be said that there are two Russias and two Germanies, a Bolshevik and an anti-Bolshevik Russia, and a pro-Bolshevik and an anti-Bolshevik Germany. Both Germanies look to Russia as their only means of regaining world power. Each keeps up its own relations with its counterpart in Russia. Either by the pro-Bolshevik or anti-Bolshevik road Germany is determined to get hold of Russia. At present doubt exists as to which will be the best hand for Germany to hold out, and which will be the best hand for them to grasp in Russia. Up to the present moment only Bolshevik Russia is ready to deal with either section in Germany. But the moment the Allies take steps which are fundamentally injurious to anti-Bolshevik Russia, and make it clear that they do not care whether it is crushed or not, both the Russian hands will be stretched out alternatively for Germany to clasp, and either in one way or another these two mighty branches of the human race will come together in effective action.[8]

Yet despite his fear of a German-Russian combination, Churchill was not nearly as quick as, for example, the Russia Department of the Foreign Office to reject as inadmissible any arrangements for German assistance to the anti-Bolshevik cause in Russia. Here, once again, was his sense of priorities. Nothing could have been further from Churchill's outlook than the Foreign Office statement that "it would be better that Petrograd should not be captured at all than that it should be captured by the Germans."[9] For Churchill, such selectivity—if the alternative were the failure of Yudenich and the probable triumph of Bolshevism—was lamentably shortsighted. Given that the Germans seemed disposed to offer Yudenich "substantial and decisive aid" in the capture of Petrograd, and that the British government had "sedulously refused to make [itself] responsible in any way for the success or failure of the operations in this theatre," Churchill posed two questions to his colleagues:

(1.) Have we the right to cut [the Russians] off from the only other form of aid that is available and

(2.) Have we the power?[10]

His own answer to both of these questions was negative. It was by no means clear that the Allies could bring to bear the necessary force to expel von der Goltz and his *Freikorps* troops (although, as we have seen, the Latvians, with British naval assistance, sub-

[8] *Idem.*
[9] Cited above, ch. VII, n. 13.
[10] From the memorandum cited in n. 6.

sequently did so); moreover, "the simple expulsion of the Germans without making any effort to fill the void will only cut off from the struggling National Russians their last hope." Churchill aimed instead at a solution more finely balanced, and therefore difficult to achieve: "an orderly and stable region between Germany and Russia in which the legitimate interests of Germany will not be ignored, but in which her influence cannot be predominant." He never spelled out, however, what these phrases meant; presumably the "National Russian" successors to the Bolsheviks, in exchange for German assistance in the capture of Petrograd, would allow German settlement, but not control, of the Baltic regions. In this arrangement, of course, there was no room for independent Baltic states. Here was a notion of appeasement: Churchill was never a believer in repressive policies as a means of preventing Germany from once again becoming a menace to its neighbors. A year later, when it was no longer possible to think that Russia would be "National," as opposed to Bolshevik, he was to shock the European public by proposing that the Germans take "a giant step upon the path of self-redemption" by assisting Poland to repel an invading Red Army; his colleagues in the British government, who had been exposed to his thinking over the intervening period, had no reason to be shocked.[11]

Churchill did not worry that German assistance to Yudenich's Petrograd campaign would help to bring about a Russian-German combination. British support to Kolchak, and to Denikin in particular, although on a scale smaller than he would have wished, had nevertheless been great enough to leave no doubts as to whom Russia would owe its ultimate debt. Such was the position in mid-September 1919. "No further large expenditure of money (other than the questionable value of surplus munitions), no assistance of troops, except a very limited establishment of technical personnel, are needed," he then wrote. "Countenance, counsel, commerce—these are the means which alone are demanded." The rewards of past policy had at last come into view. Yet they could still be lost if misguided decisions were taken.[12]

Two months later, with Yudenich and Kolchak defeated and Denikin in retreat, Churchill reflected on what he felt had been mis-

[11] See Volume III, ch. V.
[12] From the memorandum cited in n. 6.

guided decisions. On 15 December, in another memorandum, he wrote:

It is obvious . . . that the elements existed which, used in combination, would easily have been successful. They have, however, been dissipated by a total lack of combination, and this had been due to a complete absence of any definite or decided policy among the victorious Allies. Some were in favour of peace and some were in favour of war. In the result they made neither peace nor war. If they made war on one part of the front, they hastened to make peace on another. If they encouraged Koltchak and Denikin and spent both money and men in their support, they gave no encouragement to Finland, to the Baltic States or to Poland. Every proposal to establish a unified system of command and direction of the resistance to the Bolsheviks has been vetoed. In June, Koltchak was promised, on the word of the five plenipotentiaries, continuance of their support in supplies. Since that date, the withdrawal of all support from him has been continuous. Finland at two periods of this year was ready to march, in conjunction with the army of Yudenitch and the Esthonians, and occupy Petrograd. Not the slightest countenance or encouragement was given her in such an enterprise. Poland was prepared to maintain strong pressure against the Bolsheviks: she was actually discouraged.[13] As for the small States, they were told that they could make peace or not, as they liked, and that in any case they would get no help.

All these steps were perfectly compatible with a policy of peace or a policy of strict neutrality. They were certainly not compatible with a policy of war, such as was actually being carried out on other sectors of the immense circle around Bolshevik Russia.[14]

The stream of memoranda from Churchill flowed throughout 1919 (and throughout the following year as well, when new Russian problems presented themselves). Yet it evoked no countering stream —a striking indication that within the decision-making body of the Cabinet there really was no contest between Churchill and Lloyd George over Russian policy. With a few isolated exceptions, neither the Prime Minister nor any other member of the government felt it necessary to set down on paper, for circulation to the Cabinet, connected arguments against those put forward by Churchill. These opposing arguments—the weakness and reac-

[13] This and other aspects of Allied policy regarding Polish-Soviet relations will be treated in Volume III, ch. I.

[14] This memorandum, "Inter-Allied Russian Policy," 15 December 1919 (a War Office and not formally a Cabinet paper), is in W.O. 33/1004. Nearly all is in Churchill, *Aftermath*, pp. 256-59.

tionary character of the Whites, the costs of an activist Russian policy, and the unwillingness of the other Powers to share the man-power and financial burden—were taken almost for granted. This is not to say that Churchill was ignored, at least by Lloyd George: the friendship between the two men was too great for that.[15] Yet, in replying directly as the Prime Minister seems frequently to have done (always by personal letter: among the papers circulated to the Cabinet during 1919 there was not a single paper on Russia from the Prime Minister), he seems to have been motivated not so much by any felt need to rebut Churchill's arguments as by a desire to end what he considered to be a debilitating obsession that hindered the War Secretary's whole conduct of his office. "I get nothing but Russia!" Lloyd George complained in a letter to Church-ill on 30 August 1919. The "military ventures" there had cost much more than the £100 million ascribed to them, for they had pre-vented Churchill from attending to administrative deficiencies costing many scores, if not hundreds, of millions.[16] And, on 22 Sep-tember, Lloyd George wrote that every time he had called on Churchill to discuss urgent problems of military spending, Churchill had invariably promised to take matters in hand—and had then gone home and drafted another paper on Russia. He was "frankly in despair," the Prime Minister said, and continued:

I wonder whether it is any use making one last effort to induce you to throw off this obsession which, if you will forgive me for saying so, is up-setting your balance. I again ask you to let Russia be, at any rate for a few days, and to concentrate your mind on the quite unjustifiable expenditure in France, at home, and in the East, incurred by both the War Office and the Air Department. Some of the items could not possibly have been tol-erated by you if you had given one-fifth of the thought to these matters which you devoted to Russia.[17]

In this letter Lloyd George also dealt, albeit summarily, with

---

[15] On Russia and his friendship with Lloyd George, Churchill remarked to Riddell in mid-1920: "It is extraordinary that we have been able to work together on such terms of personal friendship notwithstanding the divergence of our views regarding Russia. The difference is so marked that I know exactly which foreign telegrams will please him and which will please me. I could mark them red and blue [*sic!*] before he sees them, and I should be right in every case." (Riddell, *Diary*, p. 203, entry for 12 June 1920.)

[16] Lloyd George (vacationing in Deauville) to Churchill, 30 August 1919; ex-cerpts in Frank Owen, *Tempestuous Journey: Lloyd George, His Life and Times*, London, 1954, pp. 517-18.

[17] Lloyd George to Churchill, 22 September 1919; excerpts in *ibid.*, pp. 519-22.

Churchill's substantive arguments, but he did so in a manner which emphasized just how far they were from acceptance. The White Russians had been given a fair chance: "We have kept faith with all these men." The Cabinet had faithfully discharged the obligations it had taken on and had given Churchill every possible support within the context of the policy which it had laid down and he had accepted; once or twice it had even strained that policy in the direction of Churchill's wishes. He was well aware, Lloyd George said, that Churchill was willing to spend hundreds of millions of additional pounds to carry on his Russian policies. "But," he concluded, "as you know that you won't find another responsible person in the whole land who will take your view, why waste your energy and your usefulness on this vain fretting which completely paralyses you for other work?" In this sentence was the essence of Lloyd George's political style, and of its difference from Churchill's. The anti-Bolshevik cause was lost. Lloyd George was never a fighter for lost causes. Churchill was.

❖

The Prime Minister did not make a public statement on Russian policy from the time of his speech in the House of Commons on 16 April 1919 until the Lord Mayor's Banquet at the Guildhall on 8 November. While premiers for generations had used this annual dinner as a platform for major policy addresses, the past occasions had all been at times when Parliament was in recess. But in 1919, when Lloyd George chose Russia as one of his principal topics, the press of business had forced Parliament to reconvene in October, and only three days previously Lloyd George had sat silently through a House of Commons debate on another supplement to the Army's budget, much of it made necessary by the costs of operations in Russia.[18]

In his Guildhall address the Prime Minister raised what he termed the three remaining questions of the Peace—the conflicting claims of Italy and Yugoslavia in the Adriatic, the peace treaty with Turkey, and the problem of Russia.[19] Of these, he said, the last

[18] 120 *H.C. Deb.*, cols. 1535-1642. Churchill informed the House that, including his "final packet" of £15 million for Denikin, expenditures in Russia since the Armistice had cost the country a total of £94.8 million. But this figure, he said, included £47 million worth of "non-marketable stores" which, his advisers told him, should more justly be evaluated at only one-tenth.

[19] Lloyd George's Guildhall speech was printed in *The Times*, 10 November 1919.

was the most difficult, and to it he devoted most of his speech. "There will be no peace until peace is established in Russia"—it was a line he had taken before. Earlier in the year, he reminded his listeners, he had dared to make the unpopular prediction that Bolshevism could not be suppressed by the sword.[20] Now Denikin's "brilliant drive towards Moscow" had been "temporarily checked," and the outlook, so hopeful only a few weeks before, was one of "prolonged and sanguinary struggle." Regrettably, his prediction now seemed accurate. Therefore, Lloyd George said, "other methods must finally be resorted to for restoring peace and good government in that distressed land."

The Prime Minister left his audience with little doubt about what those "other methods" might be. The Supreme Council had tried "to organise the peace among the warring sections"; it had "offered the Russian people the opportunity to decide for themselves by peaceable means" the manner in which they desired to be governed. "Unfortunately," he continued—stretching the truth—"no section of Russia was ready; all were bent on conquest." He hoped, he said, "the time is not distant when the Powers will be able to renew that attempt with better prospects of success."

Here, once again, was the Prinkipo idea, although of course Lloyd George did not use the label.[21] Quickly he moved to sidestep the obvious objection that he was deserting Britain's anti-Bolshevik allies, but in doing so he effectively wrote off their cause. He was not unmindful, he said, of the nation's obligations "to the gallant men in Russia who helped us to fight the Germans when the Bolshevist leaders were betraying the Allies." Indeed, his government had already given real proof of its sympathies in the shape of £100 million worth of material and support, and he did not begrudge a penny of it despite the heavy burdens cast upon the British domestic economy. "It was a debt of honour that we had to discharge." But Lloyd George made clear that, so far as he was concerned, the debt had been settled:

We have given them the opportunity, if Russia wished to be liberated, of equipping her sons in order to free themselves. If the Russian people wish for freedom, we can always say that we gave them the chance. . . . We have

[20] He was referring to his speech of 16 April 1919—but on that occasion his words were considerably more ambiguous. See above, ch. IV.

[21] *The Times* did, however. A sub-headline inserted in the text of his speech read: "Prinkipo Again."

held positions of danger in that country until the Russians were prepared to hold them themselves.

We cannot, of course, afford to continue so costly an intervention in an
interminable civil war.

Now nearly all British forces had left Russia. Frankly, the Prime
Minister said, he was glad of it. "Russia is a quicksand"; it had
swallowed great armies in the past. Winter was coming. Hope-
fully it would give time "for all sections there to reflect and to reconsider the situation." Then might come an opportunity for the
Great Powers to promote peace and concord.

While Lloyd George was speaking, the American ambassador
looked around and noticed the surprised expression on Churchill's
face. Later he learned that Curzon, too, had had no previous knowledge of what the Prime Minister would say.[22] There had been no
Cabinet discussion of it. Inevitably, the speech was the chief topic
of conversation in the lobbies of the House of Commons the following Monday. The Coalition backbenchers who had signed the statement calling Lloyd George to task regarding Russia the previous
April were again distinctly unhappy.[23] So, not surprisingly, was
much of the press.[24] *The Times* asserted that the original Prinkipo proposal had been conceived by "prominent Jewish financiers in
New York whose interest in Trotsky is of old standing." Now, it
implied, the Prime Minister had once again fallen into their hands;
the policies suggested in his speech would "cause the British name
to stink in the nostrils of all patriotic Russians."[25]

Neither *The Times* nor any other of Lloyd George's opponents
on the Right, however, could formulate a more realistic approach
to Russian problems than his—vague as his speech had been. These
critics agreed with the Prime Minister that, given the domestic condition of Britain or any other of the Allied countries, further
armed intervention was out of the question. *The Times* called
instead for "steady moral, political, and diplomatic encouragement"

[22] Davis (London) to Lansing, telegrams 3394 and 3486, 15 November and 3
December 1919; *Foreign Relations, 1919, Russia*, pp. 122, 128-29.
[23] So *The Times'* Lobby correspondent reported, 11 November 1919.
[24] While *The Times*, the *Daily Telegraph*, and the *Morning Post* were strongly
censorious, the *Daily Herald*, the *Daily News*, and the *Manchester Guardian* welcomed the speech, the last saying (10 November 1919): "It is a wise if all too
tardy proposal. Much will be forgiven to Mr. George if he has the courage to
carry it out."
[25] *The Times*, 10 November 1919.

to the anti-Bolshevik cause, adding that "the Russians must, indeed, work out their own salvation, but they should not be left to work it out in moral and political isolation."[26] Here was scarcely a solution. All of the "moral, political, and diplomatic encouragement" which the West possessed could not, by the autumn of 1919, save Kolchak, Denikin, or Yudenich.

The vagueness in Lloyd George's speech allowed him an easy retreat. He was never one to stand in the way of what he took to be a political tide, and on the evening of 10 November the semi-official Press Association released an obviously inspired statement that the speech "should not be taken to imply that the Allied powers have any intention of attempting diplomatic intervention" in the affairs of Russia. There was, the statement said, no question of issuing invitations to the Bolsheviks and the Whites to take part in another conference, nor was there any change in the British government's attitude toward the Soviet regime. And it continued:

What Mr. Lloyd George had in mind was . . . the possibility that with the coming of winter the contending parties in Russia might arrive at some provisional agreement among themselves, when suggestions from the Allied Powers would no doubt have a better prospect of success.[27]

Hasty retreat though this was, it did not deter the Labour Party National Executive and the Parliamentary Committee of the Trades Union Congress from passing, in a specially called joint meeting on the night of 12 November, a resolution welcoming the Guildhall speech as an indication that the government would immediately end its support of the Whites and seek means to bring about peace in Russia.[28] If Lloyd George was unsure of the meaning of his words, each section of political opinion saw in them exactly what suited it. When Sir Samuel Hoare asked angrily in the House whether the government really had not departed from past policy as laid out by Churchill in statements as recent as three days prior to Lloyd George's Guildhall address, Bonar Law, the Leader of the House, replied: "I have already said that is exactly how the speech strikes me. It is simply an expression of the hope . . . that there may be some method of obtaining peace in Russia."[29]

The Prime Minister's Guildhall speech gave rise, of course, to a

[26] *Idem.*   [27] *Ibid.*, 11 November 1919.   [28] *Ibid.*, 13 November 1919.
[29] 121 *H.C. Deb.*, col. 15 (10 November 1919).

host of Parliamentary questions, and on Thursday, 13 November, he was in the House at question hour for the first time since becoming premier three years before.[30] Instead of responding to individual questions, he read a carefully worked-out statement which he had prepared that morning in consultation with Bonar Law, Balfour, and Hankey.[31] Its essence was yet another denial that there had been a departure from past policies. As he had told the House in April, the government would supply limited assistance to the anti-Bolshevik Russians, and it had done so. There was, he implied, no intention of entering into peace negotiations with the Bolsheviks. "On the other hand," he continued,

the Government have an overwhelming sense of the importance of bringing peace to Russia. Not only is Russia a source of unrest and disturbance to all its neighbours . . . but a settlement of the Russian problem is essential to the reconstruction of the world. Russia is one of the great resources for the supply of food and raw material. The present condition of Russia is one of the contributing causes to the prevailing high prices, and high prices are undoubtedly in all lands the most dangerous form of Bolshevik propaganda.

Here was a new theme—the economic benefits that would flow from an end to civil war in Russia. It passed unnoticed in Lloyd George's statement. He returned to it, however, in a long and rambling speech on an adjournment motion four days later.[32] His government's first concern, he said, must be for its own people, "and there is no surer road to Bolshevism than financial bankruptcy." (Lloyd George was perhaps the first Western statesman to use this argument, which subsequently became a staple in the larder of fiscal conservatism.) On this occasion, he emphasized, not the positive benefits of commerce, but the negative costs of continued intervention. Great Britain, he said, had spent more money combating Bolshevism than France, the United States, and Japan put together, and he was proud of it, just as he was proud of the fact that, of all the points of view represented in the House of Commons, none was friendly to the tenets of Bolshevism. But Britain could not finance civil war in Russia indefinitely; she could not take the

---

[30] According to the *Manchester Guardian*'s Lobby correspondent, 11 November 1919.

[31] Conference of Ministers, minutes S-1, 13 November 1919, noon; Cab. 23/35. For the text of Lloyd George's statement, see 121 *H.C. Deb.*, cols. 471-75.

[32] 121 *H.C. Deb.*, cols. 715-26 (17 November 1919).

"terrible responsibility of restoring order in a country which is a continent, which is a part of two continents, which no country has ever intervened in without landing itself in disaster."

Yet, he went on to argue that, far from being a failure, intervention had thus far been a success: it had given the anti-Bolshevik leaders the means to liberate vast tracts of territory. In Siberia, on the Don, and in the Ukraine they still controlled territory containing some thirty to forty million people; if they retained the support of these people, they could hold their own, which was precisely the object of British intervention. Then there were also the peoples of the Baltic states, Finland, Poland, the Ukraine, and the Caucasus, united both in their hatred of Bolshevism and of Great Russian domination. He did not want to discuss the future of those nationalities, he said—but he mentioned, in passing, "a very great Statesman, a man of great imagination . . . Lord Beaconsfield, who regarded a great, gigantic, growing Russia rolling onwards like a glacier towards Persia and the borders of Afghanistan and India as the greatest menace the British Empire could be confronted with."

From this image Lloyd George drew no conclusions. (The White Russians did, however: both Knox, from Vladivostok, and Holman, from Taganrog, telegraphed that the Prime Minister's speech had been taken as a frank indication of British desire for a weak, divided Russia of independent states. "Such frankness as being very rare in diplomacy is much appreciated," Knox said; "it is more than the Russians expected.")[33] Indeed, the Prime Minister's whole speech was inconclusive, serving only to obscure further his previous statements. R. H. Hoare, who had returned from his post as Chargé d'Affaires at Archangel to join the Foreign Office's Russia Department, commented that from the speech British policy would seem to be "a pure negation:—'no further expenditure, no blockade, no negotiations with the Bolsheviks.' "[34] *The Times* was even harsher: its leader the following morning bore the heading, "A Pitiable Performance."[35]

No matter how inconclusive Lloyd George's statements were,

---

[33] Knox (Vladivostok) to War Office, telegram 6433, 13 December 1919; Holman (Taganrog) to War Office, telegram I.P. 3286, 27 December; W.O. 33/975, nos. 4487 and 4555.

[34] Hoare's memorandum, 22 December 1919, is in *British Documents*, vol. III, no. 619.

[35] *The Times*, 18 November 1919.

it was nevertheless clear that there would be significant changes in British policy. The signals were not lost on the Soviet leaders. From Moscow Chicherin broadcast that satisfactory Anglo-Soviet relations were quite possible despite the profound differences between the social systems of the two countries. And he went on to hint at the possibility of economic concessions, saying:

> The British customer and purveyor are as necessary to us as we are to them. Not only do we desire peace and the possibility of internal development, but we also feel strongly the need of economic help from the more fully developed countries such as Great Britain. We are ready even to make sacrifices for the sake of a close economic connection with Britain. . . . I, therefore, gladly welcome the declaration of the British Premier as the first step towards such a sane and real policy corresponding to the interests of both countries.[36]

Chicherin's statement was followed, on 5 December, by a resolution of the Seventh All-Russian Congress of Soviets formally proposing to the governments of the Allied and Associated Powers—"to all together and to each separately"—the immediate beginning of peace negotiations.[37]

Lloyd George himself, in a conversation on 24 November with Frank Polk, the head of the American delegation remaining at the Peace Conference, said that he indeed thought the time had come to see whether it was possible to reach an agreement with the Soviet government. He felt, he said, that the Bolsheviks were

[36] Chicherin's statement, broadcast by Moscow Radio on 20 November 1919, is quoted in A.L.P. Dennis, *The Foreign Policies of Soviet Russia*, London, 1924, p. 380. I have found no Russian text. However, Chicherin made an almost identical statement in an interview printed in the *Daily Herald*, 1 December 1919.

[37] The text of the resolution is in *Dokumenty vneshnei politiki*, vol. II, pp. 298-99; translation in Degras, *Soviet Documents*, vol. I, pp. 176-77. It may, perhaps, have been made partly in response to the following statement by Lloyd George in the House of Commons on 13 November: "As to the question in regard to the so-called peace advances from the Soviet Republic, the Allied Governments have always declined to take any action on communications which purported to come from the Governments of hostile countries through irresponsible agencies. They have acted only on communications coming officially and directly from such Governments. That has been the practice of the Allies during the War, and events have fully justified it. The Government do not think it advisable to depart from that practice now." (121 *H.C. Deb.*, col. 472.) This was Lloyd George's response to the charge, from Labour and the Opposition Liberals, that he had cavalierly disregarded the proposals Bullitt had brought back from Moscow; it was also his way of disposing of an interview with Lenin published in the *Manchester Guardian*, 21 October 1919, in which the Soviet leader stated that the peace terms he had offered Bullitt in March still held good.

anxious for peace, and that they were prepared to recognize their international obligations. In talking with Polk, Lloyd George did not hide his strong feeling that a unified Russia would be a danger to Europe. He hoped, he said, for Georgia, Azerbaijan, Bessarabia, the Ukraine, the Baltic provinces, Finland, and perhaps even Siberia, all to be independent. Here was the Prime Minister's answer to Disraeli's fear of "a great, gigantic, colossal, growing Russia." To John W. Davis, the American Ambassador in London, he later made the same statement: he favored the ultimate division of Russia into a number of independent states, leaving none large enough to threaten the peace, and he was not averse to treating with the Soviet government to achieve this goal.[38]

Lloyd George's views much distressed Robert Lansing, the American Secretary of State, and he cabled Davis asking him to inform "appropriate members" of the British government of his opinion that it would be utterly useless to attempt to reach an agreement with the Bolsheviks. Neither Lenin nor his immediate followers, Lansing said, would ever give up permanently the idea of world-wide revolution and enter "loyally" into friendly relations with non-communist governments. Though future generations of Russian leaders might be forced to modify this policy owing to continued hostility from the rest of the world, premature recognition would retard such an evolution. Should Lloyd George attempt to reach an understanding with Moscow, he would incur a serious moral responsibility as well as make a great tactical mistake. Furthermore, Lansing said, the United States would never support a policy leading to the dismemberment of Russia. Not only would such a policy, without the consent of the Russian people, be morally wrong, but it would remove one of the last obstacles to Japanese territorial ambition and to a revived German imperialism which would be far more menacing to the British Empire and the Western world than "a united, democratic Russia, well able to defend itself, but not disposed to attack."[39]

❖

Neither in his question-hour statement in the House of Commons

[38] Polk (Paris) to Lansing, telegram 5468, 29 November 1919; Davis (London) to Lansing, telegram 3486, 3 December; *Foreign Relations, 1919, Russia*, pp. 126, 128-29.
[39] Lansing to Davis (London), telegram 6243, 4 December 1919; *ibid.*, pp. 129-30.

on 13 November nor in his speech on the 17th did Lloyd George hint, as he did at the Guildhall, that he was contemplating "another Prinkipo." On the 13th he said simply that he looked forward to early inter-Allied meetings to deal with some of the problems left over from the Peace Conference, the Russian problem among them; on the 17th he did not raise the matter at all. Curzon assured the American ambassador early in December that "a second Prinkipo" was out of the question, and that the Prime Minister had never intended one. The idea, Curzon said, would be unacceptable to British public opinion.[40]

The meetings to which Lloyd George referred took place in London on 11-13 December, principally in order to discuss the treaty of peace with Turkey. They were essentially Anglo-French discussions, although American and Italian representatives were present for two, and Japanese for one, of the sessions. When Russia was on the agenda, Lloyd George kept any thoughts of direct dealings with the Bolsheviks, or the dismemberment of the former Tsarist Empire, very much to himself. Had he not done so, he would surely have angered the others, particularly the French, and the fact of disagreement would certainly have been made public—to Lloyd George's disadvantage. Instead, he seems to have sought out areas of agreement, glossing over those where agreement was more difficult. He was often to employ this tactic during the many inter-Allied discussions of Russian problems during 1920. Up to a point it was successful. The other parties to the discussions were generally slow to realize just how different from theirs were the premises from which Lloyd George moved in order to reach agreement with them. Only later, in most cases, did the superficial character of their agreement become apparent.

The December meetings in London were the first to deal with Russia at any length since the end of the Peace Conference the preceding June. Although the Council of Heads of Delegations had sat in Paris throughout the summer and autumn in succession to the Conference, its discussions of Russian matters were most infrequent. As we have seen, each government, in effect, carried out its own policies, with little attempt to concert them with those of the others. In this respect, if lack of consultation was an offense, the British government was a prime offender. But it was scarcely happy

[40] Davis (London) to Lansing, telegram 3486, 3 December 1919; *ibid.*, pp. 128-29.

with the results. Within the Cabinet, indeed, there was a tendency to blame the relative failure of intervention on the lack of coordination among the Allies. After Cabinet discussions on 29 July and 12 August, Curzon spelled out these thoughts in a memorandum to Balfour in Paris. The absence of a concerted Allied policy—and also, he implied, the relative inaction of the other Powers—had led to results incommensurate either with the objects of intervention or with the enormous expenditure involved. Now, Curzon wrote, the Cabinet had decided that the Allies must reach "a revised and more concerted arrangement . . . as to their future political, military, and financial responsibilities in Russia." For this purpose it proposed the early convening of a special conference at the highest level.[41]

Balfour disliked the proposal, however ("to attribute the apparent and real fluctuations in Allied policy in Russia merely to Allied stupidity and indecision is to misunderstand the situation," he wrote),[42] and he never pressed the matter in Paris. As a result, in December, when meetings finally came, they served not so much to coordinate new measures of intervention as to entomb the old. The real business of the three days was transacted by Lloyd George and Clemenceau in private seclusion on the morning of 11 December. As the Prime Minister told a hurriedly gathered meeting of British Cabinet ministers afterwards, the two found themselves in considerable agreement. Clemenceau, he said, had come to think that the Powers had made a great mistake in interfering in the Russian Civil War; the Russians were Orientals, and Western nations could not bring order out of their chaos. They had already wasted enough money in trying to do so. For that reason Clemenceau showed no interest in the proposal, recently put forward by Boris Savinkov, the colorful revolutionary leader then in Paris, for reviving the old Foch scheme aimed at creating an organized and coordinated anti-Bolshevik force from the armies of the various border states and the remaining White forces in Russia. According to Lloyd George, Clemenceau was much more concerned about future danger from Germany than he was about the spread of Bolshevism, either by force or subversion, from Russia. Therefore, while he was interested in constructing a *cordon sanitaire*, its principal purpose

---

[41] Curzon to Balfour (Paris), despatch 5556, 21 August 1919; *British Documents*, vol. III, no. 399. For the Cabinet discussions see: War Cabinet minutes W.C. 601 and W.C. 612, 29 July and 12 August 1919; Cab. 23/11.

[42] Balfour's minute (undated) is in *British Documents*, vol. III, no. 399, n. 2.

would not be to contain Bolshevism (although that would be one purpose), but to restore Russia as a counterweight against Germany.[43]

We have, of course, only Lloyd George's version of what transpired in his talk with Clemenceau, and it would not be surprising to learn that the Prime Minister had, in fact, led his guest to these conclusions—as he had led the French at the Peace Conference in Paris on so many occasions—by once again asking who would pay for a more activist anti-Bolshevik policy. Clemenceau talked of surrounding Russia with a "barbed wire entanglement," but he was really only concerned to build up Poland. As Lloyd George reported, and Balfour and Curzon later learned to their alarm, he was not in the least interested in the Baltic states except as they, too, could strengthen the barricade against Germany; in the fate of Transcaucasia he had no interest whatsoever. Since he was unwilling to devote French resources to any "border state" but Poland, the *cordon sanitaire* would be no *cordon* at all. On these issues the formal resolutions of the conference stated:

> The conference agreed that no useful purpose would be served by attempting to summon any general conference of the representatives of the anti-Bolshevik States at the present time.
> As regards the border communities with non-Russian populations which have been struggling for freedom and self-government, the Allies will give them such assistance in defending their liberties as may be found desirable in the circumstances of each case as it arises.[44]

So much for the *cordon sanitaire*. For Poland, however, there was a special resolution. Clemenceau proposed that Poland be strengthened "in order to dam up the Russian flood and to provide a check to Germany." Lloyd George agreed—in principle. But he was insistent that the Allies not give the Poles the sort of assistance that would tempt them to attack Russia: traditional anti-Polish sentiment in Russia would, in the event of a Polish invasion, only rally Russians to the Soviet regime. Clemenceau, in fact, shared

---

[43] Conference of Ministers, minutes S-5, 11 December 1919, 1 p.m.; Cab. 23/35. At this meeting, Lloyd George described in detail his preceding talk with Clemenceau; apparently no other British record was made. The two premiers recapitulated their conversation before the inter-Allied meeting the following day: "Secretary's Notes of a Conference held at 10, Downing Street, London, S.W.1, on December 12, 1919, at 11:30 a.m.," *British Documents*, vol. II, no. 56, pp. 744-46.
[44] "Text of Resolutions," *ibid.*, no. 62, p. 782.

these reservations. He commented that Churchill, in a private talk with him, had referred to Poland as "the left wing of Denikin's army," but he had been wary of the notion.[45] We will examine Polish-Soviet relations much more carefully in Volume III of this work; here it is sufficient to observe that the conference resolution on Poland was relatively weak, stating:

> The conference considered that a strong Poland was in the interests of the *Entente* Powers and left for further consideration the question of the form and the extent of the assistance to be given her for the defence of her territories.[46]

To Clemenceau, the complement of the fortification of Poland was the abandonment of any thoughts of "further direct intervention" in Russia. Here, of course, Lloyd George was in wholehearted agreement. The conference resolved, therefore, that "as to furnishing assistance to the anti-Bolshevik elements in Russia, whether in the form of troops, war material, or financial aid," the Allies would enter into no further commitments beyond what they had already promised. They would, however, be free to leave their political and military missions in Russia as long as they wished, and the Whites would still be allowed to *purchase* war material in the Allied countries. But the underlying motivation of Allied behavior would be a desire "to leave Bolshevik Russia, as it were, within a ring fence." Yet an exception to these rules was made for Siberia: the decision whether or not to continue to support the anti-Bolshevik elements there would be left to the United States and Japan, as the only interested parties.[47] In a separate Anglo-French meeting on 13 December, Curzon expressed concern over the fact that some 30,000 Japanese troops were still in Siberia, since he feared that they would encroach upon China and turn the whole Siberian Far East into a Japanese preserve. Nevertheless, he also felt that Siberia would furnish the Japanese with an outlet for their energies and their surplus population, and that their presence would be a guarantee against the spread of Bolshevism. Lloyd George and Cle-

[45] Clemenceau's comment came in the inter-Allied meeting on 12 December cited above, n. 43. Churchill was not present. That evening, however, he told the British Cabinet that Clemenceau, in their talk that morning, had *agreed* with him: Cabinet conclusions 13 (19), 12 December 1919, 6 p.m.; Cab. 23/18.
[46] "Text of Resolutions," cited above, n. 44.
[47] *Idem.*

menceau agreed that, from a purely European point of view, there was no objection to the Japanese remaining.[48]

These, then, were the results of the first of a series of inter-Allied discussions of Russia during the winter of 1919 and the spring of 1920. As Winston Churchill told the Cabinet on the evening of 12 December, the decisions which the conference had reached that day (it only remained to reach formal agreement on their precise wording the following day) signified "the abandonment of the anti-Bolshevist forces in Russia which we had supported up till now." Churchill's long statement was in the nature of a valedictory: he had not been present at the inter-Allied talks, and he knew that both within the British government and in the councils of the Allies as a whole his position had lost. But he wanted formally to go on record as dissenting from the agreed conclusions. Hoping against hope, he proposed—as ameliorative measures—that the White Russians be charged only surplus disposal prices for the war equipment they wished to buy from the Allies, that captured Russian war materials in the hands of the Germans be given back to the Whites, and that, in order not to spread demoralization among the Whites, no public announcement be made of the new Allied policies. The Cabinet took no action on these proposals. No one else, it should be noted, joined Churchill in his dissent.[49]

For Lloyd George, the London talks were entirely successful. The draft resolutions which won easy Allied approval were his. It is true that at no time was the prospect of dealing directly with the Bolsheviks even broached, although the Prime Minister certainly had it on his mind. He was concerned instead with securing general agreement to Clemenceau's notion of "walling-off Bolshevism"— this, of course, had been Britain's minimum Russian policy since the Armistice—but in doing so he made sure that the wall would neither strain British resources nor place a strait jacket around British policies. Reporting on the Allied discussions to the House of Commons the following week, he asserted that there was still "no basis for peace" in Russia. The Soviet government was no more representative of the "vast multitudes" of Russia than any of its opponents. No one could tell when Russia would "come out of this terrible con-

[48] "Secretary's Notes of an Anglo-French Conference . . . December 13, 1919, at 3:30 p.m."; *British Documents*, vol. II, no. 59, pp. 774-75.
[49] Cabinet conclusions 13 (19), 12 December 1919, 6 p.m.; Cab. 23/18.

flict." When she did, when there was "some sort of firm and steady Government with whom you can negotiate," then it would be the duty of the Allies to take the first real opportunity of making peace. But the judgment of the Allies was that the moment had not yet come.[50]

For many members of the House, and certainly for the French government, these were comforting words. Neither Lloyd George's listeners at Westminster, nor his partners in the Downing Street talks just ended, could have known from his behavior at either place that he was contemplating quite a different sort of approach to Soviet Russia, one which did not, perhaps, imply immediately making a formal peace, but one which certainly was not consistent with anything like a *cordon sanitaire*: trade. Before the War, Russia had been the source of much of the United Kingdom's imports of wheat and of nearly all its flax (for lack of which the linen industries of Belfast and Dundee were only one-half employed); by the same token Russia had accounted for British exports which, at postwar prices, would total nearly £75 million per year. Now this trade was almost completely dormant.[51] Moreover, as G. H. Roberts, a Labour M.P. who had been Minister of Labour in 1917-18 and who was now Food Controller, pointed out in a letter to Lloyd George on 2 January 1920, Britain suffered not only from the absence of direct Russian-British trade, but also from much higher world prices of foodstuffs due to their short supply. There was, Roberts said, "close inter-dependence between civil war in Russia and famine in Europe."[52]

Lloyd George, of course, fully appreciated this relationship. Throughout the period since the Armistice he had studded his remarks about Russia, both at the Peace Conference and in the House of Commons, with references to the importance of Russian trade to the economic health of Europe and, in particular, to that of Great Britain. But he had never implied that Britain might trade with a

---

[50] 123 *H.C. Deb.*, col. 765 (18 December 1919).

[51] See the statistics in the memorandum, "Economic Aspects of British Policy concerning Russia," by E. F. Wise, 6 January 1920; *British Documents*, vol. II, no. 71, n. 2, pp. 867-70. In 1912, it is worth noting, Russia exported 8.9 million tons of grain and flour—more than a quarter of the world market.

[52] Roberts sent Curzon a copy of his letter of 2 January to Lloyd George: file 168948/91/38; F.O. 371/3961. In a covering note to Curzon, Roberts wrote: "These figures [for Russian foodstuff exports, 1909-13] indicate the disastrous consequences, as regards Europe's economic life, of a continuance of civil war in Russia."

communist Russia. After all, until the mid-autumn of 1919 a White victory seemed probable. Toward the end of 1919, however, perhaps to justify his economic and—given the widespread unemployment within Great Britain—domestic-political reasons for wanting to trade with Russia, he began to combine them with the classical liberal's arguments that trade, and all of the formalities, procedures, and institutions that go with it, had a great civilizing influence which would powerfully affect the Soviet regime. This argument lay behind his brief remark, at the close of one of the inter-Allied meetings, that perhaps it was not such a bad thing that in making peace with the Baltic states the Bolsheviks would thereby gain intermediaries through which they could carry on trade between themselves and the outside world. "The Bolsheviks had talked much of propaganda," he said, but "civilisation might also undertake its peaceful penetration."[53]

The Prime Minister, therefore, took great interest in a memorandum written in early January 1920 by E. F. Wise, a former official of the Ministry of Food and at the time the principal British representative on the Supreme Economic Council, proposing the adoption of a wholly new economic policy toward Soviet Russia.[54] The paper's basic recommendations were for the ending of the blockade and for the opening of trade with Soviet-controlled areas of Russia through the medium of the Russian agricultural cooperatives, whose powerful central organization was known as Tsentrosoyuz. Despite the Bolsheviks, Wise said, the cooperatives had been able to maintain themselves over the whole of Russia, and they and Tsentrosoyuz had managed to preserve considerable freedom and independence. They could therefore serve as a means of starting the exchange of Russian agricultural produce for Western manufactured goods and clothing, even if the exchange had to be on a barter basis. Wise pointed out that Tsentrosoyuz had retained its offices in London and that its representatives were already working with British trading and cooperative organizations to prepare for the opening of trade. As for the blockade, Wise wrote, besides being open to all sorts of objections on humanitarian and legal grounds, it was now serving only to cut off Britain and France from a trade

[53] In the session of 12 December cited above n. 43 (*British Documents*, vol. II, no. 56, p. 748).

[54] Wise's paper is cited above, n. 51.

which was already being enjoyed by Germany and, in some cases, by the neutrals.

The idea of trading through the cooperatives had, in fact, been vaguely in the air for a long time. Lansing had suggested it to President Wilson in June 1918, and the President had replied that the associations might be of considerable service.[55] An American War Trade Board representative in Stockholm wrote in November 1918: "I understand these cooperative institutions are not of Bolshevik character; also that they have been very successful and have considerable power."[56] The British White Paper on Bolshevism issued in April 1919 contained a Foreign Office memorandum saying that the cooperatives had stoutly defended their independence against the Bolsheviks, and that they still represented the financial interests of a large proportion of the Russian peasantry.[57]

At that time Wise himself arranged for discussions in London between representatives of Tsentrosoyuz and the British cooperative societies in order to establish trade between the United Kingdom and those parts of Russia not under Bolshevik control; Wise's hope was that, once trading machinery through the medium of the cooperatives existed, it might be possible to extend the same arrangements to include Bolshevik-controlled territory as well.[58] "The policy of the Home Office, who deal with the matter here," said a War Office telegram in July 1919, "is to allow the Russian co-operative societies to carry on business as it is not considered they have any political significance in England, and they are a nucleus which later may be found useful."[59]

Later, in December, R. H. Hoare of the Foreign Office Russia Department proposed trade through the cooperatives as a means of getting a footing in Bolshevik Russia to convince the Russian people that the British were their friends, or, if war with Bolshevism was inevitable, to convince the British labor movement that the govern-

[55] Lansing to Wilson, 19 June 1918; Wilson to Lansing, same date; *Foreign Relations, Lansing Papers*, vol. II, pp. 363-64.

[56] Owen (Stockholm) to War Trade Board, 20 November 1918; *Foreign Relations, 1918, Russia*, vol. III, p. 169.

[57] Cmd. 8, *A Collection of Reports on Bolshevism in Russia*, 1919, p. 71.

[58] Wise described his efforts in a brief note, 26 April 1919, in file 591/1/1/8078; F.O. 608/178.

[59] War Office to G.H.Q. (Constantinople), telegram 79800, 17 July 1919; W.O. 33/974, no. 4906A. The message went on to lay down criteria for release or retention of Russian funds passing through Constantinople.

ment was making every effort to reach a compromise with the Soviet regime.[60] In a subsequent paper, written on 19 January following
a conference of experts at the Foreign Office, Hoare stated: "Such
information as we have goes to show that the Soviet Government
some time ago abandoned their repeated attempts to absorb the Cooperatives and are now looking to them to assist in the distribution
of commodities especially in recently conquered Siberia and South
Russia." Hoare went on to draw a conclusion: "If this is so it constitutes a notable victory for individualism as opposed to communism
and also goes far to explain and confirm the numerous reports that
the Soviet Government is becoming gradually acceptable to the
Russian people; in fact that it is losing most of its objectionable
features."[61]

Thus Wise was certainly not alone in considering trade with the
Russian cooperative organizations. But he was, apparently, the only
one to carry his considerations through to the stage of detailed
planning. Yet, if by January 1920 experts like Wise believed that
the Russian cooperatives were anything other than organs of the
Soviet state, they were largely mistaken. A series of decrees from
August 1918 to March 1919 had subordinated the organizations
to Narkomprod, the People's Commissariat of Supply, and had made
them the central internal distributive organ.[62] Another decree of
April 1918 had nationalized all foreign trade; since there was, in any
case, virtually no foreign trade during the period of the civil war,
this decree was easily enforced.[63] It is true that the Tsentrosoyuz
representatives abroad played an independent and even an anti-
Soviet role—including helping to arrange for trade between the West

[60] Hoare's paper, 22 December 1919, is in *British Documents*, vol. III, no. 619.

[61] Hardinge to Derby (Paris) for Curzon, telegram 77, 20 January 1920, file
172293/142549/38; F.O. 371/4032. The telegram as sent was Hoare's draft of the
previous day, unaltered. It may be noted that among the "experts" consulted were
officials of the Department of Overseas Trade—and Sir Paul Dukes, during 1918-19
the chief British intelligence agent in Soviet Russia.

[62] For the texts of these decrees, and other materials on the cooperatives, see
James Bunyan and H. H. Fisher, eds., *The Bolshevik Revolution, 1917-1918, Documents and Materials*, Stanford University, 1934, pp. 629-34, and James Bunyan,
ed., *Intervention, Civil War, and Communism in Russia: April-December 1918,
Documents and Materials*, Baltimore, 1936, pp. 428-40; also E. H. Carr, *A History
of Soviet Russia: The Bolshevik Revolution, 1917-1923*, vol. II, London, 1952, pp.
120-25, 235-40.

[63] Decree of 22 April 1918: text in *Dokumenty vneshnei politiki*, vol. I, pp. 255-
56; translation in Bunyan and Fisher, *Intervention, Civil War, and Communism*,
pp. 617-18. See Carr, *Bolshevik Revolution*, vol. II, pp. 244-45.

and those territories under the control of the Whites[64]—and it may be that this independence was responsible for the impression which Wise and others had of the cooperative organizations as a whole. The Soviet regime evidently appreciated this fact; sensing the possible usefulness of the cooperatives in opening up foreign trade, they carefully allowed Tsentrosoyuz to maintain formal autonomy.[65] But early in 1920 they moved to replace all Tsentrosoyuz representatives abroad whose loyalty to the new order was suspect.

Wise's memorandum was circulated to the Cabinet on 7 January but never discussed; so far as Lloyd George was concerned, however, it became government policy. The Prime Minister took it with him to Paris only two days later for another set of meetings of the Supreme Council. These had been arranged principally in order to discuss Adriatic questions and the draft treaty of peace for Hungary. But Lloyd George also hoped to gain from the Council a decision to begin trade with Russia—Soviet Russia—through the cooperative organizations. When he arrived, however, he found the Council seized with a much more urgent Russian problem. The last days of 1919 had seen the virtual collapse of all anti-Bolshevik resistance on the part of General Denikin's forces in South Russia. Now it suddenly seemed likely that they would be completely defeated, and that the victorious Red Army, perhaps in conjunction with the Turks, would then turn on the three infant republics of Transcaucasia. The Council would have to decide whether—and, if so, how —to help the three republics to preserve their independence.[66]

One serious aspect of the situation was dealt with by the Council of Heads of Delegations before Lloyd George and Curzon arrived. When the Council met on 5 January, it found before it a desperate request from Denikin for foreign troops as the one means of saving his armies from complete destruction. Bulgaria, he said, had offered him 40,000 equipped, armed, and officered men, and, unlike Poland and Rumania, the Bulgarians wished no territorial compensation. Further, Denikin asked that, since Bulgaria, as an enemy

[64] See the allegations made against A. M. Berkenheim (the chief Tsentrosoyuz representative abroad until his replacement in March 1920), including excerpts from a Cheka report of 28 April 1920, in *Dokumenty vneshnei politiki*, vol. II, n. 64, pp. 749-50.

[65] Carr, *Bolshevik Revolution*, vol. II, p. 240.

[66] See Lloyd George's statement to the Supreme Council, Paris, 10 January 1920, 11:30 a.m.; minutes in *ibid.*, no. 54, p. 725.

state, would have to be disarmed anyway, he should be sent its excess war materials.[67]

Not surprisingly, the Council refused to let him have the Bulgarian troops. For the Bulgarians were still in the status of enemies, and their use would raise innumerable political complications in the Balkans. Nor did the Allied delegates wish to apply pressure to Poland or Rumania. Sir Eyre Crowe, the British representative, spoke for the Council when he commented that he doubted whether anything could stop Denikin's retreat. As for the Bulgarian arms, the question was regarded as purely military: would they simply fall into the hands of the Bolsheviks? The question was referred to the Allied military representatives at Constantinople. At the same session, the delegates approved a British recommendation that the Estonian government should not be asked—as Denikin wished— to allow Yudenich's remaining troops to be transported to the South Russian front; they would almost certainly arrive too late, and such a step would violate the newly signed Soviet-Estonian armistice.[68]

From Tiflis, meanwhile, came a stream of communications to the Foreign Office from Oliver Wardrop, the British High Commissioner for Transcaucasia. Wardrop urged that the new republics of the Causasus be bolstered to withstand four dangers: Denikin's retreating armies in the north, the Soviet forces following Denikin, other Red Army units which were already moving down the shores of the Caspian to the east, and a possible Turkish attack from the south. Wardrop suggested that Georgia, Azerbaijan, and Armenia—and also the tiny republic of Daghestan astride the mountains in the north—be accorded immediate *de facto* recognition, as well as material and financial aid. These states of the Caucasus, Wardrop reiterated, formed a natural barrier separating the Bolsheviks from the Turks, two forces hostile to the British Empire. If Britain did not act quickly, he said, the Caucasian states would be forced to come to terms with the Bolsheviks.[69]

On the morning of 10 January, therefore, when the premiers and foreign ministers of Britain, France, and Italy, along with the Amer-

[67] Denikin's requests were passed to the Council by the French delegation. See the memorandum of 31 December 1919 and 4 January 1920, *ibid.*, Appendices D and E to no. 51, pp. 699-701.
[68] Minutes, Council of Heads of Delegations, Paris, 5 January 1920, 10:30 a.m.; *ibid.*, no. 51, pp. 688-90, and Appendix F, p. 701.
[69] Wardrop (Tiflis) to Curzon, telegrams 2, 3, 5, and 11 on 3, 6, and 8 January 1920; *ibid.*, vol. III, nos. 630 and 631.

ican and Japanese ambassadors, met at the Quai d'Orsay, Lloyd
George emphasized the importance of an immediate decision.[70]
Part of the problem was diplomatic: the independence of the states
of the Caucasus had not as yet been formally recognized by the
Powers. This was quickly rectified. Immediately after the larger
meeting on the 10th, the foreign ministers—acting on Curzon's
recommendation—decided upon the *de facto* recognition of the governments of Georgia and Azerbaijan. Regarding Armenia they
decided temporarily to take no action: its future was too deeply involved with the Turkish peace settlement still under discussion. Nor
did they even give consideration to the claims of Daghestan: presumably it was felt to be too small, too isolated, and economically
unviable—and, importantly, it had no representatives in Paris to
plead its cause.[71]

These measures at least partially dealt with the diplomatic problem. The more serious military problem remained. On the afternoon
of the same day, Curzon telegraphed to Hardinge in London, asking the Permanent Under-Secretary to convene a meeting of the
"Eastern Committee" (the Inter-Departmental Conference on Middle Eastern Affairs) on Monday—it was then Saturday—to discuss
the retention of British forces at Batum, the despatch to the Caucasus or Persia of British officers and aircraft and the general
strengthening of British forces throughout the region, the diversion
to the Caucasus of undelivered war materials previously promised to
Denikin, measures to protect Baku against a probable Bolshevik
advance, and the recovery from Denikin of the Caspian fleet and
either its reconstitution under British command or, failing that, its
destruction.[72]

Field-Marshal Sir Henry Wilson summed up Curzon's appeal in
one word: "ridiculous."[73] And in the Inter-Departmental Conference
on Monday afternoon he showed how completely out of accord with

[70] In the statement cited above, n. 66.

[71] Minutes, Council of Foreign Ministers, Paris, 10 January 1920; *British Documents*, vol. II, no. 65, pp. 796-97. The actual notifications of recognition of the
Georgian and Azerbaijani governments came the following day; see *ibid.*, no.
74, p. 896.

[72] Curzon (Paris) to Hardinge, sent as Derby's telegram 19, 10 January 1919;
ibid., vol. III, no. 635. The Caspian fleet had been handed over to Denikin at the
time of British evacuation of the Caucasus in August and September 1919.

[73] Wilson MS diary, entry for 12 January 1920 (Callwell, *Wilson*, vol. II, p. 221).

the realities of British power it was.[74] Merely to hold the lines from Constantinople, through Batum and Baku, and from there to Krasnovodsk and Merv on down through Enzeli and Teheran to Meshed, Wilson stated, would require seven divisions, two of them on the Batum-Baku line, as well as naval control of the entire Black Sea and all or part of the Caspian. These figures were for British forces only; the difficulties of coordinating an Allied force would necessitate larger numbers. Churchill, for his part, was adamant that, if Britain were to commit even the two divisions necessary to hold the Batum-Baku line, they should be given instead to Denikin or to the Poles for service as the spearhead of an advance upon Moscow.

To provide even these two divisions—much less seven—was out of the question, however. The British government's campaign of repression in Ireland was demanding increasingly large forces. The threat of industrial disturbances within the United Kingdom meant that garrisons at home could not be reduced. And from India, Mesopotamia (Iraq), and Egypt came insistent requests for military manpower. Wilson therefore told the Inter-Departmental Conference that the only line which could reasonably be held with available British strength was one from northern Palestine through Mosul in northernmost Mesopotamia across southern Persia to Meshed in the east. And even the Mosul-Meshed segment of this line would have to give way if strongly attacked. This meant giving up the Caucasus and even much of Persia, and concentrating on the defense of India and the oil fields of the Persian Gulf. After Wilson spoke, representatives of the Admiralty and the Air Force also affirmed that they could do nothing. That evening Wilson commented in his diary on the significance of these decisions:

It was quite true that Georgia and Azerbaijan would go Bolshevik, in spite of the fact that those fools in Paris only yesterday agreed to acknowledge the "*de facto* governments" of those countries. It was also true that we should have to clear out of Persia, in spite of the treaty Curzon has just made with Persia *without* consulting the W[ar]O[ffice] which was a scandalous thing to do. All this was agreed to by the Committee and wired to Curzon, and our wire will give Curzon and the Frocks in Paris something to think about.[75]

[74] Inter-Departmental Conference on Middle Eastern Affairs, 34th Minutes, 12 January 1920, 4 p.m.; F.O. General/216.

[75] Wilson MS diary, entry for 12 January 1920 (cf. Callwell, *Wilson*, vol. II, p. 222). "Frocks," of course, was Wilson's term for politicians. The Anglo-Persian Agreement of 9 August 1919 will be discussed at length in Volume III.

Meanwhile, Denikin's forces, wracked by disease and suffering terribly from the bitter cold of the Russian winter, their discipline almost completely gone, had retreated beyond the Don to Rostov and Novocherkaask.[76] Acting on their own authority, without reference to London, General Holman, the head of the British military mission, and Sir Halford Mackinder, who had only recently arrived in South Russia as British High Commissioner, guaranteed to Denikin on behalf of the British government that "all available ships, naval and commercial, will be used to evacuate the wives and families of Russian officers" and that "the British Military Mission will form the rearguard to ensure the safety of these wives and families."[77] Mackinder later explained that he had extended the guarantee only to families of officers because "private soldiers ran no similar risk, since they and their families could disappear into the general population."[78] In justification of his failure to consult London before making so drastic a promise, Mackinder telegraphed to Curzon on 10 January that he and Holman had done so because the White officers were becoming completely demoralized by the fear of Bolshevik reprisals against their families. "In view of the encouragement we have given to this Army," Mackinder said in his telegram, "and in view of the Archangel precedent, it seems unthinkable we could leave these women and children to be murdered."[79] After consulting with Churchill, Henry Wilson telegraphed to Holman to carry out the pledge. And to Constantinople he wired instructions that three battalions were to be held in readiness in case they were needed.[80]

❖

At just this time, the gap which separated Lloyd George from his ministerial colleagues reached its widest. Harold Nicolson has written that the diplomacy of Lloyd George was characterized most of all by its privacy—not only a privacy of method, but a privacy of

[76] For the terrible circumstances of Denikin's retreat, see Stewart, *White Armies*, pp. 338-47; a firsthand account is in Aten and Orrmont, *Rostov Bridge*, pp. 193-308.
[77] This guarantee was given to Denikin at his headquarters at Tikhoretskaya on 10 January 1920. For its text, see Appendix E to Mackinder's final report on his mission, 21 January; *British Documents*, vol. III, no. 656, p. 798.
[78] In his final report, cited in n. 77.
[79] Mackinder (Tikhoretskaya) to Curzon, telegram 1812, 10 January 1920; included by Holman in his "Final Report of the British Military Mission, South Russia," cited above, ch. VI, n. 24.
[80] Wilson MS diary, entry for 14 January 1920 (Callwell, *Wilson*, vol. II, p. 222).

aim.[81] For several days, at least, this privacy became so great that the Prime Minister, in Paris, could initiate a proposal for trade with Soviet Russia while the War Office and the Admiralty, in London, set about preparing for war. And from *both* of these enterprises the Foreign Office was excluded.

On the morning of 14 January, at a meeting with Clemenceau and Francesco Nitti, the Italian Premier, Lloyd George introduced Wise's proposals for trade with the Russian cooperatives. For reasons which are today as inexplicable as they seemed to the Foreign Office then, Lloyd George would not allow Curzon to attend, nor would he even inform him of the details of the proceedings; they were the business, he told his Foreign Secretary, of the Ministry of Food, not of the Foreign Office! Curzon knew only that the Prime Minister planned to introduce Wise's memorandum. Not until a month later, when the Cabinet secretariat finally sent over copies of the minutes of this and subsequent discussions of the trading proposals, did the Foreign Office (and the Foreign Secretary) learn precisely what had taken place. For Curzon the experience must have been deeply humiliating—but then, so was his entire relationship with Lloyd George.[82]

Whatever devious purpose the Prime Minister hoped to accomplish by this "privacy," the proceedings on the morning of the 14th were scarcely worth concealing. Besides the three premiers and

[81] Harold Nicolson, *Curzon: The Last Phase, 1919-1925*, London, 1934, p. 56.

[82] Following the announcement in the press on 17 January 1920 of the Supreme Council's decision to begin trade with the Russian cooperatives (see below), Lord Hardinge telegraphed Curzon that the Foreign Office was "particularly anxious to know the scope of the decision and the reasons which prompted it." Curzon replied, in a telegram marked "Very urgent, very confidential, not for circulation," as follows: "Decision of Prime Ministers in Paris with regard to trade with Soviet Russia was taken by them in the absence of any Foreign Office representative, and after the circulation of paper by Wise (? have) withheld account of proceedings, vide minutes as kept by Hankey. Prime Minister took line in private conversation that this was not the affair of Foreign Office, but of Food Ministry, who should control procedure. Answer (? to your) question should therefore be sought from Hankey and Wise." (Hardinge to Derby [Paris] for Curzon, telegram 77, 20 January 1920; Curzon through Derby to Hardinge, unnumbered telegram, 22 January, file 172293/142549/38; F.O. 371/4032. Both telegrams are quoted in *British Documents*, vol. II, no. 76, n. 5, p. 911. The minutes of the Paris discussions reached the Foreign Office on 16 February and were included in the same file.)

References to Lloyd George's shabby treatment of Curzon—and to Curzon's inability to bring himself to resign—are legion. See, however, Nicolson, *Curzon*, *passim*, and Taylor, *English History, 1914-1945*, p. 195, n. 2.

their secretaries, there were present two representatives of Tsentrosoyuz—Berkenheim and Krovopuskov.[83] With Lloyd George asking all the questions, they recited a long list of facts about Russian economic conditions supporting the information in Wise's memorandum; the raw materials were there if only some means could be found to collect and distribute them—an operation that would be stimulated by the prospects of foreign sales. At times, the interview sounded as if it had been rehearsed: after all these bounties had been revealed, Lloyd George asked the Russians if they felt that the proposals were "the most effective way of striking a blow at Bolshevism"; the reply came back, "absolutely."[84]

Clemenceau and Nitti were duly impressed: Nitti called it "a very remarkable proposal." The premiers then appointed a three-man expert committee, to be chaired by Wise (whom Lloyd George characterized as "one of the ablest men in the British Government Service," and to whom Curzon, in a letter to Austen Chamberlain, later referred as "that arch-Bolshevik, Wise"),[85] to consider the proposals and report back as soon as possible.

The Committee spent the following day, 15 January, discussing the trade proposals and preparing its report. In London, meanwhile, the War Office was preparing a report of its own: a public statement on the danger of impending war in all of the border lands to the south of Russia—the area which people at that time had in mind when they used the term "Middle East." According to the statement, the whole region was in a state of "subdued combustion" which could burst into flames at any time within the following three months. Sooner or later, the War Office believed, there would be a need for British military commitments on a very large scale.

---

[83] For Berkenheim, see above, n. 64. Aside from Lloyd George, the other British participants in this meeting were Wise, Hankey, Philip Kerr—and a "Mr. Leeper" (whether Reginald or Alexander is unclear; since both brothers were associated with the Foreign Office, Curzon's complaint noted in n. 82 was not strictly justified).

[84] Minutes, meeting of Heads of Governments, Paris, 14 January 1920, 11 a.m.; *ibid.*, no. 71, pp. 867-75.

[85] Lloyd George's remark about Wise is in *idem*, p. 875. Curzon's was in a letter of 13 May 1922, referring to Wise's activities at the Genoa Conference (quoted in Nicolson, *Curzon*, p. 245). By that time Wise had quit government service and was employed by Arcos, the Soviet trading organization, in its London office. Later he became a leading figure in the Independent Labour Party, and at the time of his death in 1933 he was chairman of the Socialist League.

Gloomily, the statement hinted at conflict with the Bolsheviks not only in the Caucasus but in Persia as well.[86]

Obviously such a statement could not help but create the maximum amount of sensation. Both Churchill and Henry Wilson later disclaimed any prior knowledge of it and placed all responsibility for it on subordinate officials at the War Office.[87] But it seems obvious that Churchill at least implicitly approved of it. (Wilson, anxious to reduce British military commitments, almost certainly did not.)[88] To a large Coalition demonstration at Sunderland on 3 January he had made many of the same points, if in more Churchillian language:

The ghost of the Russian bear comes padding across the immense field of snow. Now it stops outside the Conference in Paris, in silent reproach at their uncompleted task. Now it ranges widely over the enormous countries which lead us to the frontiers of India, disturbing Afghanistan, distracting Persia, and creating far to the Southward great agitation and unrest among the millions of our Indian population who have hitherto dwelt in peace and tranquillity under British rule.

Of the "defeatists" at home who would not counter Bolshevik expansionism with military power, Churchill said: "They believe in the international Soviet of the Russian and Polish Jew. We are still putting our confidence in the British Empire."[89]

Churchill's remarks were echoed by the *Morning Post*, one of his most vociferous supporters, which observed in the same issue in which it printed the text of his speech that "Lenin . . . is not in fact Lenin at all, but a secret organisation directed by Revolutionary Jews to the destruction of the world."[90] The implications of such scare journalism were clear: the world had better strike first. Indeed, during the next fortnight the *Post* and *The Times* as well were to carry so many articles about impending war, labelling them all as truth, that on 15 January the *Manchester Guardian* was moved to warn that the national press had been "drenched, from some

---

[86] All morning newspapers on 16 January 1920 carried at least a summary of the War Office statement, although it was released too late at night for most to find space to run the actual text. Curiously, the most complete version was in the *Daily Herald*.

[87] Riddell, *Diary*, p. 161, entry for 22 January 1920.

[88] Wilson did not even refer to the statement in his own diary.

[89] *The Times*, 5 January 1920.

[90] *Morning Post*, 5 January 1920.

unknown source, with what is simply war propagandist 'information' about Russia."

On the following day, the 16th, the press carried the War Office statement about the Middle East. Beside it was more concrete news: on the previous day Churchill and Walter Long, the two service ministers, together with their chiefs of staff, had suddenly been summoned to Paris, and had taken the night train from Waterloo. The unexpected nature of the summons was shown in Long's cancellation, just before departing, of a long-standing speaking engagement.[91] That same evening orders reached Malta for every available ship to take in stores and coal to its utmost capacity and set out for an unannounced destination, which correspondents took to be the Black Sea. This last piece of information was delayed in transmission and did not reach England until several days later, but the morning newspapers of the 16th, carrying both the War Office statement and accounts of the sudden movements of the service ministers and chiefs of staff to Paris, surmised that the predicted explosion in the Middle East was indeed near at hand.[92]

❖

Meanwhile, on the morning of the 16th, while Churchill and his entourage were traveling from Le Havre to Paris, the heads of the three Allied governments were privately meeting, not to plan warlike measures, but to discuss trade with Soviet Russia. Once again the devious nature of Lloyd George's diplomacy asserted itself, giving to the whole "crisis" an aspect of bizarre counterpoint.

The premiers met in order to approve the report of the committee of experts which had been considering the question of trade with the Russian cooperatives. Part of the committee's assignment had been to devise a trading scheme that would in no way imply Allied

[91] *The Times*, 16 January 1920. The *source* of the summons to Paris and the *form* that it took are quite unclear. Presumably it came from Lloyd George, but what reasons did he give? I have found no references to it whatsoever in the papers of the Cabinet, the War Office, or the Foreign Office, or in any of the private collections which were available to me. Henry Wilson's diary merely refers to the *fact* of the summons; he gave no further details. The minutes of the "Cabinet Conference" in Paris state merely that "attention was drawn" to "certain announcements" in the press that the situation in the East was so serious as perhaps to lead to the outbreak of hostilities, and that the announcements were "alleged" to have come from the War Office. (Minutes S-11, cited below, n. 96.)

[92] See, e.g., *The Times, Morning Post, Manchester Guardian,* and *Daily Herald,* 16 January 1920. The news of the sailings from Malta did not appear until 20 January.

de facto recognizion of the Soviet regime, and it was able to give assurances on this ground. Although the trade could obviously not be carried out on Russian territory without Moscow's approval, all negotiations and arrangements would take place directly between the Russian cooperatives and either their Western counterparts or private traders. However, the premiers recognized—without objection—that the opening of any sort of trade at all would necessarily imply the removal of the blockade.[93] In another meeting during the afternoon (presumably while the service ministers waited—and wondered why they had been summoned), the heads of governments approved the text of a press communiqué which stated that they had decided

to give facilities to the Russian co-operative organisations which are in direct touch with the peasantry throughout Russia, so that they may arrange for the import into Russia of clothing, medicines, agricultural machinery and the other necessities of which the Russian people are in sore need, in exchange for grain, flax &c., of which Russia has surplus supplies.[94]

In this expression of unalloyed altruism there was no mention of the Bolshevik regime. However, a concluding paragraph added: "These arrangements imply no change in the policy of the Allied Governments towards the Soviet Government."[95]

❖

Not until late in the afternoon of 16 January did Lloyd George have time to consult the ministers and military advisers he had summoned from London. And not until three days later, the 19th, did the conference as a whole seek their advice. During the intervening time the British group constituted itself, in effect, as a rump

[93] Minutes, meeting of Heads of Governments, Paris, 16 January 1920, 10:30 a.m.; *British Documents*, vol. II, no. 74, pp. 894-96. The report of the expert committee is printed as appendix 1, pp. 898-99.

[94] Appendix A to minutes of meeting of Heads of Governments, 16 January 1920, 4 p.m.; *ibid.*, no. 76, p. 912. It appeared in the press on 17 January.

[95] From Novorossiisk came a telegram from Brigadier-General Keyes, the chief political officer of the British military mission and Mackinder's successor as Commissioner, bitterly deploring the fact that both he and Denikin had had to learn about the trade decision, and also Allied *de facto* recognition of the Georgian government (see below), through newspaper accounts (Keyes to Curzon, telegram 7, 19 January 1920). Keyes's plaint was minuted by P. V. Emrys-Evans of the Foreign Office Russia Department on 26 January: "Gen. Keyes can hardly expect to learn of important decisions otherwise than through Press when this Dept. obtains the same information through the same channel." (File 173604/142549/38; F.O. 371/4032.)

Cabinet to argue and re-argue the issues which supposedly had been settled by the Inter-Departmental Conference in London on the 12th.[96]

There were, broadly speaking, three principal lines of argument put forward. One, advanced by Curzon and Walter Long, with support from Admiral Earl Beatty, the First Sea Lord, called for an Allied military effort to protect the Transcaucasian republics and Persia from a Bolshevik invasion. Curzon's arguments here were consistent with those he had made throughout the period since the Armistice and, indeed, with his lifetime of concern for the safety of Britain's eastern Empire. Denikin had failed, he said. The British government should recognize that fact and move instead "to organize the excellent defensive line of the Caucasus." Most important, for Curzon, was control of the Caspian Sea, the principal route of access from the north into Persia, which, in turn, was one of the main approaches to India. "If command of the Caspian were lost we might find that before long our whole Eastern Empire was rocking, but if we could dominate the Caspian it might alter the whole position in the East," he said.

Walter Long shared Curzon's imperial concerns. Unless "immediate steps" were taken, Britain would be in danger of losing its position in the East altogether, he said. But, as First Lord of the Admiralty, Long had a more particular interest: continued British control of the oil fields of southern Persia, which were a major source of supply for the modern oil-burning ships of the Royal Navy. For Beatty, of course, the oil was of paramount importance. Already, he said, the Navy was dependent on sources not under British control for seventy-five percent of its oil. The United States was the principal supplier, and, if it wished, it could cut off not only its own oil, but Mexico's as well. Even Trinidad, due to its location, was not a really secure source. The Naval War Staff had ascertained that, of those sources which were not controlled by another Power, the Persian fields were by far the most important. They could most

---

[96] There were three sessions of this "Cabinet Conference," as it was called, all of them in Lloyd George's room at Claridge's Hotel in Paris—16 January 1920, 5 p.m.; 18 January, 5 p.m.; and 19 January, 5:30 p.m. (Minutes S-10, S-11, and S-12; Cab. 23/35). Participants were Lloyd George, Bonar Law, Churchill, Curzon, Long, Montagu, Birkenhead, Admiral Beatty, Field-Marshal Wilson, and Hankey. In large measure, the discussions were repetitive; arguments made at the first session were made again at the last. Therefore, I have here attempted to characterize separate strands of argument, rather than describe each session.

easily be defended by controlling the Caspian Sea. Britain had handed over command of the Caspian flotilla to Denikin the previous summer; Long and Beatty now proposed that it be taken back. But Beatty insisted that Royal Navy units in the Caspian would require a secure base at Baku and secure lines of communication across Transcaucasia to the Black Sea—which, as Henry Wilson never tired of pointing out, would require the commitment of at least two divisions. Beatty thought the price worth paying. Once the Bolsheviks gained control of the Caspian—and they would certainly make an effort to do so, after the thawing of the Volga allowed them to send down their river flotilla—it would be very difficult, if not impossible, to regain it. The operations which Long and Beatty recommended would have another benefit as well: they would assure Western, as opposed to Bolshevik, control over the oil of Baku. In all their statements, however, they made clear that Baku oil was a secondary consideration, as compared with that of southern Persia.

The second main position in the discussions of 16-19 January was that of Churchill. He expressed his thoughts in an emotionally worded memorandum which should be quoted here at length because, far better than any summary could, it conveys the essence of his argument.[97] Despite Denikin's defeats, he wrote, the Volunteer Army still represented the strongest anti-Bolshevik force in the field. Yet it was in the process of being destroyed because the Allies, by acquiescing in or even encouraging the cessation of efforts against the Bolsheviks on other fronts, had allowed them to concentrate all their resources against it. Now the Allies—and the British Empire in particular—had to confront fully the consequences of their previous lack of any coherent policy. Churchill continued:

These consequences are terrible. In the hope of avoiding them at the eleventh hour, new expeditions are suggested, and the following policy has been proposed, viz., to allow Denikin's armies to be destroyed without making any further effort to help them in the field; to allow Poland, the Baltic States and Finland to remain inert and uncombined until their turn

---

[97] Churchill's untitled paper, dated 17 January 1920, is in reference file 18/OJ/2; Cab. 21/177. On the file jacket Colonel A. J. Sylvester, Hankey's assistant, wrote after returning to London on 22 January: "*Important*: This paper is *NOT* to be circulated except on instructions from Sir M. Hankey." Hankey did not so instruct, and thus the paper was seen only by the actual participants in the Paris meetings; it never became a Cabinet paper.

comes; to abandon to their fate all our present friends in Russia who have been fighting the Bolsheviks; to adopt two new protégés in the feeble and divided States of Georgia and Azerbaijan; to make new doles of arms, munitions and supplies to them; to tie up small bodies of British troops in most perilous positions along the Batoum-Baku railway line; and, finally, to put 1,200 British sailors back at the last moment into the Caspian Fleet, from which they were so precipitately withdrawn in September last.

In other words, having refused to combine any of the large factors in the struggle against the enemy, having allowed them to be smashed up one by one on the grounds that we could not face the expense or run the risk, we are now to try to make a new front out of the little weak pawns that are left to us and to lavish vainly on them resources which, applied in time and with a real "will to win" to Kolchak, Denikin, Poland, the Baltic States and Finland, concerted and combined, might well have given us victory instead of the defeat which is now upon us. . . .

I shall be asked, what is my alternative? My alternative is what it has been throughout the last year. Have a definite policy of making war on the Bolsheviks with every available resource and by every possible means. Encourage and sustain Denikin; make him improve his Government; help men like Savinkov and Tchaikovsky; foster an arrangement between him and the other anti-Bolshevik forces. Use every lever at our disposal to obtain concerted action against the Bolsheviks on all parts of the front. Aid Poland with munitions and supplies; animate her to take the pressure off Denikin. Endeavor to get the Finns to march on Petrograd. Make formal demands to the Japanese to reconstruct the Siberian front as part of a concerted scheme against the Bolsheviks.

But if it is too late to take such action, if no one else will agree to take a share in taking such action, if it is not even worth while trying to take such action, then do not let us blind ourselves to the facts which we have to face; and do not let us, in a pitiful effort to conceal those facts from our own minds or from the public at large for a few months longer, fling a few handfuls of British soldiers and sailors into positions from which it may be impossible to extricate them and where their poor lives will only be another unavailing sacrifice to the prolonged indecisions of the Allies.

Thus Churchill rejected the notion that the way to defend India against a Bolshevik incursion was to stretch a British cordon across Transcaucasia. Instead, he told his colleagues, he would attack the Bolsheviks elsewhere—from Poland and Finland, for example. In January 1920, as in January 1919, Churchill was an advocate of the "Foch plan." At present, he said, the Allies were "losing both the war game and the peace game" in Russia. If they decided to make war, they should put Foch himself at the head of a unified command which would include Denikin's forces and those of all the border states. The only alternative was to make peace and to try to induce Lenin to show some mercy toward the border states. But to attempt nothing more than shoring up Georgia and Azerbaijan against a Bolshevik attack would be "like using a piece of putty to stop an earthquake."

The third "position" in these discussions was that of Lloyd George. It is by no means easy to define. In a sense it was a compromise—by Lloyd George's lights, at any rate—between the first two. He agreed that more important than any questions regarding oil was the necessity to "establish a barrier against Bolshevism." Yet he claimed that he foresaw no great difficulty in doing so, even admitting the fact that neither the British government not any of the other Powers would (in the case of Britain, could) contribute any troops to the task. His basic premise was that the danger posed to the world by the Soviet regime was not military but political. He himself was not the least afraid, he said, of a Bolshevik attack against Mesopotamia or India. "The fundamental mistake" his colleagues were making was "to suppose that the Bolshevists were really a great military force." In the context of the civil war they had undoubtedly exhibited great superiority against demoralized opponents. But they lacked good communications facilities and munitions factories; it was therefore "absurd to talk of their undertaking an expedition against India, which we had always regarded as a very serious matter to the Russian Empire when at its strongest."

Nor, in Lloyd George's view, did the Bolsheviks offer a military threat to their closer neighbors. "Barbarians did not march after nothing," he said. And, except for the oil of Baku, there was little in Transcaucasia they would want. Rather, he said, the "real danger" posed by the Bolsheviks was political—the undermining of other societies through "gold and propaganda." So far the only Soviet "attacks" against the Allies had been by propaganda, which was "quite a legitimate method of making war," but one against which military methods were of little use. Furthermore, his "latest information" was that the Bolsheviks did not even have these aims for the present. Yet he was not averse to sending arms to the republics of the Caucasus (as the French were already doing in the case of

Poland) to make the Bolsheviks think it increasingly desirable to come to terms with them. Nor was he opposed to sending British sailors to reclaim the Caspian flotilla. If they were in danger, they could escape through the north Persian port of Enzeli (now Pahlavi); there was no necessity to send troops to hold Baku and the railway to Batum. If Beatty would take the "naval risk," Lloyd George said, he would take the "political" risk. (Exactly how he distinguished between "naval" and "political" risk is unclear, but Beatty refused: the Bolsheviks could put too great a naval force into the Caspian, he said, to allow complete reliance on Enzeli.)

These three positions were reiterated over and over again. Churchill, as in the past, was isolated; no one present supported his arguments. Curzon, we have seen, was joined by Walter Long and, in part, by Beatty. Lloyd George made his case virtually without assistance, although the few remarks which the minutes attribute to Bonar Law, Edwin Montagu, and Birkenhead indicate that they more nearly took his position than that of either of the others. Two further influences were felt. On 18 January the Minister of Labour, Sir Robert Horne, who had not been present previously, presented a gloomy account of the industrial situation in Great Britain. The extremists within the trade-union movement planned to bring the economy to a standstill by coordinated strikes in March when the economy was at its weakest, he said. The government might need to be able to raise all sorts of special forces—to take over transportation, the docks, the police—in order to cope with the situation. Thus Horne underlined Henry Wilson's contention that under no circumstances could additional manpower be spared for operations abroad.[98]

Wilson himself was the second influence. Repeatedly he gave his little lectures on logistics, underlining the relationship between resources and goals. Asked by his colleagues on the 16th to interview Georgian and Azerbaijani representatives to find out what sort of resistance their countries might present to the Bolsheviks (this was Lloyd George's solution), he reported back on the 18th that he had "traced the history of Georgia back to 1212 A.D., and could not find any case where they had not given in to every enemy." (His cynicism was greater than his historical accuracy.) And he wrote in

[98] See Wilson's diary entry for 15 January 1920 (Callwell, *Wilson*, vol. II, p. 222).

his diary: "The truth is that we would have to take over both countries, arm & feed them, run their rails & communications, & then do all the fighting—and *then* they would cart us." Regarding the discussions as a whole Wilson wrote:

I pointed out that I could not see why Lenin should not attack all the border States since Paris had filched them from Russia & Lenin might & I thought ought to claim them as part of Russia & therefore *ought* to retake them. This was unanswerable. We left the problem unsolved in exactly the state we have always left it since last Nov: year [i.e., November 1918]. L.G. is totally unable to offer a solution & simply drifts from one crisis to another.[99]

The British brought all of their disagreements with them into the Allied conference on the morning of 19 January.[100] Curzon finally broke through the confusion by suggesting that, since it was evidently impossible to send troops, the Council should abandon the idea of a military expedition and instead determine for itself whether or not the peoples of Transcaucasia, properly assisted, might be able to defend themselves. He then ushered in delegations from Georgia and Azerbaijan for questioning. Each outlined the military preparations its country had made and then—"the same ridiculous cock-and-bull stories," Wilson later wrote[101]—solemnly stated that, given Allied arms and food, it could hold off the Bolsheviks. But if it did not receive Allied assistance, it would have no alternative but to negotiate its future with Moscow. ("You would really sign an agreement with the Bolsheviks?" Clemenceau asked incredulously.) And finally (as Wilson noted, "for Lloyd George's benefit and Winston's anger")[102] both delegations observed that, in any case, they felt more confident of their ability to come to terms with the Bolsheviks than with Denikin, who would never have recognized their right to independence.

After the Georgian and Azerbaijani spokesmen had left, Foch—under sympathetic cross-examination from Churchill—once again developed his scheme for creating, with Allied support, an anti-

[99] Wilson MS diary, entry for 18 January 1920 (cf. Callwell, *Wilson*, vol. II, p. 223).

[100] Minutes, meeting of Heads of Governments, Paris, 19 January 1920, 10:30 a.m.; *British Documents*, vol. II, no. 77, pp. 914-25. The American and Japanese ambassadors were also present.

[101] Wilson MS diary, entry for 19 January 1920 (see Callwell, *Wilson*, vol. II, p. 224).

[102] *Idem.*

Bolshevik coalition of all the states on Russia's borders, from Finland to Azerbaijan. Following Churchill, Lloyd George took over in much less friendly a manner, and under his questions Foch's edifice looked scarcely imposing. When he asked whether Foch proposed that the Allies equip the Polish army for an attack against Russia, the Marshal declared that he did not; even if it were equipped, he said, it would not be up to the task. In fact, he admitted, he had in mind primarily a *political* coalition of the border states for defense against Bolshevism. The questioning continued:

MR. LLOYD GEORGE: Do you know whether the Bolsheviks are preparing to attack those countries?
MARSHAL FOCH: That one cannot know until after the event.
MR. LLOYD GEORGE: Could you now mention a single one of those countries against which the Bolsheviks contemplate a military attack?
MARSHAL FOCH: When that attack takes place, I shall be in a position to reply. I could not do so beforehand.[103]

Foch was hardly a good witness. Lloyd George thus won an easy psychological victory. As soon as he had finished with Foch, the military advisers were shown out and the heads of governments reached their decisions. They would send no troops to Transcaucasia. But on Lloyd George's urging, they decided to send arms and munitions and, if possible, food. (The Prime Minister argued that the Red Army had already captured all the war material it needed from Denikin, and that, therefore, the possibility that further supplies sent to Transcaucasia might fall into Soviet hands was not an important danger.) Finally, in order to increase the spirit of resistance among the peoples of Transcaucasia, and in compliance with the wishes of the Georgian and Azerbaijani delegations, they decided, after all, to accord *de facto* recognition to the government of Armenia, subject to the condition that such recognition in no way would prejudice the eventual decision on Armenia's boundaries.[104]

Thus the "Middle Eastern crisis," as it was called in the press, had ended, seemingly in an anti-climax. In fact, as it turned out, the War Office statement was essentially correct. The Middle East did, after a fashion, burst into flames: Azerbaijan fell to the Red Army on 28 April—almost, but not quite, within the ninety days

[103] *British Documents*, vol. II, no. 77, p. 917. Unlike most sets of these minutes, this was taken in the first person, apparently verbatim.
[104] *Ibid.*, pp. 922-25.

of the War Office's prediction. Armenia and Georgia were not long in following. And Persia, too, although on a lesser (and not mortal) scale, saw a Bolshevik invasion. But British troops—except for a few, whose activities we shall follow in Volume III—were not involved. And British interests were not fundamentally damaged. This was one chief result of the Paris discussions. As Riddell noted in his diary, "The Allies now understand the impossibility of fighting the Bolsheviks in Russia. No nation is prepared to supply troops or money."[105]

The second chief result was the decision to trade with the Russian cooperative organizations: Lloyd George had led the Allies in a long step toward normal trade relations with Soviet Russia. Indeed, as the *Manchester Guardian* noted, the decision implied an even more basic decision to make peace finally with Moscow. And it continued:

Naturally, that is not the way in which the thing is put. . . . But there is the fact, dress it up as nicely as you will. . . . Obviously, they cannot at the same time open up trade relations with Russia and go on hitting her.[106]

A Foreign Office commentary by R. H. Hoare (it will be remembered that the Foreign Office had not had knowledge that trade with the cooperatives was even under consideration) observed that the arrangement was one which could "hardly last for long." Either it would "lead to something approaching formal relations with the Soviet Government," or the Allies would instead try to use the cooperatives within Russia as a weapon against the regime. In the view of the Foreign Office (Hoare's commentary was a telegram, drafted after a meeting of Russian specialists, which Lord Hardinge subsequently signed and sent to Curzon), such an attempt would fail and would only lead the Soviet authorities to deprive the cooperatives of the independence they still had, while at the same time delaying the arrival of badly needed Russian agricultural produce in Central Europe. The Allies should therefore "avoid creating in the minds of the Bolsheviks the impression that we are looking for another weapon of offense against them."[107]

Although there had been no war, the War Office's statement and the hurried trip to Paris of the service ministers had provided a real war scare. War scares—especially ones so obviously artificial—

---

[105] Riddell, *Diary*, p. 161, entry for 22 January 1920.
[106] *Manchester Guardian*, 17 January 1920.
[107] This telegram of 20 January 1920 (the meeting was on the 19th) is cited above, n. 61.

never do their originators any good, and, if the Liberal and Labour press is any guide, a large segment of the British public blamed Winston Churchill for an anxious few days. The *Guardian* accused him of engineering a war that would serve as a *post facto* justification of the £100 million he had wasted on intervention in Russia, in order to rehabilitate his reputation.[108] Labour spokesmen made much the same allegation and then announced that their party would not regard itself as bound by "military and political commitments entered into in secret as part of a general policy against which it has never failed to protest."[109] Curiously enough, Churchill himself seems to have been most shaken by an editorial in the sober *British Weekly*, the organ of the Nonconformist churches, and one which rarely dabbled in politics.[110] "Anyone who thinks that the alarmist dispatch which has caused the trouble was the work of a mere underling," it wrote, "is more simple than Simon. We wish to see Mr. Churchill out of the Cabinet, or at least out of the War Office."[111] Lloyd George told Riddell that Churchill had been stung into wishing to issue an official explanation. He wanted to justify what he had done, and he even hinted at resigning. Lloyd George objected to the former, not the latter: Churchill could go if he wished, the Prime Minister said, but he himself would be a party to no justifications.[112] Churchill stayed.

The episode's official epilogue was written by the same authorities responsible for its prologue. On 20 January, after the shouting was over, *The Times* carried a mollifying statement from the War Office:

The particulars given last Thursday in the semi-official statement regarding the Bolshevists and Central Asia were prepared merely as a matter of routine, and had no connexion with the movements of any Ministers on that day.

✧

Another sign of the changing relationship between the British and Soviet governments—along with the decision to begin trade through the cooperatives and the concomitant ending of the blockade—was the conclusion on 12 February 1920 of an Anglo-Soviet

---

[108] *Manchester Guardian*, 17 January 1920.
[109] *Daily Herald*, 19 January 1920.
[110] So Lloyd George told Riddell; *Diary*, pp. 162-63, entry for 24 January 1920.
[111] *British Weekly*, 22 January 1920.
[112] Riddell, *Diary*, p. 163, entry for 24 January.

agreement for the exchange of prisoners. After negotiations in Copenhagen lasting nearly three months and scores of preliminary communications during the six months preceding these, Maxim Litvinov and James O'Grady, Secretary of the National Federation of General Workers and Labour member of Parliament, put their signatures to an agreement providing for the mutual exchange of virtually all prisoners and hostages, military and civilian.[113]

For both governments the agreement satisfied urgently felt humanitarian needs: for the Bolsheviks it had the added significance of being the product of the first diplomatic contacts of any kind between themselves and the Allies for more than a year, another sign of their decreasing isolation. So far as the British government was concerned, the agreement was the result of no particular policy decision: with constant pressure from Parliament and from the families of the nearly 1,000 British subjects involved, the government was always interested in getting its citizens freed, and from early 1919 British military and naval commanders began sending to the United Kingdom a few selected high-ranking Bolshevik prisoners to serve as hostages.[114] Limited exchanges, in fact, were already taking place when, in May, the British government proposed to Moscow a general exchange.[115] During the next few months the two governments agreed to negotiations in a neutral country (the British government refused to allow Soviet representatives to come to London).[116] In August, when withdrawal from North Russia was already under way, the War Office instructed Ironside to ship to England one hundred of his "most influential" prisoners in order to provide the British

---

[113] The final agreement was published as Cmd. 587, *Agreement Between His Majesty's Government and the Soviet Government of Russia for the Exchange of Prisoners*, 1920. The Russian text is in *Dokumenty vneshnei politiki*, vol. II, pp. 364-67.

[114] The leading Bolshevik hostage was F. F. Raskolnikov, Commissar of the Baltic Fleet, taken prisoner when his destroyer flagship was captured during the winter of 1918-19. On 1 February he radioed Trotsky that he and one Ninyuk, a member of the Petrograd Soviet, were being held in England as hostages for "all British civilian and military prisoners" in Bolshevik hands. His message was printed in the War Cabinet's *Eastern Report*, No. CVI, 6 February; Cab. 24/145.

[115] See *British Documents*, vol. III, no. 241, n. 3. This note also indicates that, on 26 May, Raskolnikov and Ninyuk were exchanged for a selected group of British prisoners. Raskolnikov was later to haunt his former captors: he commanded the Soviet squadron which drove British troops from the Persian port of Enzeli on the Caspian in May 1920. See Volume III of the present work. In 1921-22 he joined in the "Great Game" as Russian emissary in Afghanistan.

[116] For these arrangements, see *British Documents*, vol. III, nos. 279, 295, 344, and 355.

side with a stronger bargaining counter.[117] Finally, in mid-November, after it had been worked out that Litvinov would proceed from Reval to Copenhagen on a British warship, O'Grady—presumably because of his experience as a negotiator and his Labour Party affiliations—received his appointment as head of the British delegation. It is noteworthy that these arrangements were never the subject of Cabinet discussion. They were all handled, and questions concerning them were resolved, at departmental level. So strong were the impulses to achieve the exchange that from no quarter—within the Cabinet, the departments, or in Parliament—was there voiced the complaint that the negotiations might imply *de facto* recognition of the Soviet government. It was considered sufficient to instruct O'Grady "to refrain from all political discussion" with the Soviet representatives, and "in no way to countenance any attempt on their part to negotiate on any subjects than that of the exchange of prisoners."[118]

The negotiations themselves are of interest only as they show the immense technical complexities involved in dealing with a government which one has not recognized and with which one is in a state of undeclared war. As such, every detail—choice of location and of delegates, the powers allowed to delegates, the matters considered negotiable—was filled with a significance it would not otherwise have had. And the communications between the two governments, particularly those which took place between Curzon and Chicherin before the start of the discussions at Copenhagen, were marked with the bluntness and rudeness—from both parties, not from Mos-

---

[117] War Office to Ironside (Archangel), telegram 80255, 5 August 1919, file 608/2/12/17585; F.O. 608/203. Ironside was to turn over his remaining prisoners to "competent" North Russian authorities; lacking such authorities, he was to release them. Previously he had carried on local exchanges, subject to Churchill's dictum that: "Without previous reference here, no negotiations which might be construed as recognizing the Bolshevik Government are on any account to be entered into. Any exchange of prisoners must be purely local arrangements between commanders on the spot, and in this case also what you propose to do must be clearly specified in advance." (Churchill to Ironside, telegram 76959, 10 April 1919; W.O. 33/966, no. 1528.)

[118] O'Grady's letter of appointment and instructions from Curzon, 13 November 1919, is in *British Documents*, vol. III, no. 535. Another reason for his selection may have been his previous experience in Russia: during the spring of 1917 he was a member of a delegation of pro-war British and French socialists who toured Russia in an effort to rouse the war effort of their Russian fellow socialists—an experience hardly calculated to make him more attractive in the eyes of Bolshevik negotiators in 1919.

cow alone—which distinguished the emergence of the revolutionary Soviet regime as an actor in the world of bourgeois states.[119]

The Copenhagen negotiations themselves, conducted in the distinctly unproletarian surroundings of the Hotel d'Angleterre, nearly broke down at several points between their initiation on 25 November 1919 and their conclusion the following February. Litvinov immediately showed that he was not so much interested in Russian prisoners of war in England as he was in Bolshevik political prisoners still held by Germany and the neutrals. Unless the British government would secure the repatriation of these prisoners, Litvinov said, Moscow would only exchange with Britain noncommissioned officers and private soldiers, not officers or civilians.[120] Curzon, of course, was powerless to secure the release of prisoners held by other governments; instead, he instructed O'Grady if necessary to offer Litvinov what he termed "other concessions," from food and medical supplies to even the possibility of lifting the blockade.[121]

Litvinov, meanwhile, produced credentials giving him full powers to enter into political negotiations, and—reminiscent of his sojourn in Stockholm exactly a year before—on 9 December he circularized all of the Allied legations in the Danish capital with copies of the peace resolution passed on the 5th by the Seventh All-Russian Congress of Soviets in Moscow. These, like their antecedents a year previously, were all returned unopened.[122] On the 22nd Litvinov wrote cordially to O'Grady, extolling the mutual benefits which would come from Anglo-Soviet trade, hinting at the possibility of a debt settlement, and asserting that "there should be no obstacle to the establishment of real peace, except the bogey of revolutionary propaganda," which, he felt, could surely be dealt with. Curzon instructed O'Grady not to reply to this enticement, and the more prosaic search for the basis of a prisoner exchange continued.[123] Although

[119] See, for example, the exchange of radio messages, Curzon to Chicherin, 5 August 1919, and Chicherin to Curzon, 13 August; *British Documents,* vol. III, nos. 356 and 370. The latter is in *Dokumenty vneshnei politiki,* vol. II, pp. 236-37.
[120] See O'Grady to Curzon, sent as Copenhagen Legation's telegram 1707, 6 December 1919; *British Documents,* vol. III, no. 592.
[121] Curzon to O'Grady, telegram 1584 to Copenhagen Legation, 19 December 1919; *ibid.,* no. 608.
[122] See Grant Watson (Chargé d'Affaires, Copenhagen) to Curzon, telegram 1724, 10 December 1919, and O'Grady's letter to J. D. Gregory (Foreign Office) of the same date; *ibid.,* nos. 598 and 599. The peace resolution is cited above, n. 37.
[123] Litvinov to O'Grady, 22 December 1919, *ibid.,* no. 620; Curzon's minuted instructions are printed as n. 2.

the French minister in Copenhagen suspected otherwise, O'Grady adhered carefully to his narrowly drawn instructions.[124]

In the end, he never had to offer the concessions which Curzon proposed. The Supreme Council's decisions in January to end the blockade and to begin trade with the cooperatives had a salutary effect on Litvinov's willingness to compromise, and ultimately O'Grady convinced him that, while Britain could do nothing about Bolshevik prisoners in the hands of other governments, it could use its influence to effect an exchange between the Bolsheviks and the nearly moribund North Russian government at Archangel. On this basis, and with the British and Soviet governments each promising to return all prisoners except those "who have committed grave offences"—a concession which O'Grady offered on his own authority, to the sorrow of the Foreign Office[125]—the agreement was finally signed, and O'Grady returned to England after three months' contact with a real Bolshevik, although a singularly undoctrinaire one, unharmed and uninfected.[126] In early January, when the outcome of the negotiations was still uncertain, Litvinov himself—reflecting on his dealings with O'Grady before an audience of friends in Copenhagen (including one British intelligence agent)—is reported to have observed:

O'Grady is naturally far from being a Bolshevik. He is a Trade Unionist Philistine who is nearer to English Liberalism than Socialism. He has

[124] See Curzon to O'Grady, telegram 1524 to Copenhagen Legation, 26 November 1919 (*ibid.*, no. 566) reporting the suspicions of the French in Copenhagen that O'Grady was, in fact, discussing a whole range of political questions with Litvinov, and O'Grady's subsequent denial: Legation telegram 1665 to Curzon, 27 November (*ibid.*, no. 569).

[125] The clause caused the Foreign Office much concern, for it feared that the Soviet regime would interpret it as meaning not only offenses against criminal law, but also those which in the West would be called political. Not wishing to risk disrupting the agreement (it had already been signed), Curzon instructed O'Grady to tell Litvinov that the British government would hold him personally responsible for any reprisals in the execution of the agreement, or other acts which violated its spirit. (Curzon to O'Grady, telegram 120 to Copenhagen Legation, 16 February 1929; *ibid.*, pp. 820-21.) On 5 February the Cabinet had decided that, if Litvinov was still unwilling to accept the numerous concessions embodied in the British draft treaty, the British government should publish its terms and give Moscow one week in which to accept them (Cabinet conclusions 9 [20]; Cab. 23/20). It did so with great reluctance, however; as Hardinge pointed out in a memorandum (Cabinet paper C.P. 559; Cab. 24/97), a break in negotiations would be "an exceedingly grave step, as there would be no obvious method of securing the repatriation of the British in Russia." The Cabinet's draft agreement is printed in *British Documents*, vol. III, no. 675, n. 1.

[126] The actual workings of the exchange agreement are discussed in Volume III, ch. X.

the English characteristic of wishing to domineer, but, like all the English, he also has this quality: when he has understood a thing he is ready to talk it over with his worst enemies. He has understood the impossibility of intervention and the uselessness of the blockade. The fact alone that O'Grady would go to London with this conviction is considered by me as my greatest diplomatic victory. Naturally I know very well that all the documents and conditions of peace that I have put before him will lead to nothing. Peace is but a drop of water falling constantly on a stone; it makes at last a hole there.[127]

❖

The changing relationship between Great Britain and the Soviet regime was further reflected in a memorial presented personally to Lloyd George by a group of military officers and civil servants who had served in Russia during the intervention. Subsequently the Prime Minister circulated it to the Cabinet,[128] and on 23 February 1920 it was published in *The Times*. Among its signers were Generals Gough and Marsh, whose involvement with Yudenich's campaign we have seen, and E. M. Harvey, who had been in charge of the British effort to stabilize the currency of the Archangel government. Three, including Harvey, were partners in city banking firms. The memorial made its point directly. Its signers did not, it said, "consider that the crimes committed by the [Soviet] Russian government in the past should be regarded as a bar to its recognition now." The anti-Bolshevik regimes all over Russia had not proved themselves superior to the Bolsheviks in humanity, while in energy, cohesion, and resourcefulness they had shown themselves to be decidedly inferior. Here, of course, was no argument for recognition. But four arguments followed.

First was that of exposure: the Western Powers were afraid of Moscow's propaganda, and of the example of direct revolutionary action set by the Bolshevik regime in coming to power. This was indeed a danger. However,

[127] Report CX/P/353. 920, from "Secret Agent D.57" (Copenhagen), 6 January 1920; sent to J. D. Gregory of the Foreign Office by Sir Basil Thomson, head of the Secret Service, on 20 January (file 174866/91/38; F.O. 371/3961). In his covering note Thomson merely drew Gregory's attention to an "interesting" report. There are relatively few such items in the Foreign Office archives. Whether or not this particular report is accurate or embroidered upon is, of course, impossible to determine; certainly it has the ring of authenticity, however.

[128] As Cabinet paper C.P. 768; Cab. 24/99. On 20 February 1920 a delegation of the signers had what they described in an attached covering note as "a most successful audience" with Lloyd George.

the signatories would suggest that no protective measure would be so effectual as the reopening of Russia to commerce, intercourse, and observation. The forces of moderation in Russia would be consolidated, the fundamental differences of character, education, and economic structure between Russia and Europe would be displayed, and the misery to which great territories have been reduced would, if once disclosed, be the most impressive of warnings against precipitate and violent social changes.

Second was the need for Russian produce: it was daily becoming more clear that Europe's stability depended on the adequate feeding during the coming year of the states east of the Rhine, and it was difficult to know of any sources of food for them other than Russia. If Russian grain were not made available, there might well be famine, whose consequences would "certainly be disorder, and probably outbreaks of the kind which marked the earlier phases of Bolshevism in Russia."

Third was an argument regarding debts: trade with the Russian cooperatives would neither relieve the holders of pre-war bonds nor give them any inducement to assist in the restoration of Russia. The signers believed, however, that, once normal relations were restored, the Soviet government would be ready to consider the claims of Russia's foreign creditors; in any case, "it is evident that no class of the community can have a stronger interest in reviving Russian production," without which they would never be paid.

Finally, there was the Russo-German specter: the longer peace with Russia was delayed, the more certain it became that German influence in Russia would be reestablished, and that Russian policy would be directly antagonistic to British interests. This policy would be "to intervene on the side of the revolution everywhere; with a victorious and seasoned army at its command [Soviet Russia] could intervene effectively, bringing food as it advances."

For these reasons, given the available alternatives, the signers of the memorial believed "that peace with Russia is necessary, both on economic and political grounds, to save the continent of Europe from catastrophe." But it must come soon, before famine could make itself felt. And it must come from England: "Being as a nation less exposed than the Continental Powers to revolutionary infection, we can think with less passion; having an equal concern with them in the welfare of Europe and the peace of Asia, we speak with more authority."

These were, for the most part, not impressive arguments. They are —and they were at the time they were put forward—easily refutable. But they were impeccably liberal, the products of the rational liberalism which flourished in Great Britain before the World War, and they came from a group of respected servants of the Crown with extensive experience in the Russia of the Whites. Given the restless temper of British society in 1920 and the dissatisfaction with the Peace which already was making itself felt, their appeal is easily understandable. But their most effective enunciation came, of course, not from the signers of this memorial—its publication drew almost no comment, an indication, perhaps, of the extent to which its arguments were already generally accepted—but from its addressee, David Lloyd George. On countless occasions during the following twelve months the Prime Minister was to reiterate all these points in his effort to bring about an accord between Britain and the new Russia.

CHAPTER IX

BRITAIN AND THE RUSSIAN
CIVIL WAR

The Great Allied Powers will, each of them and all of them, learn to rue the fact that they could not take more decided and more united action to crush the Bolshevist peril at its centre before it had grown too strong.

—Winston Churchill, 14 February 1920

The capitalist circles which direct English policy are the classic home of compromise. They have raised to the pitch of perfection the art of understanding new historical forces in the course of development and of finding compromises to neutralise their effect.

—G. V. Chicherin, 7 February 1920[1]

In November 1918, at the close of the Great War and a year after the Bolshevik seizure of power, the British government found itself deeply involved in the Russian Civil War. During the months that followed, as communications through the Black Sea were opened and as resources once needed for the war against the Central Powers became available, this involvement grew, along with the apparent successes of the anti-Bolshevik Russians. By early 1920, however, with Archangel and Murmansk in Soviet hands, with Yudenich a refugee in Estonia, with Kolchak a prisoner awaiting execution in Siberia, and with Denikin's Volunteer Army—the only White force still in the field—confined to a small corner of the Kuban coast, British intervention had virtually ended, and the government in London set about the task of working out a *modus vivendi* with a Soviet regime whose prospects for immediate, if not long-term, survival could no longer be doubted. The process of reaching an accord will be the subject of the last of these three volumes. Here, however, it is useful to attempt to draw some conclusions about the

[1] Chicherin's speech, in Moscow, was reported in *The Times* of 12 February 1920; Churchill's, to his Dundee constituents, in that of 16 February.

nature of the United Kingdom's involvement in the Russian Civil War, and about the ways in which intervention was terminated once it became apparent that without massive external assistance the White cause could not possibly prevail.

At the outset, during the spring and summer of 1918, involvement of the Allied Powers came about almost inadvertently: when the decisions to intervene were made, it was not apparent to those who made them (although it may be argued that it should have been) that the commitment of forces to aid in the re-creation of the Eastern Front against the Germans would lead, in fact, to a commitment to bringing about the overthrow of Bolshevik rule. No single decision marked this transformation of objectives. When the landing of Allied forces in North Russia provoked resistance from the Bolsheviks, Allied statesmen and military commanders too easily equated it with German resistance and drew the facile conclusion that in opposing Bolshevism in Russia they were also opposing the spread of German power and influence. Once the German Empire had been defeated, this argument seemed a good deal less sound, but by then intervention had come to have a rationale as well as a momentum of its own. "Recent events have created obligations which last beyond the occasions which gave them birth," Balfour wrote in November 1918. Having fostered the growth of "new anti-Bolshevik administrations" in order to use them against the Germans, the Allies could not simply let them fall before the Bolsheviks once the War had ended.[2]

It is important here to emphasize both the rationale and the momentum. Just as the rationale was never entirely lost from sight—even those, like Churchill, who were most prone to justify intervention on explicitly anti-Bolshevik grounds were careful always to refer as well to the "obligations" incurred before November 1918—so the momentum allowed intervention to proceed in the absence of controlling decisions. Momentum, indeed, became a controlling factor in itself. November was thus a singularly unfortunate time for the war with Germany to end. In Russia the long winter was just descending. At Archangel, where the Allies were most heavily engaged in active operations against the Bolsheviks, the river and the port were beginning to freeze; unless all troops were withdrawn immediately, they would have to remain until the following spring.

[2] See above, p. 16.

And if they stayed—unless an accord were reached between the Allies and the Bolsheviks—they would come under attack and would respond. This was the momentum of intervention.

Neither was November 1918 a propitious time for a decision to withdraw these troops. Indeed, their numbers—a few brigades in North Russia, two battalions and a military mission in Siberia—were insignificant compared with those of the armies which had fought in France. They were too small to demand prolonged attention from politicians and generals with minds fatigued and sensibilities dulled by the vastly larger war which had just ended: it was all too easy to allow matters in Russia to drift on, subject only to the most general and largely meaningless guidelines laid down in London. Thus the War Office despatched two divisions to Transcaucasia almost as a reflex action; not until they were at their destination did the Cabinet's Eastern Committee begin to deliberate the question of why they should have been sent and what they would do there.

Similarly, there was little time for reasoned reflection on how intervention in Russia might be pushed to a successful conclusion, or, indeed, what "success" in such a context might mean. Until it emerged briefly in the form of the Prinkipo proposal at the Peace Conference, the idea of negotiating some sort of political settlement with the Bolsheviks was never explored. The Prinkipo idea itself was a victim of Allied disunity; so, also, was the notion of anything but a military solution to the Russian Civil War. "Success" was almost invariably assumed to comprise the destruction and total displacement of the Soviet regime. But what sort of authority should succeed it? What should be the extent of the territory which the successor regime would govern? And what actions of the Allies themselves might bring about what sorts of possible outcomes to these Russian dilemmas? All these questions deserved the most concentrated attention at the highest levels. But so—before the opening of the Peace Conference—did the Parliamentary election at home and preparations for all of the many problems which the Conference would present. And after its opening, when these potential problems and disagreements became actual, the competition for the attention and the energies of tired men continued unabated.

This is not to say that Russian problems were not among the central concerns of the statesmen at Paris.[3] Rather, it is to say that the Peace Conference, with its fitful attacks on these problems, never became a forum for decision and control. Under its auspices the several Allied governments were never able to put together the sort of tight coalition against Bolshevism which Churchill and Foch regarded as essential to their notion of "success." The various Allied positions were so far apart that the effort of producing common formulae, such as the invitation to Prinkipo or the joint statement of 27 May 1919 in support of Kolchak, tended to serve as a substitute for effective combined action and creative statesmanship. Far from transforming the environment in which the individual governments conducted their policies, as many international agreements do, they scarcely affected it. The Conference in fact gave rise to the worst of compromises: it served to restrain forthright unilateral initiatives, both political and military, while at the same time failing to produce a truly unified Allied approach to the Russian problem. The anti-Bolshevik Russians had little incentive to go to Prinkipo, for example, because the French told them they would not need to. Of course the Conference did not wholly prevent unilateral actions and decisions. During the crowded spring of 1919 the French withdrew their expeditionary force from South Russia, the British made the decision to remove their troops from North Russia and Transcaucasia, and the Americans withdrew from North Russia and confined their force in Siberia to duties which would involve it as minimally as possible in the civil war. These were all unilateral steps. But real psychological freedom of action returned only after the signature of the Treaty of Versailles in late June, when the heads of government returned to their capitals.

It should be noted that these actions and decisions, each reducing the levels of involvement in Russia of the several Allied governments, did not imply a slackening of official anti-Bolshevik fervor, nor any diminution of outward commitment to the anti-Bolshevik

[3] The central theme of Arno J. Mayer's *Politics and Diplomacy of Peacemaking* is that the related problems of Russia and Bolshevism were *the* central problems of the Peace Conference—a view vividly expressed in his subtitle, *Containment and Counterrevolution at Versailles, 1918-1919*. I find this notion suggestive and challenging, but ultimately misleading. The problem of providing for the future security of France against Germany—a problem with many ramifications at the Conference—cannot satisfactorily be explained in these terms, and it was at least as important as that of Russia and Bolshevism.

cause. Rather, they marked the ascendancy of Lloyd George's and Woodrow Wilson's position that if the Whites really *deserved* to win, they would be able to do so for themselves by attracting the support of the mass of the Russian population. Here was a fundamentally fallacious analogy—that a civil war was like an especially violent election from which the party that can attract the most popular support will emerge victorious. As a rationale for nonintervention, or intervention on a reduced scale, this argument had an understandable attractiveness. But it failed to take into account the fact that, unless the whole population of a country is mobilized, as is rarely the case and was certainly far from the case during the Russian Civil War, popular support may be less important a determinant of success or failure than the ability to combine rewards and punishments in such a way as to mold together an efficient, disciplined fighting force.

It may well sometimes be the case that the side which can create such a force can also command more popular support (of varying degrees) than its opponents. Such was probably the case in Russia. Certainly it need not have been so, however. Kolchak and Denikin were generally inept as leaders, especially in their toleration of corruption, inefficiency, and the reinstitution of the sorts of relationships between officers and soldiers which had been so poisonous an influence in the old Tsarist army. But in April and May 1920, General Wrangel, Denikin's successor and the outstanding White field commander of the Russian Civil War, was to put together in the Crimea a remarkably spirited, disciplined, and efficient force which was briefly able to inflict significant losses on the more powerful Bolsheviks. One can only wonder what Wrangel could have accomplished had he taken charge of the Volunteer Army in April 1919, before Denikin (against Wrangel's advice) launched it on its disastrously frantic plunge northward.

Yet one can also wonder—supposing that Wrangel, or even Denikin or Kolchak, had succeeded in taking Moscow and overthrowing the Bolsheviks—what the Allies would have made of the regime that would have been installed in their place. Perhaps it would have been a liberally orientated regime with roots in a reconvened Constituent Assembly. More likely, however, it would have been a restored autocracy, or a military dictatorship displaying only the barest trappings of true representative government. Would the Allies have easily come to terms with it?[4] The qualities which make for victorious generalship in a civil war do not necessarily make for wise and restrained leadership of the political entity which emerges—the dozens of regimes of every political color which since 1919 have come to power as a result of civil wars across the globe attest to the truth of this contention. As E. H. Carr concluded in a memorandum in late May 1919, after comparing the techniques for rule practiced by the Bolsheviks with those of Kolchak and his entourage: "The reasons for thinking that a Kolchak régime would be an improvement on the present Bolshevist régime do not therefore stand a very close examination." Kolchak's methods, he wrote, "do not differ sensibly from those of the Bolsheviks, in spite of any restraining influence which Allied co-operation may exercise on him."[5] Sir Esmé Howard, one of the principal British diplomatists dealing with Russian affairs at the Peace Conference, stated the dilemma in different terms. "It seems to me," he wrote, "that our best policy in Russia will be to back the saner elements of the Left." But he added: "So far, however, the moderate sane Left does not seem to have produced a single real leader."[6]

Howard's observation, of course, can be applied far beyond the Russia of 1919 to virtually all of the many instances of civil warfare in "less-developed" countries which the twentieth century has seen. The stable, "modernized," Western democratic societies have almost always hoped that out of such strife there would emerge to leadership the "moderate sane Left." (Just how one defines "moderate," "sane," and "Left," however, has been a point of considerable contention, whether in Spain in 1937, Greece in 1945, Cuba in 1958, or South Vietnam in 1968.) Civil wars are polarizing experiences; leaders who can supply the discipline and efficiency necessary to win them are not likely to be "moderate" (although they may, by most people's lights, be "sane") whether they come from the Left or the Right. In 1919 the statesmen of the West were fairly well agreed that N. V. Chaikovsky, the patriarchal sometime head

---

[4] They did, it is true, easily come to terms with Bela Kun's successors in Hungary. But Kun was overthrown primarily as a result of the Rumanian invasion, not as a result of an internal civil war.

[5] "The Proposed Recognition of the Kolchak Government," 26 May 1919, file 598/2/1/10970; F.O. 608/188.

[6] Minute in file 602/1/4/1464, 6 February 1919; F.O. 608/196.

of the Archangel government, was precisely the sort of "sane moderate Left" figure to lead in the reconstruction of Russia. Yet Chaikovsky, and others like him, such as the members of the "Directorate" at Omsk which was overthrown by the coup which brought Kolchak to power in November 1918, were ill-suited for roles as war leaders. Chaikovsky may have possessed distinguished democratic credentials, but he was notably less successful in raising and organizing a Russian fighting force than, say, Kolchak or Denikin. North Russia never became a decisively important theater of operations in the Russian Civil War precisely because of the inability of Chaikovsky and his successors to inspire a large number of Russians with a desire (or, at least, a willingness) to fight for the anti-Bolshevik cause. Thus the Allies were left with most of the weight of fighting against the Bolsheviks in the North. It was not a burden they enjoyed, and both Ironside and the War Office were therefore inclined to look elsewhere for the significant victories of the war. Yet one can argue that, in order to bring about the "moderate sane Left" in Russia which would have most served their long-term interests, the Allies would, in fact, have had to pick up this burden all over Russia and themselves do the bulk of the fighting against the Bolsheviks, at the same time working to promote the growth of representative institutions behind the lines. In this manner, perhaps, could military dictatorship have been avoided—although at the price, perhaps, of a temporary *foreign* military dictatorship during the period of institution-building. This argument implies, of course, that, in order to bring about what for them (and, one might argue, perhaps even for Russia as well) would have been a maximally advantageous outcome, the Allies would have had to take over the anti-Bolshevik cause in the Russian Civil War to a point where the effort of the indigenous anti-Bolshevik forces would have been reduced almost to insignificance.

For analytical purposes one can distinguish three stages, or degrees, of intervention by a Great Power in a foreign civil war—or, indeed, in any war between two parties with a lesser military capability than its own. The British passed through all three stages in Russia. The first stage is characterized principally by the provision of material and financial assistance. But it may also include the extension of military, economic, and political advice, and perhaps even the training of military forces. In such a situation, while the supporting

Power may significantly augment the military capability of the side it supports, the effort of fighting the war remains completely in indigenous hands. So, also, does the responsibility for strategic and tactical decision-making, although the external Power may be able to exert considerable leverage on the military and civil decision-making processes of the supported side according to the degree to which the latter is unable to find alternative sources of war materials and is unable to continue fighting without them. It is important here to stress that the supporting Power can exert leverage, but rarely control. While the regulation of the flow of materials to a belligerent may appear to afford effective controls over its policies, such is seldom the case: the party actually engaged in fighting has significant moral resources it can bring to bear against the party which is not, and this influence tends to work against effective control.[7]

[7] The degree of leverage which a foreign Power can exert depends in part upon whether its intervention is in behalf of the incumbent or the insurgent side in a civil war. Generalization is risky, but it seems reasonable to assume that it is easier to exert leverage on an incumbent than on an insurgent. The whole style of an insurgent leader usually differs fundamentally from that of an incumbent; the attitudes and impulses which have driven him to take up arms against the incumbent are likely to lead him to resist more strongly foreign attempts to exert control over the direction his movement is taking. An incumbent leader is likely to be less willing to do without foreign sources of support, upon which he (and perhaps his predecessors) may long have relied, than is the insurgent leader; unless the insurgent leader is in fact acting as the agent of a foreign power—and that is far less frequently the case than is often alleged, particularly by the propaganda of the incumbent side—he will be more experienced at improvising and getting along without external assistance. The incumbent side is also used to operating as a state in a world of states and is less likely to have the exaggerated fear of foreign domination which characterizes many insurgent leaders.

The asymmetry which usually exists between incumbent and insurgent makes the analytical scheme suggested here somewhat more relevant to the case of foreign intervention in support of an incumbent than to that of intervention in support of an insurgent. This is particularly so when the insurgents rely primarily on irregular, guerrilla warfare operating from no clearly defined territorial base. Once a civil war reaches a point (as some never do) where the insurgent side operates with regular forces from a definite territory over which it has established its administration, the degree of asymmetry between it and the incumbent is reduced and the situation, indeed, resembles that of inter-state warfare. Then the present analytical scheme can be applied to both cases.

In examining the Russian Civil War, the distinction between "insurgent" and "incumbent" is particularly difficult to draw. *Neither* side was recognized by the international community as being a legally constituted government. The Bolsheviks controlled both Petrograd and Moscow—the old and new capitals—and the bulk of European Russia. Yet their opponents, and not themselves, were looked upon by most of the international community as the rightful heirs to preceding Russian governments, and, while they were not given legal recognition,

The British government's relationship with the Kolchak dictatorship in Siberia was predominantly of this first type. With the exception of one or two minor incidents, the two British battalions attached to General Knox's military mission took no part in military operations against the Bolsheviks. Nor did they serve any very significant internal security functions. But the "Supreme Ruler" received vast quantities of British military equipment, and Knox's mission established a school at Vladivostok which trained a considerable number of Russian commissioned and noncommissioned officers. These were important contributions. Nevertheless, both Knox and the War Office in London were relatively unsuccessful in inducing Kolchak to accept British advice concerning either his conduct of the war or his administration of the territory under his power. The mountains of supplies which the British government sent to Kolchak gave it no control over him, and relatively little leverage. Nor were they sufficient to enable him to win a military victory.

The second stage of intervention is characterized by the limited participation of the supporting Power in military operations. In the Russian Civil War such a stage was exemplified by the British relationship with General Denikin in South Russia. There the British performed all the functions which mark a "first-stage" involvement, but, in addition, British "instructors" in aerial and armored warfare led their Russian pupils into battle. In some instances, the "instructors" dropped the pretense altogether and fought as autonomous British air and tank squadrons. The same was true, on a more limited basis, of artillery formations. In this second stage the supported side still bears the brunt of the military effort; the intervening Power not only supplies all of the assistance characteristic of the first stage, but it also provides direct military support, particularly by bringing to bear at the fighting front advanced military technologies which ordinarily would be unavailable, or only inefficiently available, to the supported side. The aim of this selective, limited participation in military operations is to tip an otherwise level or perhaps even unfavorable balance in the direction of the supported side.

Regardless of the greater British military role in South Russia

---

they nevertheless received many of the privileges ordinarily accorded to the agents of a recognized government—in particular, the use of Russian diplomatic properties abroad and access to sources of credit.

than in Siberia, London had no more control over Denikin than over Kolchak, and not much more leverage. Despite continued entreaties from General Holman, Denikin delayed for months the implementation of an efficient and "non-political" system for the distribution of the British military supplies. And London could not make Denikin come to terms with the secessionist republics of the Caucasus. Instead, to the despair of his British advisers, Denikin tied down significant numbers of his troops in skirmishes against Georgia. Participation by the intervening Power in military operations, of course, does much to redress the moral imbalance between the supported and the supporting side and therefore works to increase the leverage which the latter can exert. But in order for the intervening Power to get effective control, it is necessary to proceed to the third stage. Then the intervening forces become the dominant element in the war effort of the supported side. In fact, their roles are in a sense reversed: the indigenous forces do little more than support the "supporting" foreign Power and perhaps keep order outside the combat zones. The intervening Power also assumes actual if not formal command over military operations, and a concomitant control over at least the administration of the territory in which it operates, if not over the entire territory of the supported side.

The British reached this third stage in North Russia during 1918-19, when the combined Allied forces under their command outnumbered and far outfought those of the Provisional Government of the Northern Region. General Poole and his successor, General Ironside, took command of all military operations and exercised effective authority over the local Russian government in all matters which they deemed important. In such a "third-stage" situation it need not be of critical importance if large numbers of the supported indigenous forces refuse to fight or even go over to the enemy. Such desertions may demonstrate to the intervening Power that the effort it is making is not worthwhile and may thus induce it to leave (in part such desertions impelled the British to abandon North Russia in 1919), but in the third stage the interventionists have taken over the struggle to such a degree that they are still able to maintain the military effort, and perhaps even force it to a successful conclusion, without significant support from their "supported" indigenous partners.

It is important to note that, although the British passed through all three of these stages in intervening in the Russian Civil War, they did so in separate sectors. Instead of an involvement which grew over the course of time (like, for example, American involvement in South Vietnam between 1954 and 1965), the three stages of British intervention in Russia existed simultaneously: the difference was real rather than temporal. Only in North Russia—a comparatively small, isolated, and unimportant front—did British intervention reach the third stage. Yet under the British command at Archangel and Murmansk were only a score of thousands of Allied troops. Many times that number—several hundreds of thousands at least—would have been necessary for the British (or the Allies) to have played the same role on all the fronts of the Russian Civil War as they did in North Russia. Several hundred thousand Allied troops, at a minimum, would have been necessary for "success" in 1919; they could probably have defeated the Bolsheviks and installed "moderate sane" Russians in positions of control.

Merely to state such a prospect, however, is to emphasize its impossibility. None of the Powers was willing to commit even a small fraction of this number of soldiers. The Japanese, who came closest to doing so, had only a marginal interest in bringing about the downfall of the Bolsheviks. Their intervention, instead, was aimed at establishing Japan's hegemony over eastern Siberia, not at defeating the Red Army. Indeed, a weak Bolshevik regime in Moscow would have better suited Japan's purposes than a strong anti-Bolshevik regime dedicated to the reconstitution in full of the Tsarist patrimony. As for the other Powers, the United States government set out even before the Armistice of 1918 to restrict the role of American troops in Russia; although President Wilson allowed Americans under the British command in North Russia to take part in defensive actions through the winter, he withdrew them as soon as he could in 1919, and he confined the American force in Siberia to garrison duties almost from the moment of its arrival in August 1918. The French role was not much greater—two battalions in North Russia, one in Siberia, and the brief, disastrous expedition to the Odessa region—despite the strong ideological and verbal commitment of the French government to the anti-Bolshevik cause. Italy made only a token military contribution, and not much of a verbal one.

Thus, Great Britain was by default the leading participant in the intervention. Yet after the Armistice it became unthinkable to commit even a few thousand British troops to the war in Russia unless they were sent out, as were the two relief brigades of April 1919, for the limited purpose of helping to extricate forces already there. Any significantly greater level of involvement was precluded by domestic political objections to the immense costs, both human and material, which would have been engendered—and also by widespread acceptance of the view that civil wars are won ultimately by the side which attracts the most popular support, and therefore the side which "deserves" to win. This was Lloyd George's view—one shared by nearly all of his colleagues except Churchill. It was entirely proper to give the anti-Bolshevik Russians war materials of all sorts to furnish their forces with training and advice, and to maintain the blockade of Soviet territory. But, once the Whites were equipped and trained, they would have to fight for themselves; it was "their" war, and, if they succeeded in winning the active support of "the people," they would win.

The fact that this argument went essentially unchallenged made it easier for the British government to cut its commitments and extricate its forces once it had become apparent that the White armies were defeated. Just as there was no single decision to intervene, so there was no single decision to withdraw. Indeed, as we have seen, the Cabinet decided to withdraw forces from North Russia and from Transcaucasia in early March 1919, long before the outcome of the war seemed in sight and when the greatest successes of the Whites still lay in the future. Other decisions came later. The most important were those preventing further shipments of British military supplies, initially cutting off Kolchak, then Denikin. The latter decision came when Denikin was still advancing toward Moscow. He already had enough equipment on hand or en route to push his campaign through to a successful conclusion. The cutoff only affected supplies for *future* campaigning seasons. Denikin had thus been put into a position from which he could win; failure could be attributed only to his own inadequacies, not to inadequate British support. "We have kept faith with all these men," Lloyd George wrote to Churchill on 22 September 1919 when Denikin's advance was in its greatest flood and the fall of Moscow seemed near. Yet the Prime Minister felt constrained to add: "But not a member of the Cabinet is prepared to go further."[8] Civil wars were a spectator sport.

Here, of course, was a statement about British interests as well. If not a member of the Cabinet (but Churchill) was prepared to go further, it is evident that few felt that the solidification of Bolshevik power in Russia would be *fundamentally* harmful to the interests of the British Empire. Only Churchill warned that by not crushing Bolshevism in its infancy the Allies were storing up for themselves a vastly more costly confrontation in the future. Others may have had such forebodings, but they did not feel them with Churchill's certainty, and they were not persuaded of the necessity to bear more or less finite present costs in order to forestall much greater future costs when the probability of actually incurring the future costs did not seem extraordinarily high.[9] Moreover, as we have seen, many of those involved (Cabinet members and civil servants alike) did not share Churchill's certainty that a regime led by Kolchak or Denikin would be very much more desirable than one led by Lenin or his successors, despite the anti-Bolshevik rhetoric which marked almost all public pronouncements about Russia.

This attitude reflected a British tendency to discount ideology and to emphasize concrete interest: those who ruled in Moscow (or in

---

[8] The letter is cited above, ch. VIII, n. 17.

[9] One indicator of the actual costs incurred is that of casualty figures. On 13 July 1920, Winston Churchill reported to the House of Commons figures for casualties of Regular Army and Territorial Forces, Canadians, Australians, and Royal Marine Light Infantry incurred during the period from the Armistice of 11 November 1918 until the date of his announcement. He reported separate figures for North Russian operations and those in all other parts of the former Russian Empire. They were: a) Killed in action and died of wounds: North Russia, 178; elsewhere, 2. b) Wounded: North Russia, 401; elsewhere, 2. c) Missing: North Russia, 95; elsewhere, 23. Of the North Russian figures for "missing," Churchill said, 79 were subsequently reported as prisoners; all but one, who had died, had been released by the date of his announcement. (131 *H.C. Deb.*, cols. 2131-32.) It is striking how few of these Army (or Marine) casualties were incurred outside of North Russia—even in South Russia, where British "instructors" took part in combat operations.

British casualties incurred in Baltic Sea naval and air operations during the period from January 1919 to February 1920 were given in Rear-Admiral Sir Walter Cowan's report to the Admiralty published in the Fifth Supplement to the *London Gazette* of 6 April 1920, p. 4234. They were: a) Killed: Navy, 113; R.A.F., 5. b) Wounded: Navy, 42; R.A.F., 2. c) Missing: Navy, 9.

I have been able to find no other figures for naval and air operations, nor any figures for the period prior to the Armistice of 11 November 1918.

For financial costs incurred, see the Appendix to this volume.

Petersburg) would behave in roughly the same manner regardless of the political labels they wore. Furthermore, so far as the British Empire was concerned, more important than who ruled Russia was the precise extent of the territory they controlled. A Russian state whose perimeters were those of the former Russian Empire would be more likely to encroach upon British interests than one from which Poland, Finland, the Baltic states, Transcaucasia, and perhaps even (in the best of possible outcomes) Central Asia and Siberia had been separated. Thus there would be a layer of weak buffer states between Russia and the Indian Empire. British interests in Persia and Mesopotamia—and also, by extension, in the oil fields of Baku—would be made doubly secure. Similarly, the independence of Finland and the Baltic states would allow British commerce to become even more deeply established in an area which had long been of importance to the City of London.

Within the Cabinet only Churchill argued strongly against the dismemberment of the former Russian Empire. Future European stability would require a powerful Russia as a counterweight against Germany. An aggrieved Russia, he feared, would combine against the West with an aggrieved Germany. A communist Russia would be aggrieved by definition. But Churchill warned that a noncommunist Russia, also, would bear powerful grievances if stripped of its border provinces. As we have seen, he regarded British support of the governments of Transcaucasia as lamentably shortsighted. In this view he was virtually alone. British sentiment—and, over the course of history, British interest—had favored the principle of the independence of small states. Even though they feared the infection of India by Bolshevik doctrine, Curzon and others, surveying the horizon in late 1919, still felt a future conflict between the British Empire and a Great Russia, communist or noncommunist, to be a more certain danger than any of the others which Churchill so vividly delineated in his stream of memoranda.

Ultimately, the argument between Churchill and Curzon turned out to be largely irrelevant. Those who controlled the United Kingdom's resources—whether military (Sir Henry Wilson), financial (Austen Chamberlain), or political (David Lloyd George)—judged them insufficient either to ensure the victory of the anti-Bolshevik advocates of a united Great Russia or to protect the southern border states against the Bolshevik onslaught which enveloped them during 1920 and 1921. Political resources, of course, were key: given the political will, a society which for four years had maintained an average of more than thirty-five divisions at the front in France *could*—by dint of great effort—have maintained a quarter that number for a shorter time in Russia. But political will was lacking. It is true that Churchill had no trouble recruiting two brigades of volunteers for the North Russian relief force, and that a year later the government easily raised its force of "Black and Tans" for Ireland: in the aftermath of so unsettling an experience as the War had been, there are always men who cannot easily manage the transition back to civil life—or even to a peacetime army—and who yearn for the solace of violence. But they are not many. Conscription ended with the coming of peace. The War Office's infamous "questionnaire" demonstrated how unpopular—whether with conscripts awaiting demobilization or with regulars—was the notion of service in Russia. The same, indeed, was true of the entire working class. J. R. Clynes, Labour M.P., the government's Food Controller during the War, President of the National Union of General Workers, and one of the most moderate and "respectable" of Labour politicians, wrote in *The Observer* on 15 June 1919: "I doubt whether the Government appreciates the depth of feeling which exists in the minds of thousands of workers with regard to Russia." Clynes went on to condemn what he called the "skilful concealment" of the purposes and motives underlying intervention in Russia. He continued:

This art of concealment has bewildered workmen; it has created suspicion and aroused anger far greater than any other act of policy since the General Election. No reassurance can be found by merely shouting "Bolshevik!" and we still await a simple and convincing statement of our military purpose in Russia. If only a small part of what has come to us from persuasive sources is true about the Bolsheviks there is great cause for lamentation, if not for military resistance, but why should we not get at the truth? If the Government has the truth, it should reveal it in more convincing form than has yet been attempted by its spokesmen.

At the Foreign Office, Clynes's article was taken not as an argument against the government's Russian policy, but as evidence of its failure to "sell" the policy to the public effectively. Walford Selby, of the Russia Department, wrote a minute calling Curzon's attention to Clynes's "very moderate statement," and added:

There can be no doubt that there is a great deal in what he says, and that we are gradually drifting into a very difficult situation, for the reason that no properly organized campaign has ever yet been undertaken by the Government to explain our policy in Russia to the masses of the people. . . . I still remain convinced that the proper course is for the Prime Minister to give a lead, for without his authority no propaganda campaign, it seems to me, can have any chance of success.[10]

From Archangel, R. H. Hoare echoed Selby's appeal. On 16 July he telegraphed:

It may be doubted whether all that is possible and desirable has been done to convince organized labour that we have an urgent duty in North Russia. So far we have failed to convince the people that our action in Russia is not simply interference in the affairs of a people who are struggling to be free. Anti-Bolshevik propaganda has perhaps failed to convince because we have appeared to overstate the case. Working men in England have been reluctant to believe that their peers in Russia could, under Bolshevik guidance, be guilty of the horrors of which they have been accused, just as educated people in neutral countries could not believe that the atrocities in Belgium and Northern France really were part of a definite policy of terrorism, organized by the German General Staff.[11]

These attitudes extended, of course, into the Cabinet itself. There was a real sense of grievance that "the people" did not understand the motives behind the government's Russian policies and took them simply for the desire to restore the old autocracy. As Christopher Addison—by no means a supporter of intervention—told his colleagues on 25 July, the "correct answer" to the question of why Britain was intervening was "in order to establish a *stable* Government" in Russia. However, he asserted, "it would not be possible to give this answer, as it would at once be said that we were supporting a reactionary Government."[12] For Addison, the distinction between "stability" in a revolutionary situation and "reaction" was too subtle for public consumption; it should be added that, with Kolchak, Denikin, and Yudenich as the carriers of "stability," the public's confusion was not unjustified.

Within the Cabinet, one might conjecture, there was little of Walford Selby's faith that Lloyd George could lead a propaganda

[10] Minute of 18 June 1919 in file 89561/91/38; F.O. 371/3959.
[11] Hoare (Archangel) to Balfour, despatch 108, 16 July 1919, file 107652/3669/38; F.O. 371/3993.
[12] War Cabinet minutes W.C. 599, 25 July 1919, 11:30 a.m.; Cab. 23/11.

campaign that would result in a reversal of public opinion over intervention. The government was too well appraised of the depth of the Labour movement's conviction that, as Clynes put it, the only way for outsiders to combat the Bolsheviks was, not by the use of military power, but by ranging against them "the moral force of working-class opinion in Europe and America."[13] The Cabinet was well aware that this notion was naive; it was also well aware that after a long and exhausting war there were relatively narrow political limits on the extent to which it could commit British manpower and British resources to the civil war in Russia, and that domestic propaganda would not widen these limits very much.

Lloyd George himself, moreover, was not the unmitigated political asset which Selby may have imagined. The lopsided results of the election of December 1918 were misleading—as much an outpouring of gratitude that the War was over as an expression of deepfelt confidence in the man who had "won" it. By 1919 Lloyd George was no longer the brilliant reforming Radical of the first decade of the century; after his ruthless suppression of opposition during the War and his break with his old party, he seemed—and not only to Labour—more nearly the willing agent of business and financial interests, and of the Conservative politicians who were his partners. By 1919, also, Lloyd George's reputation for less than straightforward behavior was well established. Although he still was able to maintain his leadership over the rest of the Cabinet, there was about him a widening aura of mistrust which divided him not only from many of his old supporters but, not infrequently, from many of his colleagues as well. Three years later these divisions were to become so wide as to bring about the dissolution of the Coalition and to end his political career. Then his talents finally failed.

Russia, however—during 1919, at least—was not really a test of Lloyd George's leadership, for his Cabinet was largely in agreement with him. Only Churchill was in total dissent, and, as we have seen, the agreement between the Prime Minister and the rest of the Cabinet was sufficiently great so that the seeming contest between himself and Churchill was in fact no contest at all. This essential agreement—and Lloyd George's primacy—allowed him to make his Guildhall address of 8 November 1919, in effect publicly calling a halt to intervention, and two months later to impose upon

[13] In his *Observer* article of 15 June 1919.

the Supreme Council in Paris his plan to begin trading with the Russian cooperative societies, in effect ending the blockade, without in either case consulting his Cabinet or even informing his Foreign Secretary.

Curiously enough, the Russian problem during 1920 was to prove politically more difficult for Lloyd George. Although the decisions of late 1919 and early 1920 not only marked the end of intervention, but also implied a commitment to come to terms with the Soviet regime, the manner in which the Prime Minister chose to do so during the summer and early autumn of 1920 endangered his personal position to a much greater degree than did any of his earlier actions. We shall observe this process in the third volume of the present work. There, too, will be the place for more elaborate reflections on Lloyd George's personal political style, both in diplomatic negotiations and in his relations with his colleagues, and on his whole approach to the political and social transformation which took place in Russia during the period 1917-21.

APPENDIX

The Cost of British Intervention in the Period Following the Armistice of 11 November 1918

The British government published three White Papers on the cost of intervention in Russia following the Armistice. The first, Cmd. 307 (Army), issued on 14 August 1919, covered the period from the Armistice until 31 July 1919. The second, Cmd. 395 (Army), issued in November 1919, covered the period from the Armistice until 31 October 1919. These are self-explanatory; the information contained in them is tabulated on the first sheet following this note.

On 15 July 1920, however, the War Office issued a revised estimate of the expenditures between the Armistice and 31 October 1919 in the form of Cmd. 772 (Army). The White Paper explained:

> Since the statement to 31st October, 1919 (Cmd. 395), was presented to Parliament in November last, further information has become available regarding events before that date, which calls for material modification of the figures then given. . . .

> The Chief causes of alteration are:—
> 1. In columns 1 and 2 of the Statement, information as to the cost of Naval and Air operations and of sea transport, which has recently become available, has been included.
> 2. In columns 5 and 7, the full nominal values at which stores were valued, have been replaced by figures more closely representing the actual value of the articles, and allowance has been made for the fact (recently ascertained) that certain of the stores included in the original return were not handed over to the Russians.

In Cmd. 772, in other words, the magnitude of intervention has been made to appear significantly smaller by the bookkeeping device of assigning to the so-called non-marketable munitions and stores an artificial price based upon an arbitrary estimate of what they might sell for in 1920 (if buyers were available), instead of the actual costs of manufacture. For that reason, the two sets of figures have been included in this Appendix. So far as the cost of

 (Appendix continues on page 368)

Original Estimates

This information is derived from the first two White Papers issued, Cmd. 307 and Cmd. 395. The upper figure in each entry is from Cmd. 395, giving expenditures in the period from the Armistice until 31 October 1919. The figures in parentheses are from Cmd. 307, giving the same expenditures in the period from the Armistice until 31 July 1919. *Where there was no expenditure in the period 31 July–31 October, only one figure is given.*

Figures in £000

	(1) Costs of British Naval, Army, and Air Forces	(2) Sea transport	(3) Money to Provisional Government	(4) Food and supplies for Russian troops	(5) Munitions and stores for Russians (marketable)	(6) Total cash and marketable stores	(7) Munitions and stores for Russians (non-marketable)
TABLE I: Costs of British Military and Naval Operations							
Costs of Military Operations in North Russia	7,650 (5,650)	3,160 (1,940)	1,350 (750)	2,400 (1,000)	2,805 (2,800)	17,365 (12,140)	5,770
Costs of Maintaining an Army in Transcaucasia	3,000 (2,500)	410 (366)	—	—	—	3,410 (2,866)	—
Costs of Naval Operations in Black and Baltic Seas	6,350 (5,200)	—	—	—	—	6,350 (5,200)	—
Total TABLE I	17,000 (13,350)	3,570 (2,300)	1,350 (750)	2,400 (1,000)	2,805 (2,800)	27,125 (20,200)	5,770
TABLE II: Assistance to Russian Armies							
Assistance to Baltic States, including N.-W. Russian Army	205 (10)	155 (100)	—	180 (125)	530 (350)	1,070 (585)	3,400 (2,250)
Assistance to Kolchak	1,430 (1,250)	665 (590)	—	30	6,415 (6,410)	8,540 (8,280)	6,150
Assistance to Denikin	255 (150)	450 (310)	—	550	6,520 (5,840)	7,775 (6,850)	20,000 (19,200)
Total TABLE II	1,890 (1,410)	1,270 (1,000)	—	760 (705)	13,465 (12,600)	17,385 (15,715)	29,550 (27,600)

Revised Estimates

This information is derived from the third White Paper, Cmd. 772, issued in July 1920. As explained above, it presents revised estimates of expenditures in the period from the Armistice until 31 October 1919. These are the upper figures in each entry. In addition, it also presents figures for additional expenditures in the period 1 November 1919–31 March 1920. These additional amounts are prefixed with a plus (+) sign. *Where there was no expenditure in the period 1 November 1919–31 March 1920, only one figure is given.*

Figures in £000

	(1) Costs of British Naval, Army, and Air Forces	(2) Sea transport	(3) Money to Provisional Government	(4) Food and supplies for Russian troops	(5) Munitions and stores for Russians (marketable)	(6) Total cash and marketable stores	(7) Munitions and stores for Russians (non-marketable)
TABLE I: COSTS OF BRITISH MILITARY AND NAVAL OPERATIONS							
Costs of Military Operations in North Russia	9,447	3,160 +133	1,350	2,500	1,762	18,219 +133	244
Costs of Maintaining an Army in Transcaucasia	3,051 +503	410	—	—	—	3,461 +503	—
Costs of Naval Operations in Black and Baltic Seas	6,370 +2,518	—	—	—	—	6,370 +2,518	—
Total TABLE I	18,868 +3,021	3,570 +133	1,350	2,500	1,762	28,050 +3,154	244
TABLE II: ASSISTANCE TO RUSSIAN ARMIES							
Assistance to Baltic States, including N.-W. Russian Army	177 +17	338 +68	—	200	735 +157	1,450 +242	391 +109
Assistance to Kolchak	1,430 +59	1,523	—	80	5,000	7,983 +59	523.5
Assistance to Denikin	194 +246	2,295 +350	—	850 +295	5,856 +1,566	9,195 +2,457	1,794.5 +321
Total TABLE II	1,801 +322	4,156 +418	—	1,080 +295	11,591 +1,723	18,628 +2,758	2,709 +430

British military and naval operations is concerned, Cmd. 772 is doubtless a more accurate compilation (and, of course, it also covers the additional period November 1919-March 1920), but Cmd. 307 and Cmd. 395 have been included in this Appendix to show something of the ratio of expenditure before 31 July 1919 to that which came afterward.

SELECTED BIBLIOGRAPHY

UNPUBLISHED DOCUMENTS AND PRIVATE PAPERS

The most important unpublished materials used in the preparation of this volume were:

The Records of the Cabinet Office, the Foreign Office, and the War Office in the Public Record Office, London.

The Curzon Papers, formerly at Kedleston, now in the India Office Library.

The Diary of Field-Marshal Lord Ironside of Archangel in the possession of Lady Ironside.

The Diary of Field-Marshal Sir Henry Wilson in the possession of Major Cyril J. Wilson.

Other unpublished materials used were:

The Records of the Canadian Expeditionary Force, Siberia, in the Public Archives of Canada, Ottawa.

The Records of the Department of State in the National Archives of the United States, Washington.

The Asquith Papers in the Bodleian Library, Oxford.

The Balfour Papers in the British Museum, London.

The Papers of Lord Robert Cecil in the British Museum.

The Austen Chamberlain Papers in the Library of the University of Birmingham.

The Papers of Viscount Davidson of Little Gaddesden, in his own possession.

The Milner Papers, formerly at New College, now in the Bodleian Library, Oxford.

The Edward M. House Papers in the Library of Yale University.

The Roland S. Morris Papers in the Library of Congress, Washington.

The Frank L. Polk Papers in the Library of Yale University.

The Papers of Sir William Wiseman in the Library of Yale University.

Bibliography

PUBLISHED DIPLOMATIC PAPERS

Documents on British Foreign Policy 1919-1939, First Series, Vols. I-III (E. L. Woodward and Rohan Butler, eds.), London: H.M. Stationery Office, 1947-49.

Dokumenty vneshnei politiki SSSR (Documents on the Foreign Policy of the U.S.S.R.), Vols. I and II, Moscow: Ministry of Foreign Affairs, 1957 and 1958.

Papers Relating to the Foreign Relations of the United States: The Paris Peace Conference, 1919, Vols. III-VI, Washington: Department of State, 1943-46.

Papers Relating to the Foreign Relations of the United States: Russia, 1918 (3 vols.), Washington: Department of State, 1931 and 1932.

Papers Relating to the Foreign Relations of the United States: Russia, 1919, Washington: Department of State, 1937.

Paul Mantoux, *Les délibérations du Conseil des Quatre (24 mars-28 juin 1919)* (2 vols.), Paris: Editions du Centre National de la Recherche Scientifique, 1955.

PARLIAMENTARY PAPERS AND GAZETTED DESPATCHES

Cmd. 9005 (1918), *The War Cabinet: Report for the Year 1917*.

Cmd. 8 (Russia No. 1 [1919]), *A Collection of Reports on Bolshevism in Russia*, April 1919.

Cmd. 307 (Army), *Expenditure on Military and Naval Operations in Russia from the Date of the Armistice to July 31, 1919*, August 1919.

Cmd. 325 (1919), *The War Cabinet: Report for the Year 1918*.

Cmd. 395 (Army), *Expenditure on Military and Naval Operations in Russia from the Date of the Armistice to October 31, 1919*, November 1919.

Cmd. 587 (Russia No. 1 [1920]), *Agreement Between His Majesty's Government and the Soviet Government of Russia for the Exchange of Prisoners*, February 1920.

Cmd. 772 (Army), *Statement of Expenditure on Naval and Military Operations in Russia, from the Date of the Armistice to the 31st of March 1920*, July 1920.

Bibliography

Cmd. 818 (Army), *The Evacuation of North Russia, 1919*, British Blue Book, July 1920.

Cmd. 1614, *Memorandum Circulated by the Prime Minister on March 25, 1919* ("Some Considerations for the Peace Conference Before They Finally Draft Their Terms"), 1922.

Despatches to the Admiralty of Rear-Admiral Sir Walter Cowan on Naval Operations in the Baltic Sea, January 1919–February 1920, in the Fifth Supplement to the *London Gazette* of 6 April 1920.

Official Report, Parliamentary Debates: House of Commons.

Official Report, Parliamentary Debates: House of Lords.

BOOKS AND ARTICLES

Arthur E. Adams, *Bolsheviks in the Ukraine: The Second Campaign, 1918-1919*, Yale University Press, 1963.

Captain Augustus W. S. Agar, *Baltic Episode: A Classic of Secret Service in Russian Waters*, London: Hodder and Stoughton, 1963.

Captain Marion Aten and Arthur Orrmont, *Last Train Over Rostov Bridge*, New York: Messner, 1961.

Zourab Avalishvili, *The Independence of Georgia in International Politics, 1918-1921*, London: privately printed, n.d. (circa 1941).

Carl Eric Bechhofer-Roberts, *In Denikin's Russia and the Caucasus, 1919-1920*, London: Collins, 1921.

Gustav Bečvar, *The Lost Legion: A Czechoslovakian Epic*, London: Stanley Paul, 1939.

Captain Geoffrey Bennett, *Cowan's War: The Story of British Naval Operations in the Baltic, 1918-1920*, London: Collins, 1964.

General Sir Herbert Edward Blumberg, *Britain's Sea Soldiers: A Record of the Royal Marines during the War, 1914-1919*, Devonport: Swiss & Co., n.d. (circa 1927).

Robert Laird Borden, *Robert Laird Borden: His Memoirs*, New York: Macmillan, 1938, Vol. II.

George A. Brinkley, *The Volunteer Army and Allied Intervention in South Russia, 1917-1921: A Study in the Politics and Diplomacy of the Russian Civil War*, University of Notre Dame Press, 1966.

William C. Bullitt, *The Bullitt Mission to Russia: Testimony before the Committee on Foreign Relations of the United States Senate*, New York: Huebsch, 1919.

———, "The Tragedy of Versailles," *Life*, Vol. XVI, No. 13 (March 27, 1944), 98-116.

Bibliography

Alan Bullock, *The Life and Times of Ernest Bevin*, Vol. I.: *Trade Union Leader 1881-1940*, London: Heinemann, 1960.

James Bunyan, ed., *Intervention, Civil War, and Communism in Russia: April–December 1918, Documents and Materials*, Baltimore: Johns Hopkins Press, 1936.

———— and H. H. Fisher, eds., *The Bolshevik Revolution, 1917-1918, Documents and Materials*, Stanford University Press, 1934.

Major-General Sir C. E. Callwell, *Field-Marshal Sir Henry Wilson, Bart., G.C.B., D.S.O., His Life and Diaries* (2 vols.), London: Cassell, 1927.

Edward Hallett Carr, *A History of Soviet Russia: The Bolshevik Revolution, 1917-1923* (3 vols.), London: Macmillan, 1950-53.

William Henry Chamberlin, *The Russian Revolution, 1917-1921* (2 vols.), New York: Macmillan, 1935.

Winston S. Churchill, *The World Crisis: The Aftermath*, London: Thornton Butterworth, 1929.

W. P. and Zelda K. Coates, *Armed Intervention in Russia, 1918-1922*, London: Gollancz, 1935.

C. K. Cumming and W. W. Pettit, eds., *Russian-American Relations, March 1917–March 1920: Documents and Papers*, New York: Harcourt, Brace and Howe, 1920.

Jane Degras, ed., *The Communist International, 1919-1943: Documents*, Vol. I, London: Oxford University Press, 1956.

————, ed., *Soviet Documents on Foreign Policy* (3 vols.), London: Oxford University Press for Royal Institute of International Affairs, Vol. I, *1917-1924* (1951).

General A. I. Denikin, *Ocherki russkoi smuty* (Sketches of the Russian Turmoil), (5 vols.), Berlin: Russkoe natsionalnoe knigoizdatelstvo, 1921-26, Vols. IV and V.

I. Deutscher, *The Prophet Armed: Trotsky, 1879-1921*, London: Oxford University Press, 1954.

C. H. Ellis, *The Transcaspian Episode 1918-1919*, London: Hutchinson, 1963.

Louis Fischer, *The Soviets in World Affairs: A History of the Relations Between the Soviet Union and the Rest of the World 1917-1929* (2 vols.), London: Jonathan Cape, 1930 (reissued, Princeton University Press, 1951), Vol. I.

Peter Fleming, *The Fate of Admiral Kolchak*, London: Rupert Hart-Davis, 1963.

Bibliography

David J. Footman, *Civil War in the Baltic Area* (2 parts), St. Antony's College, Oxford (mimeographed), 1959, Part I: *Von der Goltz and Bermondt-Avalov*; Part II: *The North Western Army*.
———, *Civil War in Russia*, London: Faber, 1961.

General Graf Gustav Adolph Joachim Rüdiger von der Goltz, *Meine Sendung in Finnland und im Baltikum*, Leipzig: Deutsche Denkwürdigkeiten, 1920.

Vasilii Gorn, *Grazhdanskaya voina na severo-zapade Rossii* (The Civil War in North-West Russia), Berlin: Izdatelstvo Gamayun, 1923.

General Sir Hubert Gough, *Soldiering On*, London: A. Barker, 1954.

Malbone W. Graham, *The Diplomatic Recognition of the Border States*, Publications of the University of California at Los Angeles in the Social Sciences, Vol. 3, No. 2, *Finland* (1935); Vol. 3, No. 3, *Estonia* (1939); Vol. 3, No. 4, *Latvia* (1941).

Stephen Richards Graubard, *British Labour and the Russian Revolution, 1917-1924*, Harvard University Press, 1956.

William S. Graves, *America's Siberian Adventure, 1918-1920*, New York: Jonathan Cape and Harrison Smith, 1931.

A. Whitney Griswold, *The Far Eastern Policy of the United States*, New York: Harcourt, Brace, 1938 (reissued, Yale University Press, 1962).

G. K. Guins, *Sibir, soyuzniki i Kolchak. Povorotnyi moment russkoi istorii, 1918-1920 gg. (Vpechatleniya i mysli chlena Omskago pravitelstva)* (Siberia, the Allies and Kolchak. The Turning Point of Russian History, 1918-1920. [Impressions and Thoughts of a Member of the Omsk Government]), Peking: Tipo-lit. Russkoi dykhovnoi missii, 1921.

E. M. Halliday, *The Ignorant Armies*, New York: Harper, 1960.

W. K. Hancock, *Smuts: The Sanguine Years, 1870-1919*, Cambridge University Press, 1962.

Lord Hardinge of Penshurst, *The Old Diplomacy: The Reminiscences of Lord Hardinge of Penshurst*, London: John Murray, 1947.

History of the Great War Based on Official Documents, The Campaign in Mesopotamia 1914-1918 (4 vols.), compiled at the request of the Government of India under the direction of the Historical

Section of the Committee of Imperial Defence by Brig.-General F. J. Moberly, Vol. IV, London: H. M. Stationery Office, 1927.

John Ernest Hodgson, *With Denikin's Armies. Being a Description of the Cossack Counter-Revolution in South Russia, 1918-1920*, London: Lincoln Williams, 1932.

Herbert Hoover, *The Memoirs of Herbert Hoover*, Vol. I: *Years of Adventure 1874-1920*, New York: Macmillan, 1951.

——, *The Ordeal of Woodrow Wilson*, New York: McGraw-Hill, 1958.

Field-Marshal Lord Ironside, *Archangel 1918-1919*, London: Constable, 1953.

Istoriya grazhdanskoi voini v SSSR (History of the Civil War in the U.S.S.R.), Vol. III (November 1917 to March 1919), Moscow, Marx-Lenin Institute, 1957.

Général Pierre T. C. Maurice Janin, *Ma Mission en Sibérie 1918-1920*, Paris: Payot, 1933.

Firuz Kazemzadeh, *The Struggle for Transcaucasia (1917-1921)*, Oxford: George Ronald, 1951.

George F. Kennan, *Russia and the West under Lenin and Stalin*, Boston: Little, Brown, 1961.

Krasnyi Arkhiv (Red Archives) (108 vols.), Moscow-Leningrad, 1922-41.

"Anglichanie na severe" (The English in the North), Vol. 19, 1926 (No. 6), pp. 39-52.

"Interventsiya i severnaya kontr-revoliutsiya" (Intervention and the Northern Counter-Revolution), I. Mints, compiler, Vols. 50-51, 1932 (Nos. 1-2), pp. 97-115.

"K istorii interventsii na severe" (Toward the History of the Intervention in the North), N. Prokopenko, compiler, Vol. 98, 1940 (No. 1), pp. 125-44.

"Vneshnaya politika kontr-revoliutsionnykh 'pravitelstv' v nachale 1919 g." (The Foreign Policy of the Counter-Revolutionary "Governments" at the Beginning of 1919), I. Mints, compiler, Vol. 37, 1929 (No. 6), pp. 71-89.

Labour Party, *Report of the Nineteenth Annual Conference*, London, 1919.

Walter Z. Laqueur, *Russia and Germany*, London: Weidenfeld & Nicolson, 1965.

Bibliography

Commandant Joseph Lasies, *La tragédie sibérienne*, Paris: Crès, 1920.

George Lenczowski, *Russia and the West in Iran, 1918-1948*, Cornell University Press, 1949.

David Lloyd George, *The Truth About the Peace Treaties* (2 vols.), London: Gollancz, 1938.

R. B. McCallum, *Public Opinion and the Last Peace*, Oxford University Press, 1944.

Francis McCullagh, *A Prisoner of the Reds: The Story of a British Officer Captured in Siberia*, London: John Murray, 1921.

Carl Gustav Emil Mannerheim, *The Memoirs of Marshal Mannerheim*, London: Cassell, 1953.

M. S. Margulies, *God interventsii* (A Year of the Intervention) (2 vols.), Berlin: Z. I. Grjbin, 1923.

F. S. Marston, *The Peace Conference of 1919,* London: Oxford University Press, 1944.

General V. V. Marushevsky, "God na severe" (A Year in the North), *Beloe delo* (The White Cause), Berlin: Vol. I, 1926, pp. 16-60; Vol. II, 1927, pp. 21-61; Vol. III, 1927, pp. 15-52.

Major-General Sir Frederick Maurice, *The Life of General Lord Rawlinson of Trent from His Journals and Letters*, London: Cassell, 1928.

Arno J. Mayer, *Politics and Diplomacy of Peacemaking: Containment and Counterrevolution at Versailles, 1918-1919*, New York: Knopf, 1967.

Major-General Sir C. Maynard, *The Murmansk Venture*, London: Hodder and Stoughton, 1928.

Jan M. Meijer, ed., *The Trotsky Papers, 1917-1922*, Vol. I (1917-19) The Hague: Mouton, 1964.

S. P. Melgunov, *Tragediya Admirala Kolchaka*, Part III, Vol. II, Belgrade: Russkaia Biblioteka, 1931.

Isaak I. Mints, *Angliiskaya interventsiya i severnaia kontr-revoliutsiya* (English Intervention and Northern Counter-Revolution), Moscow: Gos. sots.-ek. izd., 1931.

Charles Loch Mowat, *Britain Between the Wars, 1918-1940*, London: Methuen, 1955.

G. Mymrin, M. Pirogov, and G. Kuznetsov, *Razgrom interventov i belogvardeitsev na severe* (The Defeat of the Intervention and the

White Guards in the North), Archangel: Arkhangelskoe oblastnoe izd., 1940.

Fridtjof Nansen, *Russia and Peace*, London: Allen & Unwin, 1923.

Harold Nicolson, *Curzon: The Last Phase, 1919-1925,* London: Constable, 1934.

Francesco S. Nitti, *Peaceless Europe*, London: Cassell, 1922.

George Bernard Noble, *Policies and Opinions at Paris, 1919,* New York: Macmillan, 1935.

Joseph Noulens, *Mon ambassade en Russie soviétique, 1917-1919* (2 vols.), Paris: Librairie Plon, 1933.

"Obrazovanie severo-zapadnago pravitelstva" (The Formation of the North-West Government), *Arkhiv Russkoi Revolyutsii* (Archive of the Russian Revolution), Berlin: Vol. I, No. 39, 1922.

Frank Owen, *Tempestuous Journey: Lloyd George, His Life and Times*, London: Hutchinson, 1954.

Juhani Paasivirta, *The Victors in World War I and Finland: Finland's Relations with the British, French and United States Governments in 1918-1919*, Helsinki: Finnish Historical Society, 1965.

Stanley W. Page, *The Formation of the Baltic States*, Harvard University Press, 1959.

Richard Pipes, *The Formation of the Soviet Union: Communism and Nationalism 1917-1923*, 2nd edn., Harvard University Press, 1964.

Arthur Ransome, *Six Weeks in Russia in 1919*, London, Allen & Unwin, 1919.

John S. Reshetar, Jr., *The Ukrainian Revolution, 1917-1920: A Study in Nationalism*, Princeton University Press, 1952.

Lord Riddell, *Lord Riddell's Intimate Diary of the Peace Conference and After, 1918-1923*, London: Gollancz, 1933.

Harry R. Rudin, *Armistice 1918*, Yale University Press, 1944.

Lt.-General K. B. Sakharov, *Belaya Sibir (Vnutrennyaya voina 1918-1920 gg.)* [White Siberia (Internal War, 1918-1920)], Munich: Laubereau, 1925.

G. R. Singleton-Gates, *Bolos and Barishnyas: Being an Account of the Doings of the Sadleir-Jackson Brigade, and the Altham Flotilla, on the North Dvina during the Summer, 1919*, Aldershot: privately printed, 1920.

Clarence Jay Smith, Jr., *Finland and the Russian Revolution, 1917-1922*, University of Georgia Press, 1958, Vol. II.

Bibliography

Gaddis Smith, "Canada and the Siberian Intervention, 1918-1919," *American Historical Review*, Vol. LXIV, No. 4 (July 1959), 866-77.

Boris Soldovnikov, *Sibirskiya avantiury i General Gaida (iz zapisok ruskago revoliutsionera)* (Siberian Adventures and General Gaida [Notes of a Russian Revolutionary]), Prague: Tipografia "Politika," n.d. [192?].

Sherman D. Spector, *Rumania at the Paris Peace Conference: A Study of the Diplomacy of Ioan I. C. Brátianu*, New York. Bookman, 1962.

Henry Wickham Steed, *Through Thirty Years, 1892-1922: A Personal Narrative* (2 vols.), London: Heinemann, 1924, Vol. II.

George Stewart, *The White Armies of Russia: A Chronicle of Counter-Revolution and Allied Intervention*, New York: Macmillan, 1933.

Leonid I. Strakhovsky, *Intervention at Archangel: The Story of Allied Intervention and Russian Counter-Revolution in North Russia 1918-1920*, Princeton University Press, 1944.

I. Subbotovsky, *Soyuzniki, russkie reaktsionery i interventsiya: kratkii obzor (Iskliuchitelno po offitsialnym arkhivnym dokumentam Kolchakovskogo pravitelstva)* (The Allies, Russian Reactionaries and Intervention: A Brief Outline [Exclusively from the Official Archive Documents of the Kolchak Government]), Leningrad: Gosizdat, 1926.

Sir Stephen George Tallents, *Man and Boy*, London: Faber, 1943.

A.J.P. Taylor, *English History, 1914-1945*, Oxford University Press, 1965.

John M. Thompson, *Russia, Bolshevism, and the Versailles Peace*, Princeton University Press, 1967.

Betty Miller Unterberger, *America's Siberian Expedition, 1918-1920: A Study of National Policy*, Duke University Press, 1956.

Elena Varneck and H. H. Fisher, eds., *The Testimony of Kolchak and Other Siberian Materials*, Stanford University Press, 1935.

L. E. Vining, *Held by the Bolsheviks: The Diary of a British Officer in Russia, 1919-1920*, London: St. Catherine's Press, 1924.

Robert G. L. Waite, *Vanguard of Nazism: The Free-Corps Movement in Postwar Germany, 1918-1923*, Harvard University Press, 1952.

Bibliography

Colonel John Ward, *With the "Die-Hards" in Siberia*, London: Cassell, 1920.

John Albert White, *The Siberian Intervention*, Princeton University Press, 1950.

Trevor Wilson, "The Coupon and the British General Election of 1918," *Journal of Modern History*, Vol. XXXVI, No. 1 (March 1964), pp. 28-42.

August Winnig, *Am Ausgang der deutschen Ostpolitik: Persönliche Erlebnisse und Erinnerungen*, Berlin: Staatspolitischer Verlag, 1921.

T. H. Wintringham, *Mutiny: Being a Survey of Mutinies from Spartacus to Invergordan*, London: Stanley Nott, 1936.

Jean Xydias, *L'intervention française en Russie, 1918-1919: souvenirs d'un témoin*, Paris: Les Editions de France, 1927.

Yudenich pod Petrogradam – iz belyikh memuarov (Yudenich before Petrograd – from White Memoirs), Leningrad: Gospolitizdat, 1927.

I. A. Yakushev, "Komitet sodeistviya sozyvu Zemskogo Sobora" ("Committee for the Furthering of the Convocation of the Zemsky Sobor"), *Sibirskii Arkhiv*, Prague, 1929 (No. 2), pp. 73-80.

Alfred Zimmern, *The League of Nations and the Rule of Law, 1918-1935*, London: Macmillan, 1936.

INDEX

Index

Index

Index

on danger of break-up, 106; isolated position of Churchill and other Liberals within leadership, 295; backbenchers support Churchill, 297; primacy and fragility of Lloyd George's position within, 363-64

Comintern (Third International): appeal for establishment of, 113 n. 30

Commons, House of: debates British policy in Russia, 61-62, 129-30, 141, 143-44, 153-57; and conscription, 130, 133-34; influence on policy, 175, 297; and costs of intervention, 210-11; and blockade, 292-93; and Lloyd George's Guildhall speech, 306; 117

Conservative and Unionist Party: and Bolshevism, 106; and policy re Russia, 175, 177; decisive position in Coalition leadership, 295; backbenchers support Churchill, 297; unhappy with Lloyd George Guildhall speech, 306

Constituent Assembly, 27, 351

Cook, Sir Joseph, 98

cooperatives, Russian: see Tsentrosoyuz

cordon sanitaire, 11, 98, 104, 108, 117, 136, 140, 210, 314, 317

Cossacks (Don): and Denikin, 49, 213; Lloyd George on, 220; 45, 46, 214

Council of Four: and "Nansen proposal," 158-60; and Allied support of Kolchak, 163-70; and Churchill plan to use Czechs in North Russia, 189; and blockade, 288. *See also* Supreme Council

Council of Ten: and Allied Russian policy, 101-102, 104-105, 107-109; and "Foch plan," 137, 138. *See also* Peace Conference

Crimea: falls to Volunteer Army, 215; becomes refuge for Volunteer Army, 218; 44, 48, 212

Cromie, Captain F. N. A. (British Naval Attaché), Petrograd: death a turning point in Anglo-Soviet relations, 9, 62; question of compensation for, 88

Crowe, Sir Eyre A. (Assistant Under-Secretary, Foreign Office): reluctant to protest against White pogroms, 219 n. 40; 71 n. 25; 282 n. 106

Currency scheme (North Russia, 24-26

Curzon of Kedleston, Earl (Lord President of the Council and Acting Foreign Secretary): leads Eastern Committee discussions of policy re Caucasus, 66-82; short-lived nature of conclusions of these discussions, 226; fears French in East, 69-70, 73; character of thought re international affairs, 82, 296; asserts his aim not to assume responsibility for Caucasus, 83; opposes Bolshevik representation at Peace Conference, 86; on reasons for intervention, 92-93; usually disagrees with Lloyd George re Russia, 103; and Prinkipo, 117-18; and question of recognizing Kolchak, 162-63, 205 n. 1, 249-50; and withdrawal from North Russia, 179, 183; and Churchill

plan for military link between North Russia and Siberia, 185-87; seeks mercy for North Russian Whites, 200; and office of British High Commissioner, Siberia, 208; on reactionary nature of Kolchak and Denikin administrations, 217, 260; complains that British role in Caucasus too large, 226-27; opposes offering Caucasus mandate to Italy, 228; protests against British policy in Caucasus, 230-31; orders British in Siberia not to aid anti-Kolchak movement, 240-41; asks greater U.S. support for Kolchak, 241; on O'Reilly, 244; appraisal of British policy in Siberia, 253; on Yudenich, 260, 286; and British policy in Baltic states, 260; on Finnish aid to Yudenich, 264-65; anger over formation of North-West Russian Government, 270-71; on Pirie-Gordon, 271 n. 68; tries to recall General Marsh, 272-73; attempts to block Soviet-Baltic peace, 275, 280-81, 286; role in making policy re Russia, 296; finally becomes Foreign Secretary, 296; no foreknowledge of Lloyd George Guildhall speech, 306; assures U.S. Ambassador Lloyd George intends no second Prinkipo, 312; seeks better Allied coordination re Russia, 313; anxious at continued large Japanese contingent in Siberia, 315; urges large-scale aid to Caucasus states and Persia, 323, 331; on importance of holding Caspian, 331; humiliation by Lloyd George,, 326; on exclusion of Foreign Office from Russian trade discussions, 326 n. 82; on E.F. Wise, 327; and O'Grady-Litvinov negotiations, 341-43

Czechoslovakia: in "Foch plan," 137; British "obligations" to, 155-56

Czechoslovak Corps: origin and first clash with Red Army, 6-7; British policy re, 14, 60; disillusioned withdrawal from Siberian front, 28-29, 36; decries Kolchak coup, 35-36; Churchill plan for spearhead in North Russia, 188-90; remains principal source for order on Trans-Siberian railway, 233; and anti-Kolchak movement, 235, 238, 243; and execution of Kolchak, 252; departure from Siberia, 253 n. 130

Daghestan: Curzon on, 68; Denikin attempts to overrun, 225; question of Allied recognition, 322, 323; 67 n. 22, 224

Daily Express: prints Sherwood-Kelly letter, 202

Daily Herald: prints War Office "questionnaire," 131; 202

Daily Mail: and Lloyd George disavowal of Bullitt, 151; 100, 101 n. 4

Daily News: on Bullitt mission, 141, 157

Daily Telegraph, 61

Danton: Lloyd George on, 97

Davidson, J. C. C. (now Viscount Davidson of Little Gaddesden), 118 n. 44

Index

Index

ister): urges withdrawal from Russia, 90-91; opposes intervention, 102, 103

l'Humanité, 100, 101 n. 4, 110

Hungary: establishment of Bela Kun regime, 139-40; his overthrow, 352 n. 4

India: defense of and policy re Russia, 8, 65, 66, 67, 71, 72, 77, 79, 223, 309, 324, 328, 360; government says British control of Caspian unnecessary, 78-79; Churchill and Lloyd George on threat to, 333-34

Indian Army: attitudes re "Great" vs. "divided" Russia, 223-24

intervention, Allied: origins and original purposes, 5-8, 348; differs by theater, 28-29, 357; British vs. French roles, South Russia, 46; lack of coordinated Allied policy, 171-72; question of war and peace with Bolsheviks, 293; momentum, 348-49; requirements for success, 353

Irkutsk: Japanese at, 7; anti-Kolchak movement, 235; execution of Kolchak, 252; 36

Ironside, Major-General Edmund purposes of diary, 3; on original objectives of intervention, 3-4; on disaffection of French at Archangel, 10; winter operations, 19; takes command from Poole, 20-21, 24; silences British criticism of local government, 21; own criticism of White officer corps, 22, 191; punishes mutineers, 22-23 n. 26; 191-93; distaste for propaganda, 23; distress at Mudyug Island concentration camp, 24 n. 29; pessimistic re success of intervention, 28, 171, 191; and withdrawal plans, 135, 190-93; efforts to link front with Kolchak, 180, 185, 188, 190-91; on use of gas in North Russia, 181 n. 21; despondent at mutinies, 193; relations with local government re withdrawal, 193-94; final pre-evacuation offensive, 197; offers asylum to local population, 198; and Sherwood-Kelly, 202-203; takes hostages, 340-41; effects local prisoner exchange, 341 n. 117; nature of role in North Russia, 356

Italy: contingent in Siberia, 28; question of mandate for Caucasus, 75, 227-30; favors continuation of blockade, 290

Janin, Général Pierre T. C. Maurice: commands French Military Mission, Siberia, 33, 35; rejects plan for Czech spearhead in North Russia, 189

Japan: role in Allied intervention plans, 6-7, 96; aims in intervention, 7, 8, 9, 357; troops in Siberia, 28, 30, 172; political role in Siberia, 36-40, 210, 233, 243, 315-16; support of Semenov, 38; at Peace Conference, 101 n. 5; and recognition of Kolchak, 167; troops impede Vladivostok rising, 251; departure from Siberia, 253

n. 130; Churchill on future role, 299, 333; U.S. fear of, 311

Jones, Kennedy: organizes M.P.s' telegram to Lloyd George urging no dealings with Moscow, 144, 152

Kalmykov, Ivan (Cossack Ataman): disruptive role in Siberia, 233, 241, 242

Karelia, Eastern: Finnish claims, 259, 262, 285

Kennard, Sir Coleridge A. F., 273, 276, 290 n. 126

Kerr, Philip: and Prinkipo, 115; and Churchill plan for massive intervention, 121-26; and Bullitt mission, 144-47, 149, 150; and recognition of Kolchak, 167, 168; 176 n. 7

Keyes, Brigadier-General Terence H.: advocates "Great" Russia, 223; complains Foreign Office not keeping him informed of policy, 330 n. 95

Khabarovsk: Kalmykov atrocities at, 241

Kharkov, 205, 213, 214

Kherson: French at, 47

Kiev: falls to Whites, 215

Kisch, Lt.-Colonel F. H., 13

Knox, Major-General Alfred W. F. (Chief, British Military Mission, Siberia): urges campaign against Bolshevism, 30; asks London for better troops, 31; on French policy in Siberia, 32-33; on Japanese policy, 38-39; urges support of Kolchak, 43; on Prinkipo, 114-15; and recognition of Kolchak, 169, 245; transmits British military advice to Kolchak, 183-84; on Kolchak's entourage, 206; urges cut in supplies to Kolchak, 206-207; inspires Kolchak's "liberalism," 216; criticized by Foreign Office, 216, 244; Omsk vs. Vladivostok, 233; on O'Reilly dealings with anti-Kolchak movement, 239; orders Blair to use British troops against movement, 239-40; cashiers Blair, 243; scornful of anti-Kolchak movement, 245; on Churchill appeal for Kolchak to recognize Baltic states; on Lloyd George Guildhall speech, 309; influence on Kolchak, 354

Kolchak, Admiral Aleksandr V.: brought to power in coup at Omsk, 33-34; relations with Knox, 34-35; on British and French roles in Siberia, 35; Japanese attempt to undermine, 39-40; British support of, 41-43; nature of administration, 42, 161, 164, 351, 352; Lloyd George on, 95, 104, 125, 155, 164; acknowledged as leader of anti-Bolshevik cause, 113-14, 240; and Prinkipo, 114; and "Great" Russia, 116; military successes, 161, 172, 182, 205, 232; question of recognition of, 162-70, 205 n. 1, 245-50; Chaikovsky on, 165-66; Allied conditions for support of, 168-69; retreat, 170, 185, 214; agrees to aim at North Russia link, 183-85; British military advice to, 183-84; and Churchill

Index

Index

Index

Red Army: takes control of Odessa, 48; in Baltic provinces, 55-57; strength, 97, 119 n. 46; French General Staff on, 122; collapse predicted, 160-61; offensive against Kolchak, 170, 251-52; Foreign Office view of, 176; and use of gas, 182 n. 21; in North Russia, 196-97, 201; and Denikin's Moscow campaign, 215, 250-51; victory over Yudenich, 284, 285; presses toward Caucasus, 322

Reval (Tallinn): occupied by Germans, 53; protected by British warships, 56; seat of North-West Russian Government, 270

Riddell, Sir George: role at Peace Conference, 125 n. 58; diary entries re Lloyd George, 125, 153, 303 n. 15, 339; on end of intervention, 338

Riga: British warships at, 57, 103; false reports of massacres at, 143; *Freikorps* at, 256; Bermondt-Avalov move to take, 282

Roberts, G. H. (Food Controller): on effect of absence of Russian trade, 317

Royal Air Force: see Great Britain, Royal Air Force

Royal Navy: see Great Britain, Royal Navy

Rozanov, General S. N. (Kolchak's Governor-General of Far East): and anti-Kolchak movement, Vladivostok, 238; moves Kalmykov's troops into Vladivostok, 242; suppresses rising, 251-52

Rumania: endangered, 98; British obligations to, 134, 155-56; in "Foch plan," 137, 138, 139; Allies reluctant to press re aid to Denikin, 322; invasion of Hungary, 352 n. 4

Russia: "Great" vs. "divided," 54-55, 69, 72, 77, 86, 147, 148, 166, 219, 255, 274, 279, 298-99, 309, 311, 334, 360; question of representation at Peace Conference, 86-87, 102, 103-104

Russia Department: see Great Britain, Foreign Office

Russian Civil War: weaknesses of anti-Bolshevik movement, 21-22; "Prinkipo" as solution for, 95; opposing force totals, 118 n. 46, 265; Churchill on nature of, 186; military vs. political solutions to, 349; importance of popular support, 350; distinction between "incumbent" vs. "insurgent" sides, 354 n. 7

Russian Political Conference: and Prinkipo, 110, 115; opposes "Nansen proposal," 160; and formation of North-West Russian Government, 270; 102

Sakharov, General Konstantin B., 32

Salisbury, Marquess of, 118, 152

Sazonov, Serge: serves as "foreign minister" for Denikin and Kolchak, 114 n. 37; presses Finns to aid Yudenich, 284; asks for Russian gold to subsidize Finns, 285

Second International, 176

Selby, Walford H. M.: on recognition of

Kolchak, 205 n. 1; criticizes Knox, 216; on reactionary nature of Kolchak and Denikin administrations, 216-17; calls for propaganda campaign to bolster government's policy re Russia, 361-62

Semenov, Gregorii M. (Cossack Ataman): Japanese support of, 38-40, 233; subsequent career, 252 n. 129

Sevastopol: under British and French occupation, 48

Shackleton, Sir David (Permanent Under-Secretary, Ministry of Labor): on Labour movement and intervention, 187-88

Sherwood-Kelly, Lt.-Colonel John, 202-203

Shortt, Edward (Home Secretary): and domestic revolutionary unrest, 133 n. 78, 143, 144; position re Russia in Cabinet, 295, 296

Siberia: Japanese aims and policy, 7, 9, 38-40; Allied forces, 28; U.S. policies, 28, 164; limited Allied combat role, 29-30; in pre-Armistice military plans, 30-31; British-French dispute over responsibilities, 32-33, 35; Churchill's plan to link with North Russia, 183-85; role of British High Commissioner, 208, 252-53; divisions of authority in, 233; "partisans," 233; retreat and execution of Kolchak, 251-52; Hardinge and Curzon appraise British policy in, 253; subsequent withdrawal of U.S., Czech, and Japanese troops, 253 n. 130; British and French leave responsibility to U.S. and Japan, 315-16; British view as useful outlet for Japanese energies and population, 315. *See also* Kolchak

Siberian Regional Duma, 234

Slavo-British Legion (North Russia): mutiny, 192, 194

Smuts, General Jan C.: in Eastern Committee discussions, 66, 69, 74-75; fears France in the East, 69, 74; urges Italian mandate for Caucasus, 75; supports Lloyd George over Prinkipo, 106; and Bullitt mission, 150-53

Socialist-Revolutionaries (S-R's): anti-Kolchak activities in Siberia, 233-36; seize power at Irkutsk, 251; 33, 34, 42 n. 82, 205

Sonnino, Baron Sidney (Italian Foreign Minister): and Italian mandate for Caucasus, 228, 229; 124

South Africa, Union of, 97

South Russia: theater of intervention, 8, 44-50; French policy, 46-48; opposing forces, December 1918, 49; British concentrate aid on, 207; corruption, 213-14; Mackinder mission to, 217-18; pogroms, 218-19. *See also* Denikin

Soviet government: British aim to overthrow, 9; feels more menaced by Germans than by Allies, 9; support of by population, 87, 351; peace proposals to Allies, 87-88, 107,

Index

Ukraine, Soviet government of: accepts Prinkipo invitation, 113

United States of America: aims in intervention, 7; forces in North Russia, 19, 20-21, 24, 165, 172; forces in Siberia, 28, 164, 172, 243; orders forbid combat against Bolsheviks in Siberia, 30; attempts to limit Japanese penetration of Siberia, 36-38; British effort to keep in Siberia, 210; troops concentrated near Vladivostok, 233; departure from Siberia, 253 n. 130; and recognition of Estonia, 270 n. 57; policy re blockade, 288-91; refuses export licenses for Soviet territory, 291; Churchill on future role, 299; favors "Great" over "divided" Russia, 311; role in South Vietnam compared with British role in Russia, 357

United States Senate Foreign Relations Committee: and Bullitt mission, 144, 145, 146, 150

Versailles, Treaty of: ratification and blockade, 289, 290; 171, 186

Viatka, 184

Vietnam, 352

Vladivostok: British training school, 23; and evacuation of Czechs, 189; anti-Kolchak movement, 232; perspective on civil war from, 233, 239; Allied ultimatum to Rozanov to withdraw troops, 242; abortive rising and collapse of movement, 251-52; 31

Volga River, 45, 46

Vologda, 18, 184

Volunteer Army: Tsaritsyn campaign, 161, 205, 214; Moscow campaign, 214-15; retreat to Crimea, 218, 250-51; and pogroms, 218-19. See also Denikin

Voronezh, 215

Vorovsky, V. V., 110

War Cabinet: see Great Britain, Cabinet

War Office: see Great Britain, War Office

Ward, Lt.-Colonel John: commands Middlesex Battalion in Siberia, 29, 30, 31

Wardrop, Oliver (British High Commissioner, Transcaucasia), 322

Wedgwood, Colonel Josiah: criticism of government's policy re Russia, 143, 294

Weizmann, Chaim: protests to Foreign Office against White pogroms, 219 n. 40

Wemyss, Admiral R. E. (First Sea Lord, until mid-1919): feels Navy's hands tied, 289

White, Henry: argues blockade illegal, 291

White Russian movement: weakness, 21-22; refuses Prinkipo invitation, 113-15; and nature of post-Bolshevik Russian political order, 216-18; compared unfavorably with Bolsheviks, 344-45. See also: Denikin; Kolchak; Russian Political Conference

Wilson, Harold, viii

Wilson, General Sir Henry ([after July 1919, Field Marshal], Chief of Imperial General Staff): on post-Armistice policy re Russia, 10, 11-13, 75-76; on danger of increased force commitments given needs in Empire and at home, 30, 43, 178, 199-200, 227, 232, 328, 335, 360; in Eastern Committee discussions, 74; decries absence of policy decisions, 98, 336; on post-Prinkipo policy, 118; on force totals, 119; and Churchill's intervention plans, 121, 122, 126, 128; opposes sending conscripts to Russia, 134; aims at limiting British role in Russia, 134-35; urges withdrawal from North Russia, 135, 178; and "Foch plan," 138-39; and Churchill plan for Siberia-North Russia link, 183-85, 186, 188; military advice to Kolchak, 183-84; and North Russia withdrawal operations, 190-91, 196; on lessons of North Russia, 199-200; refuses to delay withdrawal from Caucasus, 230-31; urges Finland support Yudenich, 263; defends Marsh against Curzon charges, 273 n. 72; position in Cabinet re Russian policy, 296-97; on Lloyd George's Russian policy, 298 n. 3; on proposals for aiding Caucasus states, 323-24; instructs Holman to aid Denikin evacuation, 325; disclaims prior knowledge of Middle East crisis statement, 328; on summons of self and Churchill to Paris, 328 n. 91; arguments influence Lloyd George, 335; skeptical re ability of Georgians to resist Red Army, 335-36

Wilson, President Woodrow: agrees to intervention, 7; Litvinov proposes peace to, 87 n. 50; favors sounding Litvinov, 94; opposes intervention, 105, 121, 127 n. 63, 138-40, 163; favors talks with Bolsheviks, 104-105, 107; and Prinkipo, 108-109, 111; and Kun regime in Hungary, 139-40; and Bullitt mission, 149, 150, 152; and "Nansen proposal," 157-58; and question of recognizing Kolchak, 163-65; withdraws U.S. troops from North Russia, 172; opposes Caucasus mandate for Italy, 229; says blockade illegal, 288, 289-90; but sympathizes with objects of blockade, 291; and question of degree of popular support for Bolshevism, 351

Winnig, August, 57

Wise, E. F.: memorandum recommending trade with Russian cooperatives, 318-19, 326 n. 82; chairs expert committee on question, 327; Curzon and Lloyd George on, 327; subsequent career, 327 n. 85

Wiseman, Sir William, 105

Wrangel, General Baron Piotr N.: takes Tsaritsyn, 214; succeeds Denikin, 351

Yakushev, I. A. (President, Siberian Regional Duma): organizes anti-Kolchak movement, 234

Index

Yudenich, General Nikolai N.: Petrograd campaign, 172, 175, 182 n. 21, 232, 247, 254, 285; British support of, 254, 266, 273, 283-84; takes command of Northern Corps, 255; British fear German influence on, 258, 266; relations with Finland, 258-60, 262-63, 284-85; Curzon view of, 260; and Estonia, 266, 267, 282-83; and North-West Russian Government, 267, 269, 272; 285

"Zemsky Sobor": rallying idea of anti-Kolchak movement in Siberia, 236

Zinoviev, G., 112, 175

Other books published for
The Center of International Studies,
Princeton University

Gabriel A. Almond, *The Appeals of Communism*
Gabriel A. Almond and James S. Coleman, editors, *The Politics of the Developing Areas*
Gabriel A. Almond and Sidney Verba, *The Civic Culture: Political Attitudes and Democracy in Five Nations*
Richard J. Barnet and Richard A. Falk, *Security in Disarmament*
Henry Bienen, *Tanzania: Party Transformation and Economic Development*
Cyril E. Black and Thomas P. Thornton, editors, *Communism and Revolution: The Strategic Uses of Political Violence*
Robert J. C. Butow, *Tojo and the Coming of the War*
Miriam Camps, *Britain and the European Community, 1955-1963*
Bernard C. Cohen, *The Political Process and Foreign Policy: The Making of the Japanese Peace Settlement*
Bernard C. Cohen, *The Press and Foreign Policy*
Charles De Visscher, *Theory and Reality in Public International Law*, translated by P. E. Corbett
Frederick S. Dunn, *Peace-making and the Settlement with Japan*
Harry Eckstein, *Division and Cohesion in Democracy: A Study of Norway*
Richard A. Falk, *Legal Order in a Violent World*
Robert G. Gilpin, *France in the Age of the Scientific State*
Richard F. Hamilton, *Affluence and the French Worker in the Fourth Republic*
Herman Kahn, *On Thermonuclear War*
W. W. Kaufmann, editor, *Military Policy and National Security*
Klaus Knorr, *On the Uses of Military Power in the Nuclear Age*
Klaus Knorr, *The War Potential of Nations*
Klaus Knorr, editor, *NATO and American Security*
Klaus Knorr and Sidney Verba, editors, *The International System: Theoretical Essays*
Peter Kunstadter, editor, *Southeast Asian Tribes, Minorities, and Nations*
Linda Miller, *World Order and Local Disorder: The United Nations and Internal Conflict*
Peter Paret and Gordon Craig, editors, *Selected Works of Carl von Clausewitz*
Sidney J. Ploss, *Conflict and Decision-making in Soviet Russia*
Lucian W. Pye, *Guerrilla Communism in Malaya*
James N. Rosenau, editor, *International Aspects of Civil Strife*
James N. Rosenau, *National Leadership and Foreign Policy: A Case Study in the Mobilization of Public Support*
Rolf Sannwald and Jacques Stohler, *Economic Integration: Theoretical Assumptions and Consequences of European Unification*. Translated by Herman F. Karreman
Richard L. Sklar, *Nigerian Political Parties: Power in an Emergent African Nation*
Glenn H. Snyder, *Deterrence and Defense*
Harold and Margaret Sprout, *The Ecological Perspective on Human Affairs, With Special Reference to International Politics*
Thomas P. Thornton, *The Third World in Soviet Perspective: Studies by Soviet Writers on the Developing Areas*
Sidney Verba, *Small Groups and Political Behavior: A Study of Leadership*
Karl von Vorys, *Political Development in Pakistan*
Myron Weiner, *Party Politics in India*
E. Victor Wolfenstein, *The Revolutionary Personality: Lenin, Trotsky, Gandhi*
Oran R. Young, *The Intermediaries: Third Parties in International Crises*